Healthy Young Children

SIXTH EDITION

National Association for the Education of Young Children
Washington, DC

National Association for the Education of Young Children

1401 H Street NW, Suite 600
Washington, DC 20005
202-232-8777 • 800-424-2460
NAEYC.org

NAEYC Books
Senior Director, Publishing and Content Development
Susan Friedman

Director, Books
Dana Battaglia

Senior Editor
Holly Bohart

Editor II
Rossella Procopio

Senior Creative Design Manager
Charity Coleman

Senior Creative Design Specialist
Gillian Frank

Creative Design Specialist
Makayla Johnson

Creative Design Specialist
Ashley McGowan

Publishing Business Operations Manager
Francine Markowitz

Library of Congress Control Number: 2023938494

ISBN: 978-1-952331-21-3

Item: 1167

Contents

Part Editors

Alicia L. Haupt, MD
Assistant Professor of Pediatrics
University of Pittsburgh School of Medicine
UPMC Children's Hospital of Pittsburgh
Pittsburgh, PA

Brittany Massare, MD
Assistant Professor of Pediatrics
Division of Academic General Pediatrics
Penn State College of Medicine
Hershey, PA

Jennifer Nizer, MEd
Senior Vice President for Child and Youth Programs
Armed Services YMCA National Headquarters
Woodbridge, VA

Manjula Paul, CRNP-Fam, MSN, MPH
Laurel, MD

Louis A. Valenti
Branch Chief-Licensing
Maryland State Department of Education, Division of Child Care
Baltimore, MD

Chapter Contributors

Abbey Alkon, RN, PhD
Professor
University of California, San Francisco
School of Nursing, California Childcare Health Program
San Francisco, CA

Shaun-Adrián Choflá, EdD
Butte College
Oroville, CA
Empathy Therapy
Chico, CA

Stacey C. Cook MD PhD
Medical Director, Outpatient Complex Care Services
Boston Children's Hospital
Harvard Medical School
Boston, MA

Kristen Copeland, MD, FAAP
Division of General and Community Pediatrics
Cincinnati Children's Hospital Medical Center
Professor of Pediatrics
University of Cincinnati College of Medicine
Cincinnati, OH

Nikki Gambhir, MBChB, FAAP
Department of Pediatrics
Baylor College of Medicine
Houston, TX

Ruth E. Gardner, MD
Assistant Professor of Pediatrics
Division of Academic General Pediatrics
Penn State College of Medicine
Hershey, PA

Nicole Hackman, MD, FABM
Associate Professor of Pediatrics
Medical Director of Lactation Services
Penn State College of Medicine
Hershey, PA

Banku Jairath, MD
Assistant Professor of Pediatrics
Division of Academic General Pediatrics
Penn State College of Medicine
Hershey, PA

Madiha Jamil, MD
Assistant Professor of Pediatrics
Division of Academic General Pediatrics
Penn State College of Medicine
Hershey, PA

Amy L. King, BS
Cincinnati Children's Hospital Medical Center
Cincinnati, OH

Julia Luckenbill, MA, Edu
Adult Educator/Director
Davis Parent Nursery School
Davis Joint Unified School District
Davis, CA

Terri McFadden, MD, MPH
Professor of Pediatrics
Emory University School of Medicine
Atlanta, GA

Abigail K. Myers, MD
Assistant Professor of Pediatrics
Division of Adolescent Medicine
Penn State College of Medicine
Hershey, PA

Mary Beth Pero, MD
Cincinnati Children's Hospital Medical Center
Division of General and Community Pediatrics
Cincinnati, OH

Timothy R. Shope, MD, MPH
Professor of Pediatrics
University of Pittsburgh School of Medicine
UPMC Children's Hospital of Pittsburgh
Pittsburgh, PA

Content Reviewers

Susan S. Aronson, MD, FAAP
Retired Clinical Professor of Pediatrics
University of Pennsylvania, Children's Hospital of Philadelphia
Stuart, FL

Jennifer Buchter, PhD, MSW
Eastern Illinois University
College of Education
Department of Special Education
Charleston, IL

Betsy P. Humphreys, PhD, MEd
Research Assistant Professor
Early Childhood Special Education
Institute of Disability, University Center for Excellence on Disability
University of New Hampshire
Durham, NH

Hilda Loria, MD, MPH, FAAP
Assistant Professor of Pediatrics
UT Southwestern Medical Center
Center Director
Rees-Jones Center for Foster Care Excellence
Children's Health System
Dallas, TX

Christine Lux, EdD
Associate Professor of Early Childhood Education
Montana State University
Bozeman, MT

Lori Erbrederis Meyer, PhD
Associate Professor
Department of Education
University of Vermont
Burlington, VT

Brittany Mitchell, MD
UMC Physicians
Lubbock, TX

Jodi Nerren, PhD
Texas A&M AgriLife Extension
Promoting Early Education Quality
College Station, TX

Judith Rex, PhD, RN, BC-Medical Surgical
Northampton Community College
Bethlehem, PA

Christine M. Snyder, MA
University of Michigan
Ann Arbor, MI

Deborah Palmer Watson, BS, MS
6th Year Educational Leadership
Administration & Supervision Certificate
Lead Faculty, Early Childhood Education
Charter Oak State College
New Britain, CT

Cara Wicks-Ortega, MS
Early Childhood Studies
Richard W. Riley College of Education
and Human Sciences
Walden University
Minneapolis, MN

Introduction and About the Book

Acknowledgement

NAEYC acknowledges with great appreciation and respect the contributions of Susan S. Aronson, MD, FAAP to this edition and as the Editor for the previous fourth and fifth editions of *Healthy Young Children*.

Child Development

In every early learning setting, the health, safety, and well-being of the children, educators, and staff members are among the highest priorities for the program. Educators must engage in health and safety education, modeling, promotion, planning, and prevention. These efforts take significant work and coordination between many parties, including administrative leadership, classroom teachers, all staff members, the greater community, healthcare professionals, and, of course, families. They also require that educators have a sound understanding of child development and learning to apply developmentally appropriate practice to health and safety education, policies, and goals.

Childhood is a unique period of life when physical, intellectual, emotional, and social growth all occur simultaneously and interactively. Children's bodies and minds are constantly learning how to meet challenges faced in their environment. Research shows that development of the brain (intellectual, cognitive, social-emotional) and children's physical, nutritional, and oral health are strongly linked to the quality of their early experiences. Children need protection from injury and infection, both of which can lead to discomfort, disability, or death. They also need activities that promote healthy growth and development.

Chief among the professional responsibilities of early childhood educators is the responsibility to plan and implement intentional, developmentally appropriate learning experiences across all domains of child development, including social-emotional development, physical development and health, and cognitive development, and the general learning competencies of each child served (AFSCME et al. 2020).

All domains of child development and approaches to learning are important and, as such, work together and support each other. For example, sound nutrition, regular physical activity, and sufficient sleep all promote children's abilities to engage in social interactions that, in turn, stimulate cognitive growth (AFSCME et al. 2020; NAEYC 2020).

Early childhood educators should plan and implement the health aspects of their programs to respond to the predictable developmental patterns of young children. As children progress from young infants to toddlers to preschoolers to school-age children and then to self-sufficient older children, their needs will differ and evolve. At each developmental level, early childhood professionals must simultaneously function as protectors, role models, and teachers for the children in their care. In addition, they play an important role in children's development, by supporting the families of children in their program.

Many practices in high-quality early learning programs enable learning, promote the development of strong bodies that resist disease, foster brain development, and support positive behavior. Here are some examples:

- Developing warm, positive, continuous relationships between children and caring adults and among children while doing gross motor activities
- Following recommended nutritional practices, such as offering children opportunities to choose among healthful food and beverage options and involving children in safe and sanitary practices for storing, preparing, and serving food
- Providing sufficient developmentally appropriate and vigorous structured and unstructured physical activities that promote fitness and enable children to focus better on subsequent learning activities
- Checking and tracking preventive healthcare services for children and staff members, including
  - Ensuring that they receive all recommended immunizations to control vaccine-preventable diseases so children can be present in the program for learning
  - Obtaining timely recommended screenings to detect and manage health problems to limit disabilities that can impair learning
- Following oral health practices to prevent dental illnesses that can be painful, interfere with speech and nutrition, and reduce social competence

The many hours of contact that educators have with children can be very influential. Many children remember throughout life their early childhood education experiences. Healthful routines in the early childhood program can promote this growth and development.

Risk Management and Safety

Health and safety are not external patches or optional aspects of early learning programs. Regardless of the limits imposed by constraints in funding, staffing, the environment, or the curriculum, the health and safety component of the program should be an integrated part of daily activities. The health and safety component involves risk management and continuous assessment and learning for educators. A completely risk-free and infection-proof program is neither possible nor desirable—children need to experience challenge. *Risk management* involves making choices and finding acceptable alternative approaches so children can experience challenges without significant adverse consequences. While compromise is necessary, usually it is possible to meet the seemingly conflicting objectives of risk management and risk taking. Frequent safety checks of the site, with corrective actions when necessary, can prevent injuries. Careful, regular observations of children may reveal physical health and social-emotional difficulties that respond best to early treatment. You will find specific information, procedures, and recommendations on each of these topics, as well as on many others, in this book.

The Book and National Standards

This book is based on national standards for health and safety and is grounded in research. Both healthcare professionals and early childhood professionals have participated in writing every edition of this work. The book is intended as a guide to facilitate collaboration among early childhood educators, healthcare professionals, and family members for implementing currently accepted health and safety standards. The primary reference for this book is *Caring for Our Children: National Health and Safety Performance Standards; Guidelines for Early Care and Education Programs*, fourth edition (*CFOC*), published by the American Academy of Pediatrics (AAP), and the *Caring for Our Children* online standards database maintained by the National Resource Center for Health and Safety in Child Care and Early Education (**http://nrckids.org**). In addition to *CFOC*, the text refers to guidelines from the Centers for Disease Control and Prevention (CDC) and *NAEYC Early Learning Program Accreditation Standards and Assessment Items*. These guidelines describe the conditions and practices for which sound evidence exists that following the standards will reduce an unacceptable risk of harm.

If you find it challenging to meet some of the standards in your program, implement what you can do now. Major health gains and safety measures can be achieved by taking simple steps. For example, diligently following hand-hygiene procedures (appropriate handwashing or proper use of alcohol-based hand sanitizers) and keeping everyone—children and adults—up to date with required vaccines are two strong defenses against the spread of infectious diseases.

Set targets to address the standards you cannot currently meet. Assess your priorities to avoid the most significant risks; don't expect to change everything overnight. To increase the likelihood of changes being successful, plan carefully and thoroughly, involving those who are affected, those with authority, and those with expertise related to the situation.

Some recommendations in *Healthy Young Children* may differ from those in other credible sources. Materials are published and updated in different time periods, drawing on an ever-changing base of information. Also, within the medical and scientific community, some experts differ on specific approaches. When there is a conflict, seek the *rationale* for the recommendations. Sometimes the different approaches are equally acceptable alternatives. Other times, you will have to make the best decision you can after exploring the basis for the differing points of view. If the issue involves technical information, you may want to consult a trusted local expert with the appropriate scientific background. Your state or local department of public health may be able to provide guidance or suggest where to get the help you need.

Book Organization and Chapter Features

This book is organized into four parts.

Part 1: Health and Safety in Early Childhood Education introduces the responsibilities of and collaboration between early childhood educators and healthcare professionals to ensure the health and safety of children and early learning programs overall.

Part 2: Promoting Children's Health includes chapters on specific health topics, each providing discussions, definitions, and recommendations for health promotion and illness prevention.

Part 3: Prevention, Planning, and Treatment includes chapters focused on specific guidelines and recommendations for prevention of, planning for, and treatment of certain injuries, conditions, and diseases.

Part 4: Program and Facility Management provides an overview of program and facility regulations, protocols, and guidelines for maintaining safe spaces and responding to emergencies.

Chapter Features

- **Learning Objectives.** Each chapter opens with learning objectives to guide students through the key concepts that will be discussed.
- **Special Features.** Each chapter contains special features designed to highlight specific content, provide tips, or present additional information on a specific topic.
  - **Immediate Impact.** This feature is targeted at educators and includes suggestions for implementing immediate strategies for improving health and safety in the program and classroom.
  - **Family Connections.** This feature provides tips and strategies for how educators can work with families to extend the benefits of health and safety measures taught and used in the program to the home.

Book Appendixes

Forms

Some of the chapters reference resources, such as forms and checklists, that can facilitate communication and recordkeeping. Many of these resources are provided as links within the chapters, and others are provided in the back of the book as appendixes.

Glossary and List of Acronyms

Online Resources

Online resources can be accessed at **NAEYC.org/healthy-young-children**

- A **crosswalk** of book chapters and NAEYC Early Learning Program Standards
- All **book references** are posted online and searchable.
- A **test bank** with more than 190 content-based questions for quick quizzes and exams

A note on terminology: This book uses the terms *family, parent(s), caregiver(s),* and *primary caregiver(s)* in an effort to represent diverse family structures and living situations and different contexts. In each instance, the term used refers to the person or persons responsible for the care of a child in the home.

PART 1

Health and Safety in Early Childhood Education

Health and Safety for Children and Early Childhood Educators

JULIA LUCKENBILL AND SHAUN-ADRIÁN CHOFLÁ

LEARNING OBJECTIVES

- To identify key policies and practices essential for healthy early learning programs, including child and educator health
- To consider the role administrators, educators, healthcare professionals, and advocates play as the people who introduce health education and management and explain protocols and practices
- To examine the impact of the COVID-19 pandemic on early childhood education as well as the broader community
- To locate national standards and practices for early learning programs
- To examine the difference between national and state programs that promote healthy practices

NAEYC EARLY LEARNING ACCREDITATION STANDARDS

These standards and how they relate to health and safety specifically are referred to throughout the text of this chapter (NAEYC 2019, 2022):

- **Standard 1: Relationships.** Relationships are essential foundations for safe and healthy classrooms.
- **Standard 2: Curriculum.** Educators design and present curriculum that articulates safe and healthy practices ranging from hand hygiene to how to behave in a fire drill. The content must be developmentally appropriate.
- **Standard 3: Teaching.** Educators use a variety of developmentally, culturally, and linguistically appropriate and effective teaching approach that enhance each child's learning and development in the context of the program's curriculum goals.
- **Standard 4: Assessment of Child Progress.** Knowledgeable educators are aware of child developmental milestones. They use screening and assessment to stay alert to children's physical and mental health needs and act on their findings.
- **Standard 5: Health.** Educators promote health and nutrition. They protect children from illness and injury.
- **Standard 6: Staff Competencies, Preparation, and Support.** Educators are trained in injury and illness prevention as well as pediatric first aid and cardiopulmonary resuscitation (CPR). They are aware of environmental hazards and trained to assess the least toxic way to control pests and manage chemicals.
- **Standard 7: Families.** Educators work hand in hand with families so that there are home-to-school connections around healthy and safe practices of the classroom.
- **Standard 8: Community Relationships.** Some communities have more advantages than others. The classroom can be an asset to the entire community as a center for everyone to learn and grow, where children, families, and staff members can connect with professionals who provide screenings, healthcare, dental care, mental health, and more.
- **Standard 9: Physical Environment.** The classroom is designed in a way that allows educators to supervise and interact with all children. The toys are developmentally appropriate and safe, and the site is free of toxins and other unsafe content.
- **Standard 10: Leadership and Management.** The administration of the program implements healthy and safe practices and locates and uses funding to make such practices possible.

> Two-year-old Dee toddles over to the teacher, Skylar. "Hi, Dee," Skylar says with a smile, it's handwashing time! Ready for some soap?" Dee, clearly used to the ritual, extends both hands and Skylar squirts some foaming soap on both of their hands. Together, they lather the fronts and backs of their hands, in between their fingers, and then around their thumbs as they sing a handwashing song.

The scene depicted in this vignette is a common one in high-quality early learning programs. For early childhood teachers and administrators, the health and safety of the children they serve is a top priority. The positive relationship between Dee and Skylar and their shared healthy practice are the focus of the moment captured. What isn't obvious is that it took a community—teachers, aides, administrators, and health coordinators—working together, to make this moment happen. It takes an early learning community to build a safe and healthy space for children to learn, for families to feel welcome, and for teachers to teach. A safe and healthy early learning program is one that is safe and healthy not only for children but also for their families and the educators.

In this chapter, we discuss how high-quality programs make a difference in the lives of children, their families, and the educators who work with them. First, we discuss recent and ongoing challenges within the profession of early childhood education that affect early childhood educators' opportunities to develop and implement health and safety measures that benefit the entire community. Second, we discuss how early childhood educators can manage these challenges and attend to their own health and well-being. Finally, we discuss how each day early childhood educators can and do meet these challenges to develop healthy young children through an understanding and implementation of national and state standards and resources. Despite challenges, being a part of a high-quality classroom produces an active learning buzz that is irresistible, satisfying, and rewarding.

Supporting High-Quality Programs

There has long been a call on the part of child and health organizations for the federal government to fully fund the early childhood education system to make high-quality programs available to all children and families. Educators know that access to high-quality programming affects the architecture of children's brains (High Quality Early Learning Project, n.d.) and that learning healthy practices will affect children for life. With adequate funding and a consistent set of standards applied across the nation, it would be possible to revolutionize the field, impacting millions of lives (Learning Policy Institute 2021).

ONE STEP FORWARD

In April 2023, the Biden administration signed an executive order to expand access to affordable, high-quality care and provide support for early childhood educators and family caregivers. The plan includes more than 50 directives for agencies across the government. Early childhood education and child care advocates applauded this decision.

Looking Back to Move Forward

Looking into the past shows that educating children was a role assigned to people considered "lower class" or "unskilled," and caring for the very young was considered something that anyone could do and required no training. Many of these perceptions continue to this day. In part, this is because

> terms describing those who work with children birth through grade 3, such as *provider, teacher, assistant, aide, lead teacher, child care worker, day care worker, educator, caregiver, pre-K teacher, elementary school teacher, primary teacher,* and *preschool teacher* are used across states and settings without clarity or coherence. They carry no meaning for their respective (and differing) preparation, responsibilities, expectations, and compensation levels. (AFSCME et al. 2020, 7)

Just as these terms vary from state to state and within different settings, state and national regulations and licensing requirements are not standardized. Many individuals working in early childhood education are working in states and settings where they are not required to meet even minimal educational qualifications (Whitebook 2018). At the same time, federal and state early childhood systems have raised the levels of professional preparation required for certain settings and certain people.

While kindergarten through 12th grade classrooms require standardized coursework that leads to certification to join their workforce, state licensing regulations for educating younger children are less consistent about teaching requirements. Preparation programs range in quality that leads to varying state and national credentials (AFSCME et al. 2020). Without standardization of licensing, early childhood educators are not seen as part of a unified profession.

Without a unified professional base, it has been difficult for early childhood to access federal funding. Historically, this lack of funding has created inequitable and unfair working conditions and an unhealthy work environment for many early childhood educators. The lack of funding and policies in the United States has created a situation in which early childhood educators must work long hours with few to no benefits and low pay. Insufficient funding impacts how programs manage their classes. For example, child-to-teacher class ratios and group size requirements vary by state, locality, funding stream, accreditation, and quality rating system even though these are critical standards impacting child and educator health and safety. Ratios and group sizes are cost drivers for programs and, in lieu of adequate public funding, some states have looked to loosening these standards, allowing larger group sizes and more children per educator to increase revenue and supply. Efforts to loosen regulations, driven by a goal of increasing supply and program revenue, will actually have the opposite effect by driving educator burnout and turnover even higher.

These conditions have caused educators to experience personal and financial stress. This long-term built-in inequity affects women and women of color disproportionately because of the demographic makeup of the early childhood field. As mentioned, it promotes high rates of burnout and turnover. (Whitebook 2018). Teacher turnover, particularly during the school year, also creates instability and uncertainty for children and their families and destabilizes quality improvement efforts, including those related to health and safety.

The health and well-being of the country's educators are at the heart of safe and healthy early learning programs. Sufficient funding is needed to ensure that all education professionals receive equitable compensation and professional recognition that reflect the importance of their work (AFSCME et al. 2020).

With adequate funding, the following is possible:

- Smaller group sizes, lower ratios of children to staff, and other best practices. Lower ratios and smaller group sizes are necessary to keep children safe—but they also keep educators in their programs by limiting staff burnout, turnover, and staffing shortages." (AFSCME et al. 2020).
- Increased access to infant and early childhood mental health consultants
- Highly prepared educators who can appropriately respond to children's behavior and social-emotional needs
- Increased access to individual aides, paraprofessionals, and other supports for children with disabilities to have more options for accessible care
- An increase in safe outdoor play spaces
- Increased compensation and benefits for educators and staff members with fewer financial stressors, such as the ability to access and receive healthcare
- Facilities free from lead and other hazardous materials

COVID-19 Underscored Problems in the System

The COVID-19 pandemic exposed the vulnerabilities of the early learning system in ways that hadn't previously been seen and precipitated new and greater challenges. While educators and programs were learning how to engage with children and families virtually, they had to navigate staff shortages and financial stressors. As early learning programs closed, educators lost their jobs and children were left without the in-person support that early learning settings provided, creating trauma and impacting young children's mental health. This happened at a time when children's family members were sick with and even dying of COVID-19 (Corso, Gutierrez, & Irizarry 2022; Turner 2022). Where once children had the protective buffer of an early learning setting to provide stability when the family was in crisis, many children lacked that support from a caring community and eventually returned to a classroom where educators were also emotionally exhausted (Kwartra 2020).

Even children who did not lose loved ones in the pandemic were impacted by their families' stress. The pandemic disproportionately impacted families with low income and families of color, and health disparities became even more acute. A *health disparity* refers to a higher burden of illness, injury, disability, or mortality experienced by one group relative to another. In terms of early childhood education, this can be seen in the lack of access to quality programs, healthcare, and illness prevention for children from communities of color and/or rural communities, who are single parented, or from families with low income. (See "Chapter 2: Healthcare Professionals and Educators Work Together to Support Healthy and Thriving Children" for more information.) The pandemic appears to have eliminated many positions held by parents/caregivers with lower incomes where they were required to work on-site (as opposed to working remotely). Many families with lower income found that they struggled to pay rent and access food during the pandemic. Across the globe, more families fell into poverty, and children that lost a parent/caregiver were particularly at risk. As a result, malnutrition increased, especially in countries where food insecurity was already a pre-pandemic concern (Kabir et al. 2020). When children are malnourished, their development can be stunted, both physically and cognitively. When families are stressed about food scarcity, they may not be able to be emotionally available to children.

In addition to the in-home impacts, many children experienced public health measures that may have decreased transmission of illness but replaced important practices developed in the early childhood field to support families and children around separation or to build connections in communities and classrooms. For example, in the United States, children were initially not permitted to bring transition objects into classrooms, and parents/caregivers were not allowed to join children to ease them into their classroom settings, both practices that educators know help children whose temperament leads them to withdraw. Similarly, children were guided to play in a specific area of the room with their own toys and guided away from interactive co-play, even though research shows that associative and cooperative play are skills learned through hands-on interaction. Being prevented from interacting in such ways may have impacted children's social and emotional development. This may be particularly true for children with developmental delays and disabilities, such as autism spectrum disorder (Styx 2020).

Traumatic Stress's Effects on Educators and Their Work

COVID-19 shone a spotlight on the biggest of the field's vulnerabilities and deepened the health disparities that exist in the United States. It highlighted not only the effects stress and trauma have on children and families but also on educators who experience first and *secondary trauma* because of their work.

The COVID-19 pandemic was a unique and historical event, but families experience traumatic stress every day as the result of many factors. Educators can be affected by children and families who have experienced trauma. There is stress that can cause harm to people not directly experiencing the stressor, whether they have experienced trauma themselves or not. This is called secondary trauma. Consider the following example.

> Having just attended the local state fair with their families, both Ellie and Adrian are playing in the block area, creating a new type of game for the fair. Without warning, Adrian becomes inconsolable after accidentally knocking down a structure he built. The tears streaming down Adrian's face and the shaking of his entire body indicates to his teacher, John, that Adrian is likely still processing the wildfire that destroyed his home and the town where he once lived. While commuting home that evening, John finds himself weeping just as suddenly and powerfully as Adrian was hours before. John wishes he knew what he could do for Adrian.

All young children have strong feelings that can lead to sudden and intense responses. Anyone who has spent time with children has experienced a child melt to the floor with emotion over wanting a toy or being told *no*. When these experiences stem from a traumatic experience or event, the educators working with the child can experience stress too. Consider John, in the earlier vignette, who became overwhelmed with sadness and helplessness in response to the trauma a child in his class experienced and how it was affecting him. Children and adults who have been exposed to traumatic stress and/or who have experienced adverse childhood experiences (ACEs), such as Adrian in this vignette, often develop strong emotional responses to otherwise nonthreatening, everyday situations. (See "Chapter 6: Social-Emotional and Mental Health" on social-emotional development to learn more about stress and ACEs.) These powerful and amplified emotional responses, initially associated with traumatic stress, become their standard response to all stressful situations. When people experience traumatic stress, these intense responses to stress often interfere with their daily ability to function and cooperate with others. This is why, while educators must care for children who have encountered traumatic stress, they must also care for themselves, even if they feel their trauma was less serious than that of the children that they teach.

Committing to Educator Well-Being

The strength of a high quality learning program depends on the health and well-being of its educators. Dedicated educators may ignore their own health needs because they put children's needs first and also because they lack health benefits and time off. A program's human resource policies should address and support the health, safety, and well-being of the educators in the program, but, it is also the responsibility of the educators themselves to take care of their physical and mental well-being.

Putting Our Masks on First

Anyone who has flown on a commercial airline has heard the safety announcement reminding the adults on the plane sitting next to children to—in case of an emergency—put their own masks on first before that of a child. This is sound advice for air travel, and it also symbolizes the importance of caring for one's health and safety as an educator. As the expression goes, you cannot pour from an empty cup, nor can an educator fully support a child's healthy development at the expense of their own health. That said, educators have a primary responsibility to anchor themselves first. It is nearly impossible to be a secure base that families and children need when feeling insecure.

The Role of Programs and Policies

Programs can alleviate some of these concerns by instituting policies that support educators and provide them with the safety they need to feel seen and engaged. Adequate funding would allow programs to offer benefit packages for healthcare and sick leave. Directors and programs can help educators promote their own emotional and psychological, social, physical, and intellectual safety. By doing so, educators can develop what Nicholson and colleagues (2022) dubbed *real safety* and *felt safety*, which means that adults and children alike are safe and know they are safe. For educators, this requires that they attend to their health, including setting and keeping work-home boundaries; getting regular health screenings; and making time for recreation and friendships and their families, traditions, and meals.

Here are some steps that early learning programs can take to provide support to educators.

1. **Maintain a Pool of Strong Substitutes.** Even though creating a reliable substitute policy can be challenging, substitute coverage is critical to a well-run program and allows teachers to focus on health and family concerns when needed. Here are some suggested policies and procedures to consider:
   - Hire a flexibly scheduled, permanent part-time substitute or join with other programs in hiring rotating substitutes. This allows each program some guaranteed coverage and provides dependable employment for the substitute. Even when nobody is absent, a substitute can fill in while regular staff members take breaks or attend family-educator conferences, planning sessions, or other meetings.
   - Regularly evaluate your substitute procedure to see if it needs to be updated, and keep the substitute list active.
   - Call substitutes periodically to make sure they are still available.
   - Let parents/caregivers know about the procedure for using substitutes.

2. **Schedule Regular Breaks.** Due to the cost of hiring additional staff members, most programs accommodate staff breaks by shifting assignments among regular personnel. Here are some suggestions for arranging breaks:
   - Have nonteaching staff members cover breaks on different days of the week.
   - Assign family members, higher education students, and community volunteers as floaters who can work with a regular member of the staff while a coworker takes a break.

   The key to making this plan work is regular scheduling and dependable volunteers. Volunteers should receive a thorough orientation to their duties and have the same monitoring skills and health responsibilities as regular staff members. Provide a quiet, separate, and relaxing space for staff members. Even if space is limited, a comfortable chair placed in front of a window can serve as a place to relax. If at all possible, the program should provide nutritious refreshments for staff members and enough break time so a staff member can take a short walk, preferably outdoors, to reduce the stress of the day.

3. **Promote Professional Development and Support.** Research suggests that engaging in professional development related to resilience and stress relief is restorative. In particular, researchers have found that journaling and reflective practice are the most effective professional development strategies for decreasing feelings of burnout (Roberts et al. 2020).

   In the United States, when educators participate in quality improvement programs, such as quality rating improvement systems (QRISs), Steps to Quality, and Step Up to Quality, they engage in the process of self-assessment and continual growth, working toward creating an early learning setting where people feel positive and engaged in their teaching. Tools that QRISs employ to make this possible, such as the Teachstone's Classroom Assessment Scoring System (CLASS), encourage educators to change their interactions, promoting children's mental health and learning. Programs can also work to achieve national accreditation through NAEYC; in the process, accreditation staff can answer questions and provide support.

   In many states, partnering with state QRISs can help directors improve early learning programs one step at a time. Sometimes, a QRIS will fund professional development opportunities, provide physical materials like science center tools, and bring in a coach.

Program-Level Health and Safety Practices

Educators know that their primary responsibility is the health and safety of the children they serve. After educators "put on their own mask," they can turn immediately to the care and attention of the children with a renewed sense of purpose and resolve. Educators teach math and literacy skills, yes, but they also contribute to the overall health and safety of the children in an early learning program in many other ways.

Healthy Habit How-Tos

Early childhood educators are in a position to articulate, model, and value healthy habits, such as effective handwashing, eating nutritional foods (including making sure there is access to breast milk for infants), brushing teeth, getting exercise, and staying home when ill. Think back to the first vignette in this chapter, when Skylar and Dee were washing hands together. This teachable moment is a reminder that children learn best through doing things and that adult modeling and coaching help them refine their skills. Positive relationships like the one detailed are powerful—the child can feel that the adult values the healthy routine and also engages in the practice. These key concepts should be included in the classroom curriculum and shared with families (NAEYC 2022; Standards 2 and 5). (See the chapters in Parts 2 and 3 for more on modeling healthy habits.)

As health guidance changes from year to year, educators can regularly check for healthy practice updates and adapt their practices to include current health recommendations (NAEYC 2021). By doing this, they create community expectations that set children up for success (CDC 2023). This book refers to various standards primarily from NAEYC, the American Academy of Pediatrics' *Caring for Our Children,* and the Centers for Disease Control and Prevention (CDC).

Home-to-School Health and Safety Connections

Early childhood educators must do more than engage in and model healthy and safe practices in the early learning program alone. They must build home-to-school connections so that healthy and safe practices are extended into the broader community. It is essential to respectfully communicate with each child and family, building a safe space for everyone to engage and learn. Build reciprocal partnerships with families by asking about their home languages and cultures. Learn how different cultures promote healthy and safe behaviors, including sleeping practices for infants, and, when possible, weave elements of them into the classroom routines (NAEYC 2022; Standard 1).

Partnering with Families

Partnering with families creates trust and respect, which go a long way to building strong early learning programs. Relationships and partnerships are the foundation of these programs as reflected in the first NAEYC Early Learning Program Accreditation standard (NAEYC 2022).

Families want to know that the early learning program where they send their children is safe and promotes healthy activities and interactions. How and when educators explain the program's health and safety protocols and practices to each and every family is critical. Families should receive this information when they ask about it or as soon as they join the program. It is important to share health and safety policies with families in formal written documents, such as policy and procedure handbooks. It is equally important for the program to maintain ongoing communication with families as protocols or procedures change.

Working with families with different cultural backgrounds and varied experiences can provide some communication challenges, so it is critical that educators are both clear in their understanding of the protocols and can communicate effectively to families using a range of methods, including emails, texts, phone calls, and through the help of translators when needed.

> "Hola," Noa greets 3-year-old Cian with a smile. Cian's papi begins signing in on the clipboard. "¿Cómo estás?" asks Noa. Though still learning Spanish, Noa is careful to greet the family using their home language. This is because when educators use families' home languages (and represent them using books and signs in the early learning setting), it sends a clear message that their language is valued. Before the school year began, Noa used a form that was inclusive when asking families for words in their home language. Rather than directing families to write "father's name here" or "mother's name here," the form simply asked for parents'/primary caregivers' names and pronouns. This was intentionally revised because Cian has two fathers.

Signage is also an important element in communicating policies and protocols. Signs that show national and state guidelines for health and safety actions, such as storage of poisonous cleaning supplies and how to wash hands, should be posted in classrooms and throughout the early learning program. When selecting these visual representations, administrators and purchasers should consider if materials are developmentally appropriate and equitable. For example, consider signage that conveys messaging in different languages and with visual cues (Figures 1.1 A and B).

FAMILY CONNECTIONS

"Untraditional" Families

Not all families have traditional structures, so your handouts should avoid assuming that families are headed by a mother and a father. Try *families* as a way to engage instead, and avoid using forms that assume the family structure is mother-father headed.

Many early childhood educators find that they can do even more to change lives by helping families access the things that they need, including healthy food, warm clothing, and preventive screenings. They can also help families with initial phone calls to build connections with early childhood interventionists. It can be so hard to get access to services, but with a trusted educator at their side, more families can locate what they need and follow through to get it (NAEYC 2022; Standards 2, 4, and 7).

Figure 1.1 A and B. Handwashing Posters from the CDC are available in (A on left) English and (B on right) Spanish.

FAMILY CONNECTIONS

Food and Family

Home visits are great ways to learn about the foods families value. Educators can ask families to share traditional recipes, and they can serve healthy choices that are familiar helps children feel appreciated and also comfortable eating at the program.

Helping Families with Developmental Screening

Directors can also coordinate access to developmental screenings, including physical and mental health. (See "Chapter 3: Enrollment, Health Documentation, Assessments, and Screenings" and "Chapter 10: Inclusion of Young Children with Special Healthcare Needs and/or Medical Complexity.") These may be done in collaboration with existing external organizations, such as Help Me Grow.

Educators can partner with healthcare professionals to screen children for developmental differences when they join the classroom and then use a valid and reliable assessment tool to collect data on children's growth for family-educator conferences and to guide teaching and curriculum design.

This data can be used to help families secure therapeutic intervention if necessary. (See "Chapter 6: Social-Emotional and Mental Health" and "Chapter 10: Inclusion of Young Children with Special Healthcare Needs and/or Medical Complexity.")

If families do not have access to health-based opportunities (in addition to initial screening), early learning programs are in a position to support families by locating ways to access them. Directors can identify and share directions to community clinics and promote car seat or bicycle safety events. They can help families problem solve accessing resources they need and events by partnering with programs such as Early Start (NAEYC 2022; Standard 4). (See more in "Chapter 2: Healthcare Professionals and Educators Work Together to Support Healthy and Thriving Children" and "Chapter 3: Enrollment, Health Documentation, Assessments, and Screenings.")

The health and safety protocols of any program can be extensive and, at times, complex. It is the role of administrators and teachers to set the stage and communicate with families to clarify when these details are not clear for families.

Prevention and Training

In addition to teaching healthy habits, it is important for program directors or leaders to enable preventive actions through appropriate policies and procedures. They must ensure that all staff members have completed first aid and CPR training and know the appropriate procedures for handling health and safety emergencies. Center Directors also coordinate documents and plans for daily safety checks and monthly safety drills or practices. The director should also make these plans available for families to examine (NAEYC 2022; Standard 2, curriculum). (See also "Chapter 7: First Aid and Injuries" and "Chapter 12: Emergency and Disaster Preparation and Planning.")

Training for the Worse-Case Scenario

Director Julia is in the sandbox when the police officers arrive in the program's outdoor classroom. After a whispered conversation with them, she stands up and rings the bell, cuing the preschoolers to go inside for circle time. She sits the children down and begins, "Guess what? It sounds like we're going to get to see where the big kids go to get library books! We will need to walk quietly and be very quiet when we are there because it's a library. We're waiting for my friends to tell me when to go." Just then the officers come in and whisper another request. "Oh, friends, it sounds like the plans have changed," Julia says. "We're going to walk outside and into the big kids' yard instead—we will see the big kids' playground!" Bringing the red safety backpack, Cheerios and water, a cell phone, and the roster, she guides the children to the playground of the nearby elementary school, where she continues circle time as the police officers examine and remove the pipe bomb that is in the trash can beside the center's office building. As Julia leads circle time, another educator uses the cell phone and roster to contact families and send the children home for the day. The children do not know what happened. In the coming weeks, the adults use the experience to make a better safety plan for future events, adding toys to the safety backpack.

If the teachers and staff members in this scenario had not been prepared for this event, it could have created chaos and produced trauma and stress in the children and the entire learning community.

In the United States, unlike many areas of the world, conventional wars are not a source of harm for young children, but the threat of violence places children and educators in both physical and psychological danger. The frequency of gun violence in particular has continued to increase over the past eight years, which has included an increase in injuries and fatalities of young children (Gun Violence Archive 2023). While there are some steps educators can take to promote physical safety in the event of gun violence (see section "Active Shooter Training" in "Chapter 12: Emergency and Disaster Preparation and Planning"), the problem has left many educators, families, and children understandably concerned and looking for guidance and support. Early learning program policies must effectively address these concerns and support teachers through training and professional development.

Preparing for and Eliminating Hazards

Early learning programs can help ensure the physical health and safety of children by engaging in safety checks and fire inspections, installing outlet covers, and performing other essential tasks. When a classroom space is designed with physical safety in mind and adults feel prepared to handle any possible classroom emergencies, both children and adults can colearn with and coteach one another with fewer chances of physical harm.

Teachers and program administrators must ensure that their classrooms are physically healthy and safe even before children walk in the door. When designing the classroom with a safety mindset, they ensure that all children can be supervised by sight and sound and that fire lanes are clear. They check that their cabinets are affixed to walls, that furniture is safe, and that sandboxes can be maintained free of animal feces. (See "Chapter 13: Creating a Safe Environment.")

Once children enter classrooms, educators continue to engage in the aforementioned safety checks for hazards. These include ensuring proper storage of chemicals used to clean and sanitize, using the least toxic techniques possible to control pests, and using toys appropriate for the ages of children served, with an awareness of manufacturer recalls of products and necessary actions (NAEYC 2022; Standard 9). Ideally, these safety checks happen in the morning before children arrive but are also done on an as-needed basis. For example, if the children wash their hands in the bathroom and water spills on the floor, a safety action would be to clean up the spilled water with a towel before children slip and fall. This could happen quickly if all children are easily supervised by sight and sound in a well-designed classroom.

Committing to Children's Feelings of Safety

It is relatively easy to focus on the safety of children when thinking about fire drills and hand hygiene. These protocols and procedures make a space physically safe for children. It is more complicated to address children's feelings about safety, and how these feelings effect their emotional and mental health. In addition to physical safety, children must also feel safe socially and emotionally within an early learning setting.

We have all felt "unsafe" as children and adults. Think about a time when this was true for you in any way (physically, socially, or emotionally). Imagine the moment, and think about what was going on and the range of feelings you experienced at the time. On a piece of paper, write down words or phrases that describe how you felt. Let the ideas flow. Look at the list of words you wrote and imagine a child in your program feeling those big feelings. Now consider the following vignette.

> Marco, a 4-year-old preschooler, plays in the dress-up corner, happily trying on clothes and looking in the full-length mirror while wearing a long evening dress and high-heeled shoes. Other children laugh, calling Marco names and causing the child to frantically remove the outfit that had caused so much happiness moments ago. The educator looks at Marco, who stares back tearfully.

At this moment, was Marco physically safe? Certainly. To prevent physical harm to children in their care, Marco's educators had taken all the necessary precautions in their established safety check. In fact, they spent a great deal of time doing so. However, Marco was unsafe and injured at this moment in a way that was not physically observable. The injury, although tremendously significant in Marco's life, would not find its way into an incident report, but like a cut or a broken bone, it might very well leave a lasting mark.

Educators can teach (and model) social and emotional skills, guiding children to build positive relationships and handle big feelings and stress. This can be done intentionally using many techniques (during group times and through teachable moments), so that all children can access the key concepts needed to become a member of the community and stay emotionally healthy.

Emotional or psychological safety occurs when educators are ethical, respectful, and inclusive of the unique lives of the people in their care. Creating a warm, nurturing environment, one that welcomes children and their families, sends a message to children and adults alike that they are valued and respected, as are their curiosities, interests, and cultural ways of being (Derman-Sparks & Edwards with Goins 2020). This sense of social-emotional safety sets up children to survive and thrive and has implications for what they are willing to do in the classroom. It leads them to take healthy risks and avoid harmful ones and, ultimately, influences both their learning and healthy development. This is particularly important when families are struggling with significant challenges outside of the classroom walls, such as food scarcity, homelessness, undocumented status, and/or loss of an income. It's also essential if the family has historically suffered from feelings of discrimination based on their skin color, family structure, languages spoken, or culture.

As families begin to share confidential information with administrators and educators, the administrators and educators must understand that they are mandated reporters, keeping confidentiality as much as possible but required to share key health and safety challenges, such as abuse, with Child Protective Services. By doing these things, directors, and educators plant seeds for a future where children will someday plan and take their own actions to stay safe and healthy, rather than rely on adults for guidance, support, and scaffolding. These actions build a framework for children to handle adverse experiences throughout their lifetimes.

FAMILY CONNECTIONS

Emotional Safety: A Focus on Books

How do educators select just the right books and resources for the classroom? Begin with an open mind and listen. First, partner with families. Engage in relationship planning by asking about the families' needs, values, and wishes for their children. Do this even before they join the program. How? Educators can have a conversation during a home visit or a phone or video chat with each family or invite them to write a bit about their child. Ask also for a list of key words and phrases in the families' home languages. Setting up the classroom so that the walls and shelving reflect the people walking in for the first time is a wonderful way to support feelings of belonging to a community, which are key for positive mental health.

When books in the classroom are both mirrors of the people in the space and windows into other families and communities, educators can use the conversations that follow the reading to create brave and safe spaces for conversations. What books work as windows and mirrors in your classroom? Is everyone at the table? Do books send messages that are unintentionally racist, sexist, or overly focused on cisgender lifestyles? *Bodies Are Cool,* by Tyler Feder; *Mommy, Mama, and Me,* by Lesléa Newman, illustrated by Carol Thompson; and *Julián Is a Mermaid,* by Jessica Love, are books that introduce conversations about belongingness in the classroom and community for children. Consider introducing these books and others into the classroom library. Take a moment to assess the classroom library and to pick out a few titles to add.

TRAUMA-INFORMED CARE: CREATING SAFE AND NURTURING SPACES FOR CHILDREN

One primary responsibility of all early childhood educators is to create safe and nurturing learning environments for all children. This responsibility becomes increasingly difficult when a community is in crisis (for example, due to a pandemic) or one child or family has experienced trauma and their resulting behaviors impact everyone. Either way, it is essential to consider the role of trauma and ACEs on health in order to consider how to respond and stabilize the classroom or program.

> Discussions of trauma often include the mention of adverse childhood experiences (ACEs)—potentially traumatic events that occur in childhood. This term comes from a landmark study conducted by the Centers for Disease Control and Prevention (CDC) and Kaiser Permanente from 1995 to 1997 that measured 10 types of childhood trauma (Felitti et al. 1998). Individuals participating in the

(*continued*)

study marked the adverse experiences they had been exposed to as children, which were then tallied to give them an overall ACE score. The childhood traumas listed included five personally experienced traumas and five involving family members:

> - Physical abuse
> - Verbal abuse
> - Sexual abuse
> - Physical neglect
> - Emotional neglect
> - A family member who was a substance abuser
> - A mother who was a victim of domestic violence
> - A family member who was incarcerated
> - A family member with a severe mental illness
> - Parents who were separated or divorced
>
> Researchers found that a higher ACE score put individuals at increased risk for later negative outcomes in health and well-being, including mental illness, risky behaviors such as substance use disorders, and diminished professional and educational opportunities (Sacks & Murphy 2018). (Erdman & Colker with Winter 2020, 5)

A model of trauma-informed care that expands the definition of *health and safety* to include not only the physical but all domains of a child's development, including intellectual, social, emotional and psychological, and addresses the effects of trauma and ACEs can help educators create a safe and nurturing space for children.

These domains are typically considered when doing observations in other areas of child development and early learning but not when considering health and safety. This model uses four statements to illustrate how these domains are supported by a caring and nurturing environment (Nicholson et al. 2021):

- Emotional/psychological safety—I feel supported.
- Social safety—I feel seen.
- Physical safety—I feel safe.
- Intellectual safety—I feel engaged.

"I feel supported, and I feel seen." Educators can work to ensure a learning environment is safe for and supportive of all children and families by evaluating the visual material in it. Derman-Sparks and her colleagues (2020) noted, "The toys, materials, and equipment you put out for children; the posters, pictures, and art objects you hang on the wall; and the types of furniture and how you arrange them all influence what children learn. What children do not see in the classroom teaches children as much as what they do see" (180). Checklists like the one created by author Derman-Sparks and her colleagues can guide educators to see the classroom through the lens of a wide range of families. Try assessing a classroom. Identify the strengths of the space and also places where educators could improve the visual environment.

"I feel safe." When educators are trained for emergencies and conduct regular safety drills with the children, this lets children know that there are plans to keep them safe.

"I feel engaged." Best-practice classrooms involve educators who follow the children's lead for inquiries. Such classrooms are spaces that promote a growth mindset and guide children to explore and actively engage with the materials. These "yes" spaces are essential for children as they take risks and become capable, creative, problem-solving citizens. In the following vignette, Teacher Julia uses a puppet to engage the children in considering a problem and participating in reaching the solution. This process promotes the children's sense of achievement and helps them recognize the important role they play in their own learning. Consider the following vignette.

> **Emily the Puppet is facing 18 preschoolers. From teacher Julia's lap, she comments, "I have a big problem. I'm still working on counting, and sometimes I forget numbers, or they come out wrong." Teacher Julia replies, "That's okay, Emily! We need to practice to get better at things. I bet the children can help you practice. Let's all count the vegetables together!" One child looks at the puppet. "Emily, I have a hard time counting too," he says softly. Teacher Julia replies, "It takes a lot of practice to get good at it. Let's say the numbers as we touch each vegetable together. One . . . two . . . three . . . (twenty)! We did it!" Emily the Puppet and the child who commented are both smiling. Emily comments, "I made it all the way to twenty, and we said every number!"**

Overview of National Standards and Programs

For directors and administrators, it may feel overwhelming to consider making changes to promote healthy and safe practices to a currently running program, especially if staff members are resistant to change. For educators and staff members, change can be stressful and add additional work to their already full plates.

It's okay to just pick a subset of practices and begin there, gradually expanding the quality of the program and improving each classroom. To do this systematically, first look to national standards for classroom and program practices. Here are some resources:

Physical Health and Safety

- **Federal Insecticide and Fungicide Regulation Act (FIFRA)** dictates which fungicides or insecticides can be legally used around children.

- **Head Start Early Childhood Learning and Knowledge Center's "Safety Practices" webpage** compiles best practices. It includes lists of items to focus on while improving a program's healthy and safe practices. These lists include specifics about how to keep the children in centers physically healthy and safe, covering a range of topics, including poisoning prevention, safety checks, how to respond to tornadoes, how to keep infants and toddlers safe, and more. These national standards are basic, clear, and federally mandated. (**https://eclkc.ohs.acf.hhs.gov/safety-practices**)
- **Occupational Safety and Health Administration (OSHA) guidance** dictates how an early childhood educator can safely lift play materials, descend a ladder, and more.

Behavioral Health and Safety

- **American Academy of Pediatrics' HealthyChildren.org website www.healthychildren.org**
- **California Childcare Health Program, University of California San Francisco's (CCHP UCSF) "Health and Safety Checklist for Early Care and Education Programs"**. (**https://cchp.ucsf.edu/sites/g/files/tkssra181/f/July%202020-HS-Checklist-2.pdf**)
- **Center for Early Childhood Mental Health Consultation (CECMHC)** provides free resources that support mental health and are free and easy for the public to access. (**www.ecmhc.org**)
- **Center on the Social and Emotional Foundations for Early Learning (CSEFEL)** focuses beyond physical safety and health and considers children's equally important social, emotional, and intellectual safety. It has resources that guide early childhood educators and families about effective ways to support child mental health. (**http://csefel.vanderbilt.edu**)
- **Collaborative for Academic, Social, and Emotional Learning (CASEL)** (**www.casel.org**)
- **Help Me Grow** is a national system that provides free screening and recommendations for families. These programs are funded nationally but implemented locally, partnering with state providers of early childhood intervention. (**www.helpmegrownational.org**)
- **National Association for the Education of Young Children (NAEYC)** is a professional membership organization that promotes high-quality early learning for all young children. It provides excellent guidance about program practices across every domain. Their accreditation process can guide centers to improve health and safety well beyond physical safety concerns. It also publishes articles and books that provide excellent tips for children on these topics. (**NAEYC.org**)
- **National Center for Pyramid Model Innovations' (NCPMI) Pyramid Model. (https://challengingbehavior.org/pyramid-model)**
- **National Center on Health, Behavioral Health, and Safety (https://eclkc.ohs.acf.hhs.gov/about-us/article/national-center-health-behavioral-health-safety-nchbhs)**
- **Office of Child Care's "CCDF Health and Safety Requirements Fact Sheet: Health and Safety Training" (https://childcareta.acf.hhs.gov/sites/default/files/286_1508_healthsafety_summary_training_final_0.pdf)**
- **Zero to Three. (www.zerotothree.org)**

State Programs

The previously mentioned national programs are excellent resources and guides for considering how to increase quality in early learning programs. The concepts they cover are broad and can be applied globally.

State programs vary from state to state in terms of what is provided and how programming is implemented. For example, the US Department of Health and Human Services funds a QRIS through the Child Care and Development Block Grant Act of 2014 (Public Law 113–146) for every state. This funding is intended to strengthen requirements to protect health and safety in child care. It is there to help parents/caregivers make informed choices about child care and access information to support child development. It is also meant to provide equal access to stable high-quality child care for children from families with low income and improve the quality of child care and the early childhood workforce. The money from this funding must be spent on the above topics. Within the limitations of that guidance, states or counties decide how they will implement the spending of the money.

There are also state resources to improve the health and safety of early childhood classrooms. These programs give specifics about how to implement broader national mandates. They sometimes make more rigorous guidelines and regulations than the national standards.

State Licensing

It is possible to locate useful local information through state licensing and other statewide programs. There, programs can locate specific legislation around what centers must do; for example, legal ratios and group size for the age of children served and the size of the facility. Child care licensing websites are also good sources of information when administrators have questions about new public health measures. For example, in California, there is a great deal of specific guidance on COVID-19 for classrooms on the California Department of Public Health's website (**www.cdph.ca.gov/Programs/CID/DCDC/Pages/COVID-19/Child-Care-Guidance.aspx**) and the California Department of Social Services' website (**www.cdss.ca.gov/inforesources/child-care-licensing**). If guidelines are unclear, the licensing analyst assigned to the program, or the officer of the day, can help answer questions and give tips about the rapidly changing rules concerning the pandemic that began in 2020.

Summary

> Bless has been in Charlie's full-day preschool class for a year, and drop-off time at 7:00 a.m. is generally quick and easy. Today, though, Bless cries and hangs on to her mother's leg during separation, while her mother reminds her tensely that this behavior will make her late for work. Charlie is initially confused—why would this day be different? When Bless calms down, Charlie learns that drop-off was preceded by an angry conversation during which Bless's mom said, "I wish I'd never had you." Bless is worried that her mother will not return at the 6:00 p.m. pickup time. Charlie soothes Bless and helps her to start the daily routine. Charlie realizes the stress that families can feel and decides to call Bless's mom to check on how she is feeling.

Interactions like this one remind educators about why they entered the field and why they remain. To be so deeply needed by a community and entrusted to guide its youngest citizens and support their physical and mental health is truly essential and rewarding work.

If we go back to the first vignette in this chapter and look 10 years into the future, Dee is now 12 years old. Dee washes her hands before each meal, eats fruits and vegetables, and plays on the school soccer team. Dee's first teacher helped set her on a path to healthy habits and routines that will carry throughout her life. High-quality programs make a difference in the lives of children, their families, and the educators who work with them. Early childhood education as a profession has many challenges, but through the strength of the workforce and leadership, things are changing.

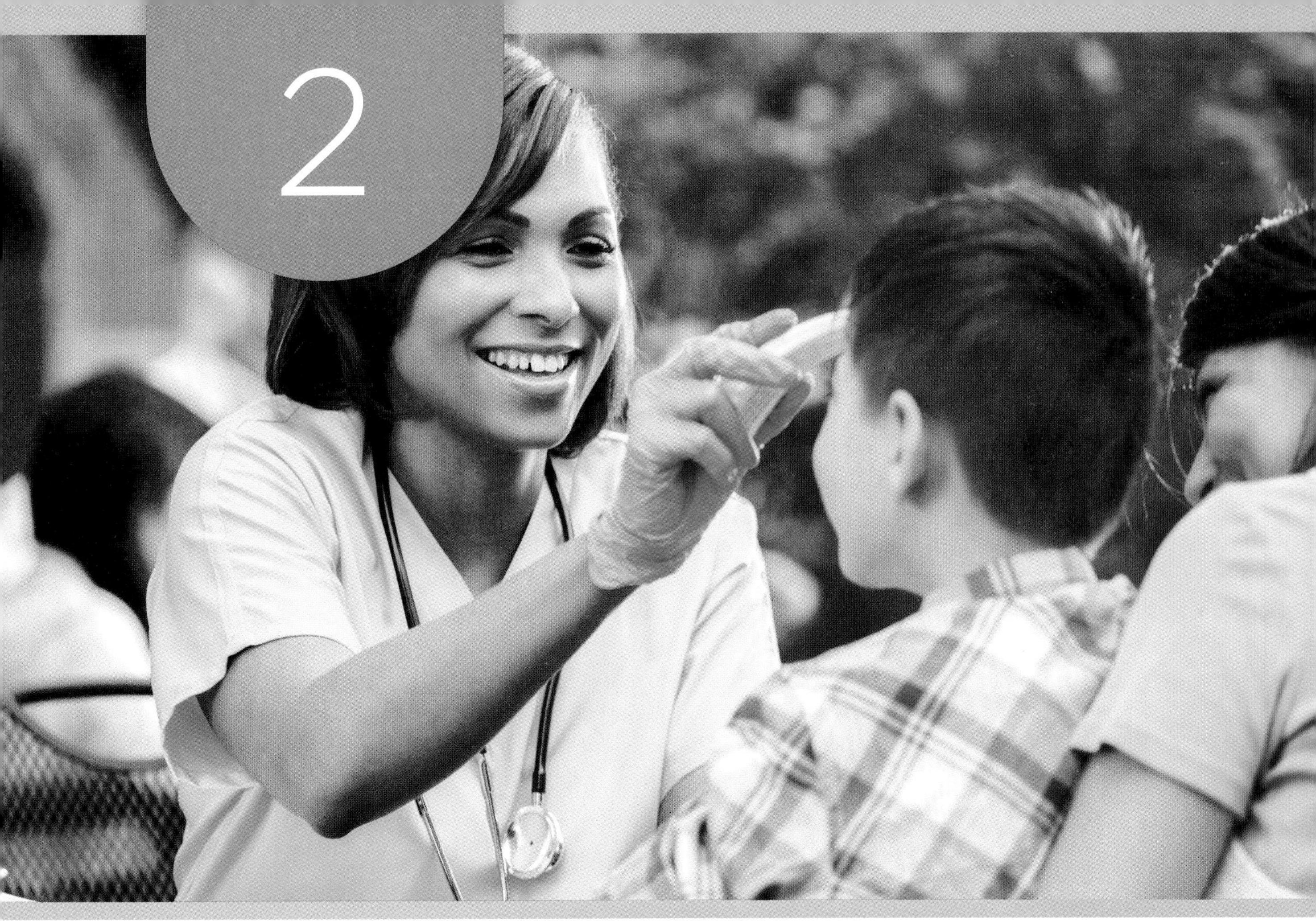

Healthcare Professionals and Educators Together Foster Children's Health and Development

KRISTEN COPELAND, AMY L. KING, AND MARY BETH PERO

LEARNING OBJECTIVES

- To understand the role of healthcare professionals in early childhood education
- To define ways for educators and healthcare professionals to work together
- To understand key child health, safety, and developmental concerns that healthcare professionals and educators share

The health of young children is multipronged and interrelational. Birth to age 8 are critical years for a child's physical, cognitive, and social-emotional development. Healthcare professionals and educators play roles in every aspect of young children's health, including illness prevention, health promotion, assessment, and treatment. Early learning programs are a critical outlet for fostering the mental and physical development of young children (Anderson et al. 2003). The developmental and educational opportunities available to children in their early years have a lasting impact on their health as adults (Campbell et al. 2014; Muennig et al. 2011; Pianta et al. 2009). The Carolina Abecedarian Project, which was a high-quality comprehensive health and development early educational program for a cohort of primarily African American children from families with low income in North Carolina born in years 1972–1977, found that the children in the study who participated in a high-quality and comprehensive early childhood education program that included healthcare and nutritional components had better health during the study (Muennig et al. 2011) and better health outcomes even three decades later (Campbell et al. 2014). Healthcare professionals and educators must understand the health and education systems as family see and experience them, particularly families who may face barriers to access, in order to be effective and assist families in navigating both systems. Most importantly, healthcare professionals, educators, and families have different perspectives and strengths but truly share the same goals that each child reaches their full potential. Educators and healthcare professionals need to understand and operate in a team-based approach to supporting children with chronic medical, developmental, nutritional, or behavioral conditions, with families being at the center of the team (respectful of families' wishes, educators' expertise, and medical professionals' expertise). By working together, healthcare professionals and educators can improve the health and safety of all children and families.

The purpose of this chapter is to discuss how pediatricians and healthcare workers can work together with educators to create safe and healthy environments for children and promote healthy living to families. To begin, we examine how early childhood educators and healthcare providers communicate and collaborate and discuss ways in which the two parties work together. Information is also provided about the specific functions of medical providers, specifically in the areas of health, development, and safety for children. We discuss the societal factors that affect children's health and families, specifically through the lens of the aftereffects of the COVID-19 pandemic, and examine what it means for educators and the healthcare community. And finally, we give an overview of potential opportunities for educators to continue to partner with healthcare professionals and the greater healthcare community.

Collaboration and Communication for Successful Partnerships

Healthcare professionals and educators understand that all child health concerns require a collaborative approach to help families and children. Given the substantial overlap between healthcare professionals and early childhood educators for effectively promoting health and development and ensuring that safe and nurturing environments are provided to young children, healthcare professionals and early educators must partner together to work with children and families.

A Child's Medical Home

It's important for educators to understand best practice for children's healthcare. The ideal way for a child to receive preventive and therapeutic services is from a trusted team of healthcare professionals and allied individuals within a primary medical home. The American Academy of Pediatrics (AAP; n.d.) defines a *medical home* as "an approach to providing comprehensive primary care that facilitates partnerships between patients, clinicians, medical staff, and families. A medical home extends beyond the four walls of a clinical practice" (n.p.). The Agency for Healthcare Research and Quality (2022) identified five key elements of a medical home:

1. Being patient-centered and based on trusted relationships
2. Providing comprehensive care including preventive, wellness, and acute care
3. Providing coordination of care across subspecialists, hospitals, and home healthcare systems
4. Having services that are highly accessible (phone, telehealth, after hours), and in the language of the patient's preference
5. Having a commitment to providing care that is evidence based, safe, and high-quality, with efforts to continuously improve the quality

Educators can provide a great service to families in meeting preventive health needs, care coordination needs, and access to subspecialty care by helping families identify a primary medical home. Educators can also help families plan for their well-child visits by providing families with the knowledge of what forms the program will need (e.g., medical form and shot record) and the actual forms required with enough time for families to schedule the visit and complete it before it is due. Giving families enough lead time is crucial to effectively partnering with healthcare professionals and the families so that children do not miss learning and families do not have to miss work or other responsibilities. Furthermore, educators can help prep families for their well-child visits by providing families with documents of any developmental or social-emotional assessments performed in the program, particularly if there are concerns for developmental delay or behavioral problems. (See "Screening and Evaluation for Development" later on in this chapter.) Educators can also help families know what to expect from their well-child visits by directing them to freely available websites, such as the **www.wellvisitplanner.org**, where families can set up an account for free and learn about what will be discussed in each well-child visit from 0 to 6 years old. If their medical home uses this service, they may also be able to fill out forms prior to their visits. Relatedly, educators can encourage families to obtain MyChart access to their child's medical record, where they can understand at any time what medications their child is on, what diagnoses were made at recent visits, when immunizations will next be due, how they can schedule appointments, and how to message the doctor's office with questions. Through MyChart, families can also send nonurgent messages outside of regular business hours and have their questions answered within 24–72 hours without having to wait on the phone. Last, educators can play a role in reinforcing and adding to health and safety topics addressed in well-child visits at the child's primary medical home. These include discussion of communicable diseases, which diseases require exclusion, and requirements for reentry into child care.

School-Based Health Centers

One way that the health and education systems work together is through school-based health centers. School-based health centers are an evidence-based model of care that improves educational and health outcomes (School-Based Health Alliance, n.d.). School-based health centers provide children and youth access to primary, behavioral, oral, and vision healthcare where they spend most of their time—at school. Working at the intersection of health and education, school-based health centers collaborate with school districts, principals, teachers, staff members, families, and children. The collaboration, care coordination, and youth engagement results in improved health outcomes as well improved health literacy for children, staff members, and the community. In addition, school-based health centers contribute to improved educational outcomes, including reduced absenteeism and disciplinary actions as well as improved graduation rates. Most school-based health centers operate as primary care medical homes with an external community medical sponsoring agency in partnership with the local education agency and offer services not only to children but also to other family and community members. The centers, then, can be a good source of primary medical and dental care for children of all ages. Children do not have to attend the school where the clinic is housed, nor do they have to be of school age. Identifying a nearby school-based health center can be a good way to establish a primary medical home for children who lack one.

Child Care Health Consultants

A role that crosses both healthcare and education is the child care health consultant (CCHC). CCHCs are healthcare professionals (e.g., nurses, physician assistants, public health workers) who are trained in health, communicable disease, and early learning settings. They consult with early childhood educators to promote the health, safety, and development of children in early learning programs. CCHCs can share their health and developmental expertise, perform assessments of children and/or staff members, and connect staff members and families to relevant community resources. CCHCs are often affiliated with the local health departments and can serve as a liaison or adviser on communicable disease and exclusion criteria for COVID-19 or other epidemics (e.g., *Shigella*, measles, Mpox). CCHCs can also provide guidance on new vaccines or boosters (e.g., COVID-19 vaccines) and where they can be obtained. CCHCs do not provide consultation or medical advice for individual children or staff members, but they can assist families in care coordination with the medical home and other health and developmental specialists. Importantly, CCHCs should collaborate with an interdisciplinary team of consultants in various fields, such as early childhood education, mental health, and nutrition. CCHCs can contribute expertise, leadership, and motivation to reach for quality in the early learning program's health component.

During site visits, CCHCs make observations, look at documents, and listen to the people who work in the program to assess strengths and identify hazards and risky practices that need to be improved. Then they collaborate with the program staff members and families to develop plans for change and provide health education. CCHCs bring knowledge of current recommendations and resources to the program for quality improvement. Each state has a different system for implementing this role. The role of the CCHC is discussed in more detail in Section 1.6 of *Caring for Our Children*. The standards in this section define the role and expertise of CCHCs, early childhood mental health consultants, early childhood education consultants, and specialized consultation for programs serving children with disabilities.

Pediatricians Provide Prevention and Health Education

Pediatric clinicians provide a multitude of preventive and therapeutic services as a part of primary care that are relevant to early childhood education. Pediatric clinics provide vaccinations and counseling on routine vaccinations, including annual flu shots. Many pediatric clinics also provide flu vaccines and COVID-19 vaccines to parents/caregivers of children who are seen by the clinic. Pediatricians also provide families with general health information and counseling on how to prevent the spread of communicable disease, including consistent handwashing before and after meals, after sneezing and coughing, and after toileting/diaper changes. Other important infectious control measures that pediatric clinicians provide counseling on are staying up to date on all recommended vaccines and boosters, including COVID-19 shots, and wearing masks indoors to prevent the spread of infectious diseases transmitted by respiratory droplets, such as COVID-19 and flu, particularly when community spread is high. Many families have the misperception that diseases are spread more easily outdoors than indoors, so pediatric clinicians provide education, and educators can help reinforce that disease is more easily spread indoors than outdoors (somewhere between 5 to 20 times more easily spread, depending on the type). For infants under 6 months old whose immune systems are still developing and who are too young for several immunizations (e.g., measles, mumps, and rubella (MMR); varicella [chickenpox]; COVID-19; and influenza), pediatric clinicians provide general infectious disease guidance, including ensuring that family members are fully vaccinated; other adults and children are not around young infants if they are exhibiting signs of sickness; and all children and adults handling or playing with the infant first wash their hands (or if soap and water not available, use a hand sanitizer).

Pediatric clinicians also direct the management of several common conditions. Some of the most common include asthma, eczema, food allergies, environmental allergies, prematurity, growth concerns, obesity, anemia, sleep apnea, lead poisoning, bed wetting, and constipation. Conditions also can be recurrent infectious diseases, such as chronic ear infections and recurrent urinary tract infections. Neurological, genetic, and environmental conditions that pediatric clinicians manage and can affect development include chromosomal-based disorders, effects of prenatal exposure to drugs, seizures, congenital heart disease, cerebral palsy, and other neurological disorders. Primary care clinician may help identify causes of inattention including poor sleep, poor hearing or vision, depression, cognitive delays, autism, learning disorders, trauma, and inattention, hyperactivity, and attention-deficit/hyperactivity disorder (ADHD).

Pediatricians and Educators Promote Nutrition and Physical Activity

Pediatric clinicians and educators promote the benefits of healthy nutrition and physical activity in young children. Early learning settings provide children with access to healthy food, and educators can also model healthy eating and consult with the Child and Adult Care Food Program (CACFP) administrator in their area for nutrition counseling for families. Healthcare providers screen and counsel on the nutritional quality of all of children's environments. Both healthcare providers and educators help families gain access to healthy food through food pantries, pop-up markets, farmers' markets, and other community assets. Educators and pediatric clinicians promote daily physical activity for children to facilitate the development of gross and fine motor skills; to improve bone health, blood pressure, and metabolic indicators (prevention of diabetes); and to help children maintain a healthy weight (Biddle & Asare 2011; FNS USDA 2023; Glenn et al. 2022; Janssen & LeBlanc 2010; Proia et al. 2021). Daily physical activity also improves mood and attention and can provide learning opportunities about science, weather, cause and effect, taking turns, and working as team. Educators can reinforce these principles by ensuring that children have daily opportunities to be physically active (running, jumping, dancing) and to go outdoors, as recommended by guidelines in *Caring for Our Children*. (See also "Chapter 5: Physical Activity.")

Social-Emotional Development and Challenging Behavior

The overlap between healthcare and education is particularly evident in terms of children's social-emotional development and challenging behavior, and the partnership of these two entities can be critical. In our experience, when the child is exhibiting challenging behavior in the classrooms, educators typically tell parents/caregivers to take their child to the doctor to have the child evaluated. When the parent sees the doctor, however, the parent isn't always able to share specifically what the challenging behavior was—just that the educators recommended visiting the doctor. Doctors' offices do, in fact, have a wealth of behavioral and mental resources to offer and are often a good first step to evaluating what additional evaluations or supports may be needed. However, there is not sufficient time to address these concerns if other concerns (e.g., well-child care, immunizations, acute illness, and so forth) are also trying to be addressed in the same visit or if the parent doesn't have a clear understanding of the problem trying to be addressed. Therefore, educators can work more effectively with physicians by

- Providing written, specific examples of the behavior the child is exhibiting in the classroom, and encouraging the parent to take a picture of this written assessment on their smartphone so they will still have this information even if they forget to bring the paperwork
- Encouraging caregivers to schedule a doctor's visit for the *sole* purpose of discussing the behavior (i.e., not adding it onto a well-check or ill visit)
- Prepping the parent for what to expect in an initial consult visit with the primary care physician. While primary care clinicians can offer support and guidance to families on their child's social-emotional and behavioral concerns, they are not trained or able to do comprehensive assessments of behavioral or developmental disorders, such as autism spectrum disorder. These comprehensive assessments often take multiple specialists and occur over several visits; however, primary care providers are the best first step for a family with a child with behavioral concerns.

Similarly, as primary care physicians have training in normal childhood development, they can work with educators to help families understand age-appropriate social-emotional skill development and ways to support their children's skill development in this area. For children 12 to 60 months old, these include potty training; temper tantrums; self-regulation skills; peer relationships and sharing; understanding and talking about feelings; discipline and praise; and sleep. The educator can specifically point to activities for social-emotional skill development in the classroom that seem to resonate for the individual child. The educator can also elucidate for parents common social-emotional challenges for each age group (e.g., parallel play versus sharing for 15 month olds, the expected attention span for a 3-year-old) to assuage parents' concerns about their children's age-appropriate behavior (Neville 2007). It is not uncommon for parents of 3- and 4-year-old children to bring up concerns to their pediatric clinician that their child is "hyperactive" because they are restless and don't want to sit still for more than 10 minutes. Or that their preschool-age child is "inattentive" because they cannot sit in circle time or write for more than 15 minutes without losing interest. Educators are well positioned to guide parents' understanding of typical social-emotional development and to discuss with parents activities and tips that are especially helpful in the classroom so that they may be reinforced at home. These may include setting and keeping to regular routines for eating, sleeping, cleaning up; providing opportunities for a certain amount of self-directed play daily; coordinating attachment building activities with adults (5 minutes of special child-directed play with an adult); ensuring the child gets adequate sleep (at least 10 hours at night and an additional two to four hours during the day, depending on age) (Paruthi et al. 2016).

RECOMMENDED REGULAR HOURS OF SLEEP BY AGE

- Infants 4 to 12 months old should sleep 12 to 16 hours per 24 hours (including naps).
- Children 1 to 2 years old should sleep 11 to 14 hours per 24 hours (including naps).
- Children 3 to 5 years old should sleep 10 to 13 hours per 24 hours (including naps).
- Children 6 to 12 years old should sleep 9 to 12 hours per 24 hours (Paruthi et al. 2016).

Connecting with Local Health Resources

Early learning programs should be aware of local health resources and make connections with health agencies, departments, and medical universities. Educators can reach out to their CCHC or the local health department about disease exclusion regulations and to the Special Supplemental Nutrition Program for Women, Infants, and Children (WIC) for nutrition/diet input, as WIC has a dietitian on staff. Their CACFP sponsor also may be a resource for dietary and cost/reimbursement questions. For specific conditions, educators can reach out disease/condition-specific organizations for training. For example, the local Epilepsy Foundation can provide training to staff members on seizures when an enrolled child has a seizure disorder, the local Autism Society can provide resources for children with autism spectrum disorder, and the American Diabetes Association can be a good resource if the program has an enrolled child with diabetes. Educators may also be able to reach out to the local child care resource and referral agency (CCR&R), CCHC or health manager (if they have one), a pediatric department, or a children's hospital with general questions about medical and dietary plans, in addition to encouraging parents to seek guidance from the child's primary medical clinician.

Partnering with Specialists

It is also possible and desirable for educators and primary care pediatric offices, which can include various specialists, to systematically and rigorously create partnerships with pediatric therapy programs in the area, including speech-language pathologists (SLPs), occupational therapists (OTs), physical therapists (PTs), and mental health specialists and counselors. As all these specialties have shared goals in fostering and guiding child development, a shared communication system would allow these specialties to share information about children and strategies that will help the children succeed. For instance, an SLP could share with a preschool teacher how she could include

LOCAL CONNECTIONS

Get to know the local players in your region/state dedicated to the health and development of young children.

- Mental health agencies, especially those who care for patients covered by Medicaid. Medicaid is public insurance for children and adults with limited income administered by each state. States receive federal support to administer this program but have discretion to set varying eligibility criteria to balance their budgets. Medicaid provides generous benefits to beneficiaries and has been associated in numerous studies with better outcomes and longevity for children and adults. Not all doctors or hospitals accept patients covered by Medicaid and not all outpatient facilities [e.g., dentists, pediatric clinics, mental health providers] accept Medicaid.
- Universities or children's hospitals; consider specifically contacting the division of general pediatrics, the division of developmental and behavioral pediatrics, the division of psychology, and the division or department of speech and language pathology
- CCR&R (local and/or state)
- Local education authority (LEA)
- School district
- Head Start administering agency or community action agency
- Public health department (local and/or state)

some strategies into the child's day, and the teacher, in turn, could share some strategies and how the child learns best or ways to keep the child on task. This type of partnership is also helpful when developmental screenings recommend further tests as discussed in the section on developmental screenings later in this chapter.

Medical Paperwork and Sharing Information

One of the most fundamental ways that educators and pediatric clinicians work together is in sharing medical paperwork and forms. Child care state licensing regulations require that children be examined by a clinician and deemed suitable for group care prior to their enrollment. (See also "Chapter 3: Enrollment, Health Documentation, Assessments, and Screenings.")

Many programs require annual checkups with the child's primary medical home and requisite documentation that these checkups have occurred and required immunizations have been administered (or documentation of parent refusal) in order for the child to stay enrolled. Medical forms are also needed for children who require medication administration in child care or who have a healthcare or dietary plan (e.g., asthma, diabetes, food allergy).

While many children have a primary medical home and are regularly seeing a physician, communication breakdowns and lost paperwork prevent the evidence of this established medical relationship making it to the educator. Without a federal or state system to enable this communication, and with privacy laws designed to protect patients' and children's private school and health information from unlawful disclosure, much of the coordination and communication between healthcare professionals and educators will rely on the child's family. Parents/caregivers ideally will bring medical reports and diagnoses letters pertinent to their educational environment from the doctor's office to educators and assessment reports from the educators to the doctor's office for the well-child visit. Yet keeping track of this paperwork, remembering to bring it, and providing it to the doctor in time for the doctor to review can be challenging for parents and healthcare professionals.

A way to make information sharing easier is to establish a process for warm handoffs from the doctor's office to early learning programs. Warm handoffs are typically used in healthcare when transferring a patient from one provider to another and involve a face-to-face meeting with the transferring and receiving providers. While face-to-face meetings are not feasible or necessary between educators and physicians, it's helpful to have a point person in the medical home and another in the educational office to handle referrals and forms.

Healthcare professionals who primarily serve families with low income who qualify for subsidized child care and Head Start may want to set up partnerships with their local CCR&Rs to establish a system of warm handoffs for families desiring child care. Pediatric clinics can assist in enrolling and keeping children enrolled in early learning programs by providing necessary paperwork, including medical forms and shot records, for enrollment and annual checkups. It is important to build into such systems automatic feedback to both the CCR&R and doctor's office in which patients were successfully enrolled so the system can be monitored and continually improved.

Large early learning programs (e.g., the local Head Start administration program, the public school district, larger chains of early learning programs) can proactively reach out to the larger clinics who take care of patients covered by Medicaid (e.g., academic health centers, school-based clinics, federally qualified health centers [FQHC], health department clinics) to ensure both are aware of the medical forms currently required for enrolling and staying enrolled in the early learning programs. Additionally, the healthcare system and pediatric clinics can work with local education programs to

FAMILY CONNECTIONS

Easy Document Retrieval and Sharing

- Suggest that families take pictures of key medical forms and assessment reports on their smartphone so they can be shared with the doctor during a visit. In the anecdotal experience of two pediatrician authors of this chapter, 100 percent of families we see bring their phones to their child's well-child visits.
- Have parents/caregivers sign a release of information so that assessment reports can be faxed to their child's doctor's office prior to their well-child visit.

ensure that medical forms submitted by their office include all the necessary information, especially for Head Start and other publicly funded programs. Many pediatric offices use an electronic medical record (EMR) that can pull pertinent information from the child's records into templated forms generated by the EMR, obviating the need for time-consuming, error prone staff member or physician efforts hand-copying information into written forms. This coordinated effort ensures that children do not miss out on education due to medical forms not being complete.

Screening and Evaluation for Development

Young children may undergo screening for development in both healthcare and educational settings, through standardized assessment tools, standardized screeners (e.g., Ages & Stages Questionnaires), and passive and active observation (educators and pediatric clinicians observing child behavior in classrooms or exam rooms and checking their observations with what families observe at home). The reasons these screenings are conducted are similar—to identify children who may be exhibiting signs of developmental delay and may benefit from additional evaluations, supports, and therapies. AAP and the Centers for Disease Control and Prevention (CDC) recommend all children from birth through 5 years old undergo routine surveillance and screening for developmental concerns (CDC 2022).

A parental concern for developmental delay is the most sensitive and specific predictor of developmental delay (Lipkin et al. 2020). These screenings begin at a very young age (as early as 2–6 months old) and happen at well-child visit, at early intervention visits, and in early learning programs. And yet, there are challenges in reliably implementing developmental screening within pediatric offices, which rely on parental awareness of their child's skills and abilities and visits with limited time (15–20 minutes to cover all medical, preventive, growth, developmental, chronic, and acute problems) (Morelli et al. 2014). Thus, despite many interventions and calls to improve developmental screening in primary care, actual screening rates remain low (30–37 percent), particularly for populations who are Black, Indigenous, and people of color (BIPOC) and who have low income (Hagan, Shaw, & Duncan 2017; Hirai et al. 2018; Meurer et al. 2022).

Therefore, developmental screening within the education setting remains crucial. Within the educational setting, educators use various screeners to assess children's development in developmental domains such as language, literacy, mathematics and science, and physical and social and emotional health (e.g., Ages & Stages Questionnaires, BRIGANCE Early Childhood Screens III, Battelle Developmental Inventory, Denver Developmental Screening Test II, Developmental Indicators for the Assessment of Learning, Infant Developmental Inventory, Parents' Evaluation of Developmental Status).

IMMEDIATE IMPACT

Sharing Results

It is very helpful for educators to provide copies of developmental screening results to the pediatric clinician to facilitate prompt referral to the appropriate specialist (e.g., SLP, developmental-behavioral pediatricians) to make the diagnosis.

Granted, screening tools are only intended to highlight areas where the child may be at increased risk for a delay and warrant further investigation. Only assessment tools administered by trained professionals can be used to diagnose a developmental delay or disability. While educators cannot make a diagnosis from a screening tool, they should share with families both the areas of the child's strengths and the areas where the child may benefit from further evaluation and skill enhancement. It is important for educators to use this specific strengths-based language to help to address families' concerns and focus on what is best for the child.

While screening and surveillance for development can occur within the primary care setting, formal evaluations for specific delays (e.g., speech or articulation delay, autism spectrum disorder) cannot. These conditions require lengthy (approximately 60–90 minute) assessments that may necessitate multiple visits and child cooperation to evaluate. Furthermore, diagnosing these conditions requires specialized training that primary care clinicians (e.g., general pediatricians, family medicine providers) lack. (These general practitioners also lack the time or legal ability to bill for this.) Therefore, while a first step in evaluating and diagnosing a developmental delay or disability may begin with a referral to the child's primary pediatric clinician, it is rarely the last or definitive step. It is important to prepare families appropriately so they do not go to their pediatric clinician expecting to receive a diagnosis during this visit.

AN IDEAL SYSTEM FOR A FAMILY AND CHILD'S JOURNEY

In an ideal situation, the parents/caregivers of a child who is demonstrating possible signs of a developmental delay or disability meet with the child's educator to discuss the concerns in the classroom and be given any copies of written assessments. Next, the parent schedules a visit with their primary medical physician specifically to discuss this issue and brings copies of the screenings done in the early learning setting and all of the program's written communication. Then the pediatric clinician will have time to perform any additional screening; provide a provisional assessment; and have ample opportunity to discuss with the parent options for further evaluation and treatment, including referrals to therapists (e.g., SLPs, OTs, PTs, and/or developmental-behavioral pediatricians), early intervention, special education evaluation from the school district, or close follow-up in primary care. At the end of this ideal situation, the medical provider puts in writing the plan that the parents share with the educational providers. Unfortunately, the journey doesn't usually take this path.

Evaluations do not stop when the referral is initially placed by the pediatric clinician at the index visit, which is the visit that precedes the appointment with the specialist. Specialists or therapists may request specific further complementary referrals for evaluations like SLP, OT, PT, feeding evaluations, and so on from the primary physician. This does not require a visit to the primary physician but does require someone to communicate referrals to the family and get appointments made.

The educational system may also request subspecialty referrals to SLPs, OTs, PTs, and developmental-behavioral pediatricians by sending a letter brought in by parent (or picture of a letter on a parent's smartphone) to the primary pediatric clinician. The letter should state specific concerns or behaviors observed in the classroom, a tentative or possible diagnosis when one is held, and suggested referrals for further evaluation. With a release of information (ROI), this may be done without a doctor's appointment. For families that face significant transportation or scheduling barriers (e.g., family's work obligations, other children's schooling), a referral handled through the medical home's office but without requiring a visit may be in the best interest of the child and family. A ROI is needed to help share across systems. In rare instances, the school nurse can be helpful in communicating to the primary care provider as it is considered provider-to-provider communication, so a release form is not legally required.

Timely Identification and Communication of Developmental Delay

Time is of the essence in initiating and conducting these assessments of language, social-emotional, and motor skills to identify developmental delays and disabilities. Research has consistently shown that early identification and intervention is essential for ensuring that children with medical diagnoses that impede their development (e.g., Down syndrome, other chromosomal abnormalities, cyanotic heart disease, autism spectrum disorder) reach their full potential in development and social-emotional wellness (Bull & AAP Committee on Genetics 2011; Hyman et al. 2020; Lipkin et al. 2020; Marino et al. 2012). It can therefore be extrapolated that children without chronic medical conditions would benefit from early detection and intervention to reach their full potential. When clinicians and educators share these results in a cohesive and timely manner, it enables faster identification of developmental concerns and facilitates prompter referral for specialists' evaluations, specific therapies, and educational adaptations. Thus, timely and effective communication systems between a child's healthcare professionals and their educators is essential. The current system of communication relies on the parents/caregivers to share information and reports. Primary care providers rarely give written reports of developmental screens to parents/caregivers. Specialty providers may give a report to the parents/caregivers, usually weeks after the visit. Therefore, while some screenings may sometimes take place in the same time frame (sometimes in the same week), sharing the screening results between systems (e.g., between the education and healthcare systems; early intervention and healthcare systems; early intervention and education systems) and communicating results to parents often does not happen or is delayed by months.

IMMEDIATE IMPACT

Simplifying Communication

In all primary care practices and educational settings, it can be helpful for clinicians and educators to each identify an administrative point person who can send and receive important medical and developmental forms via fax or electronically once parent permission is obtained.

If the child's family is provided screening results, they may not understand or agree with the findings. Screeners identify the possibility of a problem and should be followed by further evaluations. Families are then advised to seek out these evaluations and relay the findings of the screeners. If information does not get directly communicated to the primary care physician and then back to the educators, this leads to delays in diagnosis and to starting indicated therapies and interventions. If the screening tool is completed late in the healthcare professional visit, there may not be time for the pediatric clinician to evaluate and go over the results with the family.

Too often, the specifics of the concerns are lost between the doctor's office and the educational setting. Parents referred from the educational setting to their primary care doctor for developmental concerns can show up at the doctor's office unsure why they are there.

Working with Families

Developmental concerns are an uncomfortable topic for parents/caregivers and educators. Educators should exercise caution due to the potential stigma associated with developmental delays and create safe spaces and time to talk with families. Educators may lack knowledge about developmental delay or be fearful of having this conversation with the parent and how that conversation may damage their relationship with the parent. Nevertheless, healthcare professionals and educators can work together to make it easier for families to obtain timely evaluations. They can also be supportive and mutually reinforcing in encouraging families to seek treatment for possible delays.

Educators should understand the influence of families' cultures and beliefs on their children's development (Cintas 1989; Coll et al. 1996; Legare & Harris 2016; Mendonça, Sargent, & Fetters 2016). Literature has shown globally that some developmental milestones are achieved in some populations earlier than the United States and later than the United States in other populations (Kelly et al. 2006; Cromwell et al. 2014), so educators who care for children of recent immigrants may see slightly different patterns of gross or fine motor development and social-emotional development and problem solving. Children who are exposed to more than one language at home may know words in only one of the languages but have conceptual vocabularies equal to children exposed to a single language (Byers-Heinlein & Lew-Williams 2013). Educators should be prepared to offer guidance when a family seeks advice on how their child can more quickly gain mastery in these areas.

Parents of firstborn children or who have minimal experience caring for young children may similarly have misconceptions about what age certain developmental milestones are appropriate, and educators are well suited to draw from their substantial expertise and the child's classroom to enlighten families gently and sensitively on the cadence and variability in child development.

Inequitable Screening Practices and Consequences

Research demonstrates children of color, particularly Black and Latino/a children, are at risk for delayed identification of developmental disability and autism spectrum disorders, which can put them behind their peers in early learning and school success and worsen persistent long-documented racial/ethnic disparities in school achievement related to socioeconomic status, racism, and unequal educational opportunities (Paschall, Gershoff, & Kuhfeld 2018). And because educational outcomes and early educational exposures are a leading determinant of health outcomes, these disparities in developmental identification and treatment can contribute to later disparities in morbidity and ultimately life expectancy. Research suggests that Black children and Latino/a children are diagnosed on average up to two years later than their White peers due to myriad factors related to inequitable access to specialists and healthcare, stigma, and the double-stigma of the intersection of race/ethnicity with developmental delay (Dababnah et al. 2018; Guerrero & Sobotka 2022; Mandell et al. 2002; St. Amant et al. 2018). Additionally, there has been noted a tendency within the primary healthcare system to "watch and wait" children when they are demonstrating signs of possible delay. A recent study from Southern California (Elliott et al. 2022) has shown receipt of referrals and services for developmental concerns to be later for Latino/a, Black, and Pacific Islander children when compared to White children. When comparing the majority race group (Hispanic) as the reference category, referrals for children and youths who identified as White, Asian, and multiracial had higher odds of service receipt in comparison with referrals for Hispanic children and youths. These delays may be in part due to implicit racism in clinical providers. Another recent study (Sun et al. 2022) analyzed language used by clinicians in EMRs via machine language learning, and it showed that when compared to White patients, Black patients had 2.54 times the odds of having at least one negative descriptor in their EMR history and physical notes. Unfortunately for children for whom it is deemed sufficient to observe before making referrals, if these children do not return for routine or scheduled close follow-up, they can get lost and fall behind in their developmental trajectories. Therefore, too often this "watch and wait" practice in effect becomes "watch them fail."

SYSTEMIC RACISM AND FAMILY FEARS

Due to a history of systemic racism where Black parents have been implicitly and explicitly told they are not sufficient or adequate parents to their children (Glenn 1992; Gordon 1994; Roberts 2002, 2014), Black parents may be reticent to bring up developmental concerns about their child to healthcare professionals or educators. Some parents who have experienced systemic racism fear that their children may be removed from their care if their children are exhibiting corroborated signs of developmental delay (Burkett et al. 2015, 2017; Lopez, Marroquin, & Gutierrez 2020; Stahmer et al. 2019). It is important for educators and healthcare professionals to be mindful of these fears families may hold so that they can engage in productive and effective conversations when encouraging them to seek assessments, diagnoses, and appropriate therapies. Educators should be respectful and sensitive but firm and persistent in encouraging parents to seek further evaluation and/or therapies at first from the child's primary care doctor and then, as needed, from a specialist.

In our large academic center, in partnership with subspecialists from developmental and behavioral pediatrics and speech therapy, the clinics providing general pediatric care have worked jointly with these subspecialties to tackle the problem of inequitable access to patients covered by Medicaid. It is these patients who may be at increased risk for delayed identification of developmental concerns and disorders. This is part of the hospital's mission to improve patient access, and particularly in ways that are equitable to patients who have historically been underserved. These respective departments have both set up a "fast track" just for the approximately 5,000 patients in our practice (approximately 90 percent insured by Medicaid and 80 percent Black) who meet age criteria and have failed a screening assessment indicating possible developmental or speech delay. We are currently working with parents and these divisions to hasten the timeliness of these visits for more patients.

The Benefits of Early Intervention by Educators

As educators and healthcare providers have similar goals and aligned purpose to promote early childhood development and to ensure that developmental problems or differences are identified and addressed early, there are also many things educators can do to support families while the diagnosis is still being made. Early intervention programs can be helpful for children under age 3. (See "Chapter 10: Inclusion of Young Children with Special Healthcare Needs and/or Medical Complexity.")

Special education evaluations can be completed at the early learning program and implemented without medical input (but may benefit from medical input). Children may qualify for an Individualized Family Service Program (IFSP) or an Individualized Education Plan (IEP). (See Figures 10.1 and 10.2: The IFSP and IEP Processes.) Research demonstrates that earlier intervention results in better developmental and family outcomes later. The benefits of early and continued intervention and therapy is well proven (Koegel et al. 2014). Extending therapy beyond the education setting to speech therapy or occupational therapy is beneficial during the school term and especially beneficial during extended summer breaks.

These well-proven supportive therapies can be particularly helpful to families of modest or inconsistent income and families with irregular or inconsistent work schedules. Moreover, personal family challenges (e.g., transportation, getting time off work, basic problem solving, organizational skills) can delay medical or diagnostic clinical visits.

The following are some tips for how educators can be helpful to/partner with pediatric clinicians as related to developmental concerns:

- Prepare families appropriately. Recommend the child see their primary healthcare provider and ask for their assessment of whether the child needs further evaluation and referrals.
- Be aware of a tendency to "watch and wait" and prepare parents to ask for a referral to an appropriate specialist (e.g., SLPs, OTs, PTs, and/or developmental-behavioral pediatricians).
- Send all screening results to families and be sure they have a clear understanding of the results. You may want to have families take a picture of written results on their smartphone, which they will have with them at doctor's visit. Consider faxing results directly to the primary pediatric clinician's office.
- Write a brief summary of the family's and educators' concerns or the challenges the child is experiencing in the classroom. This can be particularly useful for children when the pediatrician prefers to "watch and wait" but the educators are seeing significant red flags.

- Remember that the parents are the expert on their child and that this is a process and a series of conversations. Conversations should be respectful of parents' unique expertise in their child. If possible, schedule time and a private place outside the classroom (not at pickup or drop-off) to have these difficult conversations.
- When going over developmental results, be sure to stress the child's strengths. For areas of concern, use language such as, "This is an area where your child may benefit from some evaluation and additional skill enhancement to reach their full potential." This language helps develop and maintain a positive relationship and partnership with the parent.

Societal Factors That Affect Child Health and Safety

Healthcare professionals and early childhood educators alike confront common and everyday challenges to providing care and guidance to families and children. When societal factors and extraordinary events change the healthcare landscape and educational practice in profound ways, it is important to understand child health and safety concerns and practices within these contexts.

The COVID-19 Pandemic's Impact on Child Health

COVID-19 challenged families, children, and early childhood educators in profound ways, including a loss in children's learning, a disruption in children's social-emotional development, and a suspension of family support mechanisms, such as meal services and daily child care. Likewise, the healthcare system was overburdened and under pressure to respond to the crisis. The COVID-19 pandemic catalyzed changes to the healthcare system that were already underway to increase patient access and family-centered services (right care, right time, right place), such as telehealth and home-delivery pharmacy services. It's important to acknowledge the impact that this global health event has had on the physical and mental health and development of young children.

Learning Loss

Studies have shown that children of all ages experienced learning loss during the pandemic (Engzell, Frey, & Verhagen 2021; Skar, Graham, & Huebner 2021). For example, one study (Shuffrey et al. 2022) found that infants screened during the pandemic appear to be mildly delayed in gross motor, fine motor, and personal-social subdomains, perhaps due to parental stress or lack of interaction with others. When young children enrolled or re-enrolled in early learning programs after the pandemic, early childhood educators saw children with fewer social skills, more behavior issues, and more language delays. Unfortunately, the pandemic disproportionately impacted families with low income and families of color as these families were often on the frontlines and could not work from home or find high-quality child care options for their children. On the other hand, families that could work from home saved in commuting time and expenses and were able to spend more time with their children.

Obesity, Inactivity, and Food Insecurity

During the pandemic, not only did the closure of early learning programs cut off a source of food for many children, but initially, the closure of parks and cancellation of group activities like camps and sports limited children's opportunities to be active, particularly for children who lacked a safe place to play near their homes. As a result, there has been an increase in excess weight gain and obesity among children and adults of all ages (Chang et al. 2021). Food supply shortages made healthy food difficult to reliably secure for all families globally, but even more so for families who are in food deserts, or places without affordable healthy foods. Increasing food prices and inflation in 2023 has added another hurdle to families trying to purchase healthful foods for their children. Many of the shelf-stable, inexpensive foods in food pantries are high in sodium and/or sugar and are highly refined, which research suggests contributes to obesity (Poti, Braga, & Qin 2017).

For families of modest or low income in particular, food insecurity increased during the pandemic. Before schools were closed, children from families with qualifying income in grades K–12 received at least two meals a day (breakfast and lunch) at no or reduced cost through the school lunch program (Steimle et al. 2021). Similarly, infants, toddlers, and preschool-age children received at least two meals and a snack or two snacks and a meal through CACFP in child care settings. WIC was a source of formula and food for infants and toddlers. At the beginning of the pandemic, all schools and early learning programs closed. WIC offices did not close, but they offered mostly telephone visits (recipients still had to come in to re-up their cards) and volumes dropped significantly.

By summer of 2020, child care was available for frontline workers, but there were limited spots. While some private and rural or suburban public school districts returned in the fall of 2020, many urban public school districts stayed closed for as long as a year. These closures cut off children and families from a reliable source of food for over a year, creating food insecurity for many families. While schools and community agencies distributed summer packets of food and learning materials, they were not able to meet the needs they previously had while school was in session.

Mental Health Concerns

The pandemic also created a surge in mental health concerns in children of all ages. There were increased reports of depression, anxiety, and suicidality. Children were cut off from peers and teachers, only able to see their teachers through online collaborative technologies. Many children kept their cameras off either out of need (bandwidth) or preference, so children could not see one another, and teachers could not see the children. During the worst parts of the pandemic, children were not seen in their medical home. Educators' only contact with children was through online school, which limited their ability to assess how children were doing emotionally. The children who were not able to get online were the most at risk. Whether it was from unreliable or nonexistent home Wi-Fi or lack of adult supervision to keep the children engaged online, these children were lost from the usual systems that promote their health and education. All this resulted in a weakening, and in some cases failure, of the usual systems for identification and referral for intervention for declining emotional and mental health of the children at highest risk.

Increased Vaccine Hesitancy

A trend that started pre-pandemic but that has accelerated, and perhaps for some populations has been exacerbated, by the pandemic is an increase in vaccine hesitancy. This amounts to parents/caregivers declining or delaying one or more of the recommended vaccines, including routine vaccines, flu vaccines, and COVID-19 vaccines. There was initially a drop in vaccination rates in the first six months of the pandemic as parents were fearful to bring their children into doctor's offices for ill visits or routine well-child visits. During the second and third waves of the pandemic, in-person general pediatric visits (including well-child visits) increased such that clinical volumes in August through October of 2021 were higher than typical years' volumes. Patients began returning for well-child care, but not all decided to return to getting routine vaccines. This has led to a resurgence of some vaccine-preventable diseases that were once thought to have been eradicated, including measles outbreaks in Ohio (Abbasi 2023) and polio detected in New York (Schwalbe & Varma 2022).

Backlog of Subspecialty Care

Early in the COVID-19 pandemic, all subspecialty services (everything except primary pediatric care, emergency care, and hospital/critical care) closed for about three months, providing only services by telehealth. This temporary disruption created backlogs in subspecialty care on top of backlogs that were already present due to an insufficient number of subspecialty providers seeing patients covered by Medicaid. This led to a further disparity in access for patients covered

TELEHEALTH AND NEW HEALTHCARE ACCESS METHODS: A COVID-19 SILVER LINING

Telehealth was in its infancy before the COVID-19 pandemic, but it is now a standard method of care for primary care and subspecialty care. While well-child visits cannot be performed over telehealth due to billing/legal requirements, telehealth visits can be a useful method to secure high-quality medical care without requiring transportation or care arrangements for other children or adults in the home. It is also a helpful means of delivering medical care when the single adult caregiver is under quarantine for an illness like COVID-19.

Telehealth requires that patients have access to a computer, tablet, or smartphone (which 97 percent do [Laricchia 2022]) and reliable Wi-Fi or unlimited data plans that allow for video visits. Telehealth visits are secure video visits with the physician, the patient, and any of the patient's caregivers—compliant with the Health Insurance Portability and Accountability Act of 1996 (HIPAA)—that can handle many common pediatric ill complaints, such as COVID-19 rule-out visits, rashes, pink eye (conjunctivitis), constipation, asthma follow-up, behavior, developmental follow-up (not new evaluations), and ADHD follow-up. Importantly, both the patient and their parents/caregivers must be present for the visit to take place. Also, current regulations require that telehealth visits not be done across state lines unless the physician is licensed in the state where the patient is located.

Related to telehealth, there are home-delivery pharmacy services and grocery services that can be helpful to families with transportation or child care barriers. Many communities also have mobile vans, which can be used for administering vaccines, well-child care, and ill visits in communities without a medical provider or robust transportation systems. These mobile vans are typically staffed by a physician or nurse practitioner and a medical assistant and can deliver 8 to 10 patient visits in an afternoon.

by Medicaid, including families with low income and families of color. Obtaining visits in subspecialties is particularly difficult for families who cannot take working hours off and/or who lack reliable transportation to appointments. This, in turn, creates greater disparities in healthcare access and health outcomes.

Health Disparities

A substantial body of literature (Ahmmad, Wen, & Li 2021; Alegria et al. 2002; Cunningham et al. 2017; Egede 2006; Harper, MacLehose, & Kaufman 2014) has illuminated health disparities in the United States among Black, Latino/a, and Asian adults due to racism—interpersonal, internalized, and systemic or structural racism, including health and healthcare policies. More recent literature has also demonstrated these findings among infants and children in the United States (Howell et al. 2010; Huang et al. 2012). The infant mortality rate for non-Hispanic Black infants has remained 2–2.9 times higher than the rate among non-Hispanic White infants for over a century. The rate varies by region, with higher infant mortality rates in the southeastern United States (Singh & Stella 2019). Infant mortality rates are also much higher for Native Hawaiian/Other Pacific Islanders and American Indians and lowest among non-Hispanic White and Asian populations (Jang & Lee 2022). These disparities are due to mixed factors that include racism and racial discrimination, disinvestment in the residential environments of racialized minorities, lack of medical insurance, decreased access to healthcare, low socioeconomic levels, and disparate and poor treatment at lower-quality hospitals. More possible pathways are outlined by Beck and colleagues (2020). For example, families who experience job insecurity or even homelessness likely do not have access to health resources. Many do not take advantage of Medicaid because they don't know how to apply or may again be distrustful of health and social service systems. These stressors affect every member of a family.

During an infant's first year of life, racial disparities continue to manifest in childhood in terms of frequency and length of admissions for common chronic conditions, such as asthma and diabetes mellitus (Beck et al. 2019; Correa-Agudelo et al. 2022; Maxwell et al. 2021). They also manifest in delayed diagnosis of autism and developmental disabilities among racialized populations (Mandell et al. 2002). Disparities also exist for mental health conditions (Alegria, Vallas, & Pumariega 2010), which have only worsened with the pandemic. There are also disparities in the incidence and prevalence of firearm injury (Trinidad et al. 2022), vaccination rates and uptake (Day et al. 2022), and interpersonal violence (Trinidad et al. 2023). In addition to racism and environmental factors, these disparities may be attributable to disparate exposure to trauma and ACEs experienced by both children and their parents. Traumas and ACEs include divorce/separation or incarceration of a parent/caregiver; severe illness or death of a parent/caregiver; witnessing violence; having a parent/caregiver with untreated mental illness and/or substance use; and experiencing neglect, physical, or sexual abuse. Parents who have experienced one or more of these traumas in their own childhood may be distrustful of health and social service systems and may seek medical care for their children either excessively or insufficiently as warranted by the child's presenting symptoms. Parents may be excessively protective, permissive, or authoritarian in raising their children, reflecting their unresolved trauma and fear that their children will experience the same. For educators, it is important to be mindful of parents' history with trauma and the ways in which it can manifest. (See also the section on traumatic stress in "Chapter 1: Health and Safety for Children and Early Childhood Educators.") It gets in the way of parents being able to support the social-emotional growth, resilience, and independence of their children.

Pediatric clinicians provide support to the family and child around all areas of health, including mental health, trauma, ACEs and addressing families' social determinants of health. Some clinics that care for children covered by Medicaid screen for ACEs, caregiver depression, food insecurity, housing issues, and difficulties families experience in obtaining benefits (e.g., WIC, child care vouchers, Supplemental Nutrition Assistance Program). As mandatory reporters, some pediatric clinics also screen for domestic or interpersonal violence occurring within the family or any new scary events at all visits. Many pediatric clinics have social workers and sometimes partnerships established with legal aid to help families navigate these social determinants of health related to benefits, housing, and food security. Many pediatric clinics also have co-located or integrated psychologists or mental health specialists who can screen for and promote healthy behavioral and emotional development and/or provide therapeutic mental health services for children needing it.

GET OUT THE VOTE!

Although the data on health disparities is disheartening, there is recent evidence to suggest an unusual but relatively simple way to reduce disparities and improve health outcomes: civic engagement. Recent studies have demonstrated that voter participation is related to improved health outcomes when analyzed by residential district. For example, one study (Kelly et al. 2021) found that neighborhood-level voter participation rates were associated with lower pediatric hospitalization rates after adjusting for socioeconomic deprivation, suggesting that there is a connection between voting and child health outcomes. Indeed, researchers and advocacy organizations have called on educators and healthcare professionals to promote civic engagement as that may reduce health disparities—in other words, vote like your health depends on it (Jones & Beck 2022).

Non-Partisan organizations like Vot-ER (**https://vot-er.org**) provide materials and training for educators and healthcare professionals in how to promote nonpartisan voter registration efforts, making it easy for families to register to vote and find out where they can vote.

Safe and Affordable Housing

Safe and affordable housing remains a perennial and substantial barrier to health for many families. Many pediatric clinicians screen for housing concerns and some have established medical-legal partnerships to help navigate housing issues as a substantial aspect of their work (Beck et al. 2012, 2022). Head Start programs also screen for unstable housing or homelessness and offer wrap-around supports through community action agencies and local Head Start agencies. United Way agencies also often provide these supports or partner with local community agencies to provide these supports. Last, insurance providers and some larger clinics have care managers, social workers, legal aid, and early childhood liaisons to assist family with wrap-around supports.

More Partnership Opportunities for Educators and Healthcare Professionals

There are many opportunities for educators to partner with healthcare professionals and work with the greater health community to benefit the children and families they serve. Educators and administrative staff members can seek out relationships with local clinics, including school-based clinics and pediatric offices, particularly those that serve as the primary medical home for a majority or large number of children in the program's enrolled families.

Educators may want to partner with healthcare professionals, mental health professionals, and with other agencies providing early learning programming in their community to develop a community network of health and early learning programs that are aligned on the purpose of supporting young children's development and social-emotional learning. This network would meet regularly (e.g., monthly, bimonthly) and share data on projects the network is working on (e.g., reducing time to enrollment for families, reducing child abuse and neglect, improving child and/or parent social-emotional well-being). The network would share learnings on successes and help each other learn from and troubleshoot failures. The network would work on reducing silos and barriers to parents navigating across sectors and creating a more family-centered ecosystem for early childhood.

Educators could partner with the healthcare system and specific organizations (e.g., The Epilepsy Foundation, the Asthma and Allergy Foundation, the Autism Society) for professional development opportunities. They could also work with local Child Care Resource and Referral (CCR&R) programs to coordinate training for the larger early childhood community in lieu of many individual center or program trainings.

To be certain, for educators and healthcare professionals to work together effectively, rigorous data need to be tracked and shared transparently. Data on shared goals (e.g., time to enrollment, percent of reports of child/abuse neglect) should be accessible to all parties and agencies working together on the goal. Most important, these teams should include parents/caregivers with lived experience and valuable input to understand key drivers to success and reasons for system failures. Moreover, parents should be compensated for their time and expertise in contributing to these action teams (Skelton-Wilson et al. 2021; Szczepanska 2021). A current recommended rate of $25 per hour is recommended in 2022 for cities and localities with an average cost of living, with adjustments made for localities with a higher cost of living.

When educators and healthcare professionals are working together on aligned missions, and with parents at the table driving the discussions and helping co-create solutions, collective impact is achieved.

The resources and connections with the healthcare system and public health vary by state, region, and budget year. It is often best to start locally, with similarly or complementarily aligned community partners to work to achieve the easy wins locally. Achieving these easy wins, showing up at meetings, and honoring promises made builds trust among agencies and parents. Keeping parents front and center at the decision tables not only hastens the progress toward pragmatically effective solutions but also builds trust in the community. While community change does not happen quickly, it happens authentically and effectively through relationships and trust. These relationships are built when agencies and healthcare professionals come to the table with humility and vulnerability and listen fully to others, both frontline staff members and parents with lived experience.

Summary

Pediatric healthcare professionals and early childhood educators share the same goals for the children they serve—to help each child grow to their full potential. By working as a team, pediatric clinicians and educators can help families and children understand how to manage health and development and navigate healthcare and education systems and processes. Pediatric clinicians are a great resource for child health safety and development. Improved communication and shared assessments will result in more timely referrals to evaluators and therapists. This will result in earlier interventions and improved outcomes. Health disparities, poverty, racism, lack of healthcare or insurance, and all the negative effects of the COVID-19 pandemic continue to challenge the healthcare and education of children. Developing programs and support systems that circumvent or tackle these issues head on will result in better outcomes for children. We hope that, after reading this chapter, the reader is ready to take the next steps in working together with pediatric clinicians to support healthy and thriving children.

PART 2

Promoting Children's Health

BRITTANY MASSARE AND ALICIA HAUPT

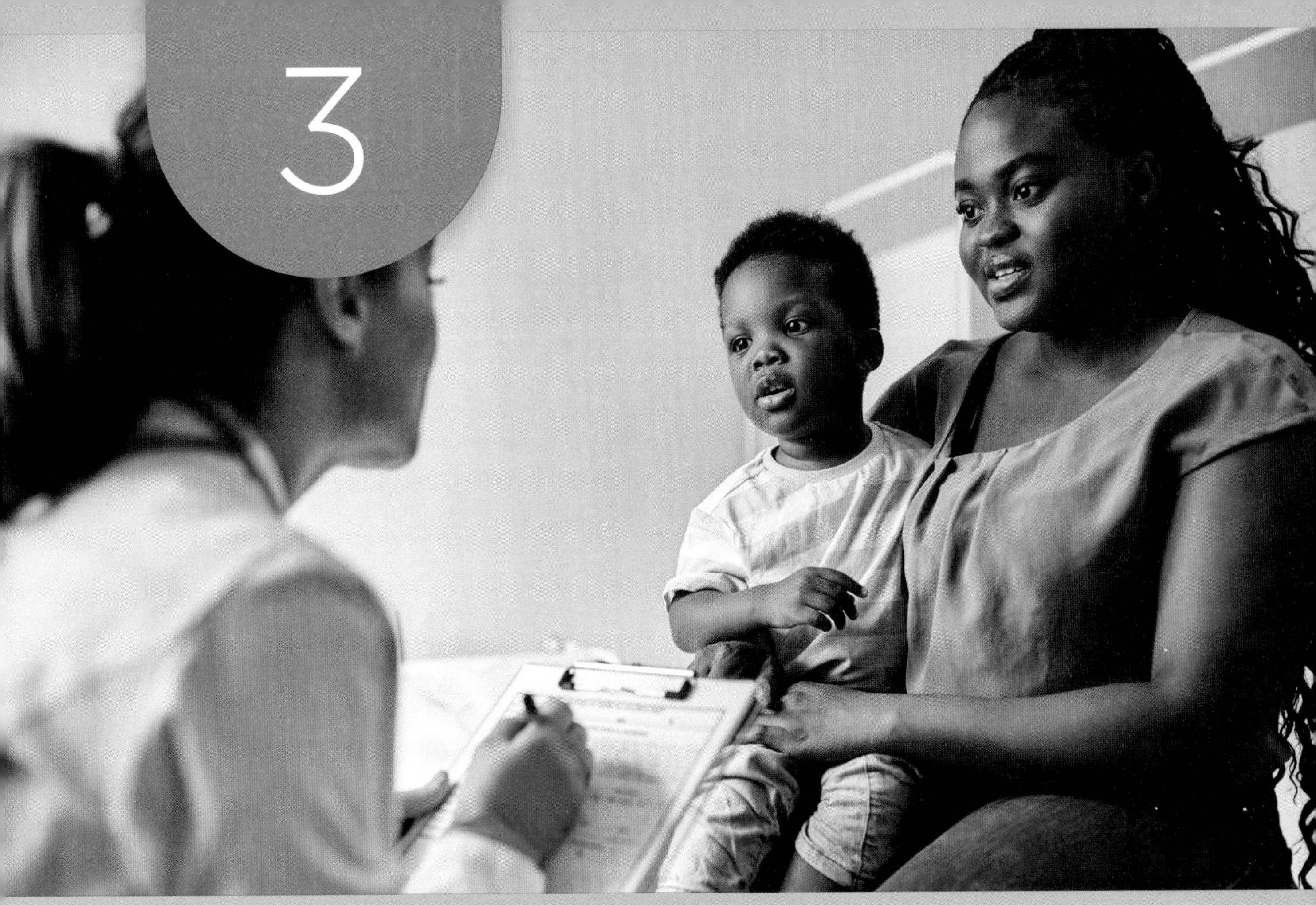

Enrollment, Health Documentation, Assessments, and Screenings

LEARNING OBJECTIVES

- To create a procedure for obtaining, reviewing, and tracking medical care information
- To understand confidentiality policy
- To define the steps required in a health assessment
- To understand the necessary health screenings, including vision, hearing, anemia, height and weight, and lead
- To analyze the role of preventive and primary care in children's health

When a family enrolls their child in an early learning program, the family must provide important information about the child's health to assist the program in preparing to care for the child. It's important for the program to know about any health concerns, medical conditions, or specific needs. Does the child have food allergies or require a special diet? Is the child on medication? Families may provide health histories and complete forms to provide this information, but additional documentation from healthcare professionals is also required including the results of medical exams, health screenings, and assessments. As mentioned in "Chapter 2: Healthcare Professionals and Educators Work Together to Support Healthy and Thriving Children," pediatric clinicians, child healthcare consultants, and early childhood professionals can provide services and support to help families manage their children's health and well-being. It is essential that healthcare providers and early childhood educators and administrators share information and communicate clearly and regularly. In this chapter, we discuss necessary health documentation for children to enroll in early learning programs and cover common health assessments and screenings. We also discuss ways that educators can help families and children by promoting supportive programs and services and by assisting families and primary caregivers in navigating the challenges that healthcare systems can present.

Families, Child Health, and Program Requirements

Families consider many factors when choosing to enroll their child in an early learning program. The health and safety of their child is of primary concern. Families will ask about health and safety protocols, and it is the responsibility of the early learning program to inform and discuss program health requirements with each family at the time of enrollment and when updates occur. Program staff must work with each family respectfully and collaboratively to ensure they understand the purpose of the requirements and help the families navigate the necessary forms and processes involved. Families should be able to ask questions, express concerns, or suggest changes to improve the program. Families may ask why the program needs certain information such as family health histories, and educators and staff must be prepared to explain why such information is important to the health of not only the child who is enrolling but also the program as a whole. The requirement to provide early learning programs with health data facilitates preventative care and treatment to ensure the health and well-being of the children. Early childhood education professionals can partner with families to empower them to ask questions and make decisions about their child's physical, developmental, and behavioral health. Educators and staff will also need to take into consideration the stressors and social and structural determinants that impact families and partner with families to protect their children's health and safety.

Enrollment and Health Documentation

When a family enrolls a child in an early learning program, the program should ask for certain information to ensure that the child can be adequately cared for and receive the attention they require. Knowing about the health of each child is key to their growth and development, and it is also important for the management of the health and safety of participants and staff in the program. Documentation of a child's health is critically important to their growth and development and helps each child reach their potential. Early learning programs should have a procedure for obtaining important health data for each child who enrolls and maintaining a record of this information. This includes health histories, health assessments, and vaccination records. It is important to begin this record at the time of enrollment, and each child in a program should have a health record that is regularly maintained and updated.

Having proper health documentation at enrollment is ideal; however, the program may offer enrollment as long as the family reports that the child has no health concerns and there is an appointment to obtain the necessary care scheduled within two weeks of the child's first day of attendance. Children who are up to date on health visits and immunizations do not need a special visit to the healthcare provider just because the child is enrolling in an early learning program. Families need only to obtain the information from their child's healthcare provider about the services the child has received so the program can ensure that the nationally recommended schedule of services are met, and the program has sufficient information and staff training to address any special needs the child may have.

The program should maintain a health record for each child until the child leaves the program. (*CFOC Standards* 3.1.2.1 and 9.4.1.2.). The child's health information should be updated at each checkup visit. The American Academy of Pediatrics (AAP) Bright Futures website provides a periodicity schedule for when updates should be done (**https://downloads.aap.org/AAP/PDF/periodicity_schedule.pdf**). The schedule requires updates every few months (typically every 3–6 months) for infants and toddlers, followed by annual updates for children once they reach age 3. This schedule is updated by the AAP from time to time. Check the website at least once a year to be sure you are using the most current version. Note that the guidelines are *minimum* requirements for healthy children having no significant health problems. When a child has special health or medically complex needs, more frequent visits may be required. If you have questions about how to check health records or whether a child is up to date with vaccines and other AAP-recommended preventive care services, seek help from your program's child care health consultant (if available) or the public health department. Health information should be considered confidential and should not be disclosed without written consent of the parent or primary caregiver.

IMMEDIATE IMPACT

Bright Futures

Many materials for parents, caregivers, and healthcare providers are available on the Bright Futures website (**http://brightfutures.aap.org**). Explore this website for handouts related to a wide variety of health promotion topics to give to families and staff.

Staff members should be informed of any health changes or issues. For example, it is easy to assume that a child who appears healthy has no health needs; however, if staff members do not know that a child is allergic to bee stings, they could face a shocking and life-threatening emergency if the child is stung. If staff members know that a child has had an extended hospitalization early in life, they may observe the child more closely to determine whether that child should receive additional support to achieve developmental progress.

Creating a Health Record

The health record (or related files) should contain at least the following information:

- Telephone numbers where primary caregivers and at least two emergency contacts can be reached at all times
- Name of the child's regular source of healthcare (child's primary care physician (PCP)/medical home) and any other usual sources of healthcare, including the name of a specific contact person, address, and telephone number
- Child's preadmission medical examination/health assessment and subsequent updates at each checkup, including immunization status
- Developmental health history (physical and developmental milestones and significant events)
- Results of all screenings and assessments
- Notations about allergies, special diet, chronic illness, or other special health needs
- Emergency permission for medical care
- All permission slips authorizing nonemergency healthcare and giving of medications
- Reports of all injuries or illnesses that occur while the child is in the program
- Medication logs
- Reports of referrals and follow-up action
- Notes about any health communication with family or healthcare providers
- Written correspondence about the child's health
- Health observations from staff members

The facility should establish and follow a procedure to obtain parental/caregiver consent, be familiar with the information in the health record, and review the information on the health record to identify gaps in service or a need to adapt the child's care.

Collecting a Health History

Health histories provide important information about the child's prior health experiences and risks for future disease. The family health history can help predict what illnesses the child may inherit or develop. Comprehensive preventive care requires a detailed health history, including information about birth, illnesses, hospitalization, all treatments, immunization status, and current health concerns.

Early learning programs should collect a health history from the family or primary caregiver that covers major physical, behavioral, and developmental concerns. Most parents can recall many details about their own child; however, the names of healthcare providers and the chronology of events may be forgotten if they are not recorded. Unless there is a specific request for it, few parents/caregivers systematically review the details of their child's nutritional, immunization, health, and family history to identify patterns that suggest a need for attention. Even the most organized parents or caregivers may innocently overlook the health needs of a rapidly changing and growing child because of other urgent or competing demands in their lives.

When an early learning program requests a child's health history, the request helps reinforce the family's and caregivers' role in keeping track of important health information. (See Appendix A.3.1: Developmental History for an example of a form that collects the type of information useful to an early learning program. Use it as a guide to develop a tool that works well in your program to gather appropriate information.) The format of the child health assessment forms your program uses may differ from the forms provided by the child's healthcare provider. What is important is that the program receives all the necessary information, no matter what format the child's healthcare provider uses. In addition to the documentation of the child's health assessment results, the report from the healthcare provider should include a written care plan for any child with special needs. If the care plan for accommodation of special health needs is not available at enrollment, then a written plan from a health professional should be prepared to cover the first two weeks of enrollment while the child's healthcare professional prepares a more definitive care plan. (See also "Chapter 10: Inclusion of Young Children with Special Healthcare Needs and/or Medical Complexity" and the section "Medical Paperwork and Forms and Sharing Information" in "Chapter 2: Healthcare Professionals and Educators Work Together to Support Healthy and Thriving Children.")

If a child has a special health need, it is not safe to enroll the child without information from the child's healthcare provider. Staff members must learn how to address specific special needs. For instance, allergies and asthma are very common in early childhood. If you have a child with allergies or asthma in your program, review the history of treatment and current medications and know when the child is due for the next follow-up visit to the healthcare provider. Ask the parents or primary caregiver how the child responds best or what they know as the best course of action during an asthma episode or allergic reaction. (See also "Chapter 8: Understanding Common Illnesses and Conditions.") Let the child's primary caregiver and healthcare provider know about any changes in the child's condition or response to possible triggers. By providing consistent information, you become part of the child's health team and facilitate continuity of care.

Confidentiality

Confidentiality of health records must be maintained to protect the child and family. *Caring for Our Children* Standard 9.4.1.3 requires early learning programs to have and implement a written policy on confidentiality of staff and child records. The policy must ensure no disclosure of material in the records (including conference reports, service plans, immunization records, and follow-up reports) without the written consent of parents or the primary caregiver for children. Such consent must specify to whom the information may be disclosed. No discussion or sharing of confidential information should be allowed beyond the limits of the consent.

Consent forms should be written in the home language of the child's family or the language spoken at the child's home, whenever possible and communicated to them in their preferred mode of communication. Language interpreters should be available to inform parents about their confidentiality rights. At the time when programs obtain prior, informed consent from the parent/primary caregiver for release of records, teachers should inform them who may be looking at the records (e.g., child care health consultants, mental health consultants, and specialized agencies providing services) (*CFOC* Standard 9.4.1.3).

Healthcare providers are required to comply with the requirements of the Health Insurance Portability and Accountability Act (HIPAA). The child's healthcare provider must have signed consent from the parents that specifies the requested information and to whom it is to be released. When an early learning program wants to obtain information about an individual child from a healthcare provider, it is possible to obtain a form for this purpose from most health professionals' offices.

Early childhood educators have an ethical, and often legal, responsibility to maintain confidentiality. Follow these guidelines for confidentiality of records:

- Health records must be kept from public access and unauthorized review.
- Information may not be shared with anyone inside or outside the facility without caregiver review and consent.
- A telephone request for information from outside parties is not acceptable unless the caregiver has previously instructed you in writing to release information or gives/has given witnessed telephone consent. This is accomplished by having two people on the telephone with the caregiver to confirm caregiver authorization to release information and then ask identifying questions of the caregiver to ensure it is the caregiver who is authorizing the release.
- Information collected by others and forwarded to you with caregiver consent becomes part of the child's record and thus the responsibility of the program.
- All releases of information should be properly logged.
- Caregivers have a right to see all information in their child's file.
- Caregivers must be made aware of the nature and type of all information collected and how it will be used.
- A caregiver may ask to speak to you in confidence, but you must receive this information in a responsible manner. This is particularly true if child abuse is suspected. Your primary responsibility is to protect the child.

Health Assessment

The medical examination is the first step in assessing the health of children. It includes collecting information from the child's family about any symptoms, concerns, family health problems, social determinants of health (such as availability of safe affordable housing and healthy food), medications, nutrition, physical activity, dental care, and vaccine history, as well as a physical examination. After the child's healthcare provider performs a complete physical examination, they arrange for necessary laboratory and screening tests. The healthcare provider can then make a health assessment of the child to begin necessary care or treatment.

Health assessment and follow-up care are often separated into three categories: screening, diagnosis, and treatment.

- *Screening* is the use of quick, inexpensive, and simple procedures to identify children who may have an issue in a specific area. Health screening tests typically produce one of three possible results: (1) the child is healthy, so no action is needed; (2) the child is possibly at risk, so the screening test is repeated; or (3) the child is at risk, so they are referred for further diagnosis and possible treatment.

- *Diagnosis* is a more detailed evaluation to find out if there is in fact a health condition and, if so, what it is. When making a diagnosis, the healthcare professional may use health histories, dietary information, laboratory test results, educator observations, radiology, consultation with subspecialists, and/or physical and psychological assessments.
- *Treatment* includes measures designed to control, minimize, correct, or cure a disease or abnormality (e.g., eyeglasses, dental fillings, therapy). *Treatment is the key to an effective early learning program.* If care for an individual does not result in whatever treatment is indicated, screening and diagnosis are meaningless.

The results of a child's health assessment should be reported to the early learning program. This could be recorded on a form that includes the necessary information from the child's electronic medical record. If the information provided by the child's healthcare provider is incomplete or does not provide a clear picture of the child's needs while in child care, the early learning program or child care health consultant should obtain caregiver consent to contact the child's healthcare provider for additional information. A program's health policies should require that the immunization record be reviewed to ensure it is up to date and that it is on file prior to the child's first day of attendance.

Health Screenings

The AAP and the US Department of Health and Human Services recommend the Bright Futures periodicity schedule for all children, as described earlier in this chapter. Head Start requires its programs to meet the well-child assessment requirements of their state's Early and Periodic Screening, Diagnostic, and Treatment (EPSDT) program, which is a component of Medicaid services. If insurance or public health services do not cover the costs of needed services, families may need guidance from the early learning program or their healthcare provider on potential resources.

Screening Tests

Most conditions respond to early treatment and intervention, which is often more effective and may also prevent the development of other issues. For instance, children with undetected hearing loss can lead to developing language, learning, and behavior problems.

Without screening, problems may go unnoticed, or if the signs or symptoms are recognized, their significance may not be understood. An abnormal screening test result means that something could be wrong and that additional testing or further questions are warranted. Abnormal results should be interpreted by the child's usual source of healthcare so that appropriate further evaluation can be planned. Premature referral to a specialist may result in overlooking the possibility that the abnormality is part of a multisystem problem.

To be valuable, a screening program must include

- Caregiver education about the screening
- Caregiver involvement and consent
- Use of a valid, reliable tool appropriate for the child's age
- A competent screener

- Screening and rescreening of children who may have a problem before making referrals
- Written information provided to the caregivers when further examination is suggested
- Caregiver choice of the healthcare professional to follow up
- Information received from the healthcare professional about examination results and treatment plans

Because children are more comfortable and secure in familiar surroundings with familiar adults, screening may be more successful if screeners come to the early learning program, as long as the screening is done properly. Prepare the children for what to expect when they will be involved in a particular screening procedure, and follow through on referrals. Be sure to notify the child's usual source of healthcare about the results of any screening test to avoid duplication and to promote follow-up and coordination of the test results with the rest of the child's health data.

Vision Screening

Healthy vision is essential to the healthy development of young children, yet up to one in five young children has an undiagnosed vision disorder. Unfortunately, uncorrected vision disorders remain common, and can impair child development, interfere with learning, reduce quality of life, and even lead to permanent vision loss. Common children's vision problems include refractive errors, strabismus, and amblyopia (Prevent Blindness 2022; Ying et al. 2014). All children should have an eye examination at birth and at each checkup visit. By age 4, this eye examination should include not only evaluation of general eye health but also near and far vision acuity as well as the ability to use both eyes together (for depth perception).

Many people believe that preschool children are too young to have their vision tested. Subjective vision screening can be done from birth by covering one eye at a time to see if the child seems to see with the uncovered eye and, by 3–4 months old, by checking whether the covered eye is out of alignment with the eye being used to see.

At age 3, most children *can* cooperate with a vision screening program that tests for visual acuity and stereopsis (checking if both eyes work together). Objective vision screening is done with an age-appropriate, standardized screening tool designed to identify some of the most common conditions found in young children. A number of tools are available. Picture identification tests are generally considered less accurate than tests with crowded letters or specific shapes, but using pictures is better than not testing. Testing whether the eyes work well together (stereopsis) is essential, yet often not done. The two types of stereopsis tests that are most popular are the Random Dot E test and the bug or butterfly test. Vision screening is frequently conducted by volunteers who have received simple training to do the screening correctly. If you are interested in performing vision screening, it is important that you receive training and learn the technique, strengths, and weaknesses of the testing methods you will use. Prevent Blindness (**www.preventblindness.org**) has information about volunteer training for how to do vision screening for young children.

If possible, it is best for children to receive competent vision screening in a medical home. When this is not possible, you can also use the Prevent Blindness website to locate a state or regional affiliate or to contact the national office for help arranging a vision screening program for groups of children that will be conducted by qualified volunteers. Alternately, ask a pediatric vision screening professional (a pediatric ophthalmologist or pediatric optometrist) or a pediatrician to help you find someone who can do competent vision screening or who will provide training for staff members so they can screen the children. For screening purposes, children 30–35 months old are expected to pass at 20/60 line on eye charts; 36–47 months old should pass at 20/50; 48–59 months old should pass at 20/40; and 60–72 months should pass at 20/20 or better (Cotter et al. 2015; Donahue et al. 2016).

Any screening program is valuable only if follow-up occurs. The first referral should be to the child's usual source of healthcare, not to a vision specialist unless the child lacks a usual source of healthcare to follow up on the vision screening results. *Do not assume that children will outgrow vision problems.* Some problems get worse. Early detection permits early treatment that will correct many conditions more easily and completely and that will cost less than later treatment. Any child who cannot perform well on a basic vision screening by age 4 should be referred to a vision specialist.

Hearing Screening

A child who does not hear clearly will have trouble imitating sounds and developing language skills. Behavior also can be affected. Learning to read and write will be difficult and frustrating for the child. Hearing problems may be hereditary, the result of certain illnesses during pregnancy or early childhood, or secondary to some medical exposures. Temporary or intermittent hearing loss may be caused by chronic and recurrent ear infection, a heavy buildup of wax in the ear, or chronic fluid in the middle ear.

Educators and caregivers should be aware of possible signs or risk factors for child hearing loss, including the following:

Signs in Babies

- Does not startle at loud noises.
- Does not turn to the source of a sound after 6 months of age.
- Does not say single words, such as "dada" or "mama" by 1 year of age.
- Turns head when he or she sees you but not if you only call out his or her name. This sometimes is mistaken for not paying attention or just ignoring, but could be the result of a partial or complete hearing loss.
- Seems to hear some sounds but not others.

Signs in Children

- Speech is delayed.
- Speech is not clear.
- Does not follow directions. This sometimes is mistaken for not paying attention or just ignoring, but could be the result of a partial or complete hearing loss.
- Often says, "Huh?"
- Turns the TV volume up too high. (CDC 2022, n.p.)

Hospitals in most states comply with universal newborn hearing screening recommendations (Wroblewska-Seniuk et al. 2017). Children need periodic hearing screening that should begin right after birth because some hearing problems can develop as the child grows. The following are typical hearing tests for young children:

- **Otoscopic exam.** The audiologist will look into the child's ear canal with an otoscope and record any findings such as cerumen (earwax), drainage, or a pressure-equalizing tube in the eardrum.
- **Tympanometry test.** This test measures the movement of the eardrum, which can help determine how your child's middle ear is functioning. An audiologists places a soft probe at the opening of the child's ear canal. Tympanometry does not measure a child's hearing, but it can detect any changes in pressure in the middle ear, fluid behind the eardrum, or a hole in the eardrum—all of which can affect a child's hearing.
- **Otoacoustic emission (OAE) test.** A small earphone will play sounds into a child's ears. A healthy inner ear will respond with otoacoustic emissions (responses), which can be recorded with a tiny microphone inside the earphone. OAE testing takes only a few minutes and is painless. (CHOP n.d., n.p.)

Measuring Height and Weight

Height and weight measurements and determination of the body mass index (BMI)—a calculation widely used to identify children who are underweight, overweight, or obese ages 2–19 years—should be carried out at each well-child visit. These measurements are one of the best ways to detect physical growth patterns that may indicate a serious problem. They should be graphed over time to show the pattern of the child's growth compared with other children of the same age. Head circumference (measurement around the head at the level of the top of the ears) should also be measured for children from birth to 24 months old. Growth measurements are usually part of a routine checkup.

Children whose length/height growth percentile differs by more than one percentile curve from their weight/growth percentile, whose growth data are below the fifth percentile curve, or whose BMI percentile is out of the expected range need further evaluation. You should receive this information with the child's physical examination report. If you want to plot the growth data yourself, you can obtain the growth charts online from the Centers for Disease Control and Prevention (CDC) at **www.cdc.gov/growthcharts**. To learn more about BMI and access BMI calculators for adults and children, go to **www.cdc.gov/healthyweight/assessing/bmi/index.html**. Using the BMI calculator may increase self-awareness among educators and caregivers about whether they or the children in their care are a healthy weight or are under- or overweight.

Anemia and Iron Deficiency

Anemia and iron deficiency in young children continue to be a public health concern in the United States (Gupta et al. 2016). Anemia results when the body does not have enough circulating red blood cells to carry oxygen from the lungs to the tissues and/or not enough *hemoglobin* (Hb) (the chemical carrying oxygen to the red blood cells) in each cell. An anemic child could appear tired, pale, and inattentive and could be susceptible to infection. Iron deficiency is the most common cause of anemia in young children. Iron is needed to form hemoglobin and also is a component of many cells in the body. Without enough iron, blood cannot carry the oxygen the body needs. Iron deficiency even without anemia can cause sleep and developmental problems.

All infants between 9 and 12 months old should be screened for anemia during a wellness visit. If a child presents with these common signs, a medical examination and blood tests are required. *Hematocrit* (Hct) and Hb measurements, as well as measurements of *ferritin,* an iron-containing substance in the body, are commonly used to screen children for anemia and problems with insufficient iron during early childhood. Hb and Hct measurements are the laboratory tests used most commonly in clinical and public health settings for screening for anemia.

Causes of iron deficiency include

- Overconsumption of milk (more than 24–32 ounces per day), resulting in low intake of other foods, particularly iron-containing foods
- Lack of high-iron, high-nutrient foods in the diet (e.g., meat, fish, beans, and green, leafy vegetables)
- Lead toxicity. Iron deficiency and lead poisoning frequently occur together. Iron and lead compete with each other for the same binding sites in the body. Iron deficiency may increase the absorption of lead from the intestine and make the toxic effects of lead worse. Therapeutic doses of iron are often required to correct the iron deficiency when it is accompanied by lead poisoning.
- Inadequate amounts of the body substance that picks up iron from the digestive system and transports it to places in the body where iron is needed

Lead Screening

Lead is widely dispersed in the environment, both in nature and in manufactured products. It is often in layers of interior paint that were put on surfaces before 1978, when lead was banned from paint for buildings. It may be in the soil around buildings painted with lead paint years ago or near highways that were heavily traveled when lead was a routine additive in gasoline. As the painted surface deteriorates or chips, lead dust is released into the air and falls onto nearby surfaces. Ingestion of a small chip of lead paint or lead dust on unwashed hands can raise the blood lead level. Lead screening is extremely important because even very low elevations of blood lead that do not produce obvious symptoms can cause developmental delay and permanent problems in learning and behavior.

The current tests for lead recommended by the AAP and CDC are a finger-stick or venous blood test (usually taken from the vein at the inside of the elbow) to most accurately detect elevated lead levels. Blood level screening should be a part of routine healthcare for children who live, play, or visit in older buildings; who play in the soil where new buildings replaced older buildings; or where the play area has soil that was contaminated by being close to highways that were heavily traveled when gasoline contained lead. According to the CDC, other nonresidential sources of lead include the following: some home remedies, some cosmetics, cookware and tableware not certified to be lead-free, some toys and toy jewelry, hot water drawn from pipes in houses with lead-soldered pipes, and stained-glass hobbies. Both the AAP and CDC recommend that risk for possible lead exposure be assessed by at least asking about possible lead exposure at children's health visits between the ages of 6 months and

6 years. It is important to note that no matter the prevalence of lead levels based on environmental factors, many state Medicaid, screening, diagnostic, and treatment programs require a universal blood lead level test at the 12-month and 24-month visits (AAP 2021).

Children should not play in bare soil where old painted buildings stand or stood at one time unless lead testing of soil samples confirms that the soil does not contain lead. In communities where lead is a known environmental problem, lead screening of infants and toddlers should be universal.

IMMEDIATE IMPACT

Ways to Decrease Lead Exposure in Early Learning Programs

- Dust windowsills regularly.
- Have children wash their hands after outside play.
- Be aware that older toys may contain lead and increase exposure.
- Keep areas where children play clear of any chipped paint or construction/renovations.

Educator Observations of Physical Health, Development, and Behavior

Opportunities for the healthcare professional to make valid observations during healthcare visits are limited by the short duration of the visit with the family and by the healthcare setting, which may not be familiar or comfortable for the child. Nonetheless, healthcare providers observe what they can and use these observations as a component of the assessment. Observations made and reported by those who care for children on a daily basis can be very helpful. Healthcare providers can learn more about the child and the family from teachers' daily observations.

Each staff member must be sensitive, conscientious, and systematic in assessing and addressing a child's health needs each day. You probably already notice such things as a new haircut or outfit as you greet a child upon their arrival, but take the time to look closely at the child's appearance. Through daily observation, you can learn a great deal about children as individuals: their typical coloring and appearance, moods and temperament, response to pain and sickness, activity level, and patterns of behavior. Each of these is a vital clue to health. Changes in the child's health from what is typical for a healthy child or for that individual child should be noted in the health record so that the information can be aggregated over time and shared when appropriate to determine a need for medical care.

While you are expected to be observant, you are not expected to be a health expert. Observe the child, record relevant data, and then report anything unusual to the appropriate person on your staff and to the caregivers. You cannot and should not offer diagnoses or treatment plans, but healthcare professionals will be able to make better judgments using the information you can provide. Health observation can be an important first step before screening, diagnosis, or treatment.

Physical Health

Physical health observations include observable signs of health or illness (e.g., coughing, vomiting, swelling, limping) and reported symptoms (e.g., nausea, headache, stomachache) or signs (e.g., refusal to do specific activities). Because young children may not be able to describe how they feel, objective observations provide essential clues. It can be helpful to use a form to record observations and symptoms and keep it as part of the health record. (See Appendix A.3.2 for a sample Observation and Symptom Record form.) Give a copy to the caregiver to give to the child's healthcare provider. When communicating your observations, whether in person or in writing, be as specific as you can. For example, say, "Jamal has a frequent dry cough, flushed cheeks, and a runny nose with thick yellow mucus," rather than, "Jamal is sick." Say, "Jennifer has a sore throat and an oral temperature of 102°F," rather than making assumptions and reporting that "Jennifer has strep throat."

Each observer has a different perspective in obtaining health information. Caregivers, for example, compare a child's appearance or behavior with what is typical for the child, or with that of the child's siblings or friends. Teachers can observe children in a group setting with many children of the same age. Child healthcare professionals use knowledge and experience from their medical practice. Each view is valuable but limited; to have a total picture of the child, all observations must be shared and seen as a whole.

Use your senses (smell, hearing, sight, touch) when making health observations. Observe clues such as the color, temperature, or texture of skin; breath odor; the appearance of a bruise; or the sound of a cough. Observe the group in general and compare individual children. For example, do most of the children of the same age get out of breath when climbing the hill on the playground? If a child has difficulty doing what the rest of the group does easily, it is worth noting and asking the caregivers to bring it up with their child's healthcare provider.

Development and Behavior

Children's physical health is only one aspect of their health and well-being. Equally important are the development of language, gross and fine motor skills, social-emotional competence, and cognition. Delays in these areas are best managed when they are identified and addressed during the early years.

1. **Developmental milestones.** Knowledge of general child development with in-depth information about children at particular ages provides a general framework to identify children whose abilities fall outside the typical range. These milestones must be viewed flexibly because a child's development is greatly influenced by childrearing styles, culture and ethnic norms, and the child's own temperament.

   Teachers can use developmental and behavioral screening tools to assess children in their care. These tools serve more than one purpose: reinforcing a sense of normal developmental pathways; identifying the child whose development is outside the range for typically developing children; and helping teachers individualize educational activities, some that are comfortable for the child and some that help the child reach for the next level of accomplishment. For information and excellent free materials about developmental milestones and screening, go to

www.cdc.gov/ncbddd/actearly/index.html. This website of the CDC, National Center on Birth Defects and Developmental Disabilities, has special sections for families and for early childhood educators, clinicians, and others.

Many observers of children are using standardized tools as a framework for assessing a particular child's placement in the range of typical childhood behaviors and developmental skills, then using the same or similar tools to measure the child's progress over time. A teacher's observations over time in the child's daily life yield much valuable information. Teachers should communicate their observations and concerns to the child's caregivers and, with caregiver consent, to the child's healthcare provider.

2. **Observation and documentation.** "Educators must have a system in place to collect, make sense of, and use observations, documentation, and assessment information to guide what goes on in the early learning setting" (NAEYC 2022, p. 20). Write down observations that might suggest concerns with a child's development or behavior. (Tip: You can keep file cards in your pocket and note on them the day, time, activity, and behavior you observe.) Ask other staff members to also observe and record the child's behaviors. Choose an appropriate developmental screening tool to use in your setting. Determine the appropriate next steps, and plan a meeting to discuss your concerns with the child's caregivers. Have the documentation in hand showing your observations.
3. **Communication.** Develop your ability to communicate concerns in a supportive, nonthreatening manner. Caregivers should be involved in discussions about concerns as soon as possible. Their input can help you identify which of your observations are appropriate for the family and culture and which are not, and which behaviors or traits are of particular concern to them. Often they may have had questions similar to yours but may not have wanted to bother the staff or to appear overly anxious about their child. By addressing these concerns in a respectful partnership, you can be a great help and support.
4. **Referral and consultation.** When concerns suggest the need to consult or make a referral, start with the child's pediatric healthcare provider. The issue may be solved at that level, or it may be necessary to seek community resources for referral and consultation. If you have used a standard development screening tool, give a copy to the caregiver to take to the child's healthcare provider. If you have not used such a tool, document your observations and concerns succinctly. Many communities have a wide array of experts on every aspect of child health and development. Develop a list of local services that families have found helpful, and keep this list at the center to share with caregivers when appropriate. (See "Chapter 10: Inclusion of Young Children with Special Healthcare Needs and/or Medical Complexity" regarding early intervention.)

Supporting Families

For many caregivers, child care staff members function as extended family. By reflecting on caregiver concerns, providing information about alternative approaches, and communicating about health issues, educators help families navigate how best to care for their children.

Just as teachers need to be informed of any concerns from caregivers at the beginning of each day, caregivers should be informed of similar information at the end of each day in child care. Illness may intensify in the evening when everyone is tired and access to professional medical care is more difficult. When caregivers call a healthcare professional for advice, they will be asked how the child ate, drank, slept, behaved, voided, and defecated during the day. Teachers need to establish an effective, routine way to communicate this information to caregivers daily using oral or written messages. This may require being able to communicate in another language; therefore, it is helpful to reach out to bilingual and bicultural staff and/or have access to language services and interpreters. Passing responsibility for a child from family to teachers and back again requires diligent attention to sharing key information that guides decisions if the child's status changes.

In addition to the daily transfer of information about the child's status and routine sharing of information at checkup time, arranging communication among teachers, family, and the child's healthcare provider is essential whenever significant health concerns arise. This ensures that the health and safety of the child—and in the case of transmissible illnesses, the health and safety of the other children and staff members—are addressed. For example, sometimes the situation may involve a caregiver's illness—as in a case of hepatitis A in an adult in the family of a child who seems well. This situation requires prompt medical intervention to protect the child, other children in the group, and staff members.

Electronic appointment and immunization tracking and reminder systems are increasingly used by clinicians, yet busy caregivers may still need support to keep up with their children's schedule for preventive service. Using the current schedule of preventive care, teachers can advocate for each child to stay up to date with immunization and screening services given at routine checkups.

Health Insurance

Lack of comprehensive health insurance coverage is a barrier to care for many families. (See the section "Health Disparities" in "Chapter 2: Healthcare Professionals and Educators Work Together to Support Healthy and Thriving Children.") Be familiar with the state Medicaid program and state Child Health Insurance Program (CHIP) referral resource telephone numbers to assist caregivers who lack health insurance.

FAMILY CONNECTIONS

Medicaid Information

Local Federally Qualified Health Centers (FQHCs) can help families navigate Medicaid so all health screenings can be completed.

The federal government created CHIP as part of amendments to the Social Security Act in 1997. This state-administered program uses a combination of federal and state funds to provide health insurance for children whose family income is high enough to make them ineligible for Medicaid but whose caregivers are unable to buy private insurance. Implementation of CHIP varies from state to state. Some states have sliding scale co-payment arrangements for CHIP that allow families to buy private health insurance at a premium cost that they can afford. Other states allow CHIP-eligible families to participate in the state's Medicaid program. To find out about your state's CHIP program, contact the office of your state's insurance commissioner or your state's office of maternal and child health, usually located in the state's health department. Federal funds support state governments to provide a telephone help line available to the public to address maternal and child health questions and to provide referrals to appropriate service providers. They give information about where women and children can receive free or low-cost healthcare and vaccines.

Summary

For early learning programs, maintaining accurate and comprehensive health information about the children it serves is important not only to the success of the program but also to the health and safety of all the children and staff members. It is essential that healthcare providers and early childhood educators and program administrators share health information and communicate clearly and regularly. Comprehensive documentation is key to maintaining accurate records and communicating effectively with caregivers and healthcare professionals about the health status of children. Educators and program administrators must support caregivers and help them to navigate the labyrinth of documentation and health requirements. Creating systems for maintaining, updating, and conveying health information should be a priority for all early learning programs.

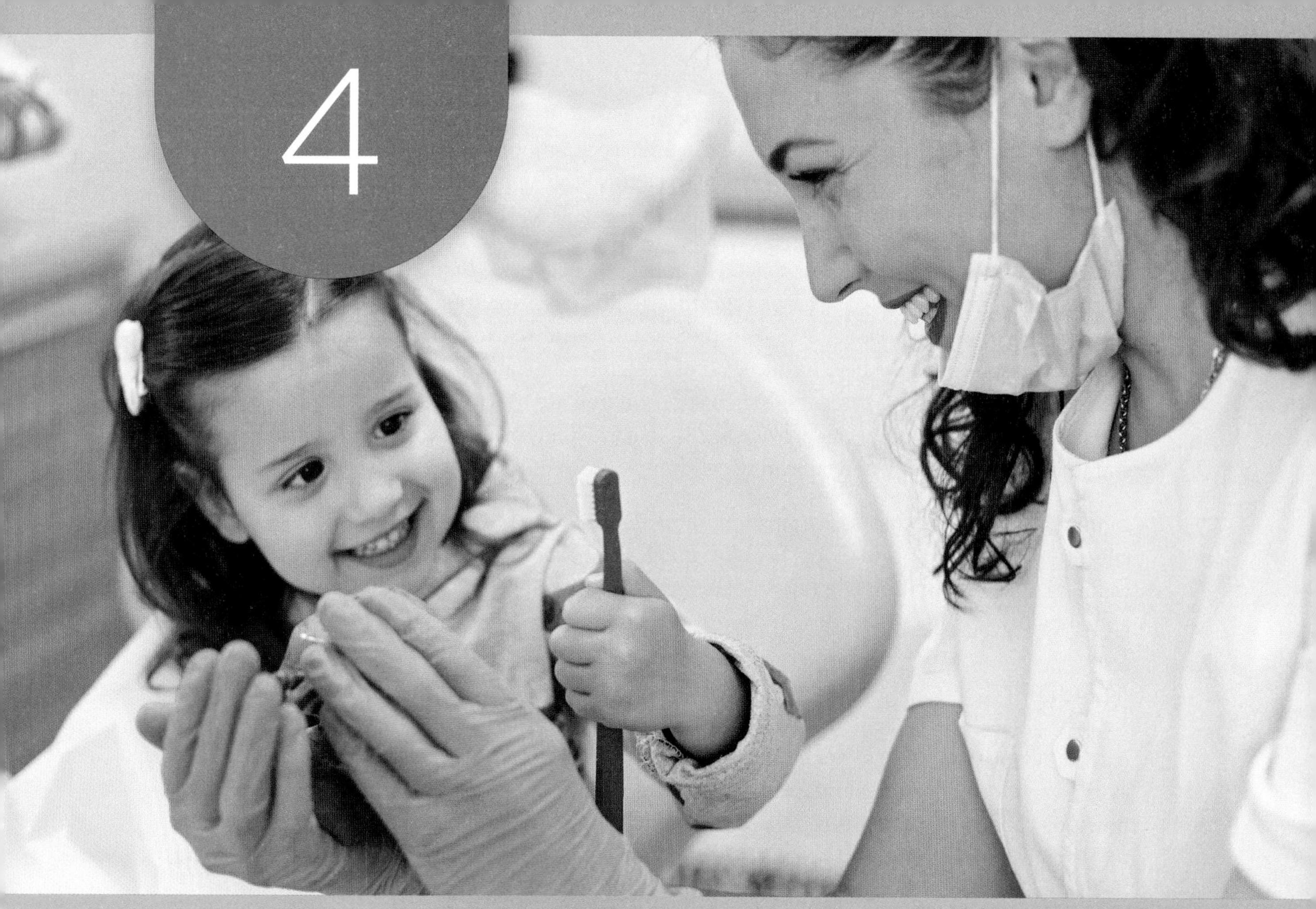

Health Education for Nutrition and Oral Health

NICOLE HACKMAN AND MADIHA JAMIL

LEARNING OBJECTIVES

- To understand basic nutrition
- To examine the benefits and concerns regarding vitamins and minerals
- To identify methods to model healthy nutritional practices
- To review best practices to maintain oral health

Good nutrition and oral health are essential in early childhood to promote healthy growth and development. Children who are hungry, malnourished, or have painful cavities will struggle to learn and play. Eating habits developed in childhood will continue into adulthood. More than half of children 5 years and younger who are not attending kindergarten will receive nonparental care, and of those 62 percent are enrolled in preschool or other center-based care (Cui & Natzke 2021). Children enrolled full time in an early learning program often spend more awake hours at the center than they do in their home. Early learning programs play a critical role in providing nutritious meals and serve as role models of healthy eating habits for children. Lessons learned here will last a lifetime!

Food insecurity, or reduced access to food at home, impacts more than 14 percent of US households with children, and the early learning program is an ideal location for children to have reliable access to nutritious foods (ERS USDA 2022). In the last few decades, overnutrition and childhood obesity have also become a public health concern that has immediate and long-term health consequences. In some communities, 60 percent of school-age children are overweight (Kleinman & Greer 2019). The early learning program can provide access to consistent, healthy, and well-balanced foods while simultaneously modeling and educating children.

In this chapter, we discuss basic nutrition for young children, how educators and programs can educate children about and model healthy eating, and how critical dental health is to the overall wellness of young children. We reference content and several standards from "Chapter 4: Nutrition and Food Service" of *Caring for Our Children*.

Basic Nutrition

Nutrition is the process that helps all living organisms develop and grow. Good nutrition and healthy eating benefit children in countless ways, including increased energy to learn, move, and play. Bad nutrition can have an equally negative effect on the development of children and increase their risk for diabetes, high cholesterol, sleep apnea, and more. Before beginning to develop healthy eating habits, it is important to understand the basics of nutrition.

Foods, Fats, Sugar, and Salt

Food can be divided into five groups: fruits, vegetables, protein foods, grains, and dairy. Foods from a variety of categories can be included in meal planning.

Categories of Foods

Fruits, such as bananas, grapes, and oranges, are part of a flowering plant or tree that encloses the seeds. Vegetables are the edible portion of a plant, such as lettuce, carrots, and broccoli. Fruits and vegetables provide important nutrients that can lower the risk for heart disease, stroke, and cancers.

Proteins are molecules made up of amino acids, and they are needed to make the body function properly. Amino acids are linked together in long chains forming important structures within the body, such as blood, hair, muscles, skin, and more. The body can make some amino acids itself, but there are nine essential amino acids that must come from foods. Seafood, beef, chicken, fish, eggs, quinoa, and soybeans are considered superfoods that contain all nine essential amino acids. Proteins will serve as structures within the cell, the building blocks of life, and work as messengers, as transporters, and in storage. Without proteins, children experience poor growth, loss of muscles, decreased immunity, and weakening of their heart and lungs.

Grains, found in foods such as pasta, breads, and cereals, are the gathered seeds from food plants like corn, oats, rice, and wheat. Fiber, B vitamins, and minerals such as iron are found in grains. There are three components to a grain seed, or kernel, and these include the bran, germ, and endosperm. Whole grains, like whole wheat flour, quinoa, brown rice, and oatmeal, have the entire grain seed or kernel (all three seed parts). Refined grains, such as those found in white flour and white bread, have been milled to remove the bran and germ part of the seed. Once milled, the remaining grain will lose some of its fiber, iron, and vitamins. For this reason, at least half of the grains that we eat should be whole grains.

Dairy products, such as cheese, yogurt, milk, and fortified soy milk, are excellent sources of protein, calcium, and vitamins. Growing children build bone at a rapid rate, and the calcium and vitamin D found in many dairy products will help promote strong bone development. Dairy products are nutrient dense, providing a high level of beneficial nutrients for low caloric intake.

Fats

Fat serves as an energy source in the body and can help absorb certain vitamins and minerals, such as vitamins A, D, E, and K. Saturated fats are tightly packed with no double bonds between the fatty acids and are usually solid at room temperature. Saturated fats can be found in animal-based foods like butter, lard, meats, and cheeses. Saturated fats increase levels of bad cholesterol (low-density lipoprotein [LDL]-cholesterol), which cause a buildup within the arteries of the heart and body, leading to heart disease and should be limited.

Trans fats are particularly unhealthy. They can reduce the levels of healthy cholesterol (high-density lipoprotein [HDL]) while increasing the levels of LDL. This combination can increase the risk for heart disease, heart attacks, diabetes, and strokes. Small amounts of trans fats can occur naturally in meat and dairy products, but since they have no nutritional value, artificial trans fats were banned by the US Food and Drug Administration (FDA) and could no longer be added to food after 2018. As of 2023 naturally occurring trans fats can still be found in baked goods, fried foods, and other processed food products.

Sugar

Sugars are simple carbohydrates with a sweet taste that provide a quick energy source for the body. It can occur naturally in fruits and vegetables, but excess sugar can hide in many prepackaged foods and beverages, such as yogurt and juices. Sugar contributes to cavities and excess weight gain, which can lead to childhood obesity. Sugar-sweetened beverages should be avoided, and children should be offered water as the preferred drink. Sweets such as candy, cakes, and ice cream should be limited. Food labels are a useful reference to review where excess sugar could be eliminated from a child's diet.

Salt

Salt, an electrolyte made up of sodium and chloride, plays a role in the human body and is found in many foods, such as soups, bread, and processed meats. Eating too much salt can lead to high blood pressure, a risk factor in heart disease and strokes. Too little salt could cause dehydration, low blood pressure, and muscle cramps. Children do not need added salt in their diets, and salty foods such as pretzels and chips should be limited. Salt-free seasonings such as herbs and spices are a great approach to flavor foods and help increase variety.

Minerals and Vitamins

Minerals and vitamins are essential substances that our bodies need to develop and function normally. Iron, vitamin D, and calcium provide great benefits to young children's health when given in correct measurements, but there are some cautions.

Iron

Iron is an important element in our bodies and is required for growth, development, and prevention of anemia. Iron helps form red blood cells, which carry oxygen throughout the body. Anemia can occur from blood loss but more frequently is due to eating too little iron. Iron-rich foods should be included in a regular healthy diet and can include fortified cereals and breads, meat, lentils, and leafy greens. Vitamin C-rich foods can help increase the body's absorption of iron, so serving these foods together is a great way to help iron absorption (e.g., eating oranges with breakfast cereal). Excessive milk intake can cause iron deficiency, and it is recommended to limit milk to less than 24 ounces per day (this includes milk consumed in a home or a school setting).

Vitamin D

Vitamin D plays an important role in the formation of strong bones, but it also plays a role in a healthy immune system. Infants should consume 400 international units (IU) of vitamin D daily, while children age 1 year and older should aim for 600 IU daily. Examples of vitamin D-rich foods include fortified milks, salmon, tuna, and some yogurts and cheeses.

Calcium

Calcium helps to maintain strong bones and teeth. Muscle and nerves also require calcium to move and send messages through the body. Calcium-rich foods are an important component of a healthy diet. Dairy products such as milk, cheese, yogurt, and cottage cheese can be good sources of calcium, but educators and staff members should review nutrition labels for individual brands and products purchased to understand the calcium content of that product.

Healthy Eating

Healthy eating means that all of the five food groups and beneficial vitamins and minerals are included regularly in the meals we eat. For children, who are developing physically and mentally, eating healthful foods are even more important. In 2011, MyPlate was developed to inspire healthy eating and replaced the food pyramid. It is designed to provide a quick reference to build healthier meals filled with the important nutrients like those found in fruits and vegetables. MyPlate's website is an excellent resource for families to learn more about the food groups and appropriate servings per age group, and it includes fun activities for children (**www.myplate.gov/life-stages/kids**).

Children will benefit from the early learning program's example of healthy eating habits, starting with an introduction to age-appropriate approaches to healthy eating. Bulletin boards, books, songs, and games can also be used to educate about healthy eating.

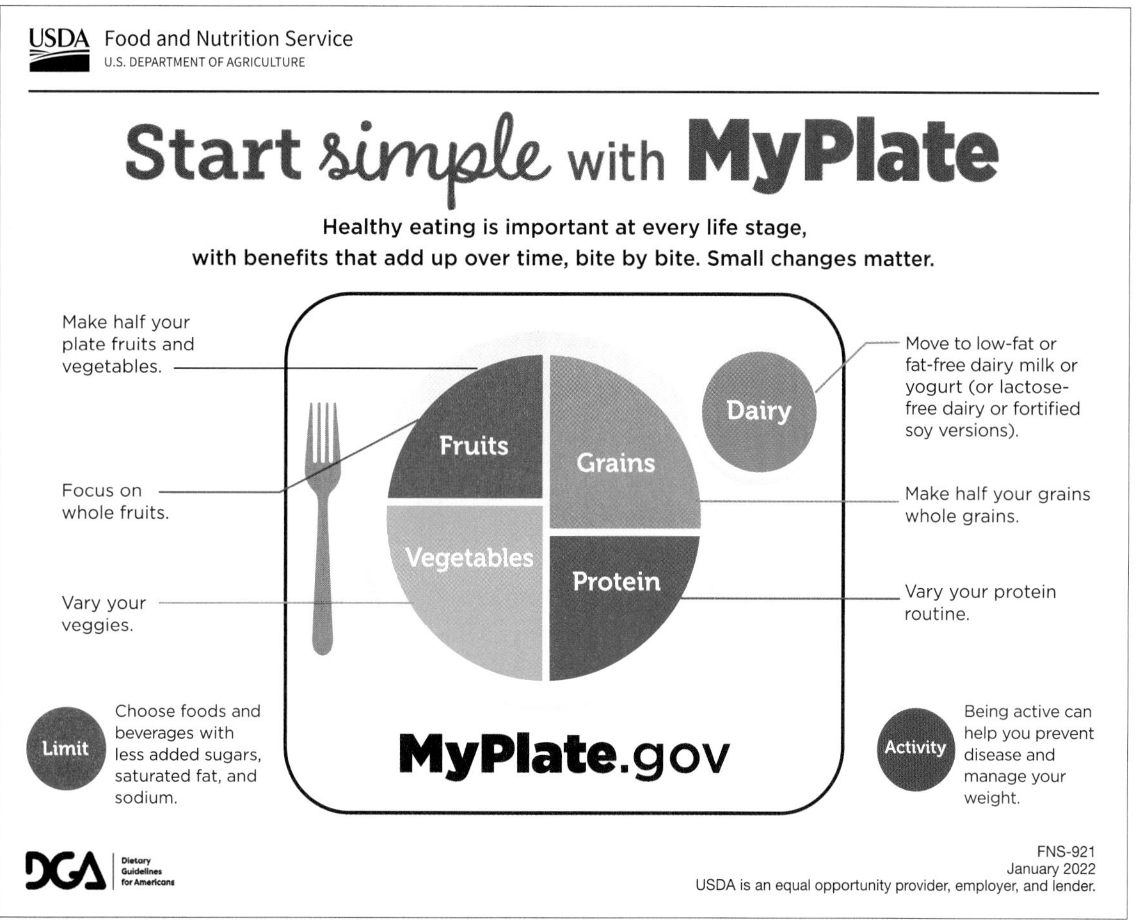

Figure 4.1. MyPlate (USDA. https://www.myplate.gov/life-stages/kids)

MyPlate reminds us that colorful fruits and vegetables should make up about half of the plate during any given meal. This will help reach the goal of eating five servings of fruits and vegetables each day (Figure 4.1).

When creating a meal plan for children, use of these themes can help create a nutritious meal:

1. **Make half your plate fruits and vegetables every day.** Fruits and vegetables contain important vitamins, minerals, and fiber, and this strategy can help to reach the recommended goal of five servings of fruits and veggies daily.
2. **Try whole grains.** Whole grains are rich in many nutrients, such as B vitamins, and zinc, and contain protein and fiber.
3. **"Think about your drink."** Low-fat milk or water are preferred beverages with specific cautions. Babies can be introduced to water at around 6 months old. Children ages 1–3 years need approximately 4 cups of beverages per day, including water or milk. This increases to around 5 cups for children ages 4–8 years and 7–8 cups for older children (Rethy 2020).

Milk

Fortified cow's milk is an excellent source of vitamin D and calcium, and it can be introduced into the child's diet after their first birthday. Milk substitutes, such as soy and almond milks, may be needed for children who have lactose intolerance or are allergic to milk. Milk substitutes may not add extra calcium or vitamin D, and the nutrition label can be reviewed to confirm.

Milk should not be given to an infant less than 1 year old because it can contribute to iron-deficiency anemia. Whole milk is generally given to children ages 1–2 years. However, there may be times when children have an elevated body mass index (BMI) and their physician will recommend a lower calorie milk (i.e., 1 percent or skim) to help promote healthy weight (*CFOC* Standard 4.3.1.7). Children older than 2 years old can be served skim or 1 percent milk.

Water

Water is the preferred beverage for children and adults, as it helps to maintain a normal body temperature, cushion our joints, and eliminates wastes in urine or perspiration. However, water should not be given to children younger than 6 months old. Water is an excellent no-calorie alternative to sugar sweetened beverages like juice or soda. It is important to make water available to children throughout the day and to help them increase their intake on hot days to prevent dehydration.

The early learning program should ensure a safe water supply and consider testing water for contaminants, such as lead and copper (*CFOC* Standard 5.2.6.3). If the early learning program water supply is fluoridated (has added fluoride), this can also help prevent cavities!

Juice

Children should drink less than 4 ounces per day or avoid juice completely. Juice and other sugar-sweetened beverages should be limited since they are high in sugar and contribute to childhood obesity and cavities; water and milk are best (Wojcicki & Heyman 2012). When possible, children should be served the fruit itself, which contains fiber and more vitamins and minerals. Children under 1 year old should not be given juice. Limits on the volume of juice consumed daily includes juice provided in other settings, such as at elementary school or in the home. The early learning program should consider if children are receiving juice in other settings prior to including it in the daily menus (*CFOC* Standard 4.2.0.7). Limit to 4 ounces for children ages 1–3 years and to 4–6 ounces for children ages 4–6 years (Heyman et al. 2017). Juice limits should also include any servings of juice at home or at school.

A child's appetite is unique to their age and their activity level. It is normal for appetite to vary throughout the day and from one day to the next. Often, toddlers will have an average of one "good" meal per day, and they might pick at their foods for other meals. Appetite will also change based on the amount of physical activity and exercise that has occurred—on busier days, children may be looking for larger portions.

Children can be guided to learn to "eat the rainbow" and incorporate colorful fruits and vegetables into their meals. Designing activities around this theme can help to reinforce the lesson. For example, videos, games, and books can make learning about healthy foods fun and engaging.

IMMEDIATE IMPACT

Use Food as Part of Lessons

Incorporate learning about and tasting fruits or veggies into lesson plans, such as sound-letter sorts using pictures or objects to represent words (like *m* is for *milk*). These food letter days also provide an opportunity for tasting days and art projects with that fruit or vegetable. Painting with a food can be a creative way to provide nutrition education and promote fine motor skill development while stimulating children's creativity. A child could also use vegetables to create a person or a funny face on a clean surface or plate. They can then eat their creation for snack. Additional ideas and resources can be found on MyPlate's website (**www.myplate.gov/life-stages/kids**).

Food habits are learned during childhood, and the early learning program is an important site for regular nutrition education to occur. The American Academy of Pediatrics (AAP) discourages the use of food for rewards or punishments and instead highlights food as a source of nourishment. Activities can be developed with early childhood educators, families, and local resources to provide opportunities for children to experience healthy foods through taste, smell, sight, and touch. Additional resources for nutrition education can be found in *Caring for Our Children* Standard 4.7.0.1. Individual state department of health programs will also provide additional nutritional resources.

IMMEDIATE IMPACT

Grow Food Inside or Out!

Children can help to plant a garden, if available, or plant seeds in pots indoors that they can help maintain. Children could eat the fruits and vegetables they grow in their program's garden!

Feeding Guidelines by Age and Special Diets

Early childhood educators and programs can model healthy behaviors, especially at mealtime. Meals and snacks should be set at scheduled times and locations. Children should be seated at an appropriate table in chairs and served appropriate portions. Portion size should be based on the child's age. Figure 4.2 includes recommendations for fruit groups, servings, and portions by age.

Food Group	Servings per Day	Portion Size for Ages 1 to 3	Portion Size for Ages 4 to 6	Portion Size for Ages 7 to 10
Fruits	2–3 servings	¼ cup cooked, frozen, or canned	¼ cup cooked, frozen, or canned	⅓ cup cooked, frozen, or canned
		½ piece fresh	½ piece fresh	1 piece fresh
		¼ cup 100% juice	⅓ cup 100% juice	½ cup 100% juice
Vegetables	2–3 servings	¼ cup cooked	¼ cup cooked	½ cup cooked
			½ cup salad	1 cup salad
Grains	6–11 servings	½ slice bread	½ slice bread	1 slice bread
		¼ cup cooked cereal, rice, or pasta	⅓ cup cooked cereal, rice, or pasta	½ cup cooked cereal, rice, or pasta
		⅓ cup dry cereal	½ cup dry cereal	¾–1 cup dry cereal
		2–3 crackers	3–4 crackers	4–5 crackers
Meats and other proteins	2 servings	1 ounce meat, fish, chicken, or tofu	1 ounce meat, fish, chicken, or tofu	2–3 ounces meat, fish, chicken, or tofu
		¼ cup cooked beans	⅓ cup cooked beans	½ cup cooked beans
		½ egg	1 egg	1 or 2 eggs
Dairy	2–3 servings	½ cup milk	½ cup milk	1 cup milk
		½ ounce cheese	1 ounce cheese	1 ounce cheese
		⅓ cup yogurt	½ cup yogurt	¾–1 cup yogurt

Adapted from Dietz WH, Stern L, eds. *Nutrition: What Every Parent Needs to Know.* 2nd ed. Elk Grove Village, IL: American Academy of Pediatrics; 2012:194.

Figure 4.2. Recommended serving and portion size by age.

Reprinted, with permission, from W.H. Dietz & L. Stern, *Nutrition: What Every Parent Needs to Know,* 2nd ed. (Elk Grove Village, IL: American Academy of Pediatrics, 2012), 194.

Infants (Birth to 1 Year Old)

A general plan for feeding infants can be found in *Caring for Our Children* Standard 4.3.1.1. Infants from birth through about 6 months old should be bottle-fed while at the early learning program, ideally receiving only breast milk. Formula may be needed for some infants as directed by the family. Breast milk, also called human milk, is considered the ideal food for infants. The AAP and the World Health Organization (WHO) recommend exclusively breastfeeding through 6 months old and that breastfeeding continue until the child is age 2 years or older. A nongendered term called *chestfeeding* is feeding milk from one's chest and may be used to describe providing human milk to infants. The AAP (2023) provides additional guidance on responsive feeding for infants.

Why is human milk best? Human milk is a living food that adjusts over the age of the infant and exposures or infections in the mother. Breast milk contains nutrients for energy, metabolism, antimicrobial factors, digestive enzymes, hormones, immune factors, probiotics, water, and micronutrients (Kleinman & Greer 2019). Breastfed infants have lower rates of ear infections, respiratory illness, gastroenteritis, hospitalization, and chronic disease like eczema, asthma, obesity, diabetes, leukemia, sudden infant death syndrome (SIDS), and more (Ip et al. 2007). Lactating individuals also benefit from breastfeeding. Women who have breastfed have lower rates of breast and ovarian cancers and reduced rates of high blood pressure and type 2 diabetes (DNPAO CDC 2021).

Breastfeeding

Breastfeeding infants and their families rely on the early learning program to help continue successful breastfeeding. Many women experience a decrease in breast milk supply when returning to work, and the support of the early learning program can help prolong breastfeeding durations. The use of paced bottle-feeding helps to mimic breastfeeding and slows the rate of the feeding.

The early learning program also benefits from supporting breastfeeding. Infants and children at the program who are fed breast milk should have fewer viral illness, fewer missed days of school and work in the future, and reduced stress on the providers and families.

Breastfeeding infants need to eat on demand, perhaps every 2 hours and 8–12 times in a 24-hour period. The breast milk handling and storage rule of 4s is a handy reminder: "4 hours at room temperature and 4 days in the refrigerator" (DiMaggio 2016, n.p.). The early learning program should consider posting human milk storage guidelines in their infant room to allow quick access to accurate information. This could be in the form of a refrigerator magnet (not recommended for use within the classroom because of choking hazards), which is available to print from the Centers for Disease Control and Prevention (CDC). Breast milk should be thawed by placing the container, bottle, or bag into a bowl of warm water. Thawed breast milk should be used within 24 hours and should not be refrozen. (See Appendix A.4.1 for CDC information on storage and preparation of breast milk.)

FAMILY CONNECTIONS

Examples of Supportive Policies and Practices

The early learning program can help families reach their goal to provide breast milk for their infants. Specific strategies to help support breastfeeding infants in early learning programs is available from the CDC at **https://www.cdc.gov/obesity/strategies/early-care-education/resource-library.html.** Early learning programs should encourage breastfeeding on site (i.e., before and after work), be trained in methods to properly handle and feed breast milk, and follow a family's feeding plan.

Formula Feeding

Formula feeding infants requires feeding on demand or roughly every 2–4 hours. Providers should prepare by washing their hands and using a clean surface. Follow manufacturer guidelines for formula preparation and use the scoop provided with that can. Ready-to-feed formula products are sterile and need to be shaken well. Formula prepared from a powder is not sterile and occasionally can be contaminated with *Cronobacter sakazakii*, a germ found naturally in the environment. Infants less than 2 months old and those that are preterm or immunocompromised are at the highest risk of infection. Educators should discuss with families of these infants if powder should be added to boiling water to kill potential bacteria and allowed to cool (CDC 2023). Safe formula preparation guidelines from WHO and the Food and Agriculture Organization of the United Nations (FAO; 2007) recommend adding the powdered formula directly to the boiled water (of at least 70°C/158°F) to kill any contaminants, then allowing it to cool to safe drinking temperature. All prepared bottles should be stored in the refrigerator for up to 24 hours and should be used or discarded within 2 hours of being removed from the refrigerator.

Bottle-Feeding Technique and Weaning from Bottle-Feeding

Formula and breast milk bottles can be warmed by placing a closed bottle into a bowl with warm water for 5–10 minutes. Do not microwave a bottle due to the risk of hot spots that can burn an infant.

The paced bottle-feeding technique should be used when feeding formula and breast milk. Through paced bottle-feeding, infants can slow the rate of their feeding, have more control over the feeding, and take breaks. Paced bottle-feeding can reduce the risk of overfeeding.

The technique for paced bottle-feeding is as follows:

1. Use a 4-ounce bottle while holding the infant in a semi-upright position, supporting the head and neck.
2. When the infant is cueing to feed (through lip smacking or suckling), place the bottle nipple into the infant's mouth and tip the milk into the nipple.

The infant will take a break during the feeding and the provider can lower the bottom of the bottle, drawing the milk out of the nipple and allowing the infant to pause. As the infant begins to suckle again, the bottom of the bottle is raised and milk returns to the nipple.

After about 6 months old when the infant is developmentally ready, or when advised by an infant's family s or physician, solid foods can be introduced. The infant should be able to sit without support and have good head and neck control, as well as loss of the tongue thrust reflex. Infants should be exposed to a variety of foods, flavors, and textures. The only food that is off limits for infants younger than 1 year old is honey. Honey should not be fed to infants until after their first birthday due to the risk of botulism.

Educators and parents can help to reduce the risk of baby bottle tooth decay and other issues related to feeding from bottles and sippy cups. Sugars interact with bacteria in the mouth to create acid, which causes tooth decay. After bottle-feeding or feeding of solids, teeth can be cleaned by wiping the mouth or brushing the teeth. Juice should not be given to a child before they are 1 year old.

Toddlers and Preschool-Age Children

A variety of table foods can be served to toddlers and preschool-age children. Careful attention to foods that are a choking hazard can help reduce the risk of an emergency. Nutritious meals with a variety of lean meats, fruits, and vegetables can help promote healthy weight. Milk and water are the preferred beverages.

School-Age Children

Healthy eating is important at all ages, and school-age children need nutritious meals and snacks while in the early learning program. Eating behaviors learned in childhood can last a lifetime, so the early learning program can play an important role in regular access to healthy food and in providing nutrition education. MyPlate can be utilized to help plan meals for older children.

Children Who Have Other Special Health Needs

Children in the early learning program have a variety of different oral motor skills and medical conditions. The early learning program may have children who feed themselves differently or are unable to chew or swallow certain textures. It is important to follow the feeding plan detailed by the family and child's physician to ensure nutritious meals that are appropriate for a child's abilities and needs.

Special Nutritional Needs and Diets

There are times when children will require a special diet due to health conditions or religious beliefs. Early learning programs should work with the family or child's physician to ensure that healthy foods appropriate to the individual child's needs will be available.

Vegetarian Diets

Children may follow a vegetarian diet due to religious or personal family beliefs. It will be important for the early learning program and family to discuss foods that are permitted and those that are not. There are many variations of diet restrictions, for example, a lacto-ovo vegetarian diet excludes meats but permits eating dairy and eggs. A vegan diet excludes foods from animal products, and the child would be meat- and dairy-free. Consider working with a nutritionist to review meal plans for children on exclusion diets. Through careful planning, all children can have nutritious meals in the early learning program.

Common Nutritional Concerns and Childhood Obesity

Understanding the basic nutritional needs of children is one step in helping them be healthy. It is also important to be able to recognize nutritional concerns surrounding children to be able to work with caregivers, families, and healthcare providers to address these concerns. In the United States, 20 percent of children are obese (NHLBI 2022). Obese and overweight children are at a higher risk for high blood pressure, type 2 diabetes, and breathing problems such as asthma (CDC 2022). Similarly, there are physical and mental development implications for children who fail to thrive or are malnourished. Children need nourishment to stimulate brain function and development and be physically active.

Childhood Obesity

Overnutrition occurs when children consume too many calories for their body's needs, which causes excess body fat to accumulate. Childhood obesity is a chronic health condition that can increase the risk for high blood pressure, high cholesterol, sleep apnea, type 2 diabetes, liver disease, and more. Extra body fat is determined using the BMI. BMI is calculated by dividing weight (in kilograms) by height squared (in meters). BMI highlights that it can be appropriate for taller individuals to weigh more while shorter individuals should weigh less. Calculators are available to help determine one's BMI, such as at **www.nhlbi.nih.gov/health/educational/lose_wt/BMI/bmi-m.htm**.

Prevention is key to reducing the health risks associated with obesity and being overweight. Interventions in nutrition, screen time reduction, and physical activity can make a tremendous difference in the long-term health of the child. (See "Chapter 5: Physical Activity.")

Failure to Thrive and Malnutrition

Failure to thrive occurs when a child is not growing at a normal rate, and they may be shorter than their peers, be underweight, or have weight loss. In general, it is not normal for children to lose weight. The most common reason for failure to thrive is not eating enough calories, but it could also be due to a medical problem or social stressors, such as food insecurity. When a child is identified as having failure to thrive, they need to be evaluated by a medical professional urgently. If the early learning program is concerned that the failure to thrive may be due to neglect or child abuse, immediate reporting to child protection agencies is mandatory. (See "Chapter 11: Child Maltreatment: What It Is and What to Do.")

Food Allergies and Intolerances

Children with food allergies or intolerances will be present in early learning programs. Eggs, milk, and peanuts are the most common food allergies in children. For a child with an allergy, the food will need to be avoided completely and careful reading of nutrition labels can reduce the risk of accidentally eating the food. Allergic reactions can range from mild (e.g., hives) to severe (e.g., anaphylaxis, or trouble breathing due to swelling of the airways and throat). If an accidental ingestion does occur, the early learning program will need to follow the allergy action plan previously provided by the family and child's physician. (See "Chapter 8: Understanding Common Illnesses and Conditions.")

Anaphylaxis is a severe life-threatening allergic reaction that occurs after exposure to an allergen (a food or item that you are allergic to such as a bee sting). Symptoms of anaphylaxis can develop within seconds and can include difficulty breathing or wheezing, increased heart rate, sweaty skin, feeling lightheaded, and even vomiting and diarrhea. If a child begins to experience these symptoms, follow your program's guidelines to activate emergency medical services. Children with severe allergic reactions may also have an epinephrine autoinjector prescribed by their doctor. This autoinjector can be given through clothing. Refer to the specific directions for use that accompany the product prescribed and from the allergy action plan provided by the child's healthcare professional. (See "Chapter 8: Understanding Common Illnesses and Conditions.")

Food intolerance occurs when a child is sensitive to eating certain foods but is not allergic. In general, a food intolerance does not cause as severe of a reaction as an allergy, but a food intolerance can be uncomfortable and disruptive to childhood. Lactose intolerance is a common example and can cause abdominal pain, cramping, changes in bowel movements, reflux, and more when a child eats dairy products like milk or ice cream. If a child is intolerant to a particular food, the early childhood educator should continue to review food labels to help the child maintain their diet free of that food ingredient.

Food Purchasing and Storage

The early learning program creates menus for children at their center. Menus can be developed to include a variety of age-appropriate foods. Nutritious meals can be developed with ideas from MyPlate or through consultation with a local nutritionist. Print or electronic versions of the menus can be shared with the children's families or primary caregivers.

Food purchasing is an important aspect of any food service. Use of a reliable food provider or local stores or programs can help reduce the risk of interruption or shortages. After food arrives at the early learning program, close attention should be paid to safe food storage. *Caring for Our Children* provides food storage guidance in Appendix V. (Appendix V (nrckids.org).)

Food Preparation and Handling

Early learning program staff members are required to have training in safe food handling and preparation (*CFOC* Standard 1.4.5.1). Good handwashing with soap and water can help reduce the risks of transmitting an infection during food handling. Hepatitis A is a very contagious infection transmitted in contaminated food and drink. Staff members should consider being vaccinated against hepatitis A to help reduce the risk of transmission within their program.

Oral Health

Oral health is an integral part of a child's well-being (Krol, Whelan, & AAP Section on Oral Health 2023). Oral health begins before the first tooth emerges, and care provided in the early learning program will promote healthy teeth and gums. Consistent oral hygiene and regular visits with the dentist can help children establish healthy habits, building a strong foundation for healthy teeth in the future.

Stages of Tooth Development

Children usually have eruption of their lower front teeth (incisors) around 6–10 months old. The upper incisors will typically come in a few months later. It is still normal if children get their teeth before or after this time. Most children will have their first tooth erupt before their first birthday, which is an important time to establish a dental home. *Dental home* refers to the ongoing relationship that children have with their dentist to continue care throughout childhood (see section on "Dental Home" for more information).

Cavities or Caries

Early childhood caries (ECC) refers to cavities, or tooth decay, in children younger than 6 years old. Dental caries are the most common disease in young children, and ECC is the greatest risk factor for cavities in adulthood. "The prevalence of total dental caries (untreated and treated) in primary or permanent teeth among youth aged 2–19 years was 45.8%. Prevalence increased with age, going from 21.4% among youth aged 2–5 to 50.5% among those aged 6–11 to 53.8% among those aged 12–19" (Fleming 2018, p. 1). ECC disproportionally affects children from families who have low socioeconomic status or who are minorities. Children with special healthcare needs, such as congenital heart disease, autism, and developmental delays, are also more likely to have cavities.

Cavities occur when bacteria in the mouth interact with carbohydrates from food, resulting in acid production. Saliva will buffer the acid to protect the teeth from damage. However, if acid production continues, tooth enamel will dissolve. Early tooth decay can appear as white spots, which can eventually turn into larger cavities. Children with cavities can have tooth pain, difficulty with concentration, and headaches. If cavities are untreated, they can result in more serious oral infection, such as abscesses and tooth loss.

Some bacteria in the mouth develop characteristics that allow them to produce large amounts of acid and adhere to the tooth enamel. This type of bacteria is termed *cariogenic*, or promoting the development of cavities. It can be passed on from generation to generation. Because the cariogenic bacteria can be transferred from person to person, it is important to avoid sharing utensils, especially if the person has poor dental hygiene. Caregivers and families should be advised against cleansing pacifiers or nipples with saliva or checking the bottle temperature by mouth.

Healthy Foods for Teeth

A balanced diet helps promote healthy teeth. This includes fruits and vegetables, grains, dairy products, and protein. (See section "Healthy Eating" earlier in this chapter for more details.) Despite how common dental caries are, it is a largely preventable disease. Gummies, fruit leathers, fruit pouches, and granola bars can stick to tooth enamel, promoting cavities. Healthy snacks, such as fresh carrots, cheese, and fresh fruits are preferred to crackers and candy. Sugary foods and sweetened beverages should be avoided. Natural sugars, such as honey and maple syrup, are just as bad for teeth as white sugar. When allowing children to have a sweet treat, offer it with a meal, followed by brushing teeth within 30 minutes.

Oral Hygiene and Brushing

Oral hygiene is the backbone of healthy teeth and gums. Here are some guidelines to remember:

- For infants, wipe gums with soft washcloth or toothbrush with water after feedings. The sugars from the milk or formula can lead to cavities.
- Once teeth erupt, begin brushing for 2 minutes twice a day with fluoridated toothpaste. The best times to brush are after breakfast and before bedtime. Any soft-bristled, age-appropriate toothbrush can be used for brushing. Children should spit excess toothpaste but not rinse. A timer, rhyme, or short song can help encourage children to brush for 2 minutes.
- A smear of toothpaste about the size of a grain of rice is recommended for children under age 3 years. A pea-size amount of toothpaste is recommended for children age 3 years and older.
- An easy position to encourage brushing and full visualization of the mouth is to hold the child upside down in the lap to brush the teeth. Early childhood educators can suggest this technique to primary caregivers and families for brushing in the evening.
- Children do not have the dexterity to brush correctly on their own until they are able to tie their shoe, or about 7–8 years old. Adults should supervise brushing to ensure that excessive toothpaste is not swallowed and to check brushing techniques.
- Once teeth start touching, flossing is recommended. The dentist will generally suggest when to begin flossing.

Dental Home

The AAP recommends that a child establish a dental home upon eruption of the first tooth, no later than 12 months (Figure 4.3). According to the American Academy of Pediatric Dentistry (2022), "the dental home is the ongoing relationship between the dentist and the patient, inclusive of all aspects of oral healthcare delivered in a comprehensive, continuously accessible, coordinated, and family-centered way" (15). A pediatric dentist completes 2 years of additional training after dental school to learn how to care for infants, children, and teenagers. These dentists are also well equipped to care for children with special needs.

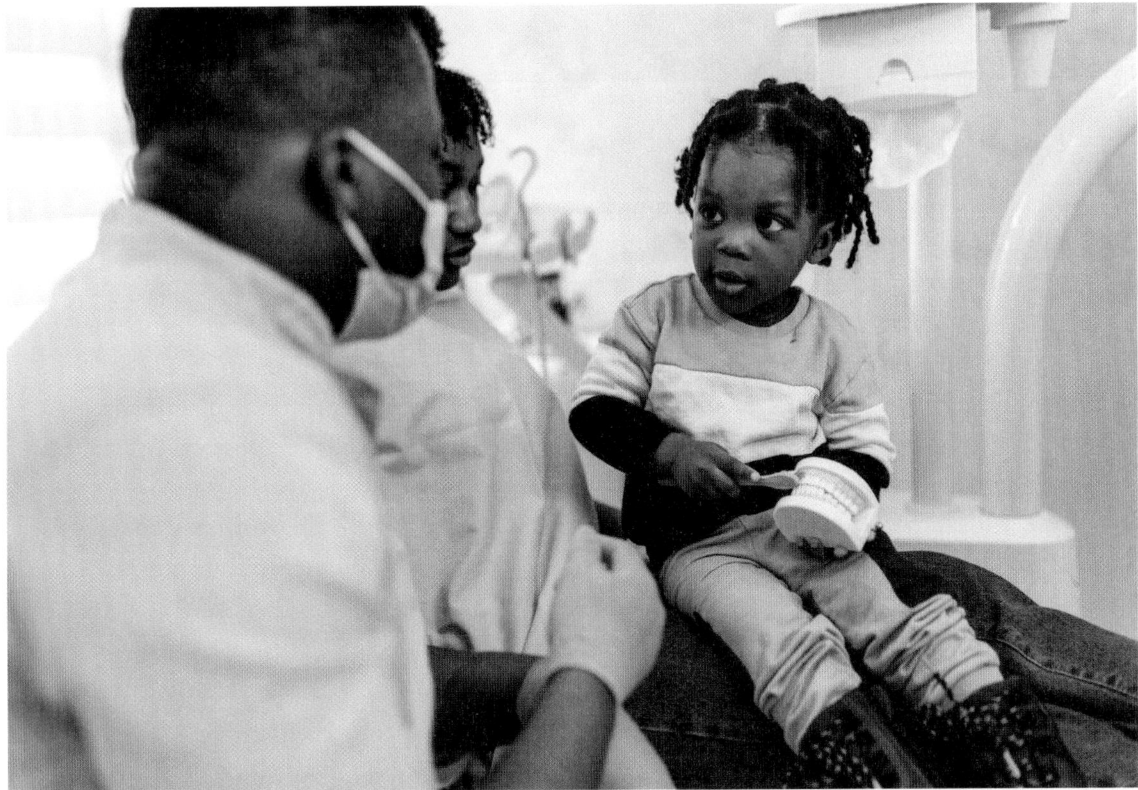

Figure 4.3. Establishing a dental home and initial dental visits for a child should start no later than 12 months old. (Copyright @ Getty.)

As soon as the teeth erupt, they are at risk of developing cavities. A cavity in the baby teeth puts children at higher risk of having cavities in the permanent teeth. Understanding and performing proper oral hygiene and dietary recommendations are crucial to preventing cavities.

The dentist will perform an oral health exam; provide preventative care (such as cleaning and fluoride treatments) and counseling; and diagnose and treat cavities, gum diseases, tooth injuries. If a dentist is not available in your area to see children, families should ask their pediatrician about routine oral healthcare, fluoride, and any concerns. Children should be seen by a dentist at least every 6 months for routine care, and more frequently as needed.

Having a positive attitude about the first dentist visit is important. If children see that others close to them are nervous about dentist visits, they will naturally follow this behavior. A favorite toy or stuffed animal can help calm children at their first visit. Keeping a positive attitude and seeing the dentist early helps children understand the importance of oral health and prevent future problems with teeth.

Oral Health Education

Early childhood educators are encouraged to invite a local dentist or public health hygienist to talk with the children about oral health. In addition, creating a community dentist list and distributing it to families can help establish the dental home.

FAMILY CONNECTIONS

Toothbrushing Routines

Toothbrushing is often difficult for families as they busily complete their morning routine. Early learning programs can offer toothbrushing as a daily educational session. Sending home flyers with reminders for families and caregivers about brushing can be helpful. Brush, Book, Bed is an AAP program that recommends that parents or primary caregivers help their children brush their teeth, read a favorite book, and go to bed at a regular time each night. In addition, there are many online oral health activities available for children. The CDC has a free oral health activity book for children ages 3–8 years at **www.cdc.gov/oralhealth/publications/dental_health_activity_book_PRINT.pdf.** In addition, the American Academy of Pediatric Dentistry has several educational handouts available on their website at **www.mychildrensteeth.org.**

Fluoride

Fluoride is a mineral that helps prevent cavities. It helps strengthen the teeth and prevents tooth decay by interfering with acid production by bacteria. Fluoride is found in both oral and topical forms. Community water fluoridation is the most cost-effective method of preventing cavities, reducing cavities by 25 percent (CDC HHS 2021).

Early learning programs are recommended to contact their local water company to find out if the water contains fluoride. If the program is on a well, the well water would need to be tested. They can then notify families regarding the status. If there is no fluoride in the water, families can discuss oral supplementation with their child's dentist and/or doctor. If using bottled water, check the label as it often does not contain fluoride.

Topical forms of fluoride include both toothpaste and fluoride varnish. Brushing with fluoride toothpaste twice daily is recommended by the AAP. Professional application of topical fluoride varnish can reduce cavities by 37 percent (Marinho et al. 2013). Varnish can be applied by both medical and dental providers.

Common Dental Concerns and Treatments

Early childhood educators may encounter children with an oral health concern. Below are some examples of some common concerns and their treatments.

- **Knocked out baby tooth.** Comfort the child, rinse the mouth with water, and apply a cool compress. Notify the dentist. Generally, a baby tooth will not be replaced into the mouth, but care has to be taken to prevent infection.
- **Knocked out permanent tooth.** Hold the tooth by the crown (top of tooth) and try to place it back into the socket of the mouth. If this is not possible, place it in a glass of milk and immediately call the dentist.

- **Chipped or broken tooth.** Rinse the mouth with water and apply a cool compress. Call the dentist immediately and bring the broken piece of tooth in water to the dentist.
- **Toothache.** Rinse the mouth with warm salt water and apply cool compress to affected area. Try to see the dentist as soon as possible.
- **Thumb-sucking and pacifiers.** Children use thumb-sucking and pacifiers as a soothing method. They likely will gradually discontinue this habit on their own. If the thumb-sucking and pacifier usage persists after age 3 years, the dentist may recommend a mouth appliance to prevent future oral alignment concerns. Try to praise the child when they are not thumb-sucking or using a pacifier, and limit the areas or times of day when a child can use them, such as right before sleep (AAP 2020).
- **Teething.** Children may be irritable and try to chew on hard surfaces. Teething rings from the fridge are recommended, as rings hard from the freezer can cut gums. Also rubbing a cool, wet washcloth on the area is soothing. Over the counter acetaminophen or ibuprofen can help with the pain. Teething tablets and gels should be avoided. Teething does not cause fever greater than 100.4°F.
- **Baby bottle tooth decay.** This type of tooth decay is most common on the upper front teeth and occurs due to prolonged exposure to milk or sugary beverages in a bottle. It often requires oral surgery with general anesthesia. Children will need to have a complete evaluation by their dental provider.
- **Discolored teeth.** This may be due to previous injury, iron supplementation, or poor oral hygiene. Recommendation to follow up with a doctor and/or dentist would be recommended.
- **Bite or cut of tongue or lip.** Rinse the mouth with water and apply pressure with gauze. Apply ice pack to area. If the injury cuts through the lip or across the edge of the tongue, it may need stitches.

Summary

Educators and programs must understand the tenets of basic nutrition and oral health to help children develop and grow physically, intellectually, and emotionally. Children enrolled in early learning programs can learn about healthy nutrition and oral health through educator modeling and program supports and services that can help families continue the education and healthy practices at home. Simple lessons like showing children and families how to use MyPlate to plan healthy meals and explaining the importance of early dental checkups can put children on a path to wellness and good health. In some situations, early learning programs are where children get their only access to healthy foods as families may experience food insecurity. This can lead to malnutrition and overnutrition in the form of childhood obesity as families must choose less expensive and less nutritious meal options. The early learning program can provide access to consistent, healthy, and well-balanced foods. Educators can make a difference in the lifelong habits of the children they serve.

Physical Activity

BRITTANY MASSARE AND ABIGAIL MYERS

LEARNING OBJECTIVES

- To describe the benefits of physical activity for children who attend early learning programs
- To apply the current *Caring for Our Children* standards for physical activity in an early learning setting
- To define the categories of physical activity and how each category applies to different age levels

Physical activity is essential for children's healthy growth and development, both physiologically and emotionally. "Young children need many opportunities throughout the day to develop their large muscles, improve their coordination, and use their limitless energy. Increasing core strength and hand–eye coordination can help preschoolers improve their gross motor abilities" (Bresson 2018, 28). This chapter discusses why physical activity is important for children, what the recommended amounts and types of activities are for children of different ages, and how early childhood educators can plan for and implement physical activity into their programs.

Benefits of Physical Activity for Young Children

Research has shown that the benefits of daily physical activity are innumerable, both for children and their caregivers, and can promote lifelong health and prevent certain health conditions. Only 24 percent of children in the United States get the nationally recommended 60 minutes or more of moderate-to-vigorous physical activity daily (CDC 2022a). This highlights the importance of normalizing routine physical activity at a young age.

Early learning programs are in a unique position to help young children make regular physical activity a lifelong habit. It is known that physical activity levels of children and among youth and caregivers are correlated; therefore, inactive caregivers will more likely have inactive children. Since many parents are not active either, early learning programs may be the only place a child has the opportunity to consistently engage in physical activity. Physical activity can include outdoor structured or unstructured activities, classroom physical activity, dedicated physical education instruction, or organized sports. All of these activities can help children increase cardiorespiratory fitness, build strong bones and muscles, maintain a healthy weight, improve sleep, and reduce the risk of developing health conditions, such as

- Heart disease
- Cancer
- Type 2 diabetes
- High blood pressure
- Osteoporosis
- Obesity

In addition, physical activity can improve children's mood and self-esteem, which can reduce symptoms of depression and anxiety (Brown et al. 2016). Providing opportunities for regular physical activity as part of the classroom schedule can improve children's cognitive performance and attention levels. Physical activity in the classroom can improve a child's self-regulatory and executive function processes, such as planning, organization, abstract problem-solving, and working memory (Strong et al. 2005). Physical activity can also benefit children who are kinesthetic learners (those who learn through movement and physical experiences). For example, children who are fidgety and unable to sit still for long periods of time may be more engaged and learn better while being physically active or if physical activity occurs just prior to learning activities. Allowing for active time improves gross motor development, decreases stress levels, and helps to promote motivation during classroom learning activities.

Recommendations for Appropriate and Beneficial Physical Activity

Many children do not reach the recommended amount of physical activity per day. For children in early learning programs, the most likely place to participate in physical activity is during their time in an early learning setting. In 2018, the US Department of Health and Human Services (HHS) published a report outlining physical activity guidelines. Activity intensity is categorized into light, moderate, and vigorous (HHS 2018):

1. *Light intensity activity* is defined as activity where a child is able to converse and there is no shortness of breath or sweating.
2. *Moderate intensity activity* is defined as when a child's heart beats faster than normal, they are breathing harder than when they are resting or sitting, they have some difficulty talking, and light sweating occurs.
3. *Vigorous intensity activity* is defined as when a child's heart is beating much faster than normal, their breathing is much harder than normal, they are unable to talk, and their face is red and sweating.

Physical Activity Recommendations by Age

Infants

For infants, physical activity is recommended several times per day, mostly through interactive, floor-based play. At least 30 minutes of supervised tummy time throughout the day while awake is important for gross motor development (HHS 2018). Educators should start by interacting with an infant on their tummy for three to five minutes, increasing time each day. *Caring for Our Children* Standard 3.1.3.1 lists ways to promote tummy time, including placing toys just out of reach of the infant in different locations or having the infant lie on the educator's chest while the educator is on their back. These will promote both lifting of the head and using the arms to lift and reach. *Caring for Our Children* Standard 3.1.3.1 also states infants should not be seated for more than 15 minutes at a time except during meals. Infant equipment (e.g., swings, bouncers, exersaucers) should be used minimally, if at all. Infants should be in an environment that allows safe freedom of movement as much as possible (*CFOC* Standard 5.3.1.10) (Figure 5.1).

Toddlers

Caring for Our Children Standard 3.1.3.1 recommends all children from birth to 6 years old participate in two to three outdoor play times, weather permitting (see the section "Safety" later in this chapter for more information), two or more structured activities that promote movement, and time to work on gross motor skills throughout the day. *Caring for Our Children* Standard 3.1.3.1 recommends children 12–35 months be allowed 60–90 minutes per eight-hour day for moderate-to-vigorous physical activity, either outdoors or indoors. For children in the early learning program for less than eight hours per day, this physical activity goal should be adjusted accordingly. Running should be part of these higher intensity physical activities. Ideally, toddlers should

Figure 5.1. Infants should have space to move and play. (Copyright @ Getty Images.)

also participate in outdoor play for at least 60–90 minutes in a day (*CFOC* Standard 3.1.3.1). Except when sleeping, toddlers should not be sedentary for more than an hour of time or for multiple times throughout the day.

Preschoolers

Children ages 3–5 years should play actively during the day in short bursts. Children should participate in physical activity of any intensity for at least three hours per day (CDC 2022b). Moderate or vigorous activity should occur for more than 60 minutes per day and vigorous activity at least three days per week (HHS 2018). Similar to toddlers, *Caring for Our Children* Standard 3.1.3.1 recommends preschoolers participate in two to three outdoor play times, two or more structured activities that promote movement, and time to work on gross motor skills throughout the day. Like toddlers, preschoolers should also be taken outside for 60–90 minutes of outdoor play daily (weather permitting). Preschoolers should participate in 90–120 minutes of moderate-to-vigorous activity and running should be part of these higher intensity activities.

School-Age Children

Children age 6 years and older should participate in at least 60 minutes per day of moderate or vigorous activity. This daily activity should be vigorous activity at least three days per week (CDC 2022b). Table 5.1 outlines activity guidelines for each age group discussed here and includes optimum time and intensity of activity.

Table 5.1. Physical Activity Guidelines

	Amount of activity	Types of activity
Infants	No set goal recommended but should not be sedentary for more than 15 minutes at a time	Supervised tummy time at least four times per day, otherwise activity recommended throughout day
Toddlers	At least 90–180 minutes per day	At least two structured occasions of 5 to 10 minutes each
Preschoolers	At least 120–180 minutes per day	At least two structured occasions, with a goal of 60 minutes of structured activity. At least 60 minutes moderate-to-vigorous activity.
School-age children	At least 60 minutes per day	Should be moderate-to-vigorous activity

Adapted from and informed by AAP, APHA, & NRC 2019; CDC 2022a, 2022b; HHS 2018; and Ward et al. 2014.

The Educator's Role

Educators can serve as role models for physical activity by encouraging children to be active with them. This can be as simple as taking a group walk. Educators should engage with children during active play times and not just be observers on the sidelines. When educators actively participate in gross motor play with children, children are more likely to participate (CDC 2022c). Educators can also use physical activity to help children who have more difficulty staying on task as well as children who have trouble controlling fidgeting or disengaging behaviors, such as excessive or disruptive talking, gazing off, or moving or getting up during a quiet activity.

Including at least two structured activities daily can encourage higher intensity levels that increase younger children's engagement in active play (*CFOC* Standard 3.1.3.1). *Caring for Our Children* Standard 3.1.3.4 encourages educators to praise children's efforts with prompts (e.g., "That was quick running," "Good catch"). Play or physical activity should not be used as a reward or punishment. Children who misbehave should not be restricted from participating in outdoor play or physical activity unless it is for a maximum of five minutes while calming down (*CFOC* Standard 3.1.3.1).

Educators can also work with families to increase physical activity at home for the whole family.

Administration and Policy

Caring for Our Children Standards 2.1.1.2 and 9.2.3.1 recommend that early learning programs have written policies for promotion of indoor and outdoor physical activity and the removal of barriers to physical activity participation. According to *Caring for Our Children* Standard 9.2.3.1, these policies should include benefits of physical activity and outdoor play, procedures to continue active play in the event of inclement weather, and the expectation of structured and unstructured play in classrooms. Educators should be provided orientation and annual training related to appropriate activities and games to encourage gross motor development during physical activity (*CFOC* Standard 3.1.3.4).

FAMILY CONNECTIONS

Share Resources for Families

There are many family resources that explain how to plan and create fun physical activities. Here are a few:

- **"Healthy Active Living for Families"** is an interactive webpage where families can learn tips and tricks for fun activities at home (**www.healthychildren.org/English/healthy-living/growing-healthy/Pages/default.aspx**).
- **"Kids and Exercise"** for caregivers explains the importance of physical activity and offers ways to incorporate into the home (**https://kidshealth.org/en/parents/exercise.html**).

Activities

Young children are naturally energetic and want to move, so to them exercise and physical activity is fun! With a little encouragement and planning, physical activities can easily be made a part of the regular classroom routine and will likely become a child's favorite time of the day. Physical activity can either be structured or unstructured. *Structured physical activity* is an activity that is planned and intentionally directed by an adult. Examples of structured physical activity include beanbag games, follow the leader, and musical chairs. *Unstructured physical activities* are sometimes called "free time" or "self-selected free play." These are activities that children start by themselves but are facilitated by the educator, who may arrange the environment to allow for play or the materials to do so. Examples of unstructured physical activity include riding a toy or bike, playing tag, imaginative games with friends, or playing on a playground. Time for both structured and unstructured physical activity should be allotted for in a child's daily schedule. Outdoor play is favored over indoor activities when weather and facilities allow for it. Children are more likely to engage in activities that require movement when outdoors compared to indoors, thus promoting physical activity (Tandon et al. 2018).

In general, when planning structured physical activities, educators should adhere to the following guidelines:

- Avoid creating a competitive atmosphere; instead, encourage children to do their best and try to do better than they did before.
- Consider the developmental abilities of the age group.
- Consider the physical abilities of each and every child.
- Make the activities engaging but not so challenging that the children become frustrated.
- Consider the length of the activity and the attention span and interest of the children.

Skills and Abilities

Children's skills and abilities are always developing and changing. Educators must understand that while physical activities are beneficial for children, the types and levels of these activities must be carefully considered and planned. For instance, organized sports like soccer or whiffle ball are not appropriate for infants and toddlers because these activities require more advanced gross motor and coordination skills and include specific rules and instructions to play that go beyond their skills and abilities. Children first need a chance to practice motor skills to enjoy certain physical activities. All activities need to fit children's abilities yet provide space to develop skills.

GROSS MOTOR SKILLS

Below are some guidelines for age ranges and gross motor skills development to help you know generally what to expect, what skills and abilities come first, and what comes next for most children:

Around 3 years old: Children can jump, kick a ball, balance on one foot for three seconds, throw overhand and underhand, switch feet when climbing stairs

Around 4 years old: Children can hop, walk backwards, gallop, walk on a balance beam, bounce a ball and catch a ball, throw to hit a target, balance on one foot for five seconds

Around 5 years old: Children can skip, kick and throw harder and with more accuracy, balance on one foot for 10 seconds (Bresson 2018, 30)

Keeping Their Attention

Attention spans for each age group can vary based on the individual, but typically infants have the shortest attention span and will move rapidly from one activity to the next. Two to three minutes is the most the child will spend with a single toy, and then they will turn to something new. By 12 months, the child may be willing to sit for as long as 15 minutes with a particularly interesting plaything, but most of the time they'll still be a body in motion. The toddler's attention span is a bit longer, about four to six minutes on average and a preschooler's attention span is even longer, eight to 12 minutes on average. These time spans are averages and may vary based on individual needs, time of day, emotional state and support, and how many distractions are nearby (Gaertner, Spinrad, & Eisenberg 2008). Again, this means that toddlers and preschoolers will usually quickly cycle through the structured physical activities that the educator has planned. After two rounds of a particular game, the educator may have some children drifting away from the game and engaging in other activities of their own choosing. Some younger age groups may need several sequential activities or multiple variations of the same activity planned for the same length of time set aside for structured physical activities, whereas educators for older age groups may only need to plan for one activity during the same amount of time. Therefore, it is important for the educator to take into account a child's attention span when planning structured physical activities.

Structured Physical Activities by Age

Infants

Early physical activities for infants involve either the infant moving their own arms and legs or the adult moving the infants' arms or legs while talking and interacting. This can occur after the diapering process is complete (allowing for grasping and kicking), upon waking from a nap (moving arms or legs before getting the infant out of the crib), or during feeding (allowing the infant to grasp the bottle while being fed). Infants thrive on repetition, so they don't mind if the physical activity is the same every time. All infants should engage in supervised tummy time, which promotes head, neck, and truncal control and increases muscle strength. Other movements to be encouraged in this age group are lifting the head, kicking, and reaching during tummy time; reaching for or grasping toys or other objects; playing and rolling on the floor; and crawling around the classroom environment. The educator should smile and praise attempts at any new skills as this will increase the likelihood that the infant will repeat them. The educator should provide an environment that allows freedom of movement as much as possible, that is safe and clean, such as an uncluttered floor space of at least 5 × 7 feet. Infant play space should be out of the caregiver's walking path, away from shelving and objects that could fall, and away from rocking chairs and other potential hazards. Infant rooms generally require caregivers and educators to cover or remove shoes before entering the room to facilitate cleanliness as infants will be spending time on the floor. Ideally, the environment should be comfortable for educators to be on the floor level when interacting with infants.

Toddlers

Toddlers are naturally active and have spurts of energy, although short attention spans. Toddlers often enjoy vigorous, high-energy activities for five to 10 minutes, followed by quieter activities or rest. Children at this age are just beginning to develop new physical skills, and each child will progress at their own rate. It is best to vary activities so that each child has challenges and successes and also to keep their attention. Physical activity should be enjoyable play for every child. The educator should spread out equipment in the classroom or outdoor space and allow plenty of room for activities.

Preschoolers

Children in the preschool age group are learning to hop, skip, and jump forward, and they are eager to show off how they can balance on one foot, catch a ball, or do a somersault. Preschoolers also enjoy playing on a playground, dancing, riding a tricycle, and swimming. The average preschooler has not mastered the basic skills needed to play a particluar sport, such as throwing, catching, and taking turns. There are activities that can help children develop and practice these skills.

School-Age Children

Children in this age group have mastered many of the gross motor skills needed to fully participate and enjoy most organized sports or more complicated games. At this age, they are working on coordination of these skills to allow for success in team or individual sports. Sports

IMMEDIATE IMPACT

Indoor Play for Rainy Days

Plan for outdoor activities two to three times a day, but make sure to have a backup plan for indoor activities if weather doesn't cooperate. For example, garbage ball/sock ball throw is a game that helps children to develop throwing and catching skills and hand–eye coordination, and it is a good indoor option when outside play is not possible.

> Garbage ball/Sock ball throw game:
>
> Create garbage balls by wadding up pieces of newspaper or wrapping paper and covering them in packing tape (for sock balls, ball up two or three socks). Mark a chalk or tape line on the floor, where children will stand. Depending on the age of the children, place a target between three and six feet away. Encourage children to aim their throws at the target. For most 3-year-olds, the target is simply there to direct children's throws. Many 4- and 5-year-olds can begin using it for accuracy. Help preschoolers develop underhand and overhand throwing techniques first, and work on accuracy later. (Bresson 2018, 28)

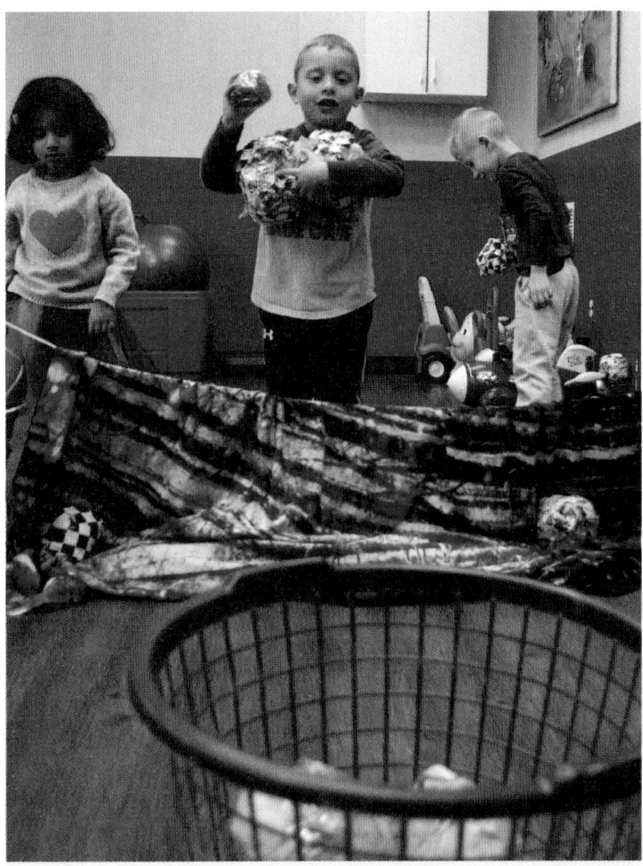

(With permission of the author, LIsa Bresson.)

Figure 5.2. Educator exercising with children. (Copyright @ Getty Images.)

that are easy to incorporate into an early learning program that require little instruction or equipment are soccer or kickball. Children in this age group should be encouraged to join games or sports that are in progress or suggest something to play with their peers. Once again, educators who participate in activities with children model good physical activity habits and sportsmanship and allow for inclusion of more children into the activity (Figure 5.2). Table 5.2 provides multiple examples of activities for children by age.

Table 5.2. Examples of Physical Activity by Age

	Infants (1 year old and younger)	Toddlers (1–2 years old)	Preschoolers (3–5 years old)
Unstructured physical activities	• Reaching and grasping for toys and other objects • Pulling up to stand on furniture or educators • Crawling around classroom • Water tables or water play (outdoors) • Banging on classroom items or pots and pans • Pushing toys when available	• Dancing • Tumbling • Running • Beanbag toss • Bubble catch • Water tables or water play (outdoors)	• Catch and throw with a ball or kicking a ball back and forth • Tag • Running/races • Dancing • Chalk drawing • Swimming (if possible)
Structured physical activities	• Tummy time	• Direction games (e.g., Simon Says; Red Light, Green Light) • Songs with action words (e.g., "Head, Shoulders, Knees, and Toes") • Obstacle courses	• Scavenger hunts or exploration walks • Obstacle courses • Follow the Leader • Musical Chairs • Duck, Duck, Goose

Safety

As with all physical activity, there is a risk for injury, bumps, and bruises. Educators should be equipped and trained to address and handle situations in which a child has been injured or experienced a medical situation during physical activity. (For more on injury prevention and treatment, see "Chapter 7: First Aid and Injuries.")

Children with Medical or Developmental Concerns

Every effort should be made for all children to be able to participate in activities, including physical activity (*CFOC* Standard 8.2). During physical activity, children with underlying medical conditions, developmental delays, or physical disabilities may need special accommodations or preparation. "Chapter 10: Inclusion of Young Children with Special Healthcare Needs and/or Medical Complexity" focuses on children with special healthcare needs and provides more information. For any child with an underlying medical condition or developmental delay, discussion with a child's healthcare provider, early intervention therapist, or a child care health consultant upon enrollment of the child in the program can help to not only accommodate but also enable a child to flourish in an early learning program. It is important to plan and try to accommodate as much as possible children with special needs who may need adaptive equipment. Overall, children with disabilities are less likely to participate in the recommended amount of physical activity and are more likely to be obese.

A common medical condition in early childhood that flares with physical activity or change in temperature or environment is asthma. An individualized care plan should be available from a child's healthcare provider that explains how to keep a child's symptoms from flaring. This may involve administering medication prior to outside or active play or if any symptoms develop. If a child is regularly showing symptoms of their asthma, the family should be instructed to talk with the child's healthcare provider as management of the illness may need to be changed. A special care plan should be available for educators to follow for all children with any medical condition or developmental delay prior to participating in physical activity.

Summary

The benefits of physical activity are numerous for children. The earlier physical activity becomes a daily part of the schedule at a child's early learning program, the more benefits for the child. *Caring for Our Children* guidelines and standards on participating in and staying safe during physical activity can help guide educators as they implement new activities. Continuing education is also important for educators to stay up to date on ways to keep children active.

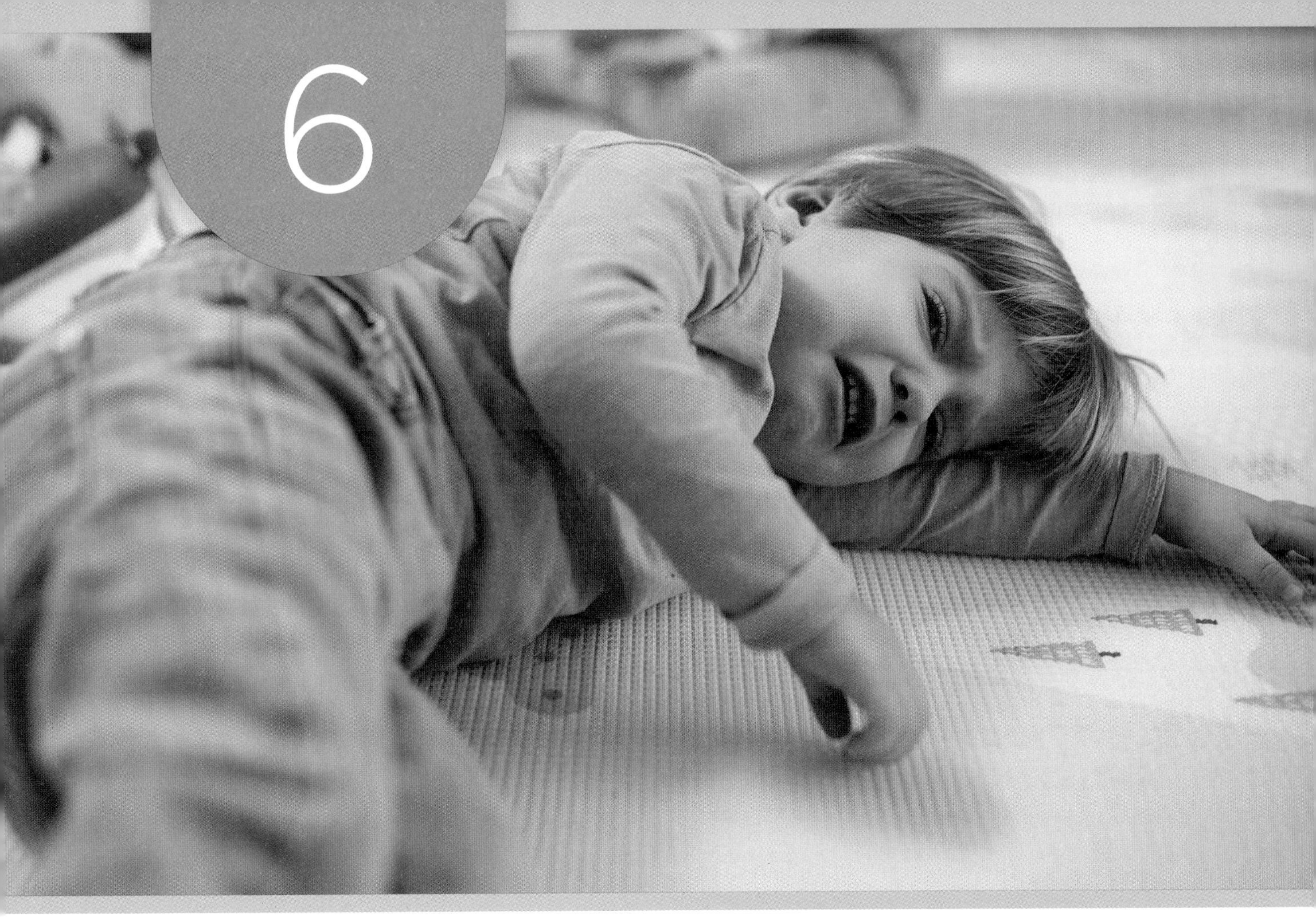

Social-Emotional and Mental Health

BANKU JAIRATH AND RUTH E. GARDNER

LEARNING OBJECTIVES

- To understand the relationship between social-emotional learning in the classroom as it relates to the development of a child's overall mental health
- To list factors that can affect a child's behavior
- To recognize common challenging behavior in young children and strategies to manage them in the classroom
- To be knowledgeable about additional resources for children with behavioral concerns, including community resources and mental health providers
- To demonstrate various strategies for how best to nurture and guide children's social-emotional learning

Children's social and emotional health affects their overall learning and development. *Social development* refers to a child's ability to establish and maintain close relationships with adults and other children, and *emotional development* involves a child's ability to express and manage their own emotions. In young children, these two types of development are very closely linked. Social-emotional skills are developed through nurturing relationships, and for children, the relationships with their families, educators, and other trusted adults are critically important. Children with strong social-emotional skills can develop the ability to recognize and understand their own feelings, manage and express strong emotions, regulate their own behavior, work through challenges, empathize with others, and establish healthy relationships. The social-emotional skills learned as a young child have a lifelong impact on a person's ability as an adult to develop and maintain relationships with family, friends, and colleagues; control their own emotions; and achieve success in other areas of life. Additionally, being able to develop strong interpersonal relationships and manage emotions can help reduce stress and other life factors that can lead to mental health concerns, such as depression or anxiety. In this chapter, we examine first how educators promote social-emotional development in children. We then discuss the signs of stress and mental health concerns in children and how educators can respond to each child's needs by developing strong family partnerships.

ADULT MENTAL HEALTH

Caregivers and educators also need to care for their own mental health needs. Caring for young children can be stressful and overwhelming at times. Often, adults may have to defer meeting their own immediate needs so they can provide competent care for children. Caregivers and educators may experience a wide range of emotions that can trigger their own feelings of sadness or anxiety or other concerns. It's important for parents, caregivers, and educators to be knowledgeable about resources to care for their own needs, such as counseling.

Educators have sources of personal stress outside of their occupation, including finances and their own relationships. Coworkers and administrators in early learning programs provide an essential peer support group for one another. Usually this support group is sufficient and enables effective operation of the early learning program. Sometimes, however, an educator or other staff member may require professional mental health resources. In such instances, the administrator or supervisor can help the staff member find a mental health professional, either in-person or virtually. Insurance coverage and ability to accept new patients varies widely.

Educators Promote Social-Emotional Development and Mental Health

Research indicates that children who are mentally healthy tend to be happier, show greater motivation to learn, have a more positive attitude toward school, more eagerly participate in class activities, and demonstrate higher academic performance than their less mentally healthy peers (Hyson 2023; Kostelnik et al. 2015).

Educators support and promote children's social-emotional development by building trusting and reciprocal partnerships with each child and their family and by organizing a material-rich environment to stimulate social interactions among children. From this perspective, teachers' starting point in nurturing social-emotional development is to focus on children's distinctive abilities rather than on what may be perceived as their deficits. How might educators' practices make the most of children's assets (Hyson 2023)?

Learn About Each Child and Family

All children do not act or react to things in the same way. "Individual differences in temperament and development result in variations in children's levels of frustration tolerance, expression of empathy, the way children respond to new situations, and how well they manage stress" (NAEYC 2022, 117). It is important to get to know each child individually and understand their family and cultural contexts. A core consideration in developmentally appropriate practice and cultural responsiveness is that practitioners learn about each child and family and intentionally adapt and respond to each child's strengths and needs (Derman-Sparks & Edwards with Goins 2020; NAEYC 2022).

ADDITIONAL HELP AND RESOURCES

The Center for Early Childhood Mental Health Consultation (**www.ecmhc.org**) developed a helpful tutorial called "Recognizing and Supporting the Social and Emotional Health of Young Children Birth to Age 5" that explains behavior expectations for children and strategies for adults to support children in social-emotional growth. This center was created with funds from the federal Office of Head Start. Its website is richly populated with observation checklists for groups of children and for individual children that teachers can use to record their observations.

Develop and Teach Empathy

Empathy is a concern for others arising from an emotional connection. Empathetic individuals apply interpersonal sensitivity to understand the experiences of others in order to provide support or assistance (Berliner & Masterson 2015). Researchers have long theorized that empathy is a critical component in teacher effectiveness in urban settings, positively impacting teachers' dispositions in interactions with children of color (Warren & Lessner 2014). It is important for teachers in all settings to model and encourage empathy to foster an inclusive and equitable classroom environment.

To develop and teach empathy, educators first have to know themselves (Derman-Sparks & Edwards with Goins 2020). It is necessary for teachers to engage in critical self-reflection to uncover implicit personal biases and assumptions and bridge understanding across cultural groups (Cooper, He, & Levin 2011; Price & Steed 2016). Whether implicit or explicit, teachers' negative perceptions about children who differ from them in terms of culture, race, or ethnic identity can impact the teachers' ability to teach effectively and create empathetic classrooms. Implement systems of support that help children practice self-regulation and provide additional supports where needed.

The following is a list of Strategies for Educators to Support Social Emotional Development

- Teachers can intentionally model and show children self-regulation and calming strategies. Remain calm. Use supportive language (e.g., "I know you feel sad, but please try to eat a little"). Provide comfort when possible. Comment on the child's behavior when they do something appropriate. Be gentle. It is easy to arouse children who are under stress.
- Provide predictable, consistent routines (but not rigid schedules with unnecessary transitions) and supportive relationships for all children, taking into consideration the range of current self-regulation abilities among the children (NAEYC 2022). Children may find routines and the usual schedules reassuring. Keep a predictable program. Do not insist that the child participate fully. Gently remind the child that they are welcome in the group.
- Encourage communication by inviting the child to talk about their feelings. Play is the language of young children. Sometimes a child will act out the stress in play or in an art activity. Use play to demonstrate some ways to handle stress. For example, use a doll to express in words sad or angry feelings. Provide positive feedback when the child's behavior is appropriate.
- Set clear and reasonable limits. Tantrums, biting, and other forms of aggression and negative behavior are not acceptable. Be ready to handle this behavior. Give the child acceptable alternatives. Focus on comforting and giving first aid to the child who was hurt as the first step. For biting, remind the biter that biting hurts and is not how we use our teeth (e.g., "We bite food, not people"). For other types of aggression tell the child, "Use your words to tell *[other child's name]* how you feel. It's not okay to hurt someone." *Caring for Our Children* Standard 2.2.0.7 describes a step-by-step approach to handle physical aggression, including biting and hitting. These steps include who should be notified when such incidents occur, a list of possible reasons a child would bite or hit, and some strategies for extinguishing aggressive behavior. For example, use positive guidance and create environments that promote positive behavior and minimize the triggers for aggressive behavior.
- Designate a place in the classroom where children can go and spend time alone. A comfort corner is a place where children choose to go. There, they can sit on beanbag chairs, pillows, or a carpeted floor. They can relax, reduce stress, and recover their composure. Stock the area with items like soft balls to squeeze, soft music to listen to through headphones, stuffed animals to hold and talk to, a basket of paper and crayons, and any other items that help children calm down.
- Reassure children that you will keep them safe and that their needs will be met. Both the child with the challenging behavior and the others in the group need to know that you are working with all those involved to make the situation better.
- Create fair and equitable pedagogy that reflects the diversity of your class or program. Supporting children's culture, gender, and ability shows each child that they are valued and welcomed.
- Find resources such as The Pyramid Model. The Pyramid Model (Fox & Hemmeter 2009) is a comprehensive framework for addressing the social and emotional outcomes of young children (Hemmeter, Ostrosky, & Fox 2006). The pyramid model includes three levels of support: universal prevention strategies for use with all children; secondary social and emotional approaches for children at risk for social and emotional delays; and tertiary individualized and function-based interventions for children with persistent challenges (Fox & Hemmeter 2009).

FAMILY CONNECTIONS

Strategies for Home

Encourage families to try these things at home!

› **Say what you mean with positive language.** Use "do" instead of "don't" whenever possible. Choose your words carefully, especially when you are guiding children's behavior. Keep sentences short and simple. Focus on *what to do* rather than what not to do. Try saying,

- "Slow down and walk" instead of "Stop running."
- "Come hold my hand" instead of "Don't touch anything."
- "Keep your feet on the floor" instead of "Don't climb on the table."
- "Use a quiet voice inside" instead of "Stop shouting."

› **Give clear, simple choices.** Toddlers can choose between a red cup and a green cup. Preschoolers can choose between playing airport and zookeeper. Give children a choice only when there is a choice. For example, saying, "It is naptime, do you want to lie down now?" is not really an option if your rule is that everyone will rest at naptime.

› **Encourage like a good coach instead of a cheerleader.** A cheerleader just shouts general praise (e.g., "What a great job!" or "What a beautiful picture"). A good coach tells you what you're doing right, uses praise as a teaching tool, and lets you know why they are proud of you. If a child sets the table, you might say, "You did such a good job setting the table! You put the spoons and forks in the right place and remembered the napkins!" When you look at a child's painting, you might remark, "This painting just glows with color. You used blue, green, red, yellow, and orange. Tell me how you did this!"

Social-Emotional and Mental Health Concerns in Young Children

Early childhood educators see children exhibit a wide range of emotions and behavior. Children can feel stress, anxiety, depression, anger, and sadness as acutely as adults do, but they are not always able to explain what they are feeling. Many times, the only way they know how to communicate feelings is through their behavior. Teachers must be able to identify when a child needs help and take care to reflect on their own behavior and expectations and the ways in which these may affect children's behavior (NAEYC 2022).

Behavioral Milestones

It is essential to understand young children's social-emotional milestones as they grow and develop to be able to recognize unusual or challenging behavior. Certain behaviors, such as responsibility and self-regulation, develop with experience and time; educators should foster such development in their interactions with each child and in their curriculum planning (NAEYC 2022). The Centers for Disease Control and Prevention (CDC; 2022) lists developmental milestones by age and provides examples of social-emotional milestones.

Why Children Develop Challenging Behavior?

Children who experience environmental stress can begin to express challenging behavior. When you become aware of these stressors, monitor the child closely for changes in mood or behavior. The child's response to stress may vary depending on the stress or the child. High-quality, nurturing relationships with caregivers and educators may lessen the effects of stress.

While children may exhibit challenging behavior for no apparent reason, there is always a reason, even if it is just to communicate frustration. The behavior can manifest as mild to severe and can vary depending on the age and the developmental stage. As you seek to better understand and handle this behavior, do not assume the family/home life is the source of all new behavior; rather, consider all factors and possibilities.

Factors That Can Affect Behavior

Transition

Transitions and changes in routine can have a significant impact on children. This includes moving to a new home and/or a new early learning program. When a family moves, children may miss their old friends or experience stress from adapting to a new culture or language. They may be transitioning from home-based care by a family member (such as a caregiver newly starting or returning to work) and attending an early learning program for the very first time. Even transitioning to a new classroom (i.e., moving from an infant to toddler classroom) can be stressful, and making these transitions gradually, when possible, can be helpful. Transition can also involve a new educator or even a new peer. All of these things take time for adjustment.

Family Relationships and Experiences

Family relationships and changes that families experience—both positive and negative, including divorce, remarriage, birth of a sibling, and death of a loved one—can change a child's behavior. Conflicts between caregivers and other family members can be very stressful for children. Children may witness problems of communication and can themselves become victims of maltreatment or abuse. The child may have difficulty trusting new adults or may be frequently afraid. These types of conflicts can sometimes lead to separation or divorce, changes in custody, and sometimes the development of two separate households.

If a caregiver becomes ill, especially with a prolonged chronic illness, or is hospitalized, the child loses physical contact and emotional support. When a loved one dies, even an extended family member, such as a grandparent, the child may experience sadness and grief. This permanent loss is challenging, especially given how little children really understand death. Similarly, mental health problems, including substance abuse (such as drugs or alcohol) can impair the caregiver's ability to care for and nurture a child. Other seemingly positive changes—such as a new sibling gained through birth, adoption, or blending of families or moving to a new neighborhood and into a bigger house—can make children feel anxious and change how they behave.

Societal Factors and Basic Needs

Societal factors (e.g., an unstable economy, racial inequity, gun violence) and natural disasters (e.g., hurricanes) place enormous stress on families and children. These factors can mean families may face loss of a job or change in income, which can lead to economic uncertainty, homelessness, or food insecurity. This uncertainty is felt and experienced by the youngest members of families and can cause stress and anxiety, resulting in a child exhibiting changes in their behavior and mood. When the basic needs of food and shelter are not met, maintaining a consistent daily routine is difficult because of changes to a family's circumstances, and children suffer physically and emotionally. For educators, it is important to be aware of resources in the community to aid families who are in need, such as information on applying for supplemental nutritional benefits, housing assistance, or medical help. (See also "Chapter 2: Healthcare Professionals and Educators Work Together to Support Healthy and Thriving Children," "Chapter 3: Enrollment, Health Documentation, Assessments, and Screenings," and "Chapter 8: Understanding Common Illnesses and Conditions.")

Children can become particularly distressed if they witness or experience violence. These adverse childhood experiences (ACEs), or potentially traumatic events that occur in childhood, can have a lifelong impact and increase the risk of behavioral and emotional problems (Erdman & Colker with Winter 2020; Sciaraffa, Zeanah, & Zeanah 2018). Reducing the incidence of these ACEs will have a positive impact on society.

THE IMPACT OF THE COVID-19 PANDEMIC ON YOUNG CHILDREN'S MENTAL WELL-BEING

COVID-19 introduced uncertainty and unpredictability in the lives of children and staff members in ways that other infectious diseases and past health crises have not. Many educators and families experienced health concerns or even death. More significantly, early learning programs suffered as an institution, which affected the children they serve. Many programs were temporarily closed or permanently shuttered due to staff member shortages and financial problems. Early learning programs were transitioned to be online/virtual-based, which led to a significant shift in how teachers interact with the young children they serve. When in-person classes were permitted again and masks were required, educators and families needed to explain and encourage the use of masks to children without causing them alarm or fear. The stressors children experience from COVID-19 and the potential of other similar types of infectious diseases may be even more complex to manage than certain ACEs due to the ongoing and erratic nature of these diseases.

Common Behavioral and Emotional Problems in Young Children

The definition of *challenging behavior* provided by the Center on Social and Emotional Foundations for Early Learning (CSEFEL; 2013):

- Any repeated pattern of behavior that interferes with learning or engagement in prosocial interactions with peers and adults
- Behavior that is not responsive to the use of developmentally appropriate guidance procedures
- Prolonged tantrums, physical and verbal aggression, disruptive vocal and motor behavior (e.g., screaming, stereotype), property destruction, self-injury, noncompliance, and withdrawal (n.p.)

Children respond to environmental stress and challenges in different ways, depending on chronological age, developmental stage, and the child's own intrinsic vulnerability. For example, crying is a normal response to pain (i.e., injury) or sadness; however, many children also cry when they are upset. Young children do not have the language skills to fully express themselves, or they experience such strong emotions that they are overwhelmed. A toddler throwing a tantrum is a good example of strong emotions that overwhelm the child.

Children may demonstrate this challenging behavior for several hours or days at a time. The following behavior and emotions should be addressed at onset, but may be cause for serious concern when they occur over long periods of time or are extreme:

- **Extreme emotions and moods.** Frequent crying with no obvious reason (i.e., no stimulus). Children may have quick changes of moods. They may become sad or withdrawn and refuse to play with other children or talk with adults. They may not seem to enjoy play, or their play may display extreme emotions.
- **Increased activity level and poor attention.** Some children may become very active and disorganized. They may not be able to concentrate on games or stories or participate in classroom activities, such as circle time. They may interrupt or have difficulty staying in their seat.
- **Problems in eating, elimination, and sleep.** Children may refuse to eat, even foods that they previously enjoyed. They may have frequent daytime accidents after toilet learning has occurred. Some children may want to sleep more than usual; others have difficulty relaxing for a nap, falling asleep at night, and staying asleep through the entire night. Sleep deprivation may add to other behavioral issues.
- **Relationship challenges.** Children may show dramatic changes in how they relate to others. They may fight with their friends. They may refuse to do the things adults ask of them. They may become extremely distressed when a caregiver or teacher has to leave. This may make it very hard for caregivers to leave their children at the early learning program. Children may become clingy. They may become afraid of being alone. On the other hand, some children become indifferent. They may go to anyone, whether it's an adult they trust or a stranger. Some children avoid eye contact, stare, and refuse to let others help them. They may isolate themselves from their friends and teachers.

- **Developmental delay or regression of skills.** Children may not achieve developmental milestones typically acquired by their age, or they may lose developmental skills they previously mastered. For example, a child who has been using the toilet may need to go back to diapers, a child who can speak in sentences reverts to single words, a child able to feed herself independently suddenly demands adult help, or a child who played independently or with other children is not able to play alone or socialize.
- **Physical aggression.** Children may throw frequent temper tantrums or become aggressive, biting and hitting. They may strike out at teachers who are trying to correct their behavior or even comfort them. Many children go through a period in which they may bite (sometimes as a learned behavior after being bitten by other children). Some hit other children. Teachers must be ready to handle and prevent this unacceptable behavior, and help the child find other ways to deal with what is causing them.

Addressing Challenging Behavior and Mental Health Concerns

"It's important for educators to understand that the behavior that challenges them is also challenging for the child" (Kaiser & Rasminsky 2021, 11). The child wants to be happy and to play and learn with their friends. Seeing the child, and not just their behavior, helps educators address challenging behavior and work with families to find solutions.

Observation and Documentation

Observation and documentation can play an important role in helping educators address and ultimately support children who exhibit challenging behavior. The following steps outline a basic process for observing and documenting behavior:

- **Observe the behavior** and document what seems to precede it, what time of day it occurs, and what seems to happen while and after it occurs.
- **Make structured observations of behavior.** Record both positive and negative behavior using checklists, such as those in the toolkits from the Center for Early Childhood Mental Health Consultation recommended earlier in the chapter. As soon as possible after a challenging behavior occurs, log when the behavior occurred, what happened before the incident, and what helped the child.
- **Talk with the family** about the child's behavior early in the process. Do not wait until the child's behavior or moods seriously deteriorate. Begin with a description of the changes you are observing. You might say to a caregiver, "I notice that Finn is crying a lot at school. It is difficult for me to comfort him." Or, if you know why the child is experiencing anxiety or stress, you might say, "Since her father has been in the hospital, Sarah has been eating poorly at school. What do you see at home?"
- **Discuss the issues with a coworker, supervisor, or mental health consultant.** After speaking with the family, arrange for someone else to observe the child who is not directly involved in providing care so that the observations can be more objective and complete.

IMMEDIATE IMPACT

Complete the Picture

Gather all necessary information regarding a child's challenging behavior, including information from family/caregivers at home, educators in the classroom, observations, and any longitudinal documentation to access a more complete picture of the child.

Using Guidance

"Guiding children's behavior is something done throughout the day, not just when a child acts in a way that is unsafe or unacceptable. [Educators] guide behavior by establishing predictable routines, setting clear rules with children, and modeling kindness and respect" (Dombro, Jablon, & Stetson 2020, 63). Young children have a hard time understanding other children's feelings, but by the time they are 4 years old they should begin to understand that when they make another child upset and angry, there are consequences for their actions. Through guidance, educators can help children learn about feelings, fairness, and communication. For example, if one child takes a toy away from another child and the second child becomes upset, it is important that "the teacher does not make one child seem like a perpetrator and the other seem like a victim. Adults can actually start bully-victim patterns if they consistently comfort the 'helpless' victim and punish the 'guilty' perpetrator" (Gartrell 2021, 10). Guidance steps include bringing the children together to talk through what happened and how they are feeling and to help them solve their own problems. Using guidance to mediate challenging situations and behavior helps "young children understand they can learn from their mistakes, and it starts with showing them how" (Gartrell 2021, 8). To give this help successfully, educators need to build relationships with every child—especially with the children who may be difficult to connect with and understand. Educators build these relationships from day one, outside of conflict situations. It is only when children know and trust us in day-to-day interactions that they will listen to us when conflicts happen (after we have helped everyone calm down).

Here is a summary of some basic reminders and tips for how best to guide children's behavior. Remember that different strategies work best at different ages.

› **Keep rules simple and easy to understand.** Discuss rules with children and write them down. Consider children's suggestions for rules. Repeat the rules often. A few rules that work well with children include

- Help each other.
- Take care of our toys.
- Say *please* and *thank you.*
- Be kind to each other.

› **Talk with children—not "at" them.** Children often don't pay attention when you are talking (or shouting) "at" them. Guidance is much more effective when you talk to children at their eye level. Look them in the eyes, touch them on the shoulder, and talk with them. Resist the urge to simply lecture. Instead, give children time to respond, and listen genuinely to their points of view.

- **Set a good example.** Children watch you all the time. They see how you talk to other children and adults. They see how you cope with anger or frustration. They watch how you deal with sadness and joy. They listen to how you say "I'm sorry." The way you handle the ups and downs of life teaches children a lot about how to behave and get along with others.
- **Encourage children to set good examples for each other.** Children also learn a great deal from each other. Encourage appropriate ways to share, play, and be kind to each other.
- **Show respect for children.** Talk to children about misbehavior in private, rather than in front of others. Remind them of reasons for rules, and discuss what they can do differently.
- **Catch children being good.** All children want attention. It is better to give them positive attention for good behavior than negative attention for misbehavior. Comment on something positive about each child each day. Better yet, strive for several times a day. And share the good news. When children have done something positive, mention it to other children and to caregivers.
- **Teach children how to correct their misbehavior.** If a child throws food onto the floor, give them a broom and show them how to clean it up. If a child draws on the wall, give them a wet cloth to clean the wall. Even if the child cannot successfully clean up the entire mess alone, participating in cleanup teaches them that their actions have consequences. Over time, experiencing consequences helps children learn self-control.
- **Use play activities to teach social skills.** Become a character in children's pretend play and show children how to use good manners and be kind. Read children's books that show how children resolve problems. Play "What If . . . ?" games. Encourage children to act out ways to work together.
- **Teach children how to resolve conflict and solve problems.** Help them recognize and name feelings, identify problems clearly, come up with ideas for solving the problem, and try possible solutions.

Mental Health Services and Professionals

Early childhood mental health professionals can help teachers address behavior of concern and significantly improve the well-being of children, staff members, and families. Many mental health professionals are skilled assessors of individual, group, and organization functioning. They can address the stress the staff members feel in working with a child, observe a child's behavior, and suggest additional strategies to try. They can also help determine whether it is necessary to refer the child for further evaluation and care.

Educators should be trained to know how and when it is appropriate to seek access to early childhood mental health experts and supports (NAEYC 2022). Programs should connect with behavioral or mental health agencies and organizations to help establish and maintain environments that will support children's mental well-being and social-emotional health and have access to such a consultant when more targeted child-specific interventions are needed (*CFOC* Standard 2.2.0.8).

To identify a qualified consultant, ask mental health and behavioral service providers in the community who does such work. The types of professionals who are likely to be helpful include psychologists, licensed clinical social workers, child psychiatrists, developmental-behavioral pediatricians, and pediatricians with a special interest in behavioral health. Developmental-behavioral pediatricians provide consultation on behavioral issues that a primary care pediatrician would not typically manage.

When children exhibit or engage in challenging behavior that cannot be resolved easily, staff members should

- Assess the health of the child and the adequacy of the curriculum in meeting the developmental and educational needs of the child
- Immediately engage the parents and caregivers in a spirit of collaboration regarding how the child's behavior may be best handled, including appropriate solutions that have worked at home or in other settings
- Access an early childhood mental health consultant to assist in developing an effective plan to address the child's challenging behavior and to assist the child in developing age-appropriate, prosocial skills
- Facilitate, with the family's assistance, a referral for an evaluation for either early intervention services for infants and toddlers or special education services for children age 3 and older (i.e., Child Find), as well as any other appropriate community-based services (e.g., child mental health clinic)
- Facilitate, along with the family, communication with the child's primary care provider (e.g., pediatrician, family medicine provider), so that the primary care provider can assess for any related health concerns and help facilitate appropriate referrals (*CFOC* Standard 2.2.0.8)

Referrals

If a mental health professional consultant is not available to work with the program staff members, the appropriate staff members must decide when it is time to refer a child to a mental health professional and have the caregiver arrange for the child to have further evaluation. One or more of the following factors may trigger a referral:

- The problems have lasted several weeks to months.
- The problems are severe or getting worse.
- Your supportive care and interventions have not helped.
- The child is unable to function successfully in the early learning setting.
- The child is not achieving age-appropriate developmental levels and tasks.
- The family is extremely distressed, or the stresses are getting worse.

Whom you refer the family to depends on the child's condition and the resources in your community. The child's usual source of healthcare is always a good starting place. The child's healthcare provider may understand the family's circumstances and be able to provide additional support. It is also easier, in many cases, to refer the child to a pediatrician or family doctor than to a psychiatrist or psychologist. However, some families appreciate an immediate referral to a mental health professional.

Know the names of professionals in your area who work with young children who have behavioral issues; do not wait until there is a crisis to identify such professionals. If the parent or primary caregiver provides written permission to share the notes of your observations and concerns with the professional, be sure to do so. Include any observation checklist data you have gathered. Sample forms can be found at **www.ecmhc.org/TTYC/index.html** under "Getting Started: Tips and Forms." Consider use of a behavior checklist ("My Teacher Has Observed") and/or observation form ("Events and Functions Associated with Problem Behavior"). Such information will help the clinician formulate suggestions that the early learning program and family can implement. It may be best to arrange a conversation with the clinician, with the parent/primary caregiver's permission, to clarify observations and recommendations. If you make a referral to a mental health professional, try to maintain the child in your program. This stability may be very helpful to the child and family.

Fact sheets from reputable sources provide helpful information that teachers can use and also share with families. The CSEFEL website (**http://csefel.vanderbilt.edu**), for example, includes tips and parent training modules, sample scenarios, and professional development tools. Another federally funded resource is the Technical Assistance Center on Social Emotional Intervention (TACSEI). TACSEI works in partnership with CSEFEL to promote adoption of The Pyramid Model for Supporting Social-Emotional Competence in Infants and Young Children. Free products, resources, and links to other useful information are available on the NCPMI website at **www.challengingbehavior.org**.

Summary

Children need adults to teach, guide, and support them as they grow and learn. Early childhood educators play an important role in guiding children's behavior in positive, supportive, and developmentally appropriate ways. The most appropriate ways to guide behavior are different for each child, depending on their age, developmental abilities, and needs. For example, 2-year-olds have limited understanding and need a lot of redirection, but 5-year-olds can learn to be good problem solvers. Effective guidance strategies also depend on the individual child's personality. Strategies that work well for one child may not be effective for another child of the same age. With your encouragement, over time, young children will develop the foundations for building long-lasting, healthy relationships and the emotional skills necessary to become successful in any of their future endeavors.

PART 3

Prevention, Planning, and Treatment

BRITTANY MASSARE AND ALICIA HAUPT

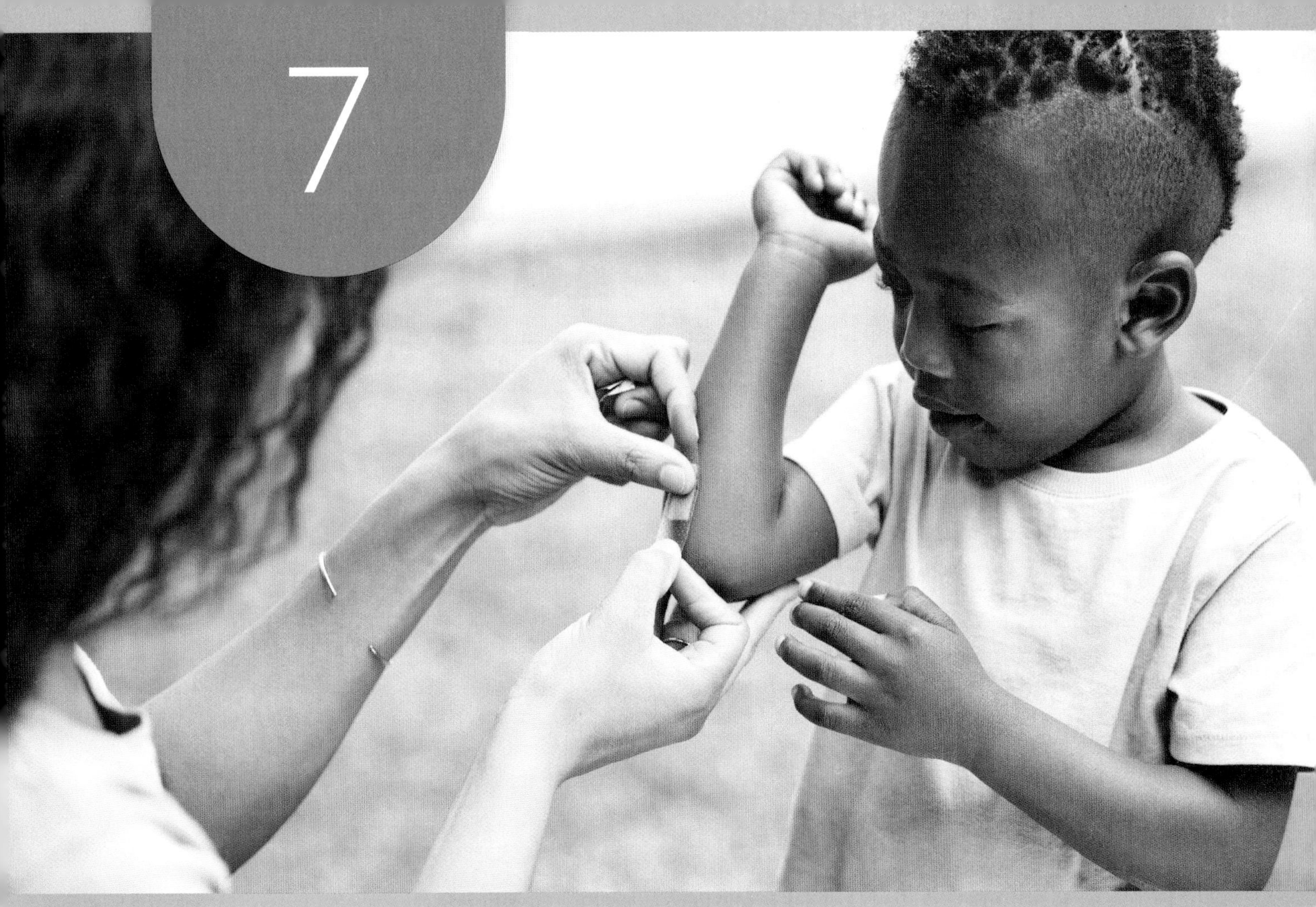

First Aid and Injuries

TERRI MCFADDEN

LEARNING OBJECTIVES

- To identify the items required in a first aid kit
- To list basic levels of first aid training required for all staff
- To identify the differences between life-threatening and non–life-threatening injuries
- To identify potential poisons located in a center (including plants, medications, carbon monoxide [CO], and other products)
- To describe procedures for addressing potential poisoning (including calling the local Poison Control Center)
- To identify potential hazards leading to common childhood injuries both inside and outside of the facility (including during transport) and list mechanisms for preventing these injuries
- To describe basic life-saving procedures such as cardiopulmonary resuscitation (CPR)

A child falls from a playground climber. A child chokes while eating a snack. A child has an allergic reaction after touching a plant. What do you do? It's a fact that children get bumps, bruises, and sometimes even more serious injuries. The key is to understand what injuries mean and how you as an educator can be prepared and best treat the children in your care.

It is important for educators to be able to make sound assessments and judgements on whether a child can be treated and monitored at the early learning program or home, or if it is important to call 911 and get emergency care. Staff training is a critical component to keeping children safe and healthy in early learning programs (AAP & NASN 2012; Alkon et al. 2015; *CFOC* Standards 9.2.4.1 and 1.4.3.1). In this chapter, basic first aid and CPR will be discussed as well as common life-threatening and non–life-threatening injuries.

First Aid

> First aid refers to medical attention that is usually administered immediately after an injury occurs and at the location where it occurred. It often consists of a one-time, short-term treatment and requires little technology or training to administer. First aid can include cleaning minor cuts, scrapes, or scratches; treating a minor burn; applying bandages and dressings; the use of nonprescription medicine; draining blisters; removing debris from the eyes; massage; and drinking fluids to relieve heat stress. (OSHA, n.d. a)

Basics

The best way to handle injuries is to be prepared before they happen. Even with careful supervision, minor accidents, illnesses, and unintentional childhood injuries may occur, however early learning program staff can play a major role in preventing injuries to children in their care, and responding appropriately when they occur. (CDC 2022f). Children may sustain scrapes, bruises, cuts, bites, and falls. It is extremely important for anyone who works with children on a regular basis to know how to properly care for them in the event of an emergency. Getting formal first aid training is the best way to know what to do in case of a medical emergency. Early learning program staff members should have basic knowledge of first aid principles and should know how to use first aid supplies (*CFOC* Standard 9.2.4.1). It is important for all programs to have basic supplies available to treat the inevitable incidents that will happen at the program (*CFOC* Standard 5.6.0.1).

Everyday Cuts, Scrapes, and Injuries

Children often get minor cuts, scrapes or abrasions, and puncture wounds through their play or during ordinary daily activities. These wounds can happen on almost any area of the body and can usually be handled with basic first aid care (Hashikawa et al. 2015).

It is important to have all necessary supplies—including a comprehensive, up-to-date first aid kit—ready and easily accessible to respond to an emergency in a timely manner (*CFOC* Standards 5.6.0.1 and 1.4.3.1). Each program should have at least one first aid kit available within the center and an additional kit, which can be taken to off-campus activities and field trips. More kits may be desired if the program has a large footprint. However, the program should have protocols to ensure that a staff member routinely inspects all kits, making sure that they are fully stocked and have no expired items. Kits should also contain protective gear for staff members to ensure that they do not come in contact with body fluids resulting from a child's illness or injury (*CFOC* Standard 3.2.3.4).

FIRST AID KIT

Basic supplies include the following:

- First aid manual
- List of emergency phone numbers including the Poison Control Center
- Nonlatex gloves for staff
- Protective eyewear for staff
- A mouthpiece for delivering CPR
- Hand sanitizer
- Sterile gauze pads
- Adhesive tape
- Scissors
- Adhesive bandages
- Cotton balls and swabs
- Tweezers
- Ice packs
- Anti-itch cream such as calamine lotion
- Soap
- Sterile water for irrigation
- Eye wash solution
- Digital thermometer
- Bandage wrap
- Splint
- Antiseptic wipes
- Flashlight and extra batteries
- Aloe vera gel
- Medications
    - Epinephrine autoinjector (e.g., EpiPen Jr.)
    - Hydrocortisone cream or ointment
    - Acetaminophen
    - Ibuprofen
    - Antihistamine (e.g., diphenhydramine)
    - Antibiotic ointment
- Graduated medication syringe or spoon
- Oral rehydration electrolyte solution (e.g., Pedialyte)

Prevention

Programs should place emphasis on safeguarding each child and ensuring that staff members are prepared and able to handle emergencies. Active supervision, including focused watching, listening, and interacting, is one of the most effective ways to keep children safe in an early learning program. Additionally, a daily safety inspection will allow the program to locate any broken or inappropriate materials as well as create the opportunity to make changes to the environment to prevent injury (Alkon et al. 2015; CDC 2022f; *CFOC* Standard 9.2.4.1; Hashikawa et al. 2015). Specific injury prevention recommendations include the following:

- Never leave an infant unattended on a bed, table, or other surface from which they could roll, scoot, or fall off.
- Always use safety straps for high chairs, strollers, or car seats.
- Follow guidelines for car seats, booster seats, and seat belts when transporting infants and young children.
- Choose age-appropriate toys. Inspect for small or loose parts, sharp edges, points, loose batteries, and other hazards.
- Keep toxic chemicals and cleaning solutions safely stored in childproof cabinets and in their original containers with labels attached.
- Make sure that infants and small children cannot reach buttons, watch batteries, high-powered magnets, popcorn, grapes, or nuts, which may be choking hazards or potentially cause other injuries.
- Do not allow young children to crawl or walk around while eating or drinking.
- Do not allow anything around an infant's neck or wrist, such as jewelry, chains, and tied pacifiers, that may be a suffocation hazard.

Instructions for accessing a higher level of care are described in each section. However, regardless of cause, seek care for

- Difficulty breathing
- Seizure
- Loss of consciousness

Assessment and Procedure

The following steps should be followed when addressing an injury:

- Remain calm and assess the situation. Make sure that the situation is safe before approaching.
- In cases of minor injury, the staff member should administer simple first aid, notify the caregivers about the injury and treatment in writing and by phone.
- Do not give medication unless there has been prior approval by the child's parent or caregiver, doctor, or other licensed prescriber.
- For more serious injuries and illness, the staff member should call the caregivers immediately.
- Do not move a severely injured or ill child unless absolutely necessary for immediate safety.
- Check the child's airway and breathing.

- If necessary, start rescue efforts with rescue breathing and CPR.
- Call 911 or your local emergency number.

Lifesaving Procedures and CPR

Lifesaving procedures are required if a child appears unresponsive, appears to have life-threatening bleeding, has another life-threatening condition, has no pulse, is not breathing, or is gasping. Providing care in these critical situations requires special training and understanding.

Staff Training and CPR

It is important to understand the ABCs (airway, breathing, and circulation) and know how to provide CPR (AAP & NASN 2012; AHA 2020; American Red Cross, n.d. a; *CFOC* Standard 5.6.01; Hashikawa et al. 2015). It is a lifesaving procedure that is performed when a child's breathing or heartbeat has stopped. This may happen after drowning, suffocation, choking, electrical shock, excessive bleeding, head trauma, lung disease, or poisoning.

CPR involves

- Rescue breathing, which provides oxygen to a child's lungs
- Chest compressions, which keep the child's blood circulating

Brain damage or death can occur within a few minutes after a child's blood stops flowing, so CPR must be continued until the child's heartbeat and breathing return, or until a trained medical professional arrives (American Red Cross, n.d. a).

Staff members should have a choking/CPR chart readily available (American Red Cross, n.d. a). A core group of staff members, if not all, should be trained in basic lifesaving skills and CPR. A child's life may depend on having trained staff members and standard procedures. Staff members should receive repeated CPR and first aid training as appropriate as procedures change with continuing evaluation of CPR techniques. CPR classes can be found at local hospitals and through the American Red Cross (American Red Cross, n.d. a). Make sure that staff training focuses on CPR for infants and children. Although staff members should be professionally trained, it is important to keep a step-by-step CPR guide with the first aid supplies and in appropriate areas of the center so that the information is easily retrievable in the event of an emergency.

IMMEDIATE IMPACT

Automated External Defibrillator

Consider adding an automated external defibrillator (AED) to the center and training staff on appropriate use. These machines have pads to place on the chest during a life-threatening emergency. They use computers to automatically check the heart rhythm and provide a sudden shock if it is needed to restore the heart rhythm. When using an AED, it is very important to follow the instructions that the machine provides exactly (AAP 2019c; AHA 2020).

INFANT CPR

- Check for unresponsiveness. Shake or tap the infant gently. See if the infant moves or makes a noise. Shout, "Are you okay?"
- If there no is a response, shout for help. Send someone to call 911. If alone, do not leave the infant to call 911 until CPR has been performed for about two minutes.
- Carefully place the infant on their back. If there is a chance the infant has a spinal injury, two people should move the infant to prevent twisting of the head and neck.
- Perform chest compressions:
  - Place two fingers on the breastbone just below the nipples. Make sure not to press at the very end of the breastbone (Figure 7.1 A).

Figure 7.1 A. (Copyright @ Getty Images.)

  - Keep the other hand on the infant's forehead, keeping the head tilted back.
  - Press down on the infant's chest so that it compresses about one and one half inches the depth of the chest.
  - Give 30 chest compressions. Each time, let the chest rise completely. These compressions should be fast and hard with no pausing. Count the 30 compressions quickly.
- If the infant is not breathing:
  - Open the airway. Lift up the chin with one hand. At the same time, push down on the forehead with the other hand.
- Listen and feel for breathing. Place your ear close to the infant's mouth and nose. Watch for chest movement. You may feel breath on your face if the infant is breathing.

- If the infant is not breathing:
  - Cover the infant's mouth and nose tightly with your mouth (Figure 7.1 B).

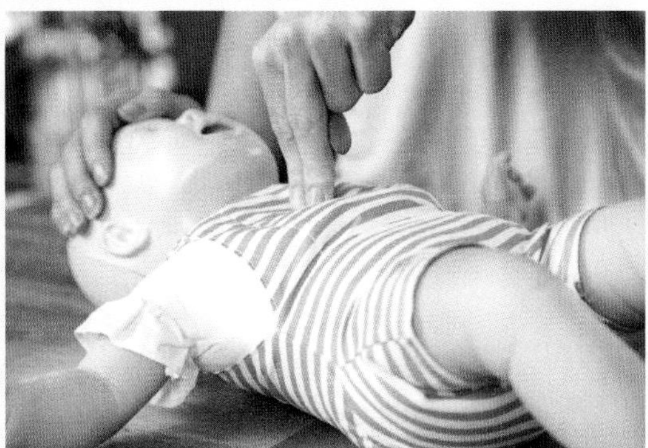

Figure 7.1 B. (Copyright @ Getty Images.)

  - Alternatively, cover just the nose, holding the mouth shut.
  - Keep the chin tilted and the head lifted.
  - Give two breaths. Each breath should take about a second and make the chest rise.
- Continue CPR (30 chest compressions followed by two breaths, then repeat) for about two minutes.
- After about two minutes of CPR, if the infant still does not have normal breathing, coughing, or any movement, leave the infant to call 911 if you are alone.
- Continue rescue breathing and chest compressions until the infant recovers or help arrives.

CHILD CPR

To be used when the child is unconscious/unresponsive or when breathing stops.

- Check for unresponsiveness. Shake or tap the child gently. See if the child moves or makes a noise. Shout, "Are you okay?"
- If there no is a response, shout for help. Send someone to call 911 and get the AED if appropriate. If alone, do not leave the child to call 911 until CPR has been performed for about two minutes.
- Carefully place the child on their back. If there is a chance the child has a spinal injury, two people should move the child to prevent twisting of the head and neck.
- Start chest compressions:
  - Place the heel of hand over the lower half of the sternum (breastbone) just below the nipples. Make sure that the heel is not at the end of the sternum. You may need to use two hands depending on the size of the child.

(continued)

- Keep the other hand on the child's forehead, keeping the head tilted back.
- Compress chest at least one-third to half the depth of the chest, or about five cm (two inches).
- After each compression, allow the chest to return to the normal position. Compress the chest at a rate of at least 100 to 120 times per minute.
- Do 30 compressions.

› Open the airway:
  - Head tilt-chin lift

› Look, listen, and feel for breathing. Place your ear close to the child's mouth and nose. Watch for chest movement. Feel for breath on your face.

› If the child is not breathing, start rescue breathing:
  - Take a normal breath.
  - Pinch the child's nose closed, and cover the child's mouth with your mouth.
  - Give two breaths, each for one second. Each breath should make the chest rise.

› Resume chest compressions.

› After about two minutes of CPR, if the child still does not have normal breathing, coughing, or any movement, leave the child if you are alone to call 911. If an AED is available use it now. You can use adult pads for a child less than 8 years, but you may need to apply them differently than shown on the pads: Apply one on the front of the chest, the other on the back, so they do not touch. Once pads are attached, follow the instructions given by the AED.

Seek a higher level of care whenever CPR is initiated. Also seek care when a child has a condition that may lead to a worsening in their health status that may require CPR, such as if they

› Appear very ill, unusually drowsy, or very fussy

› Have severe symptoms, such as a stiff neck, a severe headache, a severe sore throat, severe ear pain, unexplained rash, repeated vomiting and/or diarrhea, or difficulty breathing

› Have a condition causing immune suppression, such as sickle cell disease, cancer, or chronic steroid use

› Have a seizure

› Have a high fever

› Are younger than 3 months and have a temperature of 100.4°F or higher

› Have been in a very hot place, such as an overheated car

› Have had a serious head, neck, or back injury

› Lose consciousness

› Experience clumsiness or inability to move a body part

› Have abnormal speech or behavior

Life-Threatening Injuries

A life-threatening illness or injury involves a substantial risk of death. Life-threatening emergencies often affect a child's airway, breathing, or circulation and can be fatal if not corrected immediately (AAP 2015c). By administering immediate care during an emergency, trained center staff members may be able to save a child's life or prevent permanent harm while awaiting the arrival of emergency medical services personnel. Recognition of potentially life-threatening injuries and appropriate training for responding to these events is essential for center staff members. (See " Chapter Appendix 7.1: First Aid for Injuries" for treatment protocols.)

Choking

Young children are quite prone to choking. According to the Centers for Disease Control and Prevention (CDC), choking rates are higher among infants and decrease consistently with increasing age. Almost one-third of choking episodes in the United States occurred among infants, and more than three-fourths occurred among children age 3 years or younger (CDC 2022d). The AAP states that choking on food poses an important risk for children in the United States. Approximately, 66 to 77 children younger than 10 years old die from choking on food each year, leading the AAP to classify choking as a leading cause of both nonfatal injury and death in children 3 years or younger (AAP Committee on Injury, Violence, and Poison Prevention 2010; CDC 2021b; *CFOC* Standard 4.5.0.10; Food and Nutrition Service 2020).

Children's airways are more vulnerable to obstruction than that of adults. The airway is smaller than for adults, leading them to be more likely to experience blockage from small foreign bodies. Because of these narrow airways, even small changes in the size can lead to significant problems with air flow. Further, mucus and secretions around a foreign body form a seal around the foreign body, making it difficult to dislodge by the forced air such as with a cough or even the Heimlich maneuver (AAP Committee on Injury, Violence, and Poison Prevention 2010; AAP 2015c). The Heimlich maneuver is a simple technique used to expel an object from a child's airway by using abdominal thrusts to lift the diaphragm to dislodge the foreign object and forcefully expel it from the airway (AAP 2015c; American Red Cross 2011). Finally, the force of air generated by a child's cough may be less effective in dislodging even a partial blockage of the airway (AAP Committee on Injury, Violence, and Poison Prevention 2010).

A choking hazard is any object that can get caught in a child's throat and block their airway. This makes it difficult for them to breathe and can be life-threatening. Several edible and inedible objects can be choking hazards (AAP Committee on Injury, Violence, and Poison Prevention 2010).

It's important to closely supervise children when they are eating, as young children don't always chew their food thoroughly before swallowing. This can cause foods to become lodged in their windpipe, leading to choking.

Staff members should be aware of the high-risk foods that can lead to choking, like hard candy, nuts, whole grapes, and popcorn. Foods that are likely to become choking hazards include foods that are round and hard (*CFOC* Standard 4.5.0.10).

SIGNS AND SYMPTOMS

- Choking and gagging when object is first inhaled
- Violent coughing
- A high-pitched sound when breathing in
- Wheezing or whistling noise when child breathes out
- Being unable to cough, breathe, talk, or speak
- Face turning pale and blue-tinted
- Clutching at their throat
- Becomes unconscious

If the child is coughing and gagging but can breathe or talk, you can monitor. However, if they can't breathe, it is important to act quickly.

For young children, foods should be cut into small pieces, no bigger than half an inch. When pieces are this small, they will usually clear the child's airway even if swallowed whole.

Children younger than 4 years old should avoid eating foods that are easy to choke on, for example, raisins, marshmallows, chewing gum, and hot dogs are foods most associated with fatal choking.

While foods are a common choking hazard because they are meant to be ingested, small children often cannot tell the difference between food and other objects. They put everything into their mouths. Pick up anything off of the floor that might be dangerous if swallowed (AAP 2021b; CDC 2022d). Nonfood items that may be choking hazards for small children include

- Coins
- Marbles
- Button batteries, such as those used in watches, cameras, and small electronics
- Toys with small parts (Check for toys recalled for choking hazards on the Consumer Product Safety Commission website at **www.cpsc.gov**.)
- Pen and marker caps
- Latex balloons (Latex balloons can be particularly dangerous for young children. Young children can easily inhale the balloons while inflating them or choke on broken pieces. Latex can conform to the throat causing a blockage, which can be particularly difficult to remove [CDC 2022d].)
- Hair barrettes
- Beads

Ingested and Inhaled Poison Exposures

Young children will put almost anything into their mouths, including medications, cleaning supplies and chemicals, plants, small objects (like small toys), and household objects (see section on "Choking"). If a child ingests something accidentally, an adult needs to determine if the child's health is at risk. While many of these ingestions can cause child injury through choking (see section on "Choking"), they can also cause poisoning of the child. Overall, according to the American Academy of Pediatrics (AAP), if they are not sharp objects and don't cause choking or end up in the airway, most foreign body ingestions do not cause harm. If they pass through the esophagus, stomach, and intestines into the stool, they do not cause harm (AAP Committee on Injury, Violence, and Poison Prevention 2010; AAP 2021b; AAP 2022c). However, these objects may become stuck and may need to be retrieved by the medical team. If not removed, they may cause chronic abdominal pain, obstruction, or damage to the lining of the gastrointestinal (GI) track. However, the potential for harm with the ingestion of certain types of objects is a real concern (AAP 2022c).

There are more than two million human poison exposures reported to poison centers every year (AAP 2021c). The substances most commonly involved in poison exposures of children are cosmetics and personal care products, cleaning substances, and medications (APC, n.d. b; CCAoA 2018). According to the CDC (2023b), approximately 60,000 emergency department (ED) visits result from unintentional medication overdoses among children under the age of 5. Poisoning can occur in a variety of ways:

- **Ingestion** occurs by eating or drinking. Children are attracted to bright colorful packages, pills, and odd shapes. They often mistake pills and vitamins for candy. Approximately 85 percent of poisonings occur through ingestion.
- **Absorption** occurs when poisonous substances, such as pesticides or plants, come in contact with a child's skin or eyes. The poison is absorbed through the skin or mucous membranes and travels to the bloodstream.
- **Inhalation** occurs when children breathe fumes from CO, pesticides, certain types of art materials, or dust that may contain lead. The air is exchanged in the lungs and comes in direct contact with the bloodstream.
- **Animal and insect bites** can cause an allergic reaction or infectious disease but can also release toxins into the bloodstream (e.g., tick paralysis, envenomation from poisonous snakes).
- **Injection** occurs when there is a puncture wound. Toxins like tetanus can be released into the bloodstream in addition to blood-borne infections (see section on "Exposure to Body Fluids").

IMMEDIATE IMPACT

The Environment from a Child's Perspective

Inspect the facility for potential hazards from the child's eye view. It is easy to miss potential hazards for children when looking at things from an adult's height and perspective.

Medications

Children may take medications when no one is looking or accidentally receive a dose of medication that is too high (CDC 2023b; *CFOC* Standard 5.2.9.2). More than 90 percent of unintentional poisoning deaths are caused by drugs and medications. If you find a child with an open or empty container of a toxic substance, they may have ingested a poison. Get the substance away from the child and remove it from their mouth if visible. Always call the regional Poison Center at 1-800-222-1222 for further instructions. (APC n.d. b, CDC 2023b).

IMMEDIATE IMPACT

Easy Dos and Don'ts

- Never tell children that medication is candy.
- Keep all staff members' purses and bags out of reach of children.
- Lock up all medications.
- Read medication labels carefully and give drugs only as directed.
- Use the dosing tools that comes with the medication—never a kitchen spoon.

Plants

While plants are essential to our health and our understanding of our environment, some plants can be harmful when eaten or touched (Barbuto 2021; CHOP, n.d.; Krenzelok & Mrvos 2011). Poisonous plants contain substances that can be divided into three major groups:

- **Solanine,** which is found in food and ornamental plants, such as Jerusalem cherry, nightshade, potato sprouts, and unripe tomatoes.
- **Grayanotoxins,** which is found in plants such as azalea, lambkill, mountain laurel, and rhododendron and causes immediate effects.
- **Cardiac glycosides,** which cause changes in the rate or rhythm of the heart. Examples of where it can be found include foxglove, lily of the valley, oleander, squill.

Always call the Poison Control Center if you know or suspect a child has ingested a known or poisonous plant. Do not wait for symptoms to appear (APC, n.d. b).

IMMEDIATE IMPACT

More Easy Dos and Don'ts

- Label indoor and outdoor plants for quick and easy identification.
- Determining the toxicity of every available plant is difficult, so any unknown plant should be kept out of the children's environment.
- Cuttings, trimmings, and leaves from potentially harmful plants should be disposed of safely so children do not have access to them (Barbuto 2021; *CFOC* Standard 5.2.9.2; CHOP, n.d.).

Carbon Monoxide

Carbon monoxide (CO) is a deadly, colorless, odorless, poisonous gas. It is produced by the incomplete burning of various fuels including coal, wood, charcoal, oil, kerosene, propane, and natural gas. Products and equipment powered by internal combustion engines, such as portable generators, cars, lawn mowers, and power washers, also produce CO (*CFOC* Standard 5.2.9.5; Ritter 2020; Safe Kids Worldwide, n.d. a). CO detectors are the only way to detect this substance. It is important to install and operate correctly CO detectors and change batteries yearly. If the CO alarm goes off or children or staff members have symptoms of CO poisoning, exit the building and call 911 until the building is cleared by authorities.

Other Types of Exposures

Skin, eyes, and inhaled exposures all require evaluation by a healthcare professional (APC, n.d. a; CCAoA 2018; CDC 2023a, 2023b; EPA 2022). While awaiting care, address them as follows:

- **Skin.** Remove the child's clothes and rinse the skin with lukewarm water for at least 15 minutes.
- **Eyes.** Flush the child's eyes by holding the eyelids open and pouring a steady stream of room temperature water into the inner corners for 15 minutes.
- **Inhaled fumes.** Take the child outside or into fresh air immediately. If the child has stopped breathing, start CPR and do not stop until the child breathes on their own or until someone can take over.

Fire and Smoke Inhalation

Fires are a major concern in the United States. On average, every day 293 children are injured and at least one child dies from fire (Safe Kids Worldwide, n.d. c). The US Fire Administration claims an estimated 325 fires occur in daycares annually. Children under the age of 5 are among those at higher risk for death from fire-related injuries, and more than half of child fire deaths are children age 4 and younger (USFA 2002; USFA, n.d.). They may be unable to leave burning buildings and die as a result of smoke inhalation. Designing and regularly practicing a fire-specific emergency plan is one of the simplest ways to save lives if a fire breaks out in the early learning program (Young 2016). Although fires are a significant cause of burns in young children, actual flames and burns only account for about 30 percent of fire-related deaths and injuries. The majority of children age 4 and younger who are hospitalized for burn-related injuries suffer from scald burns (65 percent) or contact burns (20 percent) (American Red Cross, n.d. b; Cole, Crandall, & Kourofsky 2004) (see "Burns" section in this chapter).

SIGNS AND SYMPTOMS

- Cough
- Shortness of breath
- Hoarseness of voice
- Headache
- Drowsiness or confusion
- Eye irritation
- Soot in nostrils with swelling of the nasal passages

When a fire starts in a center, children can become afraid and confused. They may not understand what is happening or how they should react. With as little as two minutes to escape unharmed, there is not enough time to plan an escape route when the alarm sounds. Proper prevention methods are critical for ensuring the safety of young children should they experience a fire at the program (*CFOC* Standards 5.1.1.3 and 9.2.4.5; Safe Kids Worldwide, n.d. c).

Exposure to smoke and toxins can cause irritation or swelling in children's airways. These symptoms may occur immediately or up to several hours after exposure.

Head Injury

Head injuries are common in children. They can hurt the scalp, skull, brain, or blood vessels. Head injuries can be mild, like a bump on the head, or more serious, like a concussion. In children, most are mild and don't injure the brain; however, a head injury can be significant even without a loss of consciousness. Nonverbal children younger than 6 months will require more careful observation (AAP 2022b; CDC 2022a; Verive, Stock, & Singh 2023).

Types of head injuries include the following:

- Concussion, an injury to the head area that may cause instant loss of awareness or alertness for a few minutes up to a few hours after the incident; some concussions are mild and brief
- Contusion, a bruise to the brain
- Skull fracture, a break in the skull bone
- Bleeding

SIGNS AND SYMPTOMS

- Headache
- Vision changes
- Vomiting
- Increased sleepiness
- Confusion
- Loss of consciousness (passing out)
- Seizures (AAP 2022b; CDC 2022a; Schutzman 2021, 2022, 2023)

Submersion in Water and Drowning

Drowning is a major cause of death among children under 5 years old and is the leading cause of death of children 1–4 years old (CDC 2022e; Safe Kids Worldwide 2018; WHO 2021). Drowning can happen in almost any amount of water (as little as one to two inches), indoors or outdoors. Water safety presents a particular challenge to early childhood educators, especially of young children who are just learning to walk, and becoming active and curious. Small children have large heads in proportion to the rest of their bodies. This makes the top heavy, causing them to fall forward when they lose their balance. They also have weaker neck muscles, which makes it difficult for them to pull themselves up out of a bucket, toilet, or bathtub. Even a bucket of water can be dangerous for a small child (AAP 2019b; *CFOC* Standard 6.3.5.2; Denny et al. 2021). Drownings occur silently and quickly.

Strangulation, Suffocation, and Sudden Infant Death Syndrome (SIDS)

Suffocation and strangulation are leading causes of serious injuries in children and are leading causes of death in infants and toddlers (*CFOC* Standard 3.4.6.1). Nearly all strangulation and suffocation deaths are preventable (CSN, n.d. a). Children can easily get things caught around their necks (strangulation) or get their head or limbs stuck (entrapment) in unexpected ways. Suffocation occurs when a young child has their airway blocked by a plastic bag, dry cleaning bag, or plastic wrap but also pillows, bumper pads, or soft surfaces, such as beanbags or waterbeds. Young children can also be suffocated by being trapped in old refrigerators, freezers, trunks, or toy boxes that can trap children inside without ventilation (Moon 2022; Moon et al. 2022; Safe Kids Worldwide, n.d. b).

Sleep-related deaths are a leading cause of death in infants. Every year, around 3,500 infants in the United States die suddenly and unexpectedly while they are sleeping (Moon 2022; Moon et al. 2022). Most of these deaths are due to sudden infant death syndrome (SIDS) or accidental deaths from suffocation or strangulation. Most sleep-related deaths in early learning programs occur in the first day or first week that an infant starts attending the program (*CFOC* Standard 3.1.4 Safe Sleep; Moon 2022; Moon et al. 2022). Many of these deaths appear to be associated with prone positioning, especially when the infant is unaccustomed to being placed in that position. Infants and young children can suffocate if they get stuck under objects like boxes, pillows, bedding, or plastic bags. Blinds, cords, ropes, clothing, and hanging mobiles can be strangulation risks. Unsafe sleep practices can leave young children at risk for these injuries (CDC 2018; Moon et al. 2022; NICHQ 2020). Safe sleep practices help to reduce the risk of sudden unexpected infant death (SUID).

SIGNS AND SYMPTOMS

- Shortness of breath or difficulty breathing
- A slow heartrate
- Hoarseness
- A sore throat
- Confusion
- Loss of consciousness
- Life-threatening symptoms in infants, such as limpness, paleness, bluish color, and lack of breathing
- Visual changes

Avoidance and Prevention

There are several practices that will lessen the likelihood of sleep-related deaths as well as strangulation and suffocation (CDC 2018; *CFOC* Standard 3.1.4 Safe Sleep; CCTAN, n.d.; Moon 2022; Moon et al. 2022). They include the following:

- To prevent strangulation
  - Dress children in safe clothing.
    - Don't put necklaces or headbands on infants and toddlers.
    - Don't dress young children in clothing with drawstrings, which can get caught on furniture or other objects during playtime or while asleep.
    - Remove infants' bibs before naptime and bedtime.
    - Don't tie a pacifier around an infant's neck; instead, clip it to their clothing.
  - Create a safe environment in the program.
    - Keep mobiles out of the reach of infants and toddlers.
    - Don't hang diaper bags or purses on cribs.
    - Place cribs or toddler beds away from window blinds or curtains.
    - Secure power, phone, and cable wires so that they are not dangling or loose.
    - Tie all window blinds and draper cords up high and out of reach.
- To prevent entrapment
  - Always watch infants in strollers and strap them in to ensure that they don't slide down and trap their heads.
  - Choose a toy chest without a lid.
  - Don't use cribs with cut outs in the headboard or footboard.
  - Make sure that the crib mattresses are the right size and fit snugly in cribs.
  - Don't use bumper pads in cribs.
  - Make sure that crib slats are no more than 2⅜ inches (six centimeters) apart.
  - Avoid use of bunk beds; rails may have a narrow space beneath that can allow a toddler's head to be caught.
- To prevent suffocation
  - Remove all plastic bags and wrapping from the child activity areas.
  - Remove toy boxes, trunks, and other self-latching containers that can potentially trap young children.
  - Utilize safe sleep practices (see *CFOC* Standard 3.1.4 Safe Sleep).
- To prevent sleep-related deaths and injuries (e.g., SUID/SIDS)
  - All staff members, caregivers/guardians, volunteers, and others who care for infants in the early learning program should follow the required safe sleep practices as recommended by the AAP (*CFOC* Standard 3.1.4 Safe Sleep).

› If the child has been suffocated or strangled, immediately remove the offending object.
› Check to see if they are conscious and breathing.
› If they are not breathing, begin CPR (see section on "Lifesaving Procedures and CPR").

Pedestrian Versus Motor Vehicle Injury

Most adults know the rules of walking safely on the road, but children, especially young children, must be taught and supervised. Toddlers and young children are at greatest risk for many reasons (Safe Kids Worldwide, n.d. d), including that they

› Are impulsive and often run into the street unexpectantly
› May not realize that even though they see the driver, the driver may not see them
› May not understand the danger of traffic

IMMEDIATE IMPACT

Children as Pedestrians: Safety Tips

› Consider adding reflective vests for walkers during low-visibility times.
› Use adult staff members to assist with safe drops-off and pickups when boarding or leaving a vehicle.
› Advocate for safety features in the surrounding area, including
  - Sidewalks
  - Physical barriers between pedestrians and roads
  - Traffic-calming measures like speed humps or median barriers (CSN, n.d. b)

When young children are hit by a vehicle, the results are often fatal. Getting to a trauma center quickly is essential (AAP 2019d; AHA 2020; American Red Cross, n.d. a; CDC 2022b; *CFOC* Standards 1.4.3.1 and 9.2.4.1).

Non-Life-Threatening Injuries

In contrast to the serious injuries that can threaten a child's life or cause permanent harm, most of the injuries seen in early learning programs do not put the child's life in danger. Non–life-threatening injuries will not likely have a long-term impact on the child's life when properly treated. These injuries can typically be resolved with appropriate first aid care. However, injuries such as bites, stings, burns, and sprains require the rapid attention of teachers and staff members to evaluate the situation, provide immediate care, and determine if a higher level of care is required.

Bites and Stings

Human Bites

Human bites can be as dangerous or more dangerous than animal bites (Bula-Rudas & Olcott 2018). Although humans (especially young humans) don't have the strongest bites compared to animals, their bites can easily become infected due to the many bacteria and viruses found in the human mouth. Hands are the most common site for bites (Barrett & Revis 2021). A healthcare provider should check any human bite that breaks the skin.

Animal Bites

Animal bites and scratches that break the skin may need stiches or may heal on their own. They may also cause infection. Rarely, bites from wild animals can lead to rabies, which is a life-threatening infection. Bats, raccoons, skunks, and foxes cause most rabies cases (Mayo Clinic 2022). Most animal bites come from pets. Compared with adults, children are much more likely to be bitten on the face, head, or neck (CDC 2021a).

Insect Bites and Stings

Most insect bites and stings are mild and can be treated easily at the center (WebMD 2021a). They may cause some itching, swelling, and stinging that goes away in one to two days. Some bites and stings can transmit disease through bacteria, viruses, or parasites, and some stings from insects like bees, yellow jackets, wasps, hornets, and fire ants might cause an allergic reaction or even anaphylaxis (AAP 2018). (See "Chapter 8: Understanding Common Illnesses and Conditions" for more information about anaphylaxis.)

IMMEDIATE IMPACT

Before Children Go Outside . . .

- Prepare young children for outside playtime using age-appropriate insect repellants and other protective layers as appropriate.
- Have children dress in long sleeves and hats when playing outside during the summer.
- Tuck pants into socks when going out for walks in places with vegetation next to the walking paths (AAP 2015b, 2018; AAP & NASN 2012; *CFOC* Standards 1.4.3.1 and 9.2.4; Hashikawa et al. 2015).

Weather-Related Injuries and Concerns

Heading outside is a great way for children to explore their environment, get exercise, and blow off steam. However, children are more vulnerable than adults to the effects of heat, sun exposure, and cold weather. When they are having fun, they are less likely to recognize discomfort and ask to come inside when they are too cold or overheated. Sunburn is also of concern in both hot and cold climates. There are many reasons that young children are at greater risk to suffer effects of excessive cold and ultraviolet (UV) exposure (CDC 2019, 2023c; *CFOC* Standard 3.4.5). They have thinner skin than adults and are more sensitive to UV rays, and being smaller in size, their bodies lose heat quickly (CDC 2023c).

Cold Weather

Children exposed to extreme cold for too long and without warm, dry, breathable clothing can get frostbite or even life-threatening hypothermia (AAP 2023; Head Start 2023a). Here are some precautions for cold weather safety:

- Dress children in layers of warm clothing. If the top layer gets wet, they will still have a dry layer underneath.
- There is no set amount of time for children to play outside safely when the weather is cold. Staff should use their best judgement. When the cold becomes unpleasant, take the children in.
- Have children come indoors periodically to prevent hypothermia or frostbite. A temperature of 0°F and a wind speed of 15 miles per hour creates a wind chill temperature of –19°F. Under these conditions, frostbite can occur in just 30 minutes.
- Frostnip is an early warning sign of frostbite. The skin may feel numb or tingly and appear red. To prevent frostbite, check that mittens and socks are dry and warm. Frostbite occurs mostly on fingers, toes, ears, nose, and cheeks. The affected area becomes very cold, firm, and sometimes white or yellowish-gray in color.
- Even though it may be cold outside, it is important to use sunscreen and stay hydrated.

Warm Weather

Heat-related illness occurs when the body's temperature gets too high. Body temperature can be affected by the temperature of the air and by level of physical activity. Heat reactions are caused by a variety of factors, including exposure to high temperatures, often with high humidity; exertion from hard play; dehydration due to excessive sweating during hot weather; heat waves causing long stretches of heat exposure; exposure to a very high temperature, such as a hot car where temperatures can quickly rise to 154°F (67.8°C); and health risk factors, such as very young age or underlying medical conditions (AAP 2021a; Davies 2022; NHTSA, n.d.).

There are three main reactions to hot temperatures and heat waves (CCAoA, n.d.):

- **Heatstroke or sunstroke (serious).** Symptoms include hot, flushed skin with a high fever over 105°F (40.5°C). More than 50 percent of children with heatstroke do not sweat. Heatstroke can cause confusion, coma, or shock. Heatstroke is a life-threatening emergency. It has as high death rate if not treated promptly (Davies 2022).
- **Heat exhaustion.** Symptoms include pale skin, profuse sweating, and nausea. Dizziness, fainting, or weakness can also be signs. They can have a mild fever of 100°F–102°F (37.8°C–39°C). A person can progress from heat exhaustion to heatstroke, so all patients with severe symptoms need to be seen right away. Mild symptoms can be treated in the center with fluids and rest. If they don't resolve, these children need to be seen.

- **Heat cramps.** Severe muscle cramps in the legs (which can affect thigh muscles) and stomachache are present. There is no fever. Tightness of spasms of the hands may occur. After the child drinks fluids and cools down, they will feel better. All symptoms should go away in a few hours.

Hot weather precautions include

- Having the children rest and take breaks during exercise or outdoor play
- Avoiding the hottest part of the day (in summer 2:00 p.m. to 6:00 p.m. because the sun is hottest early afternoon)
- Drinking lots of water when exercising or playing outside during hot conditions
- Offering sports drinks during extremely high-temperature/high-humidity times

Sun Exposure

Infants and young children are at a high risk of overexposure to sunlight. Short-term consequences of excessive sunlight or UV exposure include sunburns and overheating, but there are long-term risks as well, such as aging of skin, eye damage, and skin cancers (CDC 2023c; *CFOC* Standard 3.4.5.1). Sun exposure precautions include the following (CDC 2023c; Extension Alliance for Better Child Care 2019; National Child Care Information and Referral Center 2012):

- Limit sun exposure, especially between 10:00 a.m. and 4:00 p.m. Schedule outdoor activities before and after these peak times of sun exposure as sunburns can occur quickly.
- Keep infants less than 1 year old out of direct sunlight as much as possible.
- Create shade by planting trees and/or using partial roofs, awning, umbrellas, or other covering, and plan activities in shaded areas.
- Encourage children to wear protective clothing, such as loose-fitting, long-sleeved shirts and long pants and wide brimmed hats or baseball caps with back flaps to cover the head, neck, and ears.
- Encourage use of UV protection, such as unbreakable sunglasses with 99 percent UV protection for outdoor play.
- For children older than 6 months, use sunscreen with a sun protection factor (SPF) of 15 or higher that gives protection from both UVA and UVB rays (AAP 2021d; *CFOC* Standard 3.4.5).

FAMILY CONNECTIONS

Prepping for Weather at Home

At the beginning of the program session, provide parents or caregivers with a list of precautions and recommendations for excessive or extreme weather conditions, so that their children can arrive at school ready for outside play or field trips! Be sure to remind parents and caregivers of these recommendations before any class trips.

Burns

Burns and fires are the fifth most common cause of accidental death in children and adults and account for an estimated 3,500 adult and child deaths per year (AAP 2022a). Toddlers and children are more often burned by scalding or flames. Burns can be caused by thermal, electrical, or chemical exposures. Burns are classified as first, second, or third degree depending on how deeply and severely they penetrate the skin's surface, but they are always painful (Joffe 2021).

- **First degree (superficial).** First-degree burns affect only the epidermis (outer layer of skin). The site is red, painful, dry, and has no blisters.
- **Second degree (partial thickness).** Second-degree burns involve the epidermis (outer layer of skin) and the dermis (middle layer of skin). The burn site appears red with blisters and may be swollen and painful.
- **Third degree (full thickness).** Third-degree burns severely damage or destroy the top layer of skin and may damage underlying bones, muscles, and tendons. The skin appears white or charred.

TYPES OF BURN EXPOSURES

- **Thermal.** These burns are due to heat sources that raise the temperature of the skin and tissues and cause the tissues to be damaged. Hot metals, scalding liquids, steam, and flames can all cause burns when in contact with skin (Joffe 2021; Wiktor & Richards 2022).
- **Electrical.** These burns are from electrical currents. Electrical burns can be more serious than initial appearance. The entrance wound may be small, but the electricity continues to burn as it penetrates deeper. Electrical burns can be accompanied by respiratory or cardiac arrest (O'Keefe 2023).
- **Chemical.** These burns are due to strong acids, alkalis, detergents, or solvents that come in contact with the skin or eyes (Kaushik & Bird 2022).

Fractures and Sprains

Fractures and sprains are common occurrences in childhood. It can be difficult to distinguish between the two in young children, so center staff members should have these injuries evaluated by a physician or healthcare facility (AAP 2015a, 2015d; Boston Children's Hospital, n.d. b).

Fractures

A fracture is a partial or complete break in a bone. When a fracture occurs, it is either (ASSH, n.d.)

- An open (compound) fracture, which occurs when the bone breaks through the skin or the skin has a wound which exposes the bone
- A closed (simple) fracture, which occurs when there is no wound in the skin

Fractures occur commonly in children because young children have growing bones. Growing bones tend to buckle or bend before breaking, which can lead to unusual patterns. Typically, with the proper attention, fractures will heal without complications.

SIGNS AND SYMPTOMS

Symptoms may vary among children and can also be associated with other health problems, but the most common findings for fractures and sprains include (AAP 2015a, 2015d)

- Pain
- Swelling
- Obvious deformity of the extremity or of the bone
- Trouble using or moving the extremity in the normal way
- Warmth, bruising, or redness
- Weakness

Some children may not experience any of these symptoms and may still be found to have a fracture.

Fractures can only be definitively diagnosed with an imaging study, such as an x-ray, MRI, or CT scan. If program staff members suspect a fracture based on the typical symptoms, children must be seen by a physician or healthcare facility that can order a study. First aid treatment is designed to provide comfort to the child and reduce swelling and pain while awaiting treatment.

While awaiting additional care

- Calm and comfort the child as fractures can be very painful.
- Apply gentle pressure if there is bleeding.
- Apply cold packs if there is swelling.
- Try not to move the extremity or the child unless necessary as this can cause further damage; keep the child still.
- If there is an open fracture, gently cover the area with a clean towel while awaiting treatment.
- If the child appears faint, lay them down with feet slightly higher than the head if this can be done without moving a broken extremity.

Sprains

A sprain is an injury to a ligament (elastic bands that connect bone to bone and hold joints in place), caused by tearing of the fibers of the ligament (AAP 2015d). The ligament can have a partial tear, or it can be completely torn. Ankle sprains are the most common type of sprain, although wrists, knees, and thumbs can also be sprained. Sprained ligaments often swell quickly and are painful. Distinguishing sprains from fractures in young children can be quite difficult as they can often exhibit similar symptoms.

Eye Injury

Eye injuries in children can be serious and quite painful. They are also a common cause of vision loss in children (Boston Children's, n.d. a; Head Start 2022b). Eye injuries range from corneal abrasion and chemical burns to bruising and having foreign bodies in the eye. Any injury to a child's eye should be considered a medical emergency, and immediate medical care is often necessary (AAO 2023; Head Start 2022b).

Mouth and Dental Injury

Injuries to the head, face, and mouth are common in young children (McTigue, Thompson, & Azadani 2023). Most oral injuries happen when young children are learning to walk and fall. Children may stumble or trip as they are learning to walk and when they are active. Children spend about one-third of their time in early learning programs, making them a frequent location for mouth and dental injuries (CDC 2022c; *CFOC* Standard 9.2.3.14 Oral Health). Common oral injuries include tongue or lip injuries; teeth that are chipped or cracked; teeth that are knocked out; teeth that are knocked loose, move, or are pushed into the gum; and toothaches.

Children's top front teeth are injured most often (McTigue, Thompson, & Azadani 2023). Bruises or cuts in or near the mouth are also common oral injuries. Preventing oral injuries is significant for children's long-term health. Early loss of primary teeth as a result of an oral injury or tooth decay can affect the condition of the child's permanent teeth. Any of these outcomes can affect the child's self-esteem, ability to learn, and/or ability to eat healthy food. When primary teeth are lost too early, there may not be enough space for permanent teeth to grow. Injuries to the primary and permanent teeth can affect a child's speech, nutrition, self-confidence, and overall health.

Have a plan and a first aid kit to handle oral health emergencies (AAP & NASN 2012; *CFOC* Standards 1.4.3.1, 9.2.4.1, and 9.2.3.14; Head Start 2022a, 2023b, 2023c):

› Wear gloves when attending to oral injuries to prevent exposure to body fluids.
› Have contact information for each child's dentist and a signed release form that allows the child's dentist to share information with the early learning program.
› Have a plan for transporting a child with an oral health emergency to the child's dentist or the nearest source of emergency oral healthcare.

Exposure to Body Fluids

Some children and adults may unknowingly be infected with infectious agents that can be present in blood or body fluids. Thus, the staff members in all early learning programs should adopt standard precautions for all spills of blood or body fluids (*CFOC* Standard 3.2.3.4; NC Resource Center, n.d.; OSHA, n.d. b). If blood and body fluids enter a mucous membrane (eyes, nose, mouth), standard procedures should be utilized to decontaminate the area. Blood and body fluids containing blood pose a potential risk because bloody body fluids contain the highest concentration of viruses (NCECQA 2016).

Instances where one child draws the blood of another individual during biting or otherwise gets blood from another person on mucous membranes is rare. Child bites rarely break the skin and when the skin is broken, bleeding begins a few seconds later, usually after the biter releases the bitten person. Even though biting is a common behavior of young children, transmission of blood-borne disease by biting in early learning programs has not been reported. However, if blood transfer occurs and exposes a mucous membrane to blood from another individual, this will need to be treated for an accidental exposure to a potential HIV-containing body fluid (Caring for Kids 2018; Nationwide Children's Hospital 2023; Schmitt, n.d.).

SIGNS AND SYMPTOMS

Exposure to body fluids can lead to infection, such as

- Increased pain, swelling, warmth, or redness at exposure site
- Red streaks leading from the area
- Fever
- Cough and difficulty breathing if exposed to contaminated respiratory secretions

Avoidance and Prevention

Occupational and child exposure to and acquisition of blood-borne pathogens is preventable. Staff members should be trained to use appropriate personal protective equipment, including gloves, eye protection, and masks, as appropriate to prevent transmission of infectious disease between teachers and children and from one child to another (*CFOC* Standard 3.2.3.4; NC Resource Center, n.d.). (See also *Caring for Our Children* "Appendix L: Cleaning Up Body Fluids.")

Standard precautions include

- Wearing personal protective equipment
- Handwashing
  - After diapering or toileting children
  - After handling body fluids of any kind
  - Before and after giving first aid (such as cleaning cuts, scratches, or bloody noses)
  - After cleaning up spills or objects contaminated with body fluids
  - After taking off disposable gloves
- Wearing gloves
  - During contact with blood or body fluids
  - When staff members have cuts, scratches, or rashes, which cause breaks in the skin of their hands

- Environmental sanitizing
- Proper disposal of materials

Training should be provided to all staff members who may be exposed to blood or other potentially infectious materials. All staff members should be trained to address the needs of children who have been exposed to blood or other body fluids (*CFOC* Standard 3.2.3.4; OSHA, n.d. b).

Summary

While minor injuries are common among young children, comprehensive policies and procedures can both prevent injuries, and ensure appropriate responses when they do occur. Guidelines found in *Caring for Our Children* can protect children from serious injury and prepare staff members to respond to minor events and emergencies. Ongoing education allows teachers and staff to create and maintain safe environments for young children. Further, training prepares staff members to provide timely first aid and potentially life-saving interventions.

APPENDIX 7.1

First Aid for Injuries: Specific Treatments and When to Seek a Higher Level of Care

Choking

TREATMENT

For a child younger than age 1 year who is conscious but not breathing (AAP 2015c; AAP Committee on Injury, Violence, and Poison Prevention 2010; American Red Cross 2011; CDC 2022d):

- Do not put your finger into the child's mouth to remove the object as your finger could push the object deeper into the child's throat.
- Call 911 as the airway can become fully blocked.
- Hold the child face down on your forearm supported by your thigh.
- Keep the child's torso higher than the head.
- Give forceful blows using the heel of your free hand to thump the child between the shoulder blades five times.
- Turn the child over, supporting the head and neck.
- If the object is still present:
  - Place the child on a firm surface.
  - Put two to three fingers in the center of the child's breastbone and push quickly up to five times.
  - Repeat the back thumping and chest pushes until the object comes out or the child loses consciousness.
  - If the child is still not breathing, open the airway by lifting the jaw.
  - If the child loses consciousness, perform CPR and take the object out of their mouth only if you see it.

For a child older than age 1 year who is conscious:

- Do not put your finger into the child's mouth to remove the object as your finger could push the object deeper into the child's throat.
- Call 911 as the airway can become fully blocked.
- Get the child into position.
  - Stand behind the child and wrap your arms around their waist.
  - Place a fist just above the child's belly button.
- Try to dislodge the object.
  - Hold your fist with your free hand and quickly push in and up.
  - Repeat until the object comes out or the child loses consciousness.
- Start CPR, if needed.
  - If the child loses consciousness, move the child to the floor and start CPR.
  - Take the object out of their mouth only if you see it.

WHEN TO SEEK A HIGHER LEVEL OF CARE

If the child is coughing and gagging but can breathe or talk, you can monitor. However, the child may need immediate care if:

- Unconscious
- Unable to breathe because something is blocking the airway
- Wheezing or gasping
- Unable to cry, talk, or make noise
- Turning blue in the face
- Grabbing at their throat
- Panicked

Ingested and Inhaled Poison Exposures

TREATMENT

General treatment of poisoning includes the following: (CFOC Standard 5.2.9.2)

- Get the poison away from the child.
- If the substance is still in the child's mouth, make them spit it out or remove with your gloved fingers. Keep the retrieved pill as evidence for the Poison Control Center.
- Do *not* make the child vomit.
- Call the Poison Control Center.

Medications

(AAP 2021c; CDC 2023b)

- Get the medication from the child.
- If the substance is still in the child's mouth, make them spit it out or remove with your gloved fingers. Keep the retrieved pill as evidence for the Poison Control Center.
- Do *not* make the child vomit.
- Call the Poison Control Center.

Plants

(Barbuto 2021; CHOP, n.d.; Krenzelok & Mrvos 2011:

- Look for pieces of the plant in the child's mouth.
- Remove any pieces that you can see.
- Give them small sips of water.
- Do not try to make them vomit.
- Call the Poison Control Center.

Carbon Monoxide (CO)(Safe Kids Worldwide, n.d. a)

- Remove child from location with CO exposure and get them to fresh air right away.
- Begin CPR if child is not breathing. (See "Lifesaving Procedures and CPR" in "Chapter 7: First Aid and Injuries.")
- Call 911.
- Call the Poison Control Center (APC, n.d. b).

Fire & Smoke Inhalation

(American Red Cross, n.d. b; Mlcak 2022; Safe Kids Worldwide, n.d. c)

- All children with smoke inhalation exposure should be seen at an Emergency Department.
- Remove the child from the facility as quickly as possible.
- Assess children for signs and symptoms of smoke inhalation and/or thermal burns.
- Call 911 immediately.
- Prepare to provide CPR if children are not breathing or struggling to breathe (Safe Kids Worldwide, n.d.; Mlcak 2022).

WHEN TO SEEK A HIGHER LEVEL OF CARE

Medications

- Sore throat
- Trouble breathing
- Drowsiness, irritability, or jumpiness
- Nausea, vomiting, or stomach pain without fever
- Lip or mouth burns or blisters
- Unusual drooling
- Strange odors on the child's breath
- Unusual stains on the child's clothing
- Seizures

Plants

Although childhood fatalities from plant poisonings are rare, some plant ingestions can be life-threatening to children. Seek additional care if the child

- Has collapsed or is unconscious
- Has difficulty breathing
- Is paralyzed
- Has seizures

Always call the Poison Control Center if you know or suspect a child has ingested a known or poisonous plant. Do not wait for symptoms to appear (APC, n.d. b).

Carbon Monoxide

Call 911 if child has any of the following:

- Seizures
- Loss of consciousness
- Trouble breathing
- If the child has stopped breathing, begin CPR while awaiting arrival of EMS (AHA 2020). (See "Lifesaving Procedures and CPR" in "Chapter 7: First Aid and Injuries.")

Fire & Smoke Inhalation

Signs and symptoms that are particularly concerning and require immediate attention include:

- Hoarse voice
- Difficulty breathing
- Prolonged coughing spells
- Mental confusion

Head Injury

TREATMENT

- Assess for loss of consciousness or confusion.
- Use first aid procedures to treat any bleeding from cuts or abrasions of the head or scalp.
- If no loss of consciousness or confusion
  - Place a cold pack on injured area for 20 minutes every three to four hours.
  - Observe child carefully for several hours, especially during naptime.
- If the child is complaining of headache, staff member may provide acetaminophen, provided that caregivers have given permission for medication administration.
- Alert caregivers and child's listed healthcare professional (AAP 2022b; CDC 2022a; Schutzman 2021, 2022, 2023).

WHEN TO SEEK A HIGHER LEVEL OF CARE

- All infants
- Loss of consciousness for more than a few minutes
- Continued vomiting
- Confusion
- Seizures
- Won't stop crying
- Complains of head and neck pain, or more fussy than usual if a younger child
- Won't awaken easily
- Not walking or talking normally
- Has an underlying health condition, especially a neurodevelopmental disability or bleeding disorder
- Has a ventriculoperitoneal shunt
- Fall from several feet or other severe mechanism
  - Falls greater than 1 meter for children younger than 2 years old
  - Falls greater than 1.5 meter for children older than 2 years old
- Motor vehicle crash
- Pedestrian or cyclist struck by a motor vehicle
- Head struck by an object

Submersion in Water and Drowning

TREATMENT

- Pull the child from the water and place them on their back on a firm surface.
- Check for breathing, and clear mouth and nose of any obstruction.
- Get another adult to call for emergency help.
- Begin rescue breathing or CPR as needed, if the child is unresponsive (AHA 2020; Denny et al. 2021). (See "Lifesaving Procedures and CPR" in "Chapter 7: First Aid and Injuries.")

WHEN TO SEEK A HIGHER LEVEL OF CARE

Call 911 after removing any submerged child from water. Even children who appear normal at the time they are removed from water can experience symptoms later.

Pedestrian Versus Motor Vehicle Injury

TREATMENT

When young children are hit by a vehicle, the results are often fatal. Getting to a trauma center quickly is essential.

- Call 911.
- Do not move child but provide CPR if not breathing (AHA 2020; American Red Cross, n.d. a; CSN, n.d. b). (See "Lifesaving Procedures and CPR" in "Chapter 7: First Aid and Injuries.")

WHEN TO SEEK A HIGHER LEVEL OF CARE

Call 911 immediately for all child pedestrian versus vehicle collisions as these are all likely to be life-threatening.

Bites and Stings

TREATMENT

Human bites (Baddour & Harper 2022; Barrett & Revis 2021; Bula-Rudas & Olcott 2018):

- Wear gloves.
- Try to calm the child and reassure them that you can help.
- If the bite is bleeding, apply pressure with a clean towel, cloth, or bandage.
- Wash the bite with soap and water under pressure from a faucet for at least five minutes but do not scrub.
- Dry the bite wound gently and cover with a sterile dressing. Do not tape the wound as this may trap harmful bacteria that can cause a serious infection.
- Human bites often require antibiotics to prevent infection, but the child's healthcare provider can address as needed.
- Call caregivers.

Animal bites (CDC 2021a; Mayo Clinic 2022; Schmitt, n.d.):

- Wear gloves.
- Apply pressure to stop bleeding.
- Wash the wound thoroughly with soap and water for five minutes.
- Apply an antibiotic cream or ointment and cover the bite with a clean bandage.
- Call an animal control center.

Insect bites and stings (AAP 2015b, 2018; WebMD 2021a):

- Move to a safe area to avoid more bites or stings.
- Watch for signs of a severe reaction.
- Remove any stingers.
- Gently wash the area with soap and water.
- Apply a cloth dampened with cold water or ice to the sting or bite for 10–20 minutes.
- If the injury is on an arm or leg, raise it.
- Apply calamine lotion, or 0.5–1 percent hydrocortisone cream.
- Consider giving an anti-itch medication, such as an antihistamine.
- Call the Poison Control Center for additional treatment advice.
- Call the parent or caregiver.

WHEN TO SEEK A HIGHER LEVEL OF CARE

Human bites:

Most human bites should be seen by a doctor due to the risk of infection. Also, additional evaluation may be required if the following occur:

- Bites on the hand, foot, face, scalp, or a sensitive bone or joint
- Intense swelling
- Pus around the bite wound
- The wound feels warm to touch
- The skin around the wound is red
- The child has fevers or chills or feels unwell
- Either the biter or the person who was bitten has a chronic illness, such as HIV or hepatitis B or C; both people may require testing by the healthcare professional

Animal bites:

- The bite has broken the skin.
- The bite is on the face, head, neck, hand, foot, or near a joint.
- The wound is a deep puncture or you are not sure how serious it is.
- The skin is badly torn, crushed, or bleeding significantly.
- The bite is deep or large.
- There is exposed muscle or bone.
- The wound may need stiches.
- There is swelling, redness, pain, or oozing, which may indicate infection.
- There is a concern about rabies (if the bite was caused by a cat or dog, try to confirm the animal's rabies vaccination status).
- If the bite was caused by a wild animal, consult a physician immediately.
- The tetanus status of the child is not up to date or is unknown.

Consider calling an animal control center or local police after a child is bitten if the animal

- Behaves in an odd way
- Is an unknown pet or rabies vaccination status is uncertain
- Is stray or wild

Insect bites and stings:

- Trouble breathing
- Swelling of the lips, face, eyelids, or throat
- Dizziness, fainting, or unconsciousness
- A weak and rapid pulse
- Hives
- Nausea, vomiting, or diarrhea

Weather-related Injuries and Concerns

TREATMENT

Frostbite (Nemours Children's Health 2020; WebMD 2021c):

- When frostbite is suspected, bring the child indoors to gently warm up.
- Don't rub the affected area and don't pop any blisters.
- Avoid placing anything hot directly on the skin.
- Soak frostbitten areas of the body in warm water for 20–30 minutes.
- Warm wash cloths can be applied to frostbitten noses, ears, and lips.
- After a few minutes, dry and cover the child with blankets and give them something warm to drink.

Hypothermia (AAP 2023; Head Start 2023a):

- Hypothermia is a medical emergency, so call 911.
- Take the child indoors to warm up until help arrives.
- Remove all wet clothing.
- Wrap the child in blankets or warm clothes.
- Give them something warm to drink.
- If the child stops breathing, begin CPR. (See "Lifesaving Procedures and CPR" in "Chapter 7: First Aid and Injuries.")

Sunburn (CDC 2023c; Nemours Children's Health 2022b):

- Apply cool, wet compresses to the skin to help ease pain and heat.
- Apply a moisturizing cream with aloe vera or aloe vera gel to sunburned areas.
- Consider giving acetaminophen or ibuprofen to help with pain.
- Consider diphenhydramine for itching and swelling.
- Consider using hydrocortisone 1 percent cream for children over age 2 years to help with pain.
- Do not use other topical first aid products, such as benzocaine, as they may cause skin irritation or allergy unless prescribed by a physician.
- Offer cool beverage, such as water, fruit juice, or electrolyte solution, to treat possible dehydration.

WHEN TO SEEK A HIGHER LEVEL OF CARE

Frostbite:

- Numbness and tingling do not resolve after the child is brought inside and gently warmed

Hypothermia:

- Always call 911.
- Prepare to provide CPR as needed until EMS arrives (AHA 2020).

Sunburn:

You will need to seek the help of a physician if the child is

- Younger than 1 year old
- Experiencing fever
- Experiencing chills
- Complaining of headache
- Complaining of upset stomach
- Exhibiting confusion

Burns

TREATMENT

Thermal (AAP 2022a; Joffe 2021; WebMD 2021b; Wiktor & Richards 2022):

- Remove the child from the heat source.
- Wear gloves.
- Cool the affected area with cold water or cold compresses until the pain is reduced or relieved.
- If a blister has formed, do not break it.
- Protect the burn with a dry, sterile, gauze bandage or with a clean cloth.
- If clothing is stuck to the burned area, do not attempt to remove it. Instead, cut around the clothing, leaving the burn intact, and seek medical care right away.
- Do not apply any ointments, oils, or sprays to the burned area.
- If the burn is on the hand, foot, face, eyes, or groin, or covers a large area, seek medical attention immediately.

Electrical (O'Keefe 2023; WebMD 2021b):

- All electrical burns need to be seen by a physician because electrical burns can cause damage to body parts below the skin that are not visible on the surface.
- Unplug the appliance or device that has caused the injury or turn off the electrical current.
- If the child is in contact with the electrical current, do not touch them until the current has been turned off at the source or at the circuit breaker.
- Assess the child for breathing status. If the child is not breathing, have someone call 911 and begin CPR immediately. (See "Lifesaving Procedures and CPR" in "Chapter 7: First Aid and Injuries.")
- Wear gloves.
- Cover the burned area with a sterile gauze bandage or cloth.
- Do not give the child anything to eat or drink.
- Place the child on their back unless a back or neck injury is suspected.
- If the child has vomited or has a serious injury to the face or mouth area, consider placing the child on their side.
- Keep the child warm with blankets or extra clothing.

Chemical (Kaushik & Bird 2022; WebMD 2021b):

- Wear gloves.
- Wash off the chemicals with cool water immediately.

WHEN TO SEEK A HIGHER LEVEL OF CARE

Thermal:

- Any full thickness burn
- Burns to the face, hands, feet, or groin, or burns that extend around any portion of the body
- Burns in children with chronic illnesses
- Suspected abuse
- Chemical burn
- Call the Poison Helpline at 1-800-222-1222 or the child's physician after washing off all the chemicals because the chemicals that cause burns can also be absorbed through the skin and cause other symptoms.
- Electrical injury
- Very young children

Fractures and Sprains

TREATMENT

- Evaluate the child to determine if there is broken skin, obvious deformity of the extremity, or significant swelling. If these exist, the child may have experienced a fracture and will require evaluation by a physician.
- Apply cold compresses to the area with a loose bandage or wrap.
- Elevate the injured limb above the heart if possible to limit swelling (AAP 2015a, 2015d; Boston Children's Hospital, n.d. b; Nemours Children's Health 2018b, 2022a).

WHEN TO SEEK A HIGHER LEVEL OF CARE

- There is bleeding, extreme pain, an open wound, or obvious deformity of the limb.
- The child cannot bear weight.
- There is redness.
- There is pain directly over the bones of the injured extremity or joint.

Exposure to Body Fluids

TREATMENT

When a mucous membrane blood exposure occurs (Broussard & Kahwaji 2022; NC Resource Center, n.d.; OSHA, n.d. b):

- Inform the exposed adult or the caregivers of the child who had a mucous membrane exposure to someone else's blood that
    - The adult or child was exposed to another person's blood
    - The risk of transmission of HIV is small
    - The exposed adult or the caregivers of the exposed child should notify the primary care physician of the exposure
    - The person who was exposed to blood should have a baseline test for HIV. Inform the person whose blood was involved (or caregivers if that person is a child) about the incident and ask
        - If the person whose blood is involved ever had an HIV test and if so could results can be shared with the exposed adult or caregivers of the exposed child
        - If that person does not know or has never had an HIV test, ask if that person would be willing to have one and share results with the exposed adult or the caregivers of the child who was exposed

WHEN TO SEEK A HIGHER LEVEL OF CARE

Body fluids can be contaminated with a variety of infectious diseases. All body fluid exposures should be referred to a healthcare professional to determine level of risk and necessary testing and treatment to mitigate risk.

Eye Injury

TREATMENT

Minor eye irritation (AAO 2023; Head Start 2022b; Nemours Children's Health 2018a):

- Wash hands before attending to the child.
- Wear gloves.
- Keep the child from rubbing their eye.
- Rinse the eye.
  - Hold the child's head over a sink, facing down and to the side, and hold the eye open.
  - Gently pour water over the eye for five minutes and see whether the object is out. Repeat up to two more times if the object does not come out of the eye.
  - If the eye remains irritated, take the child to see a physician.

Object stuck in eye (AAO 2023; WebMD 2022):

- Protect the eye.
  - Tape a paper cup over the eye.
  - Do not try to remove the object.
  - Go to the ED.

Minor cut or scratch around eye (AAO 2023; WebMD 2022):

- Wear gloves.
- Stop the bleeding.
  - Hold gauze on the wound for 10 minutes.
- Clean the injury.
  - Cover the eye with a cloth for protection, and wash the area with clean water for a few minutes.
- Apply antibiotic ointment if the wound is not too close to the eye and there is no danger of getting the ointment in the eye.

Black eye, bruising, or swelling (AAO 2023; Nemours Children's Health 2018a):

- Check for further injury.
  - Look for signs of broken bones in the face, damage to the eye, or a head injury. If you suspect any of these, go to the ED.
  - If the black eye was caused by something hitting the eye, it needs to be evaluated by a physician.
- Apply cold such as placing a cold pack on the area for 20 minutes each hour to lessen swelling. Repeat for four hours. Don't press on the eye.
- Consider giving pain medication like acetaminophen if allowed by the parent or caregiver.

Chemical exposure (AAO 2023; Nemours Children's Health 2018a; Kaushik & Bird 2022):

- Wash hands before attending to child.
- Wear gloves.
- Prevent rubbing of the eye.
- Immediately rinse the eye.
  - Hold the child's head over a sink, facing down and to the side, and hold the eye open. If outside, use whatever clean water source is closest.
  - Pour water over the eye for 15–20 minutes.
  - If the chemical is both eyes, rinse them in a shower if available.

WHEN TO SEEK A HIGHER LEVEL OF CARE

- An object, such as a piece of glass or metal or a pencil, was stuck in an eye
- Problems seeing after an eye injury
- Chemicals splashed into eye
- Younger than 1 year old
- Hit in the eye with an object
- Has continuing tearing
- Eye is extremely sensitive to light
- Child keeps blinking
- Painful, swollen, or red area near the eye
- Cut on the eyeball or eyelid

Mouth and Dental Injury

TREATMENT

Toothache (AAP 2019a; CDC 2022c; Head Start 2022a, 2023b, 2023c):

If a child has a toothache, the tooth is likely decayed. Contact the caregivers to schedule a dental appointment as soon as possible. If there is permission to provide an over-the-counter pain reliever, such as acetaminophen, provide the child with an age-appropriate dose.

Tongue or lip injury (AAP 2019a; McTigue, Thompson, & Azadani 2023):

- Wear gloves.
- Clean the injured area and press a clean piece of gauze or a cotton swab on it to stop the bleeding.
- Keep the child's head up and facing forward to prevent choking.
- Put ice wrapped in a lean cloth on the area to reduce swelling.

A chipped or cracked tooth (AAP 2019a; Keels & the Section on Oral Health 2014; Silk 2021):

- If a child's tooth is chipped or cracked, contact the child's caregivers and dentist immediately.
- Clean the injured area and if the child can rinse, have them rinse with water.
- Press a clean piece of gauze or a cotton swab on the gum around the tooth to stop any bleeding.
- If there are other injuries around the mouth, apply ice wrapped in a clean cloth on the area to reduce swelling.

A knocked out tooth (AAP 2019a; Keels & the Section on Oral Health 2014; Silk 2021):

- Check the child's health record to see if it is a primary tooth or permanent tooth.
- Do not try to put the tooth back into the mouth.
- Clean the injured area.
- If there is bleeding, have the child bite on a clean piece of gauze on the area for 15–30 minutes to stop it.

Keep the tooth moist by transporting it in milk or the child's saliva or by wrapping the tooth in a wet cloth.

Tooth loosened, moved or pushed into the gum (AAP 2019a; Keels & the Section on Oral Health 2014; Silk 2021):

- Contact caregivers and dentist immediately.
- Wear gloves.
- If the child can rinse, have them rinse with water.
- Press a clean piece of gauze or a cotton swab on the gum around the tooth to stop bleeding.
- If there are other injuries around the mouth, put ice wrapped in a clean cloth on the area to reduce swelling.

WHEN TO SEEK A HIGHER LEVEL OF CARE

- When a child has sustained a serious injury to the tonsils, soft palate, or back of the throat (e.g., injuries sustained from falling with a pencil or toothbrush in the mouth)
- Bleeding from the tongue or lip does not stop after 30 minutes
- Child is having trouble breathing
- Gaping cut of the lip, tongue, or inside the mouth that may need stitches
- Severe pain with no improvement two hours after taking pain medicine
- Trouble swallowing fluids or spit
- Cannot fully open or close the mouth
- Younger than 1 year old
- Fever and mouth looks infected
- Any dental injury requires immediate dental care.
- Any knocked out tooth should ideally be seen by the dentist within one hour.
- Permanent tooth (usually erupt between ages 6 and 8), contact the parents and dentist immediately

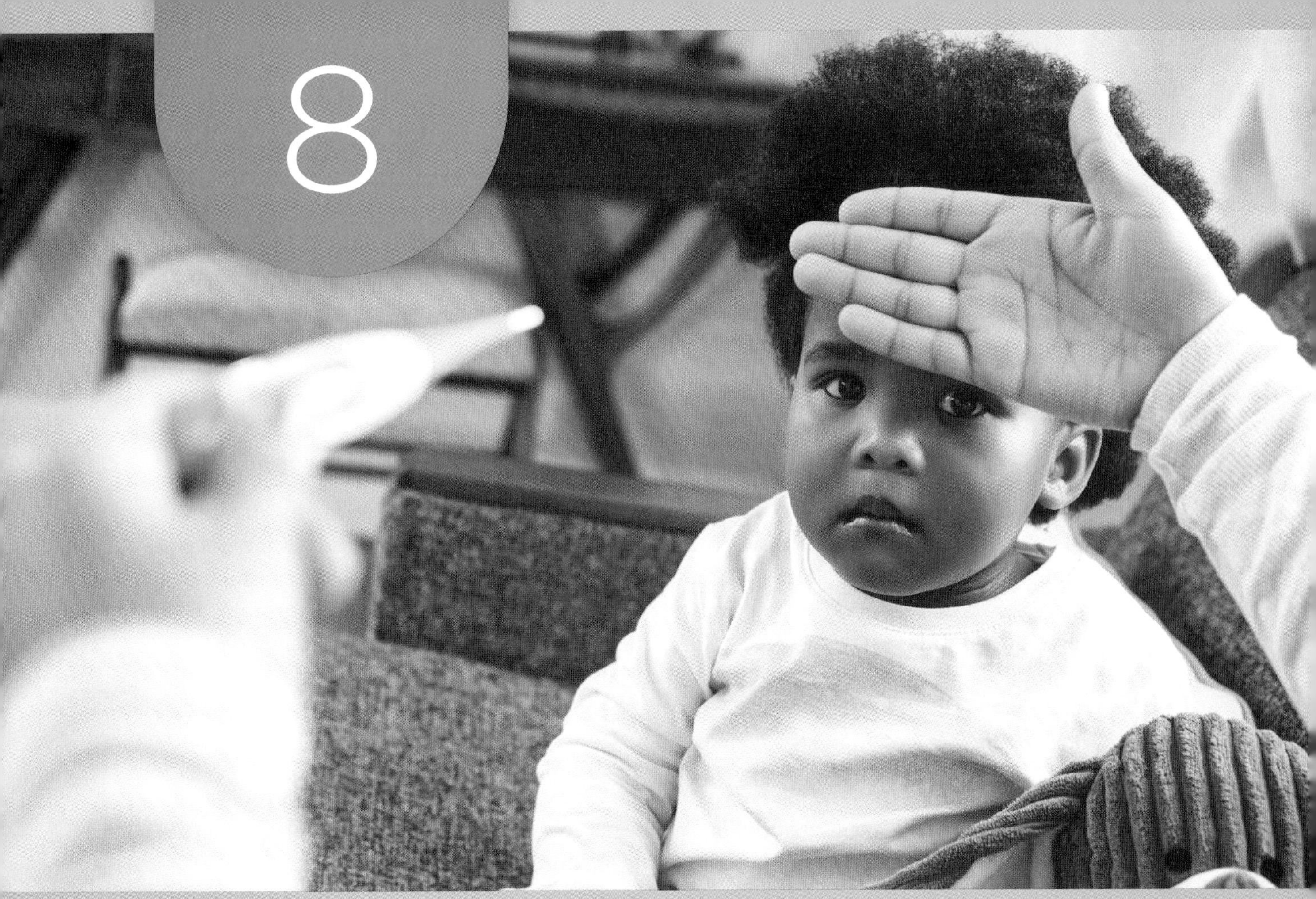

Understanding Common Illnesses and Conditions

TERRI MCFADDEN

LEARNING OBJECTIVES

- To understand typical signs and symptoms of several common illnesses
- To recognize potential risks and triggers for illnesses within the early childhood education environment
- To identify best practices to prepare staff members to manage illnesses in the early learning program
- To describe both basic assessment and intervention for ill children and understand the illnesses that require immediate intervention by healthcare professionals
- To understand when cough and fever require next levels of care

Children can exhibit different health symptoms or conditions that can be innocuous or serious. Fevers, coughs, and nosebleeds are common conditions that all educators will see in children. Viral illnesses also occur frequently in young children and are quite contagious (Tesini 2022). Knowing when these symptoms or conditions are more serious (e.g., when a cough is more than perhaps the common cold) is important for educators to understand so that they are better able to maintain the health and safety of the children they serve. This chapter discusses several common illnesses and conditions and describes how educators can identify and treat them (Shope & Hashikawa 2023).

Fever

Fever is a common issue among young children, but fever itself causes little harm and actually can be a good thing. It is often the body's way of fighting infections (AAP 2022a; Nemours Children's Health 2022). Body temperatures normally fluctuate throughout the day, but fever occurs when the rectal temperature is elevated above 100.4°F (38.0°C) (CDC 2017a; Stanford Medicine Children's Health 2019). Exercise, warm clothing, and hot weather can cause a small rise in temperature, but normal temperatures do not exceed 100.4°F (38°C). The average normal body temperature is 98.6°F (37°C), with a normal range between 97.5°F (36.4°C) and 99.5°F (37.5°C) (AAP 2015b; CDC 2017a; Nemours Children's Health 2022).

A child who has a fever may be fussy, uncomfortable, warm to the touch, flushed, and sweaty. If the child is older than 6 months and has a fever, they may not need to be treated for the fever unless they are uncomfortable. If they are drinking, eating, sleeping normally, and able to play, it may be appropriate to observe before providing treatment (Stanford Medicine Children's Health 2019).

Thermometers and Taking Temperature

Early learning program staff members should be properly trained to take an accurate temperature. There are many types of thermometers, each with recommended usage and accuracy.

Follow all program guidelines regarding exclusion from the program for illness based on *Caring for Our Children* Standard 3.6.1.1 regarding exclusion (see also Table 9.1) and inclusion criteria. Since most fevers in young children are caused by infectious diseases, often viral illnesses, children will need to be dismissed to caregivers for temperatures greater than 100°F to keep themselves and their classmates safe (AAP 2018, 2022a, 2022c; *CFOC* Standards 9.2.4.1, 3.1.1.1, and 3.6.1.1).

Types of Thermometers

Always use a digital thermometer to check someone's temperature. Because of the potential for mercury exposure or ingestion, glass mercury thermometers have been phased out and are no longer recommended. Various types of digital thermometers are available (AAP 2020, 2022a; Mayo Clinic 2022).

Different types of thermometers measure temperatures using different areas of the body.

- Rectal thermometers are used in the rectum.
- Oral thermometers are used in the mouth.

- Temporal artery thermometers use an infrared scanner to measure the temperature of the temporal artery in the forehead.
- Armpit (axillary) and ear (tympanic membrane) thermometers are less accurate.

No matter which type of thermometer you use, take these precautions when using it:

- Read the instructions that came with the thermometer.
- Clean the thermometer before and after each use with rubbing alcohol or soap and lukewarm water.
- Don't use the same thermometer for both oral and rectal temperatures. Get two and label which is to be used in each location.
- Never leave a child unattended while taking their temperature.

How to Take a Temperature Using Different Types of Thermometers

- **Temporal Artery Temperature**
  - Turn on the digital thermometer. Gently sweep it across the forehead and read the number (Figure 8.1).

Figure 8.1. Taking a temporal artery temperature. (Copyright @ Getty Images.)

- **Oral Temperature**
  - Turn on the digital thermometer. Place the thermometer tip under the tongue.
  - Close the mouth around the thermometer for the recommended amount of time or until the thermometer beep indicates it's done.
  - Remove the thermometer and read the number.
- **Armpit Temperature**
  - Turn on the digital thermometer. Place the thermometer under the armpit, making sure it touches skin, not clothing.
  - Hold the thermometer tightly in place until the thermometer beep indicates it's done.
  - Remove the thermometer and read the number.
- **Ear Temperature**
  - Turn on the digital thermometer. Gently place it in the ear canal no further than indicated by the instructions that came with the device.
  - Hold the thermometer tightly in place until the thermometer beep indicates it's done.
  - Remove the thermometer and read the number.
- **Rectal Temperature (for Infants)**
  - Turn on the digital thermometer and dab petroleum jelly or another lubricant on the tip of the thermometer.
  - Lay the child on their stomach or side, with knees flexed.
  - Carefully insert the tip a half to one inch (1.3 to 2.5 centimeters) into the rectum.
  - Hold the thermometer and child still until the thermometer beep indicates it's done. To avoid injury, don't let go of the thermometer while it's inside the child.
  - Remove the thermometer and read the number.

Temperature cutoffs for fever can also vary according to the type of thermometer used (Mayo Clinic 2022). The following thermometer readings generally indicate a fever:

- Rectal, ear, or temporal artery temperature of 100.4°F (38°C) or higher
- Oral temperature of 100°F (37.8°C) or higher
- Armpit temperature of 99°F (37.2°C) or higher

More than a Cough

A cough is the sound made when the body's reflex clears the airway of mucus or irritants. Coughing protects children by removing mucus, irritating substances, and infections from their respiratory tract. Coughing can be voluntary or involuntary and can be sudden and acute or chronic. Children can cough several times a day or have coughing episodes lasting up to a couple of weeks if they have a viral infection. The majority of children have brief repeated periods of coughing due to viral upper respiratory tract infections, such as the common cold (AAAAI 2020). Since healthy preschool-age children attending early learning programs have been found to have up to eight viral respiratory

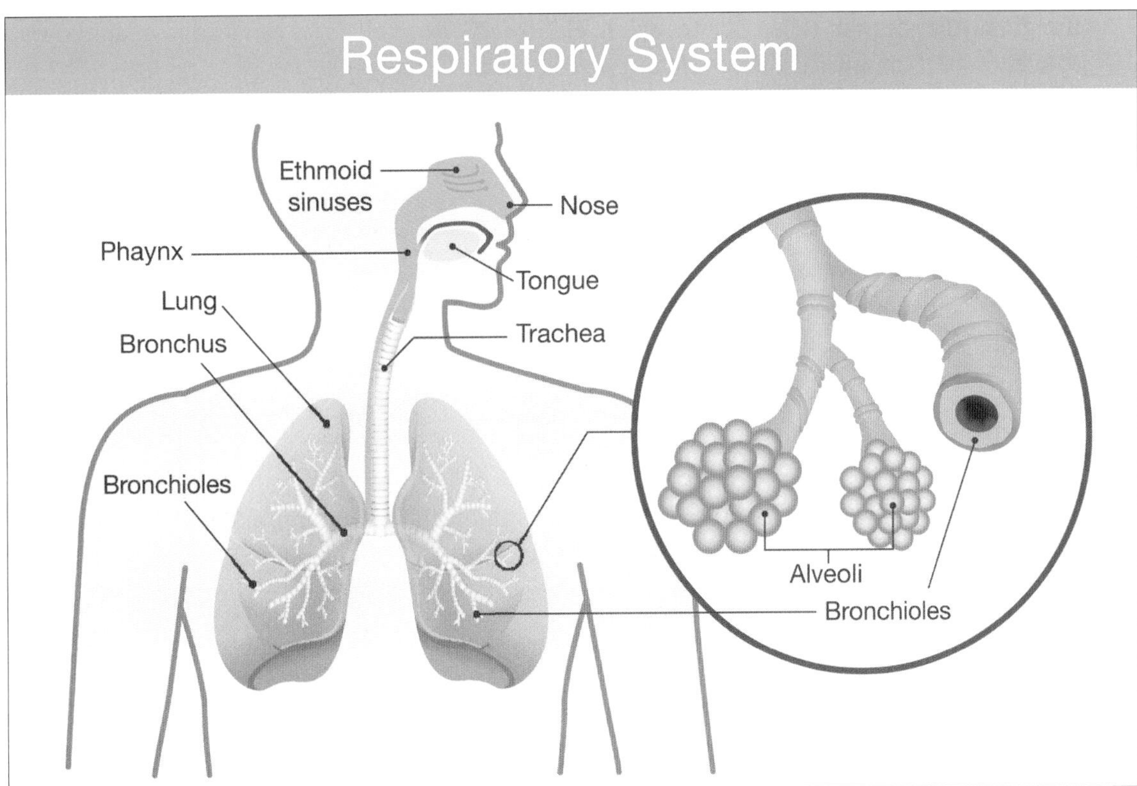

Figure 8.2. (Copyright @ Getty Images.)

infections with cough each year (AAAAI 2020), coughing is a common finding in the program. Although painless, coughing may leave children fatigued and may make breathing difficult if it is continuous.

There are many different causes for coughing in young children, both common and innocuous and more serious (AAAAI 2020; Seattle Children's Hospital 2022). Typically, self-limited causes of cough are as follows:

› **Common cold.** Most coughs are a part of a cold that includes the lower airway (lungs). The young child may have viral bronchiolitis or bronchitis, which is inflammation of the mucous membrane in the bronchus and its tiny branches, the bronchioles. The bronchus delivers air to the lower airway leading to the lungs (see Figure 8.2).
› **Irritants.** For example, tobacco smoke, automobile exhaust, or air pollution.
› **Nasal and sinus disease.** Postnasal drip caused by rhinitis (runny nose) from a cold, allergies, or sinusitis (sinus infection) can cause cough. Usually, other symptoms are present, but sometimes cough is the only symptom.
› **Stomach and esophageal conditions.** In some children, stomach acid can move up into the throat. This is called *reflux* and may occur silently without heartburn. Some children may develop a hoarse voice or signs of choking.
› **Post-viral infections.** After having a viral respiratory infection, some children can have cough that lasts for weeks but will eventually go away.

- **Allergies.** Allergies can cause a dry cough in children. Serious allergies can lead to anaphylaxis (see section on "Anaphylaxis").
- **Habit cough.** This is a persistent cough that has no clear physical cause. The cough is usually dry and repetitive. It typically happens when the child is awake, not while asleep.

Serious causes of cough include

- **Asthma (see "Asthma").** Most children with asthma have inflamed or swollen airways, which commonly cause wheezing. However, sometimes the only symptom of asthma is a cough that is made worse by viral infections or that happens when the child is asleep, exercising, or exposed to cold temperatures (CDC 2022b).
- **Pneumonia.** A child may develop pneumonia from viruses, bacteria, or fungi. Bacterial infections can lead to fever, rapid breathing, grunting, wheezing, or chest pain.
- **Viral bronchiolitis.** Bronchiolitis is a common viral infection in infants and children younger than 2 years old. Swollen small airways (bronchioles) make breathing difficult, causing wheezing and cough (see section on "Respiratory Syncytial Virus [RSV]") (Justice & Le 2022).
- **Inhaled foreign body.** Foreign bodies, such as toys and foods, can be accidentally inhaled by young children. This type of cough can persist for weeks or months (Concepcion 2018).
- **Pertussis.** Pertussis, which is also known as whooping cough, is a highly contagious bacterial infection that can be very serious, especially for babies. Pertussis is known as whooping cough because of the "whooping" sound that people can make when gasping for air after a fit of coughing. These coughing fits can go on for up to 10 weeks or more (CDC 2022c; *CFOC* Standard 7.3.7).

SIGNS AND SYMPTOMS

Coughing is the body's way of responding to irritation in the throat or airways and results from the sudden movement of air from the lungs through the throat. It can be accompanied by

- A runny nose
- A feeling of liquid dripping into the back of the throat
- Frequent throat clearing and sore throat
- Hoarseness
- Wheezing and shortness of breath
- Heartburn or reflux
- Coughing up mucus or phlegm
- Coughing up blood (rare)

See "Chapter Appendix 8.1: Common Illnesses and Conditions: Specific Treatments and When to Seek a Higher Level of Care" for treatment protocols.

Asthma

Asthma is the most common chronic disease among children who attend an early learning program. These children have an increased risk of asthma due to early respiratory infections (CDC 2017b; NHLBI 2008). Asthma occurs in 7 to 10 percent of all preschool and school-age children, so it is highly likely that the program will have at least one child with asthma in their care. Asthma is also the leading cause of school absences—10.5 million missed days of school were documented in 2010 (CDC 2022a, 2022b). Furthermore, there have been high levels of indoor allergens noted in early learning programs. Most notably, pet dander is present even when there are no animals on site (EPA 2022).

An asthma flare-up (attack) is when the child develops asthma symptoms like coughing, wheezing, or mild breathlessness. When children have an asthma flare-up, the air passages of their lungs become temporarily narrowed, swollen, and inflamed. They also produce a thick mucus, causing the child to have difficulty breathing. The symptoms usually resolve with treatment and/or removal of asthma triggers. Asthma cannot be cured but can be controlled with appropriate care.

Children with asthma can be grouped into three categories: mild (infrequent) intermittent asthma, frequent intermittent asthma, and persistent asthma (NHLBI 2007).

Children with *infrequent intermittent asthma* usually need treatment only for asthma attacks. They may not need medication between attacks unless the attacks are severe. Children with *frequent intermittent asthma* might have an intermittent cough or a wheeze or cough triggered by exercise. These children may need to use a prevention medication each day. Children with persistent asthma have symptoms at least once per week, and they may need to take one or several prevention medications each day.

SIGNS AND SYMPTOMS

Although the signs and symptoms of asthma may vary by child, common signs and symptoms include the following (NHLBI 2007):

- Coughing (children often have a cough as an early or only symptom of asthma)
- Complaint of tightness in the chest
- Wheezing (a high pitched, whistle-like sound when exhaling)
- Rapid breathing or difficulty breathing
- Unusual tiredness
- Difficulty playing, eating, or talking

Signs and symptoms of a severe asthma episode include

- Flaring nostrils or open mouth
- Bluish color to the lips or nails (late sign: call 911)
- Sucking in chest or neck muscles (retractions)

Asthma medications can be divided into two categories. *Rescue medications,* such as albuterol, help to open the air passages during an asthma attack. *Controller medications,* such as inhaled steroids, are used to prevent an attack or settle the lungs after an attack. Asthma medications are generally safe, and children usually experience only minor side effects, such as tremulousness or fast heart rate (Bush & Fleming 2015; CDC 2023a).

Triggers and Prevention

Asthma flare-ups (attacks) are usually started by a trigger that causes the asthma to flare. Examples of asthma triggers include (CDC 2017b; CDC 2022b; NHLBI 2008)

- Allergies to substances, such as pollen, mold, cockroaches, animal dander, or dust mites
- Allergies to a particular food (see section on "Anaphylaxis")
- Infections like colds or other viruses
- Irritants, such as cigarette smoke, cleaning supplies, air pollutants, or other airborne substances (e.g., some arts and crafts supplies)
- Cold air or sudden temperature or weather changes
- Exercise or overexertion
- Strong emotions, such as laughing, crying, and/or stress

To prevent asthma flares, staff members should ask about and document medical history (Bush & Fleming 2015; CDC 2022b, 2023a; EPA 2020). (See also "Chapter 3: Enrollment, Health Documentation, Assessments, and Screenings.") It is important for staff members to learn about the child's triggers, symptoms, and treatment. Every child with asthma needs an asthma control and management plan. The documentation should include medications, indications for using medications, directions for use, and dosages. Specific questions include the following:

- What is the severity of the child's asthma? Are there any previous hospitalizations or emergency department visits? How many asthma attacks occurred in the last year?
- How should the severity of an episode be judged? Is rest or treatment needed? When should the parent or caregiver be called?
- Other:
    - What are the triggers for asthma flare-up?
    - What medications does the child routinely take?
    - How is their spacer or nebulizer used?
    - What are the next steps if symptoms do not resolve with the treatment?
    - What are the standard emergency protocols and procedures?

Controlling Triggers

See *Caring for Our Children* standards regarding controlling asthma triggers. These include *Caring for Our Children* Standards 3.3.0.1 regarding routine cleaning, 5.2.8.1 regarding integrated pest control, and 5.2.1.15 regarding the quality of outdoor and indoor environments.

Staff members should work to do the following:

- Control dust mites.
  - Keep surfaces including furniture and floors clean of dust.
  - Wash small rugs, nap mats, blankets, bed linens, and fabric toys in water 130°F (54°C) weekly.
  - Enclose beds and pillows children sleep on in allergy-proof covers.
  - Avoid soft mattresses and upholstered furniture.
  - Avoid clutter.
- Prevent and control mold and mildew.
  - Provide ventilation and airflow in rooms and hallways.
  - Use exhaust fans in bathrooms, kitchens, and basements to help remove humidity.
  - Remove wet carpeting and padding that does not dry within 24 hours.
- Avoid and control additional allergens (CDC 2022b; *CFOC* Standard 5.2.9.7; EPA 2020; NHLBI 2008).
  - Avoid use of latex gloves and other latex products.
  - Clear play areas of fallen leaves and cut grass.
  - Consider closing windows during times of high-pollen count.
  - Do not allow smoking on premises.
  - Use arts and craft materials with fragrance in well-ventilated areas.
  - Avoid air fragrance sprays and air fresheners.
  - Avoid cleaning supplies with strong smells when children are present.
  - Shampoo rugs and upholstery with low emission, fragrance-free products and dry thoroughly.

Anaphylaxis

Anaphylaxis is a potentially life-threatening allergic reaction that affects the whole body. It involves a group of symptoms that can affect multiple organ systems in the body and happens when the body has an intense response to an allergen (Linzer 2022; Shaker et al. 2020). The most dangerous of these symptoms include breathing problems and a drop in the blood pressure, or shock, and they can be fatal. Symptoms usually happen within minutes of contact with the allergen or allergy-causing substance. Exposures to foods and stinging insects are responsible for the majority of these potentially life-threatening allergies, although drugs and latex are also potential offenders (Shaker et al. 2020).

Approximately 1 to 2 percent of the general population are at risk of anaphylaxis from food allergens and insect stings, with a lower prevalence for drugs and latex. Food allergy occurs in 2 to 8 percent of children (AAFA & EAF 2022; *CFOC* Standard 4.2.0.10; Shaker et al. 2020). It is important to note that children with asthma have a higher risk of anaphylaxis after exposure to an allergen (AAFA & EAF 2022; *CFOC* Standard 4.2.0.10; Shaker et al. 2020). As a result, they should be monitored closely for potentially life-threatening allergic events. Fortunately, deaths from anaphylaxis are rare, with approximately 50 deaths related to anaphylaxis caused by insect stings and 100 food-related anaphylaxis deaths each year (Shaker et al. 2020). However, quick recognition and action can save lives.

SIGNS AND SYMPTOMS

Symptoms of allergic reactions can include

- Hives
- Itching (of any part of the body)
- Swelling (of any part of the body)
- Red, watery eyes
- Runny nose
- Vomiting
- Diarrhea
- Stomach cramps
- Change of voice-hoarse or high-pitched
- Coughing
- Wheezing
- Throat tightness or closing
- Difficulty swallowing
- Difficulty breathing
- Sense of doom
- Dizziness
- Fainting or loss of consciousness
- Skin or mouth become pale or blue appearing

Educating Staff on Prevention Strategies

Avoidance of specific allergens is the critical foundation for preventing anaphylaxis. The foods that most commonly produce allergic reactions are peanuts, tree nuts, shellfish, fish, milk, eggs, soy, and wheat (AAP 2019a; Food and Nutrition Service 2001). Reactions to peanuts, tree nuts, fish, and shellfish tend to be life-long problems and are more likely to cause severe reactions. While it is difficult to completely avoid allergenic foods because they may be hidden or accidentally ingested, it is possible to reduce exposure within the school setting (AAFA & EAF 2022; AAP 2019a; *CFOC* Standard 4.2.0.10; Food and Nutrition Service 2001). Understanding the specific allergies of individual children is critical to avoid unintentional exposures. Staff members should also receive training about common terms for allergenic foods. Ingredient statements should be carefully read before giving the child any food (Figure 8.3).

Staff members should receive training to increase their knowledge about allergies to food, medications, insect bites and stings, and other products and learn the difference between anaphylaxis and milder symptoms of allergies and anaphylaxis (AAP 2019a; AAP & NASN 2012; *CFOC* Standard 1.4.3.1; Linzer 2022; Shaker et al. 2020; Trella 2019).

IMMEDIATE IMPACT

Tips for Avoiding Exposure to Allergens

- Children should not be allowed to trade foods or eating utensils.
- Surfaces should be washed clean of contaminating foods, and food used for lessons should be carefully reviewed for potential allergens.
- Handwashing should occur after food handling (AAFA & EAF 2022; *CFOC* Standard 3.2.2.1).

Allergy Advice
Contains: Egg, Mustard
May contain:
Nuts, Peanuts, Sesame Seeds, Celery, Wheat, Barley, Fish, Soybeans, Milk, Sulphites and Cereals containing Gluten.

Figure 8.3. Food labels contain information about possible allergens. (Copyright @ Getty Images.)

Food service staff should be instructed to utilize necessary measures to prevent cross-contamination. Refer to the US Department of Agriculture Food and Nutrition Service's (2001) guidance document entitled, "Accommodating Children with Special Dietary Needs in the School Nutrition Programs: Guidance for School Food Service Staff."

Treatment

Treatment protocols are critical components to the management of anaphylaxis, as accidental exposures can happen despite avoidance strategies. Program staff members should have written instructions from the child's physician signed by the caregivers providing easy-to-follow steps for recognizing a reaction and administering medication (AAP & NASN 2012; *CFOC* Standards 1.4.3.1, 4.2.0.10, 9.2.4.1; Shaker et al. 2020; Trella 2019). Food Allergy Research & Education (FARE) has developed an allergy and anaphylaxis Treatment Plan Food Allergy & Anaphylaxis Emergency Care Plan (FoodAllergy.org).

All teachers and staff members responsible for the care of children should have familiarity with basic first aid and resuscitation techniques (*CFOC* Standards 1.4.3.1, 3.6.3.3, and 9.2.4.1) (see "Chapter 7: First Aid and Injuries."). It is critical that training include the delivery of standard emergency procedures for children with known allergies, such as using an epinephrine autoinjector (e.g., EpiPen Jr.) (Shaker et al. 2020). They should receive training in the emergency administration of epinephrine autoinjectors or other medications that are prescribed by the child's healthcare provider and are permitted by caregiver consent. Follow guidance for medication administration provided in *Caring for Our Children* Standard 3.6.3.1 (Figure 8.4).

Epinephrine is the first drug that should be used in the emergency management of a child having a potentially life-threatening allergic reaction. Epinephrine is available in several self-delivery administration devices, which program staff members should be trained to use. There are no

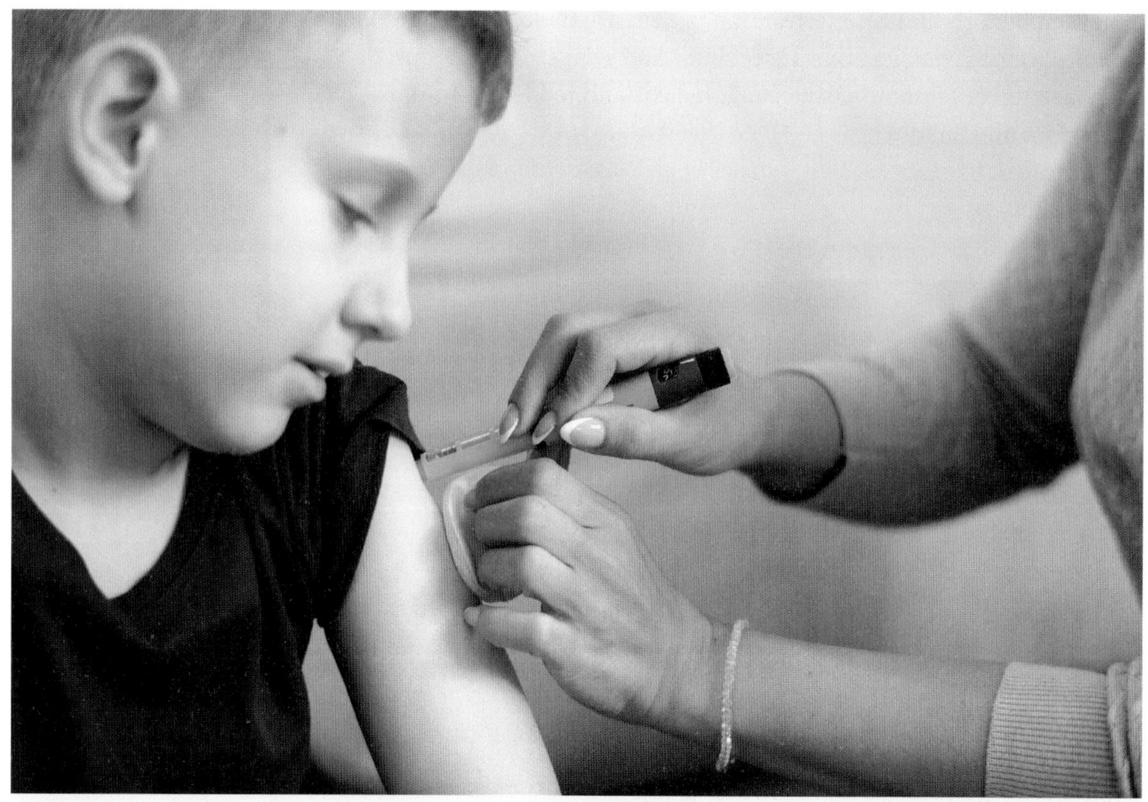

Figure 8.4. Knowing how to correctly use an epinephrine autoinjector (e.g., EpiPen Jr.) is critical to managing potential life-threatening allergic reactions. (Copyright @ Getting Images.)

contraindications to the use of epinephrine for a life-threatening allergic reaction (Cleveland Clinic 2022). It is recommended that epinephrine be given at the start of any reaction occurring in conjunction with exposure to a known or suspected allergen. If there has been a previous history of severe cardiovascular collapse in response to an allergen, the physician may request administration of epinephrine immediately after an insect sting or ingestion of the offending food and before any reaction has begun (Shaker et al. 2020).

If prescribed, every child should have the epinephrine autoinjector labeled with their name and classroom. Epinephrine should be kept in locations that are easily accessible and not locked away. Teachers should be instructed about the location of the device and instructed regarding its use. Ideally, the device should be kept in the classroom and passed along to individuals responsible for activities outside of the classroom. Expiration dates should be checked regularly.

When to Seek a Higher Level of Care

Medical supervision is needed for at least four hours after an episode of anaphylaxis (Shaker et al. 2020). Emergency medical services (EMS) should be called immediately for any child with a suspected episode of anaphylaxis. All children who have received emergency epinephrine should be immediately transported to a hospital even if symptoms appear to have resolved. In most cases, epinephrine will be effective after one injection; however, further treatments may be required. Additional doses may be given every 15–20 minutes during transport, ideally under the direction of a medical provider (AAP 2019a; Shaker et al. 2020).

Ear Infection

Ear infection is the most common childhood illness other than the common cold and one of the most frequent reasons that young children visit healthcare providers (CDC 2021; Talathi et al. 2017). There are two major forms of ear infection that often affect children—*otitis media*, affecting the middle ear, and *otitis externa* (swimmer's ear), affecting the external ear canal (CDC 2021). Although these distinct types of ear infections exist, most commonly, references to ear infections are focused on infections of the middle ear, also known as *acute otitis media* (AOM).

Acute ear infections are defined as viral or bacterial infections of the middle ear—the space behind the eardrum. Many times, an ear infection happens after a cold or respiratory infection and are considered a possible complication of a cold. When a child has an ear infection, the middle ear space fills with infected fluid that pushes against the eardrum, potentially causing fever and pain. If the pressure in the middle ear builds too high, the eardrum can rupture (Cleveland Clinic 2020a).

Risk Factors

Children develop ear infections much more often than adults for a variety of reasons related to their anatomy and potential exposures. Young children more commonly experience ear infections because

- They have shorter, more horizontal eustachian tubes that allow viruses and bacteria to grow when drainage is impaired by a respiratory infection
- They have large glands called adenoids that interfere with the opening of the eustachian tubes
- Their immune systems are not fully developed, and they may not yet have protection against some of the common viruses and bacteria

SIGNS AND SYMPTOMS

Signs and symptoms of ear infection can be nonspecific but include

- Ear pain, which may manifest in young babies as rubbing or tugging at ears, crying more than usual, difficulty sleeping, and/or irritability
- Loss of appetite, which may be noticeable in younger children especially with bottle-feeding, which may cause pressure or pain and decreased desire to eat
- Irritability
- Poor sleep
- Fever
- Drainage from the ear
- Trouble hearing

Ear infections occur most often in children who are between 3 months old and 3 years old and are common until age 8. In the United States, 23 percent of children experience at least one episode of AOM by age 1 year, 60 percent experience an AOM before age 3 years, and up to 24 percent have three or more episodes (Kaur, Morris, & Pichichero 2017). Ear infections tend to happen more often in the fall and winter, as this is the time when children are more likely to be exposed to cold and flu viruses.

Prevention

There are many factors implicated in the prevention of ear infections, such as breastfeeding beyond 6 months old and keeping immunizations up to date (Chonmaitree et al. 2016). Vaccines have resulted in a decline in overall cases of AOM, and surgeries are performed for chronic AOM (Hu et al. 2022; Kaur, Morris, & Pichichero 2017).

Further prevention strategies include (NIDCD 2022)

- Vaccinating children against the flu
- Vaccinating children with the 15-valent pneumococcal conjugate vaccine or current version. The vaccine is strongly recommended for children attending early learning programs (*CFOC* Standard 7.2).

Treatment

Treatment of ear infections depends on the age of the child, the severity of the infection, the nature of the infection (first versus repeated or ongoing), and the presence of fluid in the ear for a lengthy period of time.

Middle ear infections often clear up on their own after a few days without specific treatment, but children younger than 2 years old will likely require antibiotic treatment (CDC 2021, Frost et al. 2021). Also, treatment can be determined by the type and severity of the ear infection, frequency of infections, length of the infection, and likelihood that the infection can affect hearing long-term. If a doctor prescribes an antibiotic, most children will require a 10-day course, but some may be prescribed a course of five to seven days depending on the type of infection and the choice of antibiotics based on the age of the child. (CDC 2021).

Some children with ongoing or frequently occurring ear infection may be required to have tympanostomy tubes placed in their ears (Hoberman et al. 2021). Small plastic or metal tubes can be inserted into the eardrum to help drain fluid. Children who have tubes will need to have the outer ear kept dry and free of dirty water, such as lake water, until the eardrum heals completely. (See also "Appendix 8.1: Common Illnesses and Conditions: Specific Treatments and When to Seek a Higher Level of Care" at the end of the chapter.)

Return to the Early Learning Program

Ear infections are common in young children and are not considered to be contagious. However, the common viral illnesses that can lead to ear infections are quite contagious. *Caring for Our Children* Standard 3.1.1 references the importance of using the daily health check, which should be conducted as soon as possible after children enter the program, serving as an opportunity to identify illness and to reduce the transmission of infectious diseases. Children with ear infections can return to the early learning program when they can participate in all of the program's activities and the child's care does not require more than the staff members can provide without putting the health and safety of other children at risk (AAP 2022d).

Conjunctivitis

Conjunctivitis is an inflammation or irritation of the conjunctiva, the membrane that lines the inside of the eyelids and covers the eyeball. Conjunctivitis is also known as pinkeye because the eye looks pink or red (Stanford Medicine Children's Health, n.d.). Although conjunctivitis is uncomfortable and can be extremely contagious, it usually resolves without treatment. Conjunctivitis is the most common cause of red eyes in children (Rainsbury et al. 2016) and can be divided into two groups: *newborn conjunctivitis* and *childhood conjunctivitis*. Newborn conjunctivitis involving babies less than 1 month old can be caused by a variety of exposures to the newborn during the birth period and usually requires immediate assessment to rule out serious illness (CDC 2019b). This type of conjunctivitis is not typically managed by the program staff and should be evaluated by a healthcare professional.

The swelling and irritation of the conjunctiva seen in childhood conjunctivitis is typically caused by viruses, bacteria, allergies, and occasionally irritants (CDC 2019a). If the conjunctivitis is caused by an infection, it is highly contagious and can spread from one eye to the other or to other children and adults who may touch infected fluid from the eye (CDC 2019a; *CFOC* Standards 7.1 and 7.5.1). While viral and bacterial conjunctivitis infections are both very contagious, viral infections remain contagious for the entire time that the child has symptoms. Bacterial conjunctivitis can remain contagious for 24 to 48 hours after starting treatment (Stanford Medicine Children's Health, n.d.). Conjunctivitis happens frequently in young children, and large outbreaks can occur in group settings as the infection can spread easily from one child to another (CDC 2019a; Stanford Medicine Children's Health, n.d.). While highly contagious, the vast majority of cases of viral conjunctivitis are self-limited and can be thought of like the common cold (AAP 2015a). Although often treated with antibiotics, some cases of bacterial conjunctivitis may resolve completely without treatment (CDC 2019a). The need for treatment will be decided by the child's healthcare professional after considering the child's specific history and condition.

Types of Conjunctivitis

Healthcare professionals will need to determine the underlying cause of conjunctivitis, but tips for distinguishing the different types are shown in the "Sign and Symptoms" box on page 172 (AAP 2015a; CDC 2019a).

Treatment

Treatment depends on the child's symptoms, age, and general health. It will also depend on the underlying cause of the conjunctivitis. *Bacterial infections* may be treated with antibiotic eye drops and should resolve in five to seven days. *Viral infections* usually do not need treatment; however,

SIGNS AND SYMPTOMS

Typically, children with any form of conjunctivitis will have some degree of eye discomfort (AOA, n.d.).

Viral conjunctivitis causes pink, watery, and itchy eyes, but it can be difficult to determine whether a child has bacterial or viral conjunctivitis. It may affect one or both eyes, and may initially involve only one eye then often spreads to the other eye in one to two days. Symptoms usually get worse over the first three to five days then gradually improve

Bacterial conjunctivitis causes red, itchy, and often painful eyes. It can affect one or both eyes and is often accompanied by yellowish discharge and mild swelling.

Allergic conjunctivitis causes itchy, watery, pink eyes that tend to occur in a seasonal nature. It generally affects both eyes.

Irritant conjunctivitis occurs as pink, watery eyes after contact with an eye irritant (such as sand or chlorine). It resolves quickly without treatment, although contact with some irritants may require eye washing.

Other signs and symptoms include

- Gritty feeling in one or both eyes
- Swelling of the eyelids
- Redness of the conjunctiva
- Mild pain when looking at a light
- Burning in the eyes
- Eyelids that stick together in the morning
- Clear, thin drainage from the eyes
- Sneezing and runny nose
- Stringy discharge from the eyes
- Ear infection
- Sore on eyelids with a crusty appearance

in some cases, antibiotic eye drops may be used to prevent a secondary bacterial infection. *Allergic reactions* may be treated with oral medications or allergy eye drops. Irritant reactions should resolve quickly after removal of the irritant but may require an eye wash (CDC 2019a). (See also "Appendix 8.1: Common Illnesses and Conditions: Specific Treatments and When to Seek a Higher Level of Care.")

Preventing the Spread of Infection

Conjunctivitis can easily spread within the early learning program. Staff members can help to prevent the spread by recognizing and notifying designated staff members for decision making about inclusion in the program (*CFOC* Standard 3.1.1.1).

- Notify parents or caregivers of affected child.
- Alert family members of potentially exposed children.
- Use gloves and good handwashing/sanitizing before and after touching child's eyes.
- Wipe tears or discharge from the child's eye from the inside out and in one direction only. Use a clean portion of the tissue or wipe only.
- Wash staff member's hands and child's hands very carefully after touching or wiping their eyes (*CFOC* Standard 3.2.2.2).
- Do not share towels or washcloths, which can spread infection.

Return to the Early Learning Program

According to the Centers for Disease and Prevention (CDC), schools should allow infected children to remain at the program once any indicated therapy is implemented, except when viral or bacterial conjunctivitis is accompanied by systemic signs of illness. Children can return to the program once they have seen a doctor. If the child is taking an antibiotic, they can return after 24 hours of treatment. Use procedures as outlined in *Caring for Our Children* Standard 3.6.1.1 regarding inclusion and exclusion.

However, infected children should refrain from attending the program if their behavior is such that they cannot avoid close contact with other children. Program staff members should follow *Caring for Our Children* Standard 3.6.1.1 regarding exclusion criteria for early learning. No exclusion should happen unless

- The child is unable to participate, and staff members determine they cannot care for the child without compromising their ability to care of the health and safety the other children in the group
- The child meets other exclusion criteria
- There is a recommendation from the local health department or the child's healthcare professional
- Antibiotics are not required to return to the program

When exclusion criteria are resolved, the child is able to participate and staff members determine they can care for the child without compromising their ability to care for the health and safety of the other children in the group.

Nosebleeds

Nosebleeds are a common childhood occurrence and involves bleeding from tissues inside the nose after small blood vessels break (Johns Hopkins Healthcare 2021; Tunkel et al. 2020). Nosebleeds, also known as epistaxis, usually stop on their own or can be cared for with minor interventions. Nosebleeds are common in children and are usually not serious. They happen most often in the front part of the nose close to the nostrils. This part of the nose has many tiny blood vessels that can be damaged easily. They also happen most often in winter and when the air is dry. While most children will outgrow nosebleeds by their teen years, this is a common issue facing teachers and staff members (Johns Hopkins Healthcare 2021; Yan & Goldman 2021).

Common causes of nosebleeds include the following (Tunkel et al. 2020):

- Dry air
- Picking the nose
- Blowing the nose too hard
- Injury to the nose
- Colds and allergies
- Object in the nose
- Trauma to the nose or face

In many cases, no specific cause for a nosebleed is found.

SIGNS AND SYMPTOMS

- Main symptom is blood dripping or running from the nose
- Usually painless (unless injured or has a sore in the nostril)
- Usually comes from one nostril only

Addressing a nosebleed requires basic first aid management and treatment including (AAP 2019b; *CFOC* Standards 3.2.3.4 and 9.2.4.1; NCECQA 2016)

- Wearing gloves and washing hands after treating a child with a nosebleed.
- Sanitizing any surfaces that come in contact with the child's blood or other nasal secretions.
- Disposing of blood-contaminated waste in double plastic bags and in a manner consistent with program policies.

Respiratory Syncytial Virus (RSV)

Respiratory syncytial virus (RSV) is one of many viruses that can cause major respiratory problems for young children. Although some children will only develop symptoms consistent with a common cold, others can develop significant respiratory disease and even respiratory failure. Unlike viruses that only affect the upper respiratory tract (nose, mouth, and throat), RSV can cause infections deep into the lungs (pneumonia) and breathing passages (bronchiolitis). RSV is the most common cause of inflammation in the lower respiratory tract (AAP 2022b; CDC 2022d), often leading to blocked air passages and difficulty breathing in young children (Piedra & Stark 2021).

RSV is extremely contagious and spreads through droplets expelled from a sick person's coughing or sneezing. The virus can live on hard surfaces (e.g., toys, bedrails, countertops, doorknobs) for hours and on hands for up to 30 minutes (CDC 2022d). Children can easily pick up the virus from direct contact or touching an object that a sick child or adult has also touched. According to the CDC (2022d), people infected with RSV are usually contagious for three to eight days and may become contagious a day or two before they start showing signs of illness. Some infants and people with weakened immune systems can spread the virus even after they stop showing symptoms for up to four weeks (AAP 2022b).

Most children will experience RSV before age 2 years and repeated infections are common throughout childhood (CDC 2022d). The virus can easily spread through the program as sick children spread the disease to others. Young infants can also be exposed to staff members or older siblings who may only have common cold symptoms. However, in the youngest children, the disease can be much more significant. Sometimes RSV can cause inflammation and narrow the breathing passages leading to wheezing (a whistling noise heard with breathing) and difficulty breathing (CDC 2022d). Some children can experience disease that is so severe that they require oxygen and other support to help their breathing. Fortunately, these children are in the minority (AAP 2021; CDC 2022d). The severe illnesses, such as pneumonia or bronchiolitis, will usually resolve in about a week, but cough may persist for weeks. RSV is typically seen in the fall, but these patterns can shift based on seasonal changes and variations according to geography. Outbreaks can also occur outside of typical seasonal patterns (AAP 2021; CDC 2022d).

SIGNS AND SYMPTOMS

Most children with RSV will experience symptoms typical of the common cold including

- Stuffy or runny nose
- Sore throat
- Mild headache
- Cough
- Fever (Note that fever may not always occur with RSV infections.)
- Decreased appetite
- General feeling of illness

In very young infants (younger than 6 months old), the only symptoms of RSV may be (CDC 2022d)

- Irritability
- Decreased activity
- Decreased appetite
- Apnea (pauses in breathing more than 10 seconds)

Treatment

Most cases of RSV will resolve without additional interventions in one to two weeks. While there is no specific treatment for RSV, there are options for preventing RSV in the highest risk children, such as extremely premature babies (AAP 2021, 2022b). Treatment focuses solely on supportive care and providing comfort to the young child (CDC 2022d; Piedra & Stark 2022).

Staff members can manage fever by providing fever reducers, such as acetaminophen or ibuprofen. While acetaminophen and ibuprofen can be used for most children, all aspirin or products containing aspirin should be avoided for children with a viral illness. Aspirin has been associated with the development of Reye syndrome (a condition that causes swelling of the brain and liver) when given to children with some viral illnesses (NINDS 2023b).

Staff members should be trained to handle a medical emergency per *Caring for Our Children* Standard 9.2.4.1 as, on rare occasions, a child with RSV can develop respiratory distress and, potentially, respiratory failure. Getting formal first aid training is the best way to know what to do in case of a medical emergency. Staff members should be trained to administer cardiopulmonary resuscitation (CPR) in case the child develops a respiratory or circulatory emergency. CPR is a lifesaving procedure performed when a child's breathing or heartbeat has stopped (AHA 2020; American Red Cross, n.d.). (See "Chapter 7: First Aid and Injuries" and "Chapter Appendix 8.1: Common Illnesses and Conditions: Specific Treatments and When to Seek a Higher Level of Care.")

Prevention

Outbreaks of RSV are common in early learning programs. *Caring for Our Children* Standard 3.1.1 references the importance of using the daily health check, which should be conducted as soon as possible after children enter the program, as an opportunity to identify illness and to reduce the transmission of infectious diseases. *Caring for Our Children* Standard 3.6.1.1 cites specific inclusion/exclusion/dismissal criteria of ill children, stating that exclusion is needed for some infectious diseases to control contamination and spread, and these diseases need criteria for a child's return. Children with known RSV can return to the program when (AAP 2022d; *CFOC* Standard 7.3.8)

- The child can participate in all the program's activities
- The child's care does not result in more care than the staff members can provide without putting the health and safety of other children at risk

Early learning programs can limit the spread of RSV by (AAP 2018)

- Using good hand washing techniques
- Not allowing children to share food, bottles, toothbrushes, or mouthed toys
- Teaching children and staff members to cover their cough and sneezes
- Throwing away used facial tissues after one use
- Cleaning and sanitizing surfaces regularly and more often during outbreaks

Roseola

Roseola, also known as sixth disease or exanthema subitem, is a viral illness that causes fever and a skin rash. The illness is typically mild and occurs most commonly in children younger than 3 years old, especially in the 6-month to 2-year age range. Older children and adults will commonly develop lifelong immunity after acquiring infections early in childhood (Mullins & Krishnamurthy 2022; Nemours Children's Health 2019). In most children, roseola begins as a mild upper respiratory illness, followed by a high fever. The rash usually develops three to five days into the illness as the fever subsides (Tesini, Epstein, & Caserta 2014). The rash frequently begins on the abdomen or torso, then spreads to the limbs and face. Children with roseola develop small spots or patches that tend to be flat but may be raised. The rash is not itchy or painful (Mullins & Krishnamurthy 2022). Roseola is very contagious and is believed to spread from person to person, usually from an infected person's saliva from a cough or sneeze. Children are most contagious during the period of high fevers before the rash occurs. The illness typically happens in the spring and fall, and most cases are self-limited. While most instances of roseola will resolve with nothing more than supportive care, some children may develop febrile seizures. Febrile seizures occur in about 10 to 15 percent of young children who have roseola (Cleveland Clinic 2020b; Mullins & Krishnamurthy 2022). Sometimes roseola can be confused with measles (rubeola). Roseola and measles both cause rashes and are common during childhood (CDC, 2020). However, measles can develop at any age, while roseola rarely affects adults (Figure 8.5).

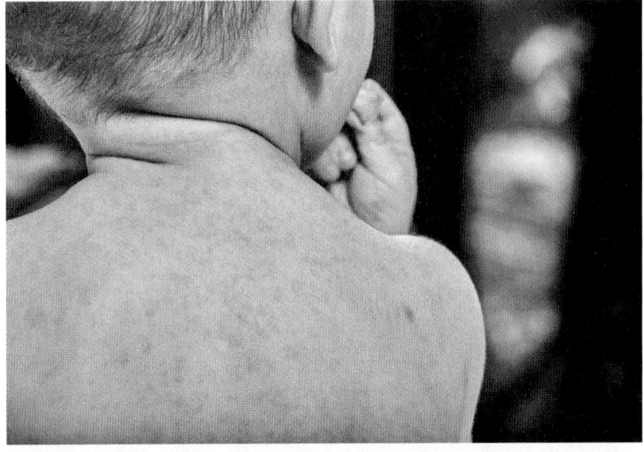

Figure 8.5. Young child exhibiting typical red spots of the Roseola virus. (Copyright @ Getty Images.)

SIGNS AND SYMPTOMS

Signs and symptoms of roseola can be nonspecific and similar to other cold viruses. However, the rash, which "blossoms" after the fever is resolving, is a timeline that is classic of roseola. Symptoms include

- High fever that may start abruptly and last for three to four days
- Irritability
- Swelling of the eyelids
- Rash
- Swollen lymph nodes in the neck
- Occasionally, sore throat, cough, runny nose, and mild diarrhea

Treatment

There is no specific treatment for roseola, thus the goal of care is to help decrease the severity of symptoms. (See also "Chapter Appendix 8.1: Common Illnesses and Conditions: Specific Treatments and When to Seek a Higher Level of Care.")

Preventing the Spread of Infection

Per *Caring for Our Children* Standard 3.1.1.1 on health checks, it is important for the program to have a standard procedure for evaluating children as they sign into the program and for addressing illnesses that occur during the day. Most children with roseola are no longer contagious 24 hours after the fever subsides. Staff members should follow *Caring for Our Children* Standard 3.6.1.1 regarding inclusion/exclusion criteria (see also Table 9.1). Children with roseola (exanthema subitum) or clinical evidence of infection with human herpes virus 6 or 7 need not be excluded from the program as long as they are able to participate in normal activities comfortably and staff members find they can care for the child without jeopardizing the health or safety of other children.

Summary

Minor illnesses and infections in young children are a common occurrence in the early learning setting, and children are at risk of acquiring an infectious disease because (1) young children may exchange secretions frequently due to poor cough/sneeze etiquette and poor handwashing habits, (2) children and adults with potentially infectious diseases are not always excluded from the program, and (3) staff members may have challenges when enforcing recommended measures for reducing infection transmission (*CFOC* Standard 7.1). With a strict focus on following best practices around prevention and clear guidance and training regarding recognition and treatment of minor illnesses, the program can partner with caregivers to keep young children healthy and safe.

APPENDIX 8.1

Common Illnesses and Conditions: Specific Treatments and When to Seek a Higher Level of Care

Fever

TREATMENT

Simple interventions include (AAP 2022c; NINDS 2023a):

- Offer plenty of liquids to avoid dehydration.
- Give acetaminophen or ibuprofen based on the physician's recommendation. Follow *Caring for Our Children* Standard 3.6.3.1 regarding medication administration
- Always look carefully at the label on the medication and follow the directions. Each type of medication has different directions based on the age and weight of a child.
- Do not give aspirin due to concern about Reye syndrome.
- Let the child eat, but do not force them.
- Allow the child to rest.

WHEN TO SEEK A HIGHER LEVEL OF CARE

Seek additional care if the child (AAP 2022a):

- Is less than 3 months old
- Is very irritable or sleepy
- Has trouble breathing or is breathing fast
- Has a seizure
- Has a rash
- Has dry lips, tongue, or mouth
- Is vomiting
- Has not had a wet diaper in 8 eight hours
- Has a chronic health condition, such as asthma or diabetes
- Is 3 to 6 months old and has a temperature greater than 101° F(38.3 °C)
- Is older than 6 months and has a temperature greater than 103° F(39.4° C)
- Is not alert when awake (lethargic)

Cough

TREATMENT

- Determine if the child is in distress (AAAAI 2020; CDC 2023a):
  - Struggling for breath or short of breath
  - Tight breath, so unable to talk or cry
  - Ribs are pulling in with each breath (retractions)
  - Breathing has become noisy (wheezing)
  - Breathing is much faster than normal
  - Lips or face are blue
  - Using accessory muscle in neck and chest
- Determine if the child has fever.
- If the child has asthma, treat according to their asthma action plan.
- If the child is not in distress and does not have fever or signs of serious illness
  - Do not give a cough suppressant.
  - Have them stop active play and sit quietly.
  - Consider providing a warm, clear liquid slowly.
  - Consider clearing nasal passages with suction bulb or saline wash.

WHEN TO SEEK A HIGHER LEVEL OF CARE

Cough should be self-limited. Call a healthcare professional if the child (AAAAI 2020):

- Has trouble breathing
- Is breathing fast
- Is wheezing
- Makes a whooping noise when coughing
- Has a fever
- Appears or acts ill
- Has a cough that does not resolve after a few minutes
- Has lips or face that appear blue during coughing
- Coughs with a harsh sound
- Is complaining of earache or has ear drainage
- Is less than 6 months old
- May have swallowed a foreign body

Asthma

TREATMENT

When an asthma episode occurs, the staff members should follow the protocol to manage the episode (Bush & Fleming 2015):

- Remove the child from known triggers if possible.
- Help the child rest in a sitting position to allow easy breathing.
- Keep the child relaxed by staying calm and calming them.
- Administer medications as directed using the guidance provided by the asthma action plan.
- Call emergency contacts if the child gets worse or does not respond to medication in 15 minutes.
- Stay with the child; observe closely until help arrives.
- Document the episode and use of medication.

WHEN TO SEEK A HIGHER LEVEL OF CARE

An asthma flare-up can progress to become life-threatening. Seek additional care if (Bush & Fleming 2015):

- Lips or face have turned bluish during coughing
- Wheezing is not improved 20 minutes after receiving a nebulizer or inhaler treatment
- Breathing is much faster than normal
- Nonstop coughing that is not improved after receiving a nebulizer or inhaler treatment
- Severe chest pain
- Need to use asthma medicine more often than every four hours
- Fever greater than 104°F (40°C)
- Child looks or acts very sick
- Wheezing and life-threatening allergic reaction to similar substance in the past (see section on "Anaphylaxis")
- Start to wheeze suddenly after a bee sting, taking medicine, or eating a food they are allergic to
- Severe trouble breathing or struggling for each breath and/or can barely speak or cry
- Fainted
- Lips or face bluish when not coughing

Anaphylaxis

See the main chapter section.

Nosebleeds

TREATMENT

As nosebleeds are typically self-limited, initial treatment includes supportive care (AAP 2019b; Tunkel et al. 2020):

- Comfort and calm the child as nosebleeds can be scary.
- Have them sit up and bend forward slightly. Do not have the child lie down so that they do not swallow the blood. Swallowing the blood may cause vomiting. Do not have the child put their head between the knees as this can make bleeding worse.
- Tell the child to breathe out of their nose. Gently pinch the nostrils closed for five to 10 minutes. Do not stop pinching to check if the bleeding has stopped.
- Apply a cold compress or ice pack to the bridge of the nose, which may reduce blood flow. Do not put tissues or gauze in the child's nose.
- If the bleeding does not stop, repeat the above steps.
- Once the bleeding stops, tell the child not to rub, pick, or blow their nose for two to three days. This will allow the broken blood vessels to heal.

WHEN TO SEEK A HIGHER LEVEL OF CARE

For nosebleeds that do not respond to the intervention, seek additional care if (Tunkel et al. 2020):

- Nosebleed does not stop after 20 minutes
- Nose bleeds again
- Child has an injury to the nose or face
- There is a large amount of blood
- Child looks or feels faint, weak, ill, or has trouble breathing
- Child is bleeding from other parts of the body, such as in the stool, urine, or gums, or bruises easily
- Child is vomiting blood or a brown substance that resembles coffee grounds
- Child has an object stuck in the nose

Ear infection

TREATMENT

Follow instructions of child's healthcare provider (AAP 2022d; Frost et al. 2021):

- Administer treatment as prescribed by the child's healthcare provider, following medication administration guidelines as described in *CFOC* Standard 3.6.3.1.
- Manage pain and fever using fever reducers, such as acetaminophen or ibuprofen, if prescribed by the child's healthcare provider and permitted by parent or caregivers. Follow *CFOC* Standard 3.6.3.1.
- Do not give aspirin (NINDS 2023b).

WHEN TO SEEK A HIGHER LEVEL OF CARE

Very rarely, children can develop complications from ear infection; however, it is important to seek care when (AAP 2022a):

- Fever
  - Child is younger than 3 months and has a fever of 100.4°F or greater
  - Temperature is above 102.2°F (39°C) for any child
  - Fever for greater than one day in child younger than 2 years old
  - Fever for greater than three days in any child
- Severe pain
- Pus, discharge, or blood draining from the ear
- Child has a stiff next
- Child acts sluggish, looks, or acts sick
- Child's walk is unsteady or looks weak
- Symptoms lasting more than two to three days
- Hearing loss

Conjunctivitis

TREATMENT

Most cases of conjunctivitis should be self-limited, but routine care may consist of (CDC 2019a):

- Referring the child to their healthcare provider to determine the underlying cause of conjunctivitis and treatment plan (newborns should be seen urgently).
- Wearing gloves when touching the child's face and secretions.
- Washing hands before and after contact.
- Administering treatment as prescribed by the child's healthcare provider, following medication administration guidelines as described in *CFOC* Standard 3.6.3.1.
- Referring the child back to healthcare provider if there is no improvement in their condition after two to three days.

WHEN TO SEEK A HIGHER LEVEL OF CARE

Urgent follow-up is required if (CDC 2019a, 2019b):

- Thick white or discolored discharge or fever in an infant younger than 3 months old
- Child is younger than 1 month. old
- Child seems unwell and has a fever, rash
- Moderate-to-severe eye pain
- Nonstop tears or blinking
- Any type of vision problem
- Fever lasts for more than three days
- Fever returns after being gone for more than 24 hours
- Child appears ill

Respiratory syncytial virus (RSV)

TREATMENT

Most cases will resolve after one to two weeks, thus treatment focuses on supportive care (CDC 2022d; Piedra & Stark 2022):

- Manage fever using fever reducers if prescribed by the child's healthcare provider and permitted by caregivers. Follow *CFOC* Standard 3.6.3.1.
- Do not give aspirin (NINDS 2023b).
- Provide prescription medication as recommended by child's healthcare provider (*CFOC* Standard 3.6.3.1).

WHEN TO SEEK A HIGHER LEVEL OF CARE

Children should be seen urgently for (AAP 2022b):

- Symptoms of bronchiolitis
  - Fast breathing
  - Flaring of the nostrils and head bobbing with breathing
  - Rhythmic grunting during breathing
  - Belly breathing, tugging between the ribs and/or the lower neck
  - Wheezing
- Symptoms of dehydration (fewer than one wet diaper every eight hours)
- Pauses or difficulty breathing
- Gray or blue color to tongue, lips, or skin
- Significantly decreased activity and alertness
- Symptoms that worsen or do not start to improve after seven days
- A fever (with a rectal temperature of 100.4°F or higher) and they are younger than 3 months old (12 weeks old)
- A fever that rises above 104°F repeatedly for a child of any age
- Poor sleep or fussiness, chest pain, ear tugging, or ear drainage

Roseola

TREATMENT

There is no cure for this viral illness, so treatment involves lessening symptoms and discomfort, including (Mullins & Krishnamurthy 2022):

- Increase fluid intake to avoid dehydration.
- Give acetaminophen for fever as directed by child's healthcare provider and caregivers following *CFOC* Standard 7.7.3.
- Avoid all aspirin products (NINDS 2023b).

WHEN TO SEEK A HIGHER LEVEL OF CARE

Child should be seen urgently for (Cleveland Clinic 2020b; Mullins & Krishnamurthy 2022):

- Fever greater than 103°F (39.4°C)
- Rash does not improve in three days
- Rash is itchy and painful
- Fever returns
- Child is lethargic
- Child refuses to eat and/or has signs of dehydration
- Child has a seizure
- Child has a compromised immune system

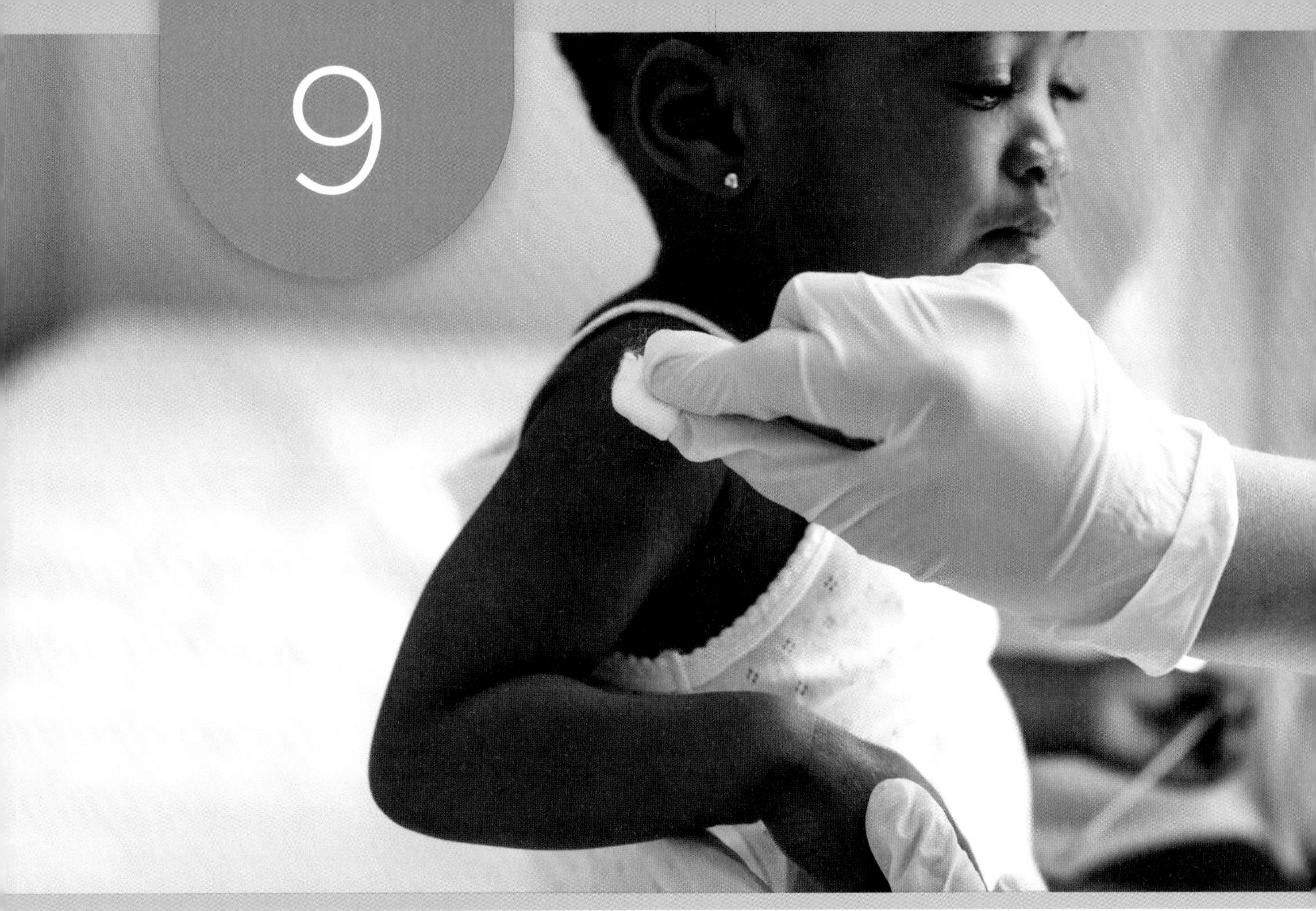

Preventing and Managing Infectious Diseases

ABBEY ALKON AND TIMOTHY R. SHOPE

LEARNING OBJECTIVES

- To explain the routes of transmission of infectious diseases in early learning programs
- To identify healthy habits and prevention strategies to reduce the spread of infectious diseases in early learning programs
- To determine the health and administrative practices that reduce the spread of infectious diseases in early learning programs
- To collaborate with the program's child care health consultant (CCHC) or health manager, administrator, staff members, and local public health department to identify infectious diseases and reduce the spread in early learning programs

Young children want to play with and touch people and things, resulting in them picking up and spreading germs. When they have runny noses, cough, diarrhea, and certain skin sores, germ spread is even more common.

Educators, parents, caregivers, and healthcare professionals are concerned about infectious diseases because they are easily spread in early learning programs, and it is a challenge to screen for and prevent them. An infected child may pass germs on to other children, adults who work in the program, and families of other children and workers. When children become ill in a group setting, they may require more attention and need to be sent home. Having an infected child, who temporarily cannot participate in the program, is costly and burdensome to families and for employers. Family members may miss workdays to care for sick children. It is important to understand how infectious diseases are spread and how these diseases can affect children and adults.

Infectious diseases are illnesses caused by germs such as viruses, bacteria, fungi, or parasites that get into the body. *Infectious* means capable of causing an infection. Contagious or communicable diseases are infectious diseases that can spread from one person to another. Most germs are harmless and only cause mild illness, while others can be more severe.

Infectious diseases are spread when there is an agent (germ), a susceptible host (person), and an environment (early learning program) that brings the host and agent together. The presence of germs does not cause illness in everyone. Infectious diseases occur when vulnerable *people* (hosts) succumb to disease-causing *germs* (agents) in the *places* (environment) where there are enough germs or the right conditions to overcome barriers to infection. To *reduce the risk of infection* we must modify the people, germs, and places in the following ways:

- Increase people's resistance to disease-causing germs through measures that foster health and well-being, such as immunization, nutrition, good sleep habits, and physical fitness activity.
- Reduce the number of disease-causing germs by ventilating spaces and by cleaning, sanitizing, and disinfecting surfaces and materials.
- Modify the places people occupy to reduce their contact with illness-causing germs.

The purpose of this chapter is to explain the types of infectious diseases that can be transmitted between children and/or staff members in early learning programs and how to decrease the spread of these infectious diseases. *Caring for Our Children: National Health and Safety Performance Standards, Guidelines for Early Care and Education Programs* (AAP, APHA, & NRC 2019) and *Managing Infectious Diseases in Child Care and Schools: A Quick Reference Guide* (Shope & Hashikawa 2023) provide evidence-based best practices to support the guidance in this chapter.

How Infectious Diseases Spread

The germs that cause infections and contagious diseases are spread in different ways: by droplets or aerosols carried in the air; by direct contact with body fluids; by direct contact with people with infections or surfaces where there are germs; and by nonhuman sources, such as insects or animals.

Respiratory Route: Droplets and Aerosols Carried by the Air

Most respiratory droplets expelled during breathing, coughing, singing, or sneezing fall out of the air onto surfaces within three to six feet. Smaller droplets, called aerosols, may travel farther and are more common with certain infectious diseases. Air currents from fans and wind can carry these aerosols even further across a room or into adjacent rooms (Figure 9.1).

Respiratory tract diseases include

- The common cold
- Pink eye
- Strep throat
- Croup/laryngitis
- Bronchiolitis/bronchitis
- Pneumonia

Most respiratory tract diseases are mild, but some are serious (bacterial meningitis), and we have developed immunizations against most of these. Respiratory tract diseases are spread from germ-laden droplets or aerosols traveling from the infected individual to another person's eyes, nose, or mouth. Additionally, surfaces (e.g., tables, doorknobs) or objects (e.g., toys, utensils) may get germs on them from an infected person's droplets falling on them or from their hands touching their nose or mouth, then touching the surfaces or objects. The germs on the surfaces and objects can then be touched by a healthy individual, who then transmits the germs to the mucous membranes of their eyes, nose, or mouth, causing an infection.

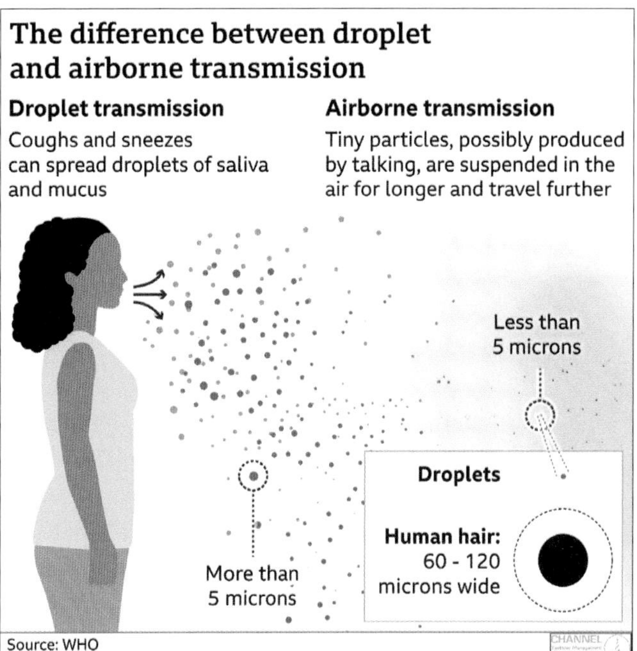

Figure 9.1. The difference between airborne and droplet transmission.

People touch their hands to their mouths, noses, and eyes all day long—especially young children. They have constant physical and oral contact with objects around them, increasing opportunities for the spread of disease-causing germs. Each time they touch their mucus membranes with contaminated hands, they allow the germs they have picked up from touched surfaces to get into their bodies. As a result, respiratory tract diseases spread easily among young children in group settings.

Direct Contact with Body Fluids, Including Fecal-Oral and Blood-Borne Routes

Some diseases are spread directly from one person to another by touching infected body fluids like saliva, vomit, stool, or blood, and then touching an uninfected person's eyes, nose, or mouth. Diseases spread through the intestinal (fecal-oral) tract are caused by viruses, bacteria, or parasites that multiply in the intestines and pass out of the body in the stool or vomit. When infectious vomit or stool gets on hands, the germs can be transferred into that individual's mouth or onto food or objects that are then touched by other people, who in turn may transfer germs to their mouths, causing an infection. Programs that care for children in diapers or children who are not able to successfully use a flushing toilet all the time are especially at risk because staff members and children can get some fecal material on their hands. Germs spread by the fecal-oral route most commonly cause diarrhea and vomiting. Diarrhea outbreaks can occur among staff members and children in early learning programs. For some diseases, a small number of germs is enough to cause an infection, and children or staff members with disease-causing germs in their stool may not act or feel sick or have diarrhea. That is why practicing good infection control, especially handwashing, is so important to reduce the spread of diarrheal illnesses and outbreaks.

Diseases spread through blood include hepatitis B and human immunodeficiency virus/acquired immunodeficiency syndrome (HIV/AIDS). These are serious viral infections that can be spread when infected blood encounters a broken surface of a mucus membrane (such as the inside lining of the mouth, eyes, nose, rectum, or sex organs). This can also happen when the skin is accidentally or intentionally punctured by a contaminated needle. An infected mother can pass on a virus to her child during pregnancy or childbirth or by breastfeeding. Once these viruses enter a body, they may stay for months or years. An infected person may appear to be healthy, but can spread the virus. Fortunately, the risk of spreading HIV and hepatitis B is extremely low in early learning settings.

Direct Contact with Surfaces with Germs on Them

Superficial infections and skin infections—impetigo, herpes (cold sores), ringworm, scabies, and head lice—are caused by bacteria, viruses, fungi, or parasites. They are common and usually are not serious. They are spread by direct contact with infected skin areas, secretions, or infested items. Because young children in early learning programs constantly touch their surroundings, their peers, and their educators, these infections can spread easily. The direct-contact method of disease spread is illustrated in these examples:

- A child with oozy sores on their arm brushes against another child. A small amount of ooze gets on the other child's arm and into a cut or scratch on their skin.
- Two children huddle over a project. A louse on the head of one child crawls onto the head of the other child.

In addition to skin infections, respiratory or fecal-oral germs may spread by an infected child or adult touching items or surfaces (e.g., toys, utensils, food, doorknobs, countertops), and then those items are touched by a healthy person, who then puts their hands in their nose, mouth, or eyes. For example,

- A child with a runny nose handles a toy. Another child later handles the toy, rubs their eyes, and puts their finger into their nose or mouth. The second child develops a runny nose, cough, and eye discharge.
- A child and/or adult gets sick after ingesting food that is contaminated or not refrigerated properly. Consider food contamination as the source of illness if staff members and children experience stomach cramps, vomiting, diarrhea, and/or dizziness at the same time.

Other Infectious Conditions Not Transmitted Person to Person

Some infectious diseases caused by bacteria, viruses, fungi, or parasites come from nonhuman sources and do not spread from person to person. For example, ticks and mosquitoes can transmit infections like Rocky Mountain spotted fever, Lyme disease, malaria, and Zika virus. Certain types of animals kept as pets, those encountered during visits to petting zoos, or some animals that are ingested may transmit infections to humans.

Strategies to Reduce the Spread of Infectious Diseases

There are many ways to reduce the spread of infectious diseases in early learning programs through practicing healthy habits, ensuring high immunization rates, and focusing on the routes of transmission.

Start with Healthy Habits and Prevention Strategies

Young children learn healthy habits from adults who serve as their role models. Healthy habits support optimal nutrition, hydration, hand hygiene, physical activity, sleep, and oral hygiene. A healthy body can be a key defender against infectious disease. Encourage adults and children to follow practices that help their bodies resist infections. For example, the program should ensure these healthy habits for children:

- **Nutrition.** Eat nutritious foods and drink enough water, while avoiding beverages containing sugar. These strategies help the whole body better resist infection.
- **Support breastfeeding.** Encourage and support breastfeeding for infants enrolled in the early learning program, through 12 months old if possible. Breast milk has components, not present in infant formula, that increase immunity against infections.
- **Encourage adequate sleep.** The program should provide an opportunity for, but not require, sleep and rest. The program should make available a regular rest period and an age-appropriate sleep/nap environment for all children (*CFOC* Standard 5.4.5.1). Facilities that offer infant care should provide a safe sleep environment (*CFOC* Standard 3.1.4.4).
- **Ensure optimal hand hygiene.** Require frequent, thorough hand hygiene for both staff members and children before any activity that involves food or touching the mouth and whenever contact with stool may have occurred. Handwashing is best, but staff members and children over 24 months old may use alcohol-based hand sanitizers if their hands are visibly clean and running water is not available.

Programs should ensure that early childhood education staff members:

- Promote excellent infection control and prevention. Follow guidance on hygiene, cleaning, sanitizing, and disinfecting, including procedures for diapering and changing soiled underclothing (*CFOC* Standard 3.2.1.4).
- Do not allow sharing of personal items (e.g., toothbrushes, washcloths, teething rings, pacifiers, cups).
- Separate children into three groups whenever possible by age and diapering needs—infants, older diapered children, and children who use the toilet reliably. Try to have a staff member work with only one group to avoid carrying germs from one group to another. (Note: Because this type of grouping may not meet a particular program's administrative or child development needs, directors often consider a variety of factors when grouping children and assigning staff members. If mixing staff members and child groups is necessary, minimize the number of people involved and emphasize careful hand hygiene when moving from group to group and within mixed groups.)

Promote Immunization

The most important method to reduce or prevent infectious diseases in early learning programs is ensuring children and educators are up to date on their immunizations. Before immunizations existed against diseases like measles, mumps, rubella, polio, pertussis (whooping cough), diphtheria, tetanus, Hib, chickenpox, pneumococcus, and rotavirus, children and adults suffered high rates of complications, hospitalizations, and death. Vaccines enable people to make protective antibodies that prevent severe disease when people are exposed to these germs. Fortunately, in the United States, rates of immunizations are high against these diseases, so many parents and educators have not experienced these infections in their lifetimes. But this lack of experience can cause some parents to undervalue immunizations and, in some cases, decline the required vaccines for their children. In areas of the United States where immunization rates are low, outbreaks of vaccine-preventable diseases have unfortunately recurred.

Early learning programs are especially at risk because some children may be too young to be fully immunized and because close contact allows easy spread of any infectious disease. Programs with staff members born after the late 1950s are at particular risk because this age group does not have natural immunity from having caught some of the diseases during childhood (e.g., measles, polio). Immunity wanes without natural infection or vaccine boosters. So, throughout life, people need immunizations to help their bodies respond to an exposure that, without a vaccine, would make them sick.

Make sure all children and adults who are involved with early learning programs are immunized as completely as possible for their age (*CFOC* Standard 7.2.0.2). Detailed up-to-date information about immunization schedules and individual vaccines is available at **www.cdc.gov/vaccines**. Among the recommended vaccines for children from birth to age 7 are those that prevent tetanus, diphtheria, pertussis (whooping cough), Hib infections (e.g., ear and blood infections, cellulitis, abscess, and meningitis), pneumococcal infections (e.g., ear and blood infections, meningitis, and pneumonia), polio, hepatitis B, rotavirus (diarrhea in infants), varicella (chickenpox), measles, mumps, rubella, influenza, and COVID-19. At age 11, children need a booster dose of the tetanus, diphtheria, and acellular pertussis vaccine. In addition, the human papilloma virus vaccine series starts at age 9, and the meningococcal vaccine starts at age 11. Thereafter, people of all ages should continue to receive annual influenza vaccine and booster doses of certain vaccines.

Three vaccines deserve special emphasis for adults who work with children:

1. Tdap vaccine for pertussis (whooping cough)
2. Influenza vaccine
3. COVID-19 vaccines (and boosters)

Very young children are at risk for severe disease if infected with these diseases because they do not have immunity. Infants are especially vulnerable to pertussis in their first 6 months of life. They can have severe and sometimes fatal cases, and they are not fully immunized until 15 months old. Infants get pertussis from adults; therefore, adults should receive a dose of the Tdap vaccine, women should receive Tdap during each pregnancy, and Tdap should be repeated every 10 years.

Influenza vaccine is especially important for educators (although the vaccine is recommended for everyone) because young children are known to infect their peers in early learning programs as well as their families and others in their community (Hurwitz et al. 2000a, 2000b). Influenza kills thousands of people, including more than 150 children, every year, even people who are healthy with no medical problems (CDC 2022). Infants younger than 6 months old are the most likely to suffer severe influenza infections, and they cannot receive the vaccine until 6 months old. The Centers for Disease Control and Prevention (CDC) reports that, each year, an average of 20,000 children younger than age 5 are hospitalized because of flu-related complications.

SARS-CoV-2 (one of the coronaviruses) is the virus that causes COVID-19. Since 2019, the world has experienced the COVID-19 pandemic, and several vaccines have been developed to reduce the risk of severe disease. COVID-19 vaccines are available for everyone 6 months old and older. The dosage schedule varies by manufacturer and age. There may be different vaccines developed based on the COVID-19 subvariants in the future. Children generally have mild COVID-19 disease; however, infants under 6 months old cannot receive the COVID-19 vaccine and are at higher risk for more severe infections. Children can be hospitalized and die from COVID-19 at rates like influenza. So, for these diseases, we must protect young children by immunizing the adults that educate them.

Too often, immunization schedules are delayed or disrupted because of illness or missed appointments for well-child checkups, often requiring a special "catch-up" schedule that may involve fewer doses with specified intervals between doses. When a child or adult is not immunized as recommended, there is a risk of exposure to the other people in the program. Unfortunately, myths and misperceptions, not supported by science, about the risks of vaccines have been promoted widely. Children and adults who lack vaccines for medical reasons should be excluded from the program if an outbreak of that disease occurs in the group setting for their own protection.

Three sources of accurate information about immunizations are shown as follows. Each of the websites provides additional information.

- **www.aap.org/immunization.** The AAP's Recommended Immunization Schedules for Children and Adolescents provides up-to-date schedules for childhood immunizations. The website provides education and resources for parents and caregivers and pediatricians on immunizations.

- **www.cdc.gov/vaccines.** This CDC site provides information for healthcare professionals and parents and caregivers about all aspects of immunization, including vaccine recommendations, understanding vaccines and their purpose, vaccine misconceptions, and answers to commonly asked questions about vaccines.
- **www.immunizationinfo.org.** The National Network for Immunization Information's mission is to provide the public, healthcare professionals, policymakers, and the media with up-to-date, scientifically valid information related to immunization to assist with understanding the issues so that informed decisions can be made.

Because the national schedule of recommended vaccines for children and adults is complex, the CDC has online tools at **www.cdc.gov/vaccines** to review an individual's immunization record. There is another CDC website (**www2a.cdc.gov/vaccines/childquiz**) that helps you identify what vaccines a child may need. The CDC's recommended vaccines for adults can be found on the website at **www.cdc.gov/vaccines/schedules/downloads/adult/adult-combined-schedule.pdf**.

Remember that the current online CDC Adult Immunization Scheduler may not consider some vaccines recommended for adults who work in group early learning settings for children. Check with the public health authorities in your area to find out what vaccines are currently recommended for adults working in early learning programs.

Checking for and Monitoring Vaccine Status

Because children need many vaccines in early childhood, a child who is up to date when admitted to an early learning program may become due or overdue for vaccines over time. In addition to checking at admission, tracking for necessary vaccine updates must be done throughout the period a child remains enrolled. Checking and tracking up-to-date status in early childhood education settings will continue to be necessary until there are community-wide vaccine-tracking registries that have follow-up capacity. These exist in some areas of the country now.

Information about which vaccines children and adults have received should appear on their health assessment from their healthcare provider. A child care staff health assessment form should be completed, and an example can be found in *Caring for Our Children* "Appendix E: Child Care Staff Health Assessment" (**https://nrckids.org/files/appendix/AppendixE.pdf**). (See "Chapter 8: Understanding Common Illnesses and Conditions" for a discussion of routine preventive care for children.)

There are very few true medical contraindications to immunizations. They include having an immune deficiency condition, as the result of an infection such as AIDS, or as a side effect of immunity-suppressing medications used for cancer treatment or to prevent rejection of a tissue transplant. Some vaccines are not recommended during pregnancy or when someone is moderately to severely ill. Some states may allow religious or philosophical objections to immunization. However, each early learning program can have its own immunization requirements that exceed the state requirements. Staff members and children who are un- or underimmunized may be able to prove immunity by prior infection through laboratory testing for some diseases. The significance and duration of protection from previous COVID-19 infection is changing as the virus changes.

Ensuring that immunizations are up to date and handling contraindications, exemptions, and objections can be complex, so educators are encouraged to use a CCHC if available and encourage adherence to recommended well-child checks to validate these issues.

Reduce Routes of Transmission

Because respiratory diseases like influenza and COVID-19 primarily spread through droplets and aerosols, efforts to reduce spread should focus on preventing these droplets and aerosols from landing on other peoples' noses, mouths, and eyes. Germ-laden droplets also land on surfaces and objects where they can stay alive for enough time that another person can touch them and infect themselves or others by touching their hands to the eyes, nose, or mouth of an uninfected person. Finally, efforts should be undertaken to avoid nonhuman sources of infectious diseases, such as pets, animals, mosquitos, and so on. This section will address how to reduce transmission, considering the various routes.

Air: Reduce the Chances of Aerosols and Droplets Reaching Uninfected People

There are strategies and methods for reducing the spread of aerosols and droplets in the environment.

Ventilation, Temperature, Humidity, and Barriers

Address ventilation, heating, and cooling equipment, if possible:

Air circulation helps to clear infectious disease droplets and aerosols that are released in early childhood education settings when children and adults talk, sing, shout, cough, and sneeze. Exchanging indoor air with outdoor air reduces the density of infectious particles in the air. Even in winter, some form of ventilation is necessary to ensure sufficient air exchange. Fans; heating, ventilation, and air conditioning (HVAC) systems; open windows; and time spent outdoors can all reduce the risk of transmission through droplets and aerosols. (See "Chapter 13: Creating a Safe Environment" for information on ventilation, temperature, and humidity recommendations and requirements.)

- Become familiar with standards and resources for your facility, including *Caring for Our Children* Standard 5.2.1: Ventilation, Heating, Cooling and Hot Water, which provides standards on Ensuring Access to Fresh Air Indoors (*CFOC* Standards 5.2.1.1–5.2.1.15), Indoor Temperature and Humidity (*CFOC* Standard 5.2.1.2), and Heating and Ventilation Equipment Inspection and Maintenance (*CFOC* Standard 5.2.1.3). There is a graphic poster of the key elements of healthy air indoors and outdoors (titled "Healthy Air in Your Child Care Facility") on the University of California San Francisco California Childcare Health Program (UCSF CCHP) website (**https://cchp.ucsf.edu/content/posters**). For more information, contact American Society of Heating, Refrigerating and Air-Conditioning Engineers (ASHRAE), the Environmental Protection Agency's (EPA) Public Information Center, the American Gas Association (AGA), the Edison Electric Institute (EEI), the American Lung Association (ALA), the US Consumer Product Safety Commission (CPSC), and the Safe Building Alliance (SBA).

Provide fresh air:

- Allow children to play outdoors as often as possible. The concentration of germs outdoors is much less than in closed spaces.
- Space children at least three feet apart while they rest or nap to reduce the number of germs passed from one child to another. Alternating cots or sleeping mats head to toe can increase the space between each child's head to six feet, which reduces the chance that a cough or sneeze will find its target.
- Use fans. Child-safe portable fans or ceiling fans increases the circulation of fresh air from open windows. Placing a fan by an open window to blow inside air out encourages airflow throughout the room.

IMMEDIATE IMPACT

Open Windows to Keep Air Moving

Ventilate all rooms with fresh outdoor air as much as possible. If the program has operable windows, open them whenever the weather permits. Routinely open the windows to allow fresh air in and recirculate stale air whenever the room is not being used.

Create barriers:

- Masking may be recommended during a pandemic (COVID-19) or severe influenza season. Wearing face masks helps reduce the respiratory particles in the air from leaving one person and from entering mouths and noses of other people. Wash hands when putting on and off masks for adults and children (Murray et al. 2022).
- Cohorting children in specific rooms and preventing children or early childhood educators from traveling from one room to another effectively creates a barrier to prevent germs from spreading. However, this is not always possible due to staffing needs early and late in the day.
- Because coughs and sneezes often come too quickly to cover the mouth and nose with a tissue, teach children and staff members to cough or sneeze toward their shoulder or elbow. This will hopefully prevent droplets and aerosols from getting into the air.

Physical Environment

Design, organize, and maintain the space and furnishings to reduce the ways people are likely to be contaminated by disease-causing germs.

- **Sufficient space for the group.** Research-based recommendations are that 42 to 54 square feet per child is best to foster child development, minimize challenging behavior, and reduce infectious diseases.

- **Separate areas and personal items.** To decrease the spread of germs from one group to another, separate groups of children with full walls that minimize contact between the groups. Provide storage that keeps clothing and bedding used by one person from contact with those of another person. Bedbugs and skin infections spread when personal items are improperly stored. If cubbies are too small to completely contain personal articles, hang a bag in each child's cubby to hold them. Provide more than several arm's lengths of distance between food preparation/handling areas and areas and surfaces used for toileting/diapering.
    - Each room in which diapers, disposable training pants, or soiled underwear are changed should have its own changing area adjacent to a handwashing sink, even when there is a hand sanitizer dispenser. Changing areas should not be shared by more than one group of children to prevent sharing of disease-causing germs across groups.
    - Skill, practice, and a good setup make it possible to follow the healthful practices recommended for sanitary changing while also using the opportunity to interact with each child one-to-one, fostering warm, positive relationships.
    - Keep supplies off the changing surface but have them neatly and accessibly stored on open shelves nearby. Occasionally, some extra supplies are needed during the change. They should be in a location that does not require opening cabinet doors to reach them.
    - Everything touched, such as cabinet doors, door handles, and supply containers, will need to be cleaned daily.
    - Changing tables need to be cleaned and disinfected after each use.
- **Choose surfaces wisely.** When installing surfaces, carefully select those that people will touch. They should be easy to clean and disinfect.

Figures 9.2 A and 9.2 B include examples of a school poster on diapering procedure in English and Spanish that can be used in the program.

Germs: Modifying the Presence and Spread of Germs on Surfaces

Respiratory Etiquette

Programs should have routine procedures to handle common runny noses and coughs to prevent infected droplets or mucus from landing on surfaces and infecting others.

- If someone sneezes or coughs into a tissue or hand, properly dispose of the tissue and wash hands.
- Wipe runny noses and eyes promptly, dispose of the used tissue, and wash hands afterward.
- Use disposable towels and tissues. If your program prefers single-use cloth towels and handkerchiefs, these will need to be laundered (which will have a consequent labor and environmental impact).
- Dispose of towels or tissues contaminated with nose, throat, or eye fluids in a hands-free covered container with a plastic liner. Keep waste cans away from food and classroom materials. Teach children to drop tissues into the waste receptacle and not to poke around in waste cans.

DIAPERING PROCEDURES

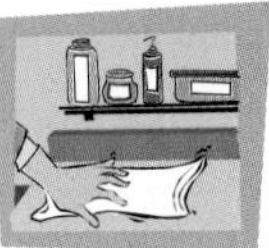

1. **Get prepared.**
   - Gather all diapering supplies so they are within reach, including a diaper, wipes, a plastic bag for soiled clothes, and a plastic-lined, hands-free, covered can.
   - If diaper cream is needed, put some on a piece of facial tissue before you begin.
   - Cover the diapering surface with disposable paper.
   - Put on disposable gloves.

2. **Place the child on the diapering table.**
   - Remove bottom clothes and any soiled clothing.
   - Remove socks and shoes that cannot be kept clean.
   - Avoid contact with soiled items.
   - ALWAYS KEEP ONE HAND ON THE CHILD.

3. **Unfasten the diaper and clean the child's diaper area.**
   - With the soiled diaper under the child, lift the child's legs to clean the child's bottom.
   - Clean from front to back with a fresh wipe each time.

4. **Dispose of the diaper and soiled items.**
   - Put soiled wipes in the soiled diaper.
   - Remove the diaper and dispose of it in a plastic-lined, handsfree, covered can.
   - If the disposable paper is soiled, use the paper that extends under the child's feet to fold up under the child's bottom.
   - Remove gloves and dispose of them in hands-free can.
   - Use a fresh wipe to clean your hands.
   - Use a fresh wipe to clean the child's hands.

Rev. 06/2022

California Childcare Health Program
cchp.ucsf.edu

DIAPERING PROCEDURES

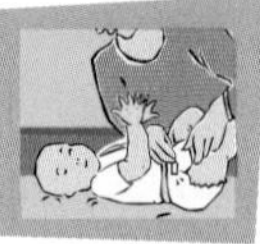

5. **Put on a clean diaper and dress the child.**
   - Put a clean diaper under the child.
   - Apply diaper cream with a tissue as needed.
   - Fasten the diaper, and dress the child.

6. **Wash the child's hands.**
   - Moisten hands and apply liquid or foam soap to hand surfaces from finger tips to wrists.
   - Rinse with running water.
   - Dry with a single use paper or cloth towel.
   - Return the child to a supervised area away from the diapering table.

7. **Clean and disinfect the diaper changing surface.**
   - Discard the paper liner.
   - Remove any visible soil with soap and water.
   - Apply EPA-registered disinfectant and use according to label instructions.
   - Be sure to leave the disinfectant on the surface for the required contact time.

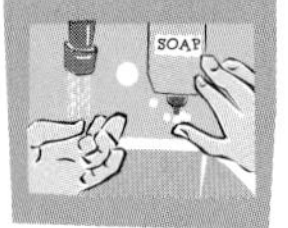

8. **Wash your hands with soap and running water, and record the diaper change in a report for parents.**
   - Include the time of diaper change and diaper contents.
   - Note any problems such as skin redness, rashes, or loose stool.

Rev. 06/2022

California Childcare Health Program
cchp.ucsf.edu

PROCEDIMIENTOS PARA CAMBIAR PAÑALES

1. **Prepárese.**
   - Reúna todos los materiales para cambiar el pañal de modo que estén al alcance de la mano; esto incluye un pañal, toallitas húmedas, una bolsa plástica para la ropa sucia y un bote de basura con tapadera de pedal con una bolsa plástica.
   - Si se necesita pomada para pañales, ponga un poco en un pañuelo de papel facial antes de empezar.
   - Cubra la superficie para cambiar pañales con papel desechable.
   - Póngase guantes desechables.

2. **Coloque al niño en la mesa para cambiar pañales.**
   - Quítele la ropa de la parte inferior del cuerpo y la ropa que esté sucia.
   - Quítele las medias y zapatos si no puede mantenerlos limpios.
   - Evite el contacto con los artículos sucios.
   - SIEMPRE DETENGA AL NIÑO CON UNA MANO.

3. **Desprenda el pañal y limpie el área donde estaba puesto el pañal.**
   - Con el pañal sucio debajo del niño, levántele las piernas para limpiarle el trasero.
   - Limpie del frente hacia atrás con una toallita limpia cada vez.

4. **Deseche el pañal y los artículos sucios.**
   - Coloque las toallitas húmedas sucias dentro del pañal sucio.
   - Quite el pañal y deséchelo en un bote de basura con tapadera con bolsa plástica de pedal.
   - Si el papel desechable se ensució, agarre el papel desde debajo de los pies del niño y dóblelo hasta debajo del trasero del niño.
   - Quítese los guantes y deséchelos en el bote de pedal.
   - Utilice una toallita limpia para limpiarse las manos.
   - Utilice una toallita limpia para limpiar las manos del niño.

Rev. 06/2022

Facultad de Enfermería de UCSF
Programa de Salud en Centros de Cuidado Infantil en Californiacchp.ucsf.edu

PROCEDIMIENTOS PARA CAMBIAR PAÑALES

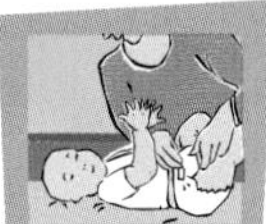

5. **Póngale un pañal limpio y vista al niño.**
   - Coloque un pañal limpio debajo del niño.
   - Aplíquele crema para rozaduras con una servilleta según se necesite.
   - Ajuste el pañal y vista al niño.

6. **Lávele las manos al niño.**
   - Humedezca las manos del niño y aplíquele jabón líquido o en espuma en las superficies de las manos desde las puntas de los dedos hasta las muñecas.
   - Enjuáguelas bajo el agua corriente.
   - Séquelas con una toalla desechable o de tela.
   - Lleve al niño de vuelta al área supervisada lejos de la mesa para cambiar pañales.

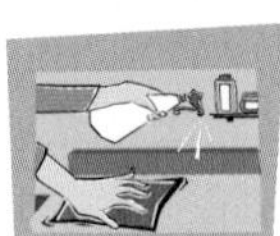

7. **Limpie y desinfecte la superficie para cambiar pañales.**
   - Deseche el revestimiento de papel.
   - Limpie lo que esté visiblemente sucio con agua y jabón.
   - Aplique un desinfectante registrado con la EPA y úselo conforme a las instrucciones de la etiqueta.
   - Asegúrese de dejar el desinfectante en la superficie durante el tiempo de contacto requerido.

8. **Lávese las manos con jabón y agua corriente y anote el cambio de pañal en un informe para los padres.**
   - Incluya la hora del cambio de pañal y el contenido del pañal.
   - Anote los problemas observados, como enrojecimiento de la piel, sarpullidos o heces sueltas.

Rev. 06/2022

Facultad de Enfermería de UCSF
Programa de Salud en Centros de Cuidado Infantil en California
cchp.ucsf.edu

Figures 9.2 A and 9.2 B. UCSF CCHP diapering procedure posters in English and Spanish.

Hand Hygiene

Hand hygiene is the first line of defense against infectious diseases because hands carry and spread germs and children frequently put their hands in their mouths.

WHEN TO PRACTICE HAND HYGIENE

Everyone should follow the procedure for hand hygiene at the following times, as outlined by *Caring for Our Children*. Standard 3.2.2.1:

a. On arrival for the day, after breaks, or when moving from one child care group to another

b. Before and after

   1. Preparing and handling food or beverages or feeding a child
   2. Giving medication or applying a medical ointment or cream in which a break in the skin (e.g., sores, cuts, scrapes) may be encountered
   3. Playing in water (including swimming) that is used by more than one person

c. After

   1. Diapering
   2. Using the toilet or helping a child use a toilet
   3. Handling bodily fluid (e.g., mucus, blood, vomit) from sneezing, wiping and blowing noses, mouths, or sores
   4. Handling animals or cleaning up animal waste
   5. Playing in sand, on wooden play sets, or outdoors
   6. Cleaning or handling the garbage
   7. Applying sunscreen and/or insect repellent

d. When children require assistance with brushing, caregivers/teachers should wash their hands thoroughly between brushings for each child.

Reprinted with permission, from American Academy of Pediatrics, American Public Health Association), & National Resource Center for Health and Safety, Caring for Our Children: National Health and Safety Performance Standards, Guidelines for Early Care and Education Programs, 4th ed. (Itasca, IL: American Academy of Pediatrics, 2019), 118.

You may want to display a handwashing poster near every sink as a reminder. Find handwashing posters on the CDC website (**www.cdc.gov/handwashing/posters.html**) or search online to find others that work well in early learning programs. Switch out posters periodically to catch the attention of everyone about this important procedure. Review all the procedures for hand hygiene with everyone—and monitor staff members and children to ensure that the procedures are followed.

There are six important handwashing components:

1. Use running water that drains—not a stoppered sink or container. Using a common container of water spreads germs.
2. Use liquid soap for children and preferably for adults too. Bar soap gathers germs from the users. Antibacterial soap is not recommended because it may kill healthy bacteria that keep bad bacteria in balance.
3. Rub your hands together for at least 20 seconds. Aim for 20 seconds, but do not settle for less than 10 seconds of rubbing. The point is to rub long enough to loosen any adherent soil on the skin before rinsing. Friction helps remove soil that holds germs. Use the lather time to teach math, music, or poetry. To count off the seconds, children can either chant twice ("Bubble one, bubble two, bubble three, bubble four . . . bubble ten") or sing a song. Children can sing the ABC song once or sing one of the following songs twice: "Happy Birthday," "Row, Row, Row Your Boat," or (to the tune of "Row, Row, Row Your Boat") "Wash, wash, wash your hands; sing this handy song. Scrub and rub, rub and scrub. Germs go down the drain!"
4. Rinse hands, fingertips down, from wrists to nails, under running water until all soil and soap are gone.
5. If the faucet does not turn off automatically, turn off the faucet with a paper towel or your hand or forearm. A hands-free faucet is best. Ideally, throw the paper towel into a lined, covered, hands-free trash container.
6. Have hand lotion available for staff members to apply to their hands and to use (with parent or caregiver consent) with children after their hands have been washed. Lotion prevents dry or cracked skin. Dry skin traps germs, so using lotion is not only for comfort, but also for germ control.

Sinks should be located near all diapering, toileting, and food areas. Refillable soap dispensers must be regularly cleaned and sanitized. A sink should be a priority piece of equipment for every child area in the program.

The critical features for hand hygiene are

- Clean *running* water—not a common basin
- Water temperature between 60°F and 120°F (water between 80°F and 100°F is comfortable and may encourage washing)
- Collection of contaminated water out of the children's reach
- A system safe for children
- Readily available liquid soap
- Single-use (disposable or cloth) towels

When handwashing with running water is impossible, such as on a field trip, use disposable wet wipes to clean visible soil and then, for children over 24 months old, use an adult-supervised application of an alcohol-based hand sanitizer. Disposable items such as paper towels, diaper table covers, wet wipes, gloves, and hand sanitizers are expensive. Consider buying in bulk from medical or paper supply companies. Use centralized buying whenever possible. If the program is not part of a system or large agency, ask other programs to join in bulk purchases. It is worth it!

Hand sanitizers. Handwashing is essential for hand hygiene if there is visible soil on the hands. However, as an alternative to handwashing, children over 24 months old and adults may use alcohol-based hand sanitizers if their hands are visibly clean. Hand sanitizers should contain at least 60 percent alcohol (ethanol) to be effective. When using hand sanitizer, be sure to use the amount recommended by the manufacturer. Rub both hands together to distribute the sanitizer on all hand and finger surfaces. Then let the hands air-dry. Keep the hand sanitizer out of the eyes, nose, and mouth. Supervise children very closely when they are using hand sanitizers and limit children's independent access to containers of this toxic, flammable chemical. *Caring for Our Children* Standard 3.2.2.5: Hand Sanitizers provides guidance on the maximum size and safe placement of hand sanitizer dispensers in early learning programs.

Premoistened disposable cleansing cloths. These types of cloths do not effectively clean hands. There are only two allowable situations when these disposable cleaning cloths can be used as a substitute for hand hygiene with soap and running water or an alcohol-based hand sanitizer: (1) When changing diapers, disposable training pants, or soiled underwear, you may use a disposable wipe for your hands and the child's hands when all soiled materials have been discarded, and before putting a clean diaper or underwear and clothing on the child. (Hand hygiene with soap and water or alcohol-based hand sanitizer must still be done for the child before returning the child to the group, and for the educator, after completing the disinfecting step for the changing surface.) (2) If you are out on a trip and handwashing sinks are not available, you can use some premoistened disposable cleansing cloths to remove visible soil and then apply hand sanitizer. Follow up with a handwashing sink as soon as one is available.

Disposable gloves. Wearing gloves is never a substitute for hand hygiene; however, gloves can provide a protective barrier that significantly decreases exposure of the wearer's skin to germs that cause infections. However, they do allow some germs to get through to the skin. They are optional for diaper-changing unless contact with blood is expected. Wearing gloves while changing diapers, disposable training pants, or soiled underwear reduces the amount of skin contact between the educator and the diaper's contents. Gloves do not need to be used when handling or cleaning up spilled breast milk unless the educator has open skin wounds on their hands.

Always wear disposable gloves in these situations:

- When contact with blood or blood-containing fluids is likely (such as when providing first aid or changing a diaper with bloody diarrhea), particularly if the educator's hands have open cuts or sores
- When cleaning surfaces that are contaminated with blood or body fluids (such as large amounts of vomit or feces)
- When cleaning an aquarium
- When changing the diaper of a child with diarrhea or a diagnosed gastrointestinal disease

Try to use disposable gloves made of latex-free vinyl or nitrile to protect staff members who might become or are already allergic to latex. However, if using latex gloves, choose the powder-free gloves with reduced protein content. Remove and dispose of gloves properly after handling infectious material and each time they are used in food handling. There is a proper technique for removing used gloves. See the graphic poster titled "Gloving" on UCSF CCHP's website, which shows how this is done (**https://cchp.ucsf.edu/content/gloving**). After removing the gloves, you still need to wash your hands. In addition, any skin surfaces that are contaminated by blood or other body fluids should be cleaned immediately and thoroughly.

Remember: You may wear reusable utility gloves for cleaning and disinfecting toilet equipment. After use, wash them with soapy water, and then dip them in disinfectant solution up to the wrist. Allow the gloves to air-dry.

Cleaning, Sanitizing, and Disinfecting

The best way to reduce germs is to create a regular schedule for cleaning, sanitizing, and disinfecting surfaces and objects in the program (See *Caring for Our Children* "Appendix K: Routine Schedule for Cleaning, Sanitizing and Disinfecting" at **https://nrckids.org/files/appendix/AppendixK.pdf**). Cleaning, sanitizing, and disinfecting result in progressively higher levels of germ reduction and require different products, product concentrations, or contact time. See the following definitions (*CFOC* Standard 3.3.0.1; EPA 2023; Western States Pediatric Environmental Health Specialty Unit 2021):

- Cleaning removes dirt and debris by scrubbing and washing with a detergent solution and rinsing with water. The friction of cleaning removes most germs and exposes any remaining germs to the effects of a sanitizer or disinfectant used later.
- Sanitizing (not hand sanitizing) kills bacteria on inanimate surfaces using chemicals to levels considered safe by public health codes or regulations
- Disinfecting kills 99.9 percent of bacteria and viruses on any hard nonporous surfaces or objects

Reduce germs on surfaces and objects:

Here are some general principles for establishing a good germ reduction program:

- **Develop a policy, using two key documents.** (1) *Caring for Our Children* "Appendix K: Routine Schedule for Cleaning, Sanitizing and Disinfecting" (**https://nrckids.org/files/appendix/AppendixK.pdf**) for developing a schedule by method (e.g., clean, sanitize, disinfect) and timing by surfaces, objects, and area; and (2) *Caring for Our Children* "Appendix J: Selection and Use of a Cleaning, Sanitizing, or Disinfecting Product" (**https://nrckids.org/files/appendix/AppendixJ.pdf**) for determining which products to use.
- **Establish a schedule.** Set a schedule for cleaning, sanitizing, and disinfecting.

Direct Contact with Body Fluids: Fecal-Oral Germs/Blood-Borne Pathogens

How to Reduce the Spread of Intestinal Tract Diseases

Children and staff members who have intestinal tract diseases do not always feel sick or have diarrhea, so the best method for preventing the spread of disease is to have a prevention program at all times, not just when there is an outbreak. However, during an outbreak, it is especially important to strictly follow the best prevention practices and enhance them.

Diarrhea is defined as stools that are more frequent, watery, unformed, and looser than normal. Some judgement is required because diarrhea can occur from noninfectious causes, such as drinking excessive amounts of fruit juice, eating more than usual amounts of certain foods, having a disease that makes it difficult for the body to absorb nutrients (e.g., a food allergy or food intolerance), toxins in spoiled foods, or using some medications. Note that infants who are not yet eating solids normally have unformed and frequent stools. Similarly, it is common for infants to spit up often or have gastroesophageal reflux without having an infection. However, a child who vomits and appears ill is always assumed to have an infection.

Routine prevention program:

- Require frequent, thorough hand hygiene for both staff members and children before any activity that involves food or touching the mouth, whenever contact with stool may have occurred (*CFOC* Standard 3.2.2.2; see "Hand Hygiene" section).
- Follow guidance on hygiene, cleaning, sanitizing, and disinfecting, including procedures for diapering and changing soiled underclothing (*CFOC* Standard 3.2.1.4; see "Chapter 13: Creating a Safe Environment").
- Do not allow sharing of personal items (e.g., toothbrushes, washcloths, teething rings, pacifiers, cups, utensils).
- Separate children into three groups whenever possible by age and diapering needs—infants, older diapered children, and children who use the toilet reliably. Try to minimize combining staff members or children from other groups or rooms because it may increase the spread of infectious diseases.

Heightened prevention for diarrheal outbreaks:

- *Strictly enforce* all hand hygiene, diapering, toileting, cleaning procedures, and group separation.
- *Exclude* children with diarrhea that is not explained by a change of diet or use of medication and who have (1) two or more stools above their normal frequency or (2) diarrhea not contained in the diaper or toilet without accidents. The rationale for excluding children who have two or more stools above their normal frequency is that such frequent need to be changed or use the toilet may cause more work for the staff members than they can provide while maintaining sanitary conditions.
- *Report* diarrheal outbreaks to the local health department if two or more staff members or children have diarrhea symptoms. Diarrhea caused by *Giardia, Shigella, Cryptosporidium, Campylobacter,* and *norovirus* and other organisms can cause outbreaks and be difficult to eradicate in early learning settings. Laboratory tests may be indicated during an outbreak at the direction of the local health department but are not normally done by pediatric healthcare providers. It is especially important to report, investigate, and request laboratory studies in cases of bloody diarrhea, because it is most often caused by *Shigella* and known for difficult-to-stop outbreaks.

How to Reduce Spread from Contact with Blood and Other Potentially Infectious Body Fluids

Although the spread of disease does not always occur on contact with blood or body fluids, *you should treat all contact with blood and body fluids as if these fluids might cause infection* (*CFOC* Standard 3.2.3.4). People can be infected by contaminated materials or contact with body fluids, such as nasal discharge, feces, blood, drainage from sores or wounds, and urine on materials such as tissues, toilet paper, soiled diapers, bandages, soiled clothing, and surfaces in the facility. Cuts and scrapes are the usual sources of blood spills in early childhood settings. Biting is not a common method of transmitting infection because biters do not usually have bleeding mouth or gums that can transfer blood to someone they are biting. Additionally, when one child bites another, it rarely draws blood from the bitten child into the mouth of the biter. If bleeding occurs, it usually happens after the biter's mouth is no longer in contact with the bitten child. No case of transmission of HIV by biting in early childhood programs has been reported. Hepatitis B spread by biting is unlikely because most children have received the hepatitis B vaccine.

Educators are subject to Occupational Safety and Health Administration (OSHA) regulations for handling anything that might involve contamination with blood. OSHA uses the term *universal precautions* to describe the measures that the CDC calls standard precautions. OSHA can impose heavy fines on any employer who fails to comply with OSHA regulations. These regulations include having written policies, procedures, and training about the procedures to manage exposure to blood-borne pathogens, and steps to make sure staff members follow the procedures. Compliance with these requirements must be documented. Regional OSHA offices can provide interpretation of the requirements. Find your regional OSHA office online or in the telephone directory with other federal offices.

General procedures for reducing germ spread from contaminated surfaces:

- Keep changes of clothing handy. Place soiled disposable diapers in a tightly covered, hands-free lidded container that is lined with a disposable plastic bag.
- Clean and sanitize toys. As part of scheduled cleaning, sanitizing, and disinfecting, establish a routine to clean (wash and rinse) and sanitize all mouthed toys before they pass from one child to another. One easy way to manage mouthed toys is to put a soiled toy into a dishpan labeled clearly *soiled* on a counter when the child is no longer using it. Use a diluted solution of dishwashing detergent and water for soaking. These toys should be thoroughly cleaned and sanitized by the end of the day. If toys are dishwasher-safe, use a dishwasher that meets the requirements of the public health authorities as explained in *Caring for Our Children* Standard 4.9.0.11: Dishwashing in Centers. Other toys can be washed by hand, rinsed, and sprayed or soaked in an EPA-registered sanitizing product. Adequate numbers of toys should be available to correspond with the washing frequency.
- Use a dishwasher that meets regulatory requirements.
- Do not own anything that cannot be washed in a dishwasher, by hand, or in a laundry machine. Allow such an item only if it is a child's personal belonging that will not be shared.
- Label all toothbrushes and children's personal items. Make sure they are used only by their owners and that objects such as toothbrush bristles do not touch any surface other than the child's mouth.

- Avoid carpets in areas used by children. While carpets can help reduce the level of noise, they absorb moisture from infectious body fluids and dust; they are difficult to thoroughly clean and sanitize. Where rugs are needed, use those with nonslip backing that are of a size that staff members can remove and wash often. Do not use carpets or rugs in toilet, diaper-changing, or food-handling areas. Follow the procedure for cleaning carpets that are contaminated by body fluids outlined in *Caring for Our Children* "Appendix L: Cleaning Up Body Fluids." Routinely shampoo or steam-clean wall-to-wall or large area rugs at least every six months or when otherwise soiled.
- Practice regular hand hygiene (see section on "Hand Hygiene"), especially after handling body fluids.
- Always use disposable tissues or towels for wiping and washing. Single-use cloth towels are acceptable as long as they are placed in a hands-free container after they are used and then laundered before being used again. The environmental impact of doing that much laundry should be weighed against that of using disposable paper towels.
- Never use the same tissue or towel for more than one child.
- Dispose of used tissues and paper or single-use cloth towels in a lined and covered hands-free container that is stored away from food and classroom materials.
- Ensure each child has their own crib or mat and never switch unless all surfaces are cleaned first. Sheets and mats should be kept clean and stored so that sleeping surfaces do not touch each other.
- Do not allow children to share personal items, such as combs, brushes, blankets, pillows, hats, or clothing, without cleaning them before used by another child.
- Do not allow children's stored clothing or bedding to touch. If storage cubbies or hooks are too small or too close together, use a large laundry bag to store each child's articles separately. Store each child's dirty clothing separately preferably in paper bags and send it home for laundering. If plastic bags are used, they should be kept out of reach from the children to avoid suffocation.
- Promptly wash and cover sores, cuts, and scrapes. Report rashes, sores, and severe itching to the child's parents or caregivers so they can consult their child's usual source of healthcare.

Specific procedures for reducing germ spread from handling blood and body fluids:

- Ensure that as few people as possible handle contaminated items.
- Separate people involved with handling body fluids from those associated with handling food.
- Do *not* rinse or wash soiled cloth diapers or clothing at the early learning program. Place the soiled items in a paper or plastic bag (reminder to keep plastic bags out of children's reach), close it tightly, label it with the child's name, keep it out of the reach of children, and ask the family to launder the items at home.

Other Infectious Conditions Transmitted from Nonhuman Sources

Infectious conditions can be transmitted in other ways besides person-to-person contact. Some animals and vermin can transmit diseases by way of germs on surfaces and through bites. Likewise, insects can transmit disease through stings and bites.

- **Limit exposure to animals and vermin.** Limit exposure to pets, insects, wild mice, rats, and other vermin that may transmit disease-causing germs to people. Some pets are not appropriate for early childhood education settings because they or their habitat have disease-causing germs that pose risks for young children. Check with a veterinarian or look on the website of the CDC before bringing any animal into the setting, even just for a visit. (You can browse animal-related diseases at **www.cdc.gov/healthypets**.)
- **Prevent insect bites.** Some insects transmit infections when they bite. Reducing the risk of insect bites is the first line of defense. When possible, stay indoors at dawn and dusk because these are times of day when disease-carrying insects are most active. Use screens on windows. Eliminate from children's play areas any standing water, fruit trees, and open trash because they attract biting and stinging insects. When children do get insect bites, the swelling of body tissues or scratching may lead to secondary infection by bacteria on the skin. This is a common cause of impetigo—superficial, crusty infections of the skin. DEET (N,N-diethyl-3-methylbenzamide) is the most effective insect repellent; it is safe when used properly, even for very young children. (See also "Chapter 7: First Aid and Injuries.")

Managing People, Procedures, and Policy

If a child or staff member is ill, the policies and procedures of a program or center take over. It is important to refer to all policies and procedures, and for educators and administrators to work together in these situations.

First Steps for Educators: Set Expectations

At a child's enrollment, educators should set expectations and reassure families about common infections. Explain that their child in an early learning program will have more illnesses than they would if they were at home. Explain the program's policies and practices on screening for illness, excluding ill children, and return to care criteria.

FAMILY CONNECTIONS

Reassuring Families About Frequent Illnesses

Reassure families that every child is handled equitably and in the best interests for everyone's health. Explain that despite more frequent illnesses, especially in the first year of early childhood education, children rapidly develop immunity to common infectious diseases and by kindergarten age, those who have been in group care since infancy have fewer illnesses than children cared for only at home. Research demonstrates that early exposure to frequent mild illnesses has some beneficial effects on the development of the immune system and may reduce the risk of some allergic conditions like asthma (Swartz et al. 2018).

Daily Health Check

When the child comes to the program each day, use the daily health check procedure to quickly gather information on the child's health status and decide whether the child should enter the program for the day. If the child develops symptoms after the parent or caregiver leaves, then a new health check is necessary to make the decision about what to do and to tell the parent/caregiver about the change in the child. Performing daily health checks and excluding children when doing so will reduce the risk of exposure of others to illness-causing germs.

Early childhood educators must follow the most stringent guidance by comparing the state and local public health regulations with the national agencies and experts about actions to take when a child is ill. If the regulations are not consistent with current recommendations of national health experts, consult with the child's healthcare professional. For guidance on child and staff member exclusion for illness, see *Caring for Our Children* Standard 3.6.1.1.

Working Together to Reduce the Risk of Infectious Disease

Educators, families, and healthcare providers need to work together to help reduce preventable infectious diseases. Educators need to establish and monitor vaccination requirements for children and staff; monitor for illness at the daily health check and throughout the day, and notify parents or caregivers if illness occurs, and exclude children when necessary. Educators occasionally need input from pediatric healthcare providers about a child's illness. Families need to comply with immunization and health maintenance requirements, report new symptoms at the daily health check, and take their children to health checks when necessary. Pediatric healthcare providers should recommend and give the required immunizations and preventative care, and inform families and educators when children can safely return to care in some cases by using evidence-based recommendations.

Occasionally, outbreaks of serious diseases may occur. If precautions are not taken, these serious diseases can spread quickly. Educators and healthcare providers should contact the local health department for any condition that might pose a threat to the group or is reportable according to state regulations such as most vaccine-preventable diseases (e.g., chickenpox, measles, and whooping cough). For reportable infectious diseases, the health department has the legal authority to make final determinations about what the program must do, for example, during outbreaks of some types of diarrhea and COVID-19.

Sometimes programs receive what seem to be conflicting opinions from different healthcare providers about how to address a particular health issue. Usually, these conflicts are best resolved with the help of the program's CCHC or health manager. CCHCs are trained professionals with expertise in health and safety issues, regulations, and resources specific to early learning programs. Many states fund CCHCs through their health or education departments, but some CCHCs are independent contractors or employed by other agencies. CCHCs have skills in assessing the quality of an early learning program, connecting child care administrators and educators with resources, providing educational workshops, and writing health and safety policies (*CFOC* Standard 1.6.0.1).

Recommended health practices and policies are essential tools in the management of infectious diseases. Written program policies should describe expectations for staff members and families. Even with clear and appropriate written policies, practices must be regularly monitored to ensure that they are followed.

Exclusion of Children and Staff When Ill

Contrary to popular belief and practice, only a *few* illnesses require sick children and staff members to be sent home ("excluded") to protect other children and staff members. Children and adults in group learning settings are exposed to one another's germs all the time. The signs and symptoms of illness often appear days after the germs causing the illness have already spread from the infected person. So, before someone has any symptoms, other people may have been exposed to that person's disease-causing germs. Additionally, after symptoms resolve, a person can continue to be infectious, or spread germs to others. We can't have all children and educators at home for the entire duration of their contagious period—we can't identify them before they get sick and keep them out for days after they feel well again, that would be too much time. The most common symptoms young children with infectious diseases experience are runny nose, cough, congestion, fever, eye discharge, and rash. Diarrhea and vomiting occur much less frequently than respiratory symptoms. Mild symptoms do not usually require exclusion if the child is able to participate in activities and is not requiring too much care. Table 9.1 lists symptoms that do not require exclusion and those that require temporary exclusion. For more information and complete recommendations, see *Caring for Our Children* Standard 3.6.1.1. If a child develops an excludable condition, the parents or caregivers should remove the child from care as soon as possible. In the meantime, the ill child should receive appropriate care in an area where the child will not expose previously unexposed individuals.

ANOTHER AAP RESOURCE

A helpful resource is the Quick Reference Sheets in *Managing Infectious Diseases in Child Care and Schools: A Quick Reference Guide* (Shope & Hashikawa 2023). Each of the Quick Reference Sheets gives a succinct, easy-to-understand summary for a specific symptom or diagnosis. The publisher gives permission to copy the Quick Reference Sheets and distribute them to families and staff members. These resources make clear not only when to exclude a child or staff member, but also when the child can return based on the condition, the symptoms, or the treatment.

Early learning programs should avoid unnecessary exclusion of mildly ill children whenever possible. Studies show unnecessary exclusion is common. When children are inappropriately sent home, it can have a negative financial consequence that disproportionately affects families with low income. Exclusion of mildly ill children forces parents and caregivers to make alternative arrangements on short notice; many take their ill children to work or leave them in make-do arrangements. These alternate arrangements may be less appropriate than the ill child's group learning setting. As previously indicated, for many illnesses, children have already exposed others

Table 9.1. Conditions That Do Not Require Exclusion (AAP 2021; Shope & Hashikawa 2023)

Conditions	Notes
Common cold, runny nose, and cough	No exclusion regardless of color or consistency of nasal discharge.
Cytomegalovirus infection (CMV)	No exclusion required.
Diarrhea	No exclusion if stool is contained in the diaper, there are no toileting accidents, and there are no more than two stools per day above the normal for that child.
Eye drainage	No exclusion unless the child has watery discharge that is yellow or white; without fever, eye pain, or eyelid redness.
Fever	Temperature above 100.4°F (38°C) (axillary, temporal, or oral) is a fever. Children over 4 months old without signs of illness do not need to be excluded. Only take a child's temperature if the child seems ill. (During outbreaks such as COVID-19, follow CDC or local health department recommendations.)
Fifth's disease (parvovirus B19 or slapped cheek disease)	No exclusion for children who have normal immune systems and who don't have an underlying blood disorder like sickle cell disease.
Hand, foot, and mouth (Coxsackie virus)	No exclusion unless the child has a fever with symptoms, mouth sores, and constant drooling, or if recommended by public health authorities to control an outbreak.
Hepatitis B virus, chronic	No exclusion required.
HIV infection	No exclusion required.
Impetigo	Cover skin lesions until the end of the day if there is no fever or changes in behavior. If medical treatment starts before returning the next day, no exclusion is needed.
Lice or nits	Treatment may start at the end of the day. If treatment starts before returning the next day, no exclusion needed.
Methicillin-resistant (MRSA) and methicillin-sensitive (MSSA) colonization	Colonization is the presence of bacteria on the body without illness. Active lesions or illness may require exclusion.
Molluscum contagiosum	No exclusion or covering of lesions is needed.
Pink eye	No exclusion needed if pink or red on the white of the eye with or without drainage, without fever or behavioral change (AAP 2021).
Rash without fever or behavior changes	No exclusion necessary.
Ringworm	Cover skin lesions until the end of the day. If medical treatment starts before returning the next day, no exclusion is needed.
Roseola	No exclusion needed unless there is a fever and behavior changes.
Scabies	Treatment may be delayed until the end of the day. As long as treatment starts before returning the next day, no exclusion is needed.
Thrush	No exclusion needed. (The signs of thrush are white spots or patches in the mouth, cheeks, or gums.)

before becoming obviously ill and therefore do not need to be excluded because of the risk of contagion. However, when a child's illness meets the criteria for exclusion, then the family will need to use a preplanned, alternative care arrangement.

In general, children can return to their early learning program after an illness without a primary care provider note if they are getting better and are able to participate in their usual activities. In a few specific instances, a healthcare provider's note is needed to provide instructions when the child or adult needs continued special care or arrangements while in the group setting, but should not be routine for excluded children.

Exclusion criteria are based on sound science, and in some cases may be different than common health beliefs. In general, for a condition to require exclusion, it should meet all three of the following conditions: it must be harmful, capable of spread from one person to another, and there should be evidence exclusion might reduce the spread. For example, pink eye—or bacterial conjunctivitis—characterized by redness in the whites of the eyes and green or yellow discharge, resolves on its own without antibiotic drops and children are usually only mildly ill. The bacteria that cause it are present in the noses of nearly half of young children who are not having symptoms, so excluding the children with symptoms will not reduce the spread significantly. Similarly, children infected with hand-foot-and-mouth disease have the virus in their secretions long after the rash is gone, and many children become infected without ever developing a rash, so excluding only children who have the rash is ineffective at reducing the spread. These conditions, although they spread from one person to another, are not harmful, and there is no evidence exclusion would reduce the spread.

With the same exceptions that apply to children, staff members who are well enough to perform their role as expected do not need to be excluded. As with the decisions regarding exclusion of children, someone should be designated to decide when a staff member who wants to work needs to be excluded for illness. Criteria for when staff member should be excluded can be found in *Caring for Our Children* Standard 3.6.1.2.

Notification of Exposure to Infectious Diseases

Inform staff members and families about exposure to infectious diseases that are present in higher numbers in the program. "Appendix A.9.1: Sample Letter to Families about Exposure to Communicable Disease" provides a sample letter to families that can be used and adapted. Make this information available to staff members as well. One online source for up-to-date fact sheets about infectious diseases (not specific to the early childhood setting) is **www.cdc.gov/diseasesconditions/index.html.** See the latest guidance from the CDC regarding COVID-19 at **www.cdc.gov/coronavirus/2019-ncov/community/schools-childcare/k-12-childcare-guidance.html**.

Reportable Diseases and Outbreaks

Every state has laws requiring early learning programs to report the occurrence of certain infectious diseases to the state's public health authorities. The CDC and state health departments maintain a list of *notifiable diseases*. Sometimes called *reportable diseases,* these are conditions for which public health authorities need timely information when someone has the health problem so they can institute measures to prevent and control disease. The list of notifiable diseases varies from state to state. Contact your local health department for the current list. *Be sure to include this list and a reporting procedure in your facility's health policy.* Even though the healthcare facility that makes the diagnosis is required to report to the state, early learning programs should report to the state promptly when a child has a disease on the state's list to make sure that public health authorities can take appropriate action to protect others in the group.

For some diseases (e.g., hepatitis and meningitis), any occurrence must be reported to health authorities. Other diseases must be reported when an *outbreak* occurs—that is, when two or more children or adults involved in the program become ill. Keep track of the number of cases of diarrhea, and when *two or more* people in the program have diarrhea, ask the health department or your CCHC to determine what additional steps are necessary.

Generally, an *epidemic*—a large number of cases in a short period—should be reported, even if the disease is not on the list of notifiable diseases. For example, outbreaks of COVID-19, flu, mononucleosis, the rapid spread of severe conjunctivitis, or pneumonia should be reported promptly so public health authorities can offer advice about preventing additional cases. All programs should have a written plan for seasonal and pandemic influenza that includes approaches for coordination among program staff members, families, and public health authorities; infection control policies and procedures; communication procedures; and maintenance of child learning and program operations. During illness outbreaks, programs may need to sanitize, or disinfect surfaces more often and should refer to state, local, tribal, or territorial health authorities and child care licensing for more information (*CFOC* Standard 3.3.0.1). See the latest guidance from the CDC regarding COVID-19 at **www.cdc.gov/coronavirus/2019-ncov/community/schools-childcare/k-12-childcare-guidance.html**.

Summary

Program administrators can create and implement certain policies and procedures that will optimize the ability of educators to reduce the spread of infectious diseases. These policies and procedures can be thought of as affecting the behavior of *people*, the presence and spread of *germs*, and the *environment* in which germs may thrive. There are sample policies available in *Caring for Our Children* and on state health department and other organizations' websites. Policies are needed for exclusion criteria for ill children, reporting outbreaks and illnesses to the local health department, respiratory etiquette, hand hygiene, diapering, food safety, gloving, cleaning, sanitizing, and disinfecting. Educators and staff members must be knowledgeable of all policies and trained to follow carefully all procedures. Policies should be shared with families at enrollment in a booklet or online, so they are aware of the steps the program takes to reduce the spread of infectious diseases and feel reassured that children are handled equitably. The following checklists of action items can help program administrators and educators and staff to manage infectious diseases.

Plan in advance and use the following steps to plan for unexpected illnesses.

For program administrators:

- Ensure parents, caregivers, and educators understand the policies for infectious control and their roles and responsibilities.

- At least annually, provide creative, attention-getting reminders for all staff members, children, and families about hand hygiene, cough and sneeze control, and the need to obtain influenza vaccine each fall.
- Choose a CCHC who knows about infectious disease in early childhood settings.
- Prominently post telephone numbers of local and state departments of public health.
- Make sure children's adult staff immunizations are up to date at program entry and regular intervals. If an outbreak of a vaccine-preventable disease does occur, identify children who are not protected—either because they are not old enough to have received all their doses or because their families have not obtained the recommended vaccines for them—and exclude them if necessary.
- Inform staff members, parents, and caregivers of any contagious disease to which they or their children might have been exposed so they can watch for symptoms and alert their own healthcare professionals about the exposure.
- Report to your local health department if more than two people from a group experience food contamination with gastrointestinal symptoms (e.g., stomach cramps, vomiting, diarrhea, and/or dizziness) at the same time.

For educators:

- Develop procedures for handling child illness, including a safe, separate resting area, care plans and establishing designated individuals who will use the inclusion/exclusion criteria to make final decisions.
- Learn and follow guidelines for hand hygiene, cleaning/disinfection, and ventilation all the time, but especially during spring, fall, and winter, when illness seems more common.
- *Be watchful!* Learn to look for signs of infectious disease. Call or send a note home if you suspect a health concern.

Inclusion of Young Children with Special Healthcare Needs and/or Medical Complexity

ALICIA HAUPT AND STACEY COOK

LEARNING OBJECTIVES

- To define what characterizes a child as having special healthcare needs and/or medical complexity
- To recognize how inclusion of children with special healthcare needs into the early learning program benefits both the children and their families
- To understand why the integration of children with special healthcare needs in the early learning program enriches the educational experience for typically developing children, teachers, and staff members

(continued)

LEARNING OBJECTIVES (*continued*)

- To identify the key components of the Individuals with Disabilities Education Act (IDEA)
- To appreciate how early learning programs must prepare and modify their structure and environment to appropriately integrate children with special healthcare needs
- To identify some of the services and resources that exist for children with chronic medical conditions
- To understand the importance of open and frequent communication among all individuals involved in the care of children with special healthcare needs

Teachers are not expected to be experts in special healthcare or nursing procedures. Usually, the child's parents or caregivers have a wealth of information to share about what works and what doesn't work for their child. Families of young children with special healthcare or complex medical needs are active and contributing participants in the education and development of their children. Early childhood educators must know the definitions and medical terms associated with the situations of these children, yet understand that these definitions do not define the children themselves. Each child is an individual. Educators must use a strengths-based approach and learn what is unique about each child and family with a focus on abilities, inclusion, and support to promote "opportunities for development and learning, and a sense of belonging for every child" (DEC & NAEYC 2009, 1). The purposes of this chapter are to introduce the responsibilities for educators who work with children with special healthcare and medical needs and to emphasize the importance of inclusion and support systems.

Definition and Description of Special Healthcare Needs in Children

Children and youth with special healthcare needs (CYSHCN) or *children with medical complexity* (CMC) constitute an increasing population within private early learning programs as well as within the public school system. Both distinct terms encompass a diverse group of developmentally and medically complex children who have specialized educational needs. Traditionally, the term *CYSHCN* has referred to anyone younger than 21 years old who has any chronic medical, psychological, and/or developmental condition. Examples of CYSHCN might include children with asthma, type 1 diabetes, or autism. A better way to describe this important population was outlined by McPherson and colleagues (1998): "Those [children] who have or are at increased risk for a chronic physical, developmental, behavioral or emotional condition and who also require health and related services of a type or amount beyond that required by children generally" (138). This interpretation broadly covers all children with special needs or disabilities, not just those children with conditions conventionally thought to require chronic medical management. The Developmental Disabilities Act defines *developmental disability* as a severe, chronic disability of a child over 5 years old that is due to a mental and/or physical impairment that is likely indefinite in nature and results in functional limitations in daily activity.

In contrast, the term *CMC* refers to the most medically complex, technology-dependent children who often require additional clinical support both at home and at school. An example of a child with a medical complexity is a child with seizures and a gastrostomy tube. Full participation in an early learning program outside the home for this child may include the assistance of a skilled nurse to help manage medications, meals, and mobility.

However, both populations (CYSHCN and CMC) may additionally be classified as having a disability, which is defined by the Americans for Disabilities Act (ADA) as "a person who has a physical or mental impairment that substantially limits one or more major life activity." Thus, the groundbreaking legislation of ADA, which went into full effect in 1992, helped develop a common language for organizations to use when identifying vulnerable individuals. Even more importantly, ADA provided a legal framework that could address the many social inequities disabled adults and children experience in a wide range of settings, including educational programs. ADA states that people with disabilities are "entitled to equal rights and protections in employment, in receipt of state and local public services, and in access to public accommodations such as preschools, child-care centers, and family child-care homes." Stated plainly, schools, both public and private, must account for the entire spectrum of medical complexity and developmental disability by accommodating the needs of each individual child.

Inclusion of Children with Special Healthcare Needs Within the US Educational System

Prior to 1975, children with significant neurodevelopmental disabilities, that is children with abnormalities in the brain's nervous system, were educated away from typically developing children. However, a movement toward inclusion within educational systems began gaining steam in the late 1960s, culminating with the passage of the IDEA (see section "The Individuals with Disabilities Education Act (IDEA)" for further specifics). This federal action had an enormous impact on the lives of families who have a child or family member with specialized needs as it established the right of all children with disabilities in the United States to have access to publicly funded, free, appropriate education and related services. Essentially, no child could be denied an educational experience due to disability. The law requires that programs must provide services with *reasonable accommodation*. Each child's needs must be *evaluated on an individual basis* to determine whether a program can *reasonably accommodate* the child's needs.

Once IDEA and ADA established the illegality of limiting access, the practicality of providing this safety net became a new focus for educators. A central ethos in this discussion was the concept of inclusion, which as a value, supports the right of all children—regardless of their diverse abilities—to participate actively alongside their peers. It is important to remember that prior to IDEA, families had no legal standing to advocate for their children to be accommodated in early learning programs.

Meeting the child's and family's needs while caring for other children may seem overwhelming to those working in potentially short-staffed and inadequately financed programs. The challenge of educating such a large spectrum of children with varying needs cannot be overstated, but the benefits make this endeavor worthwhile and meaningful for all children, educators, and the communities they live in.

Inclusion Is Essential

While it may be challenging to meet the needs of a diverse population of children, both typically developing children and CYSHCN benefit from shared learning environments that allow them to learn together. Studies looking at the impact of inclusive instruction have consistently demonstrated the benefit to CYSHCN and CMC. The gains these children experience in diverse early learning programs are wide ranging and include academic, developmental, and social-emotional well-being. CYSHCN, when given the chance to interact with their peers, learn more about themselves and their abilities while also advancing life skills. Likewise, outcomes data has shown the educational experience for neurotypical children in the classroom is equally enhanced through inclusive educational practices. They grow to embrace any differences, find ways to support one another, and participate in the same activities—all with a positive outlook. These findings were contrary to earlier-held beliefs that children with disabilities would funnel attention and resources away from other children. Instead, the last 60 years since IDEA was ratified has shown that when programs are designed with consideration of CYSHCN and their needs, it allows for resources and environments within the institution to be richer for all (Pfeiffer & Reddy 1999).

Inclusion of children with special healthcare needs also has clear benefits for educators and staff members (Dinnebeil et al. 1998; Tarantino, Makopoulou, & Neville 2002). A key to ensuring success for any early learning program is to provide suitable training and support for all educators regarding the developmental and medical challenges faced by CYSHCN. From a professional standpoint, working with CYSHCN provides an opportunity for teachers to broaden their skills, gain valuable insight into neurodevelopment and collaborate more meaningfully with their special education colleagues. Providing adequate resources to teachers and caregivers enables them to have a comprehensive approach to a child's education.

Lastly, the parents and caregivers of CYSHCN and CMC undoubtedly benefit from integrated educational practices and programs. Early learning programs provide a safe, structured setting for children with special healthcare needs, allowing caregivers to maintain meaningful employment and financially support the child at home. Without this resource, families suffer not only financially, but they become socially isolated from the local community ultimately leading to suboptimal care for the child. One of the most important functions of early learning programs is to allow for consistent and easy access to essential therapies by developmental specialists. For instance, lack of regular physical therapy can have devastating health consequences for children with spastic quadriplegia or cerebral palsy.

Finally, inclusion of CYSHCN and CMC in all educational settings creates a network for caregivers and families, and the positive impact of this community cannot be underestimated. It is essential, however, to realize that priorities differ between families. A perfect example is weighing the benefits and risks of participation in early learning programs during the COVID-19 pandemic. To allow for a truly family-centered plan for educating a child with special healthcare needs, an individualized approach is necessary to help the family navigate competing concerns for education and health. Therefore, it is important to maintain open and frequent communication with all providers and participants involved in the child's educational plan over time. This requires a multidisciplinary approach and allows for consideration of a child's needs, strengths, and abilities while also respecting the concerns of the parents or caregivers. In an ideal scenario, the educational plan for CYSHCN and CMC should be individually determined, agreed upon by all participants, and reassessed regularly. Coordination of efforts is both a challenge and a critical requirement for meeting the needs of CYSHCN and CMC.

The Individuals with Disabilities Education Act (IDEA)

Under IDEA, a federal law, state or local school systems are responsible for providing services to children with specific types of special healthcare needs.

As explained in the previous section, IDEA, most recently amended in 2004, affords caregivers and teachers a unique opportunity to support children with disabilities in the early learning program. Federal funds subsidize the cost of providing these services. Medicaid and private health insurance, including the state- and federally subsidized Child Health Insurance Program (CHIP), pay some but usually not all of the expenses of daily care for children with special healthcare needs or chronic medical conditions. Federal tax credits and deductions are available to for-profit early learning programs to help defray some types of costs associated with serving CYSHCN. Early learning programs can play a significant role in optimizing a child's developmental potential by making sure that families whose children are eligible for subsidized services apply and receive care.

Part C of IDEA: Infants and Toddlers

Part C of IDEA provides for a comprehensive system of early intervention services for eligible infants and toddlers from birth to age 3 years and their families. Depending on the child's needs, early intervention services might include family training, counseling, and home visits; occupational, physical, or speech therapy; hearing loss services; health, nutrition, social work, and assistance with service coordination; assistive technology devices and services; and transportation. Additionally, Part C also aims to transition children to appropriate, effective preschool services. Essentially Part C of IDEA allocates federal funds for states to implement an interagency system of early intervention services for eligible infants and toddlers in natural settings.

> When parents request early intervention services, either by contacting their state's system directly or having a medical doctor or school staff member do so on their behalf, an early intervention representative asks the parents about their child's development to decide the next steps. This is called a *referral* to early intervention. Before anyone from the early intervention system can evaluate or work with their child, the parents must give their written permission. (Brillante 2017, 11)

Before Part C services start, an Individualized Family Service Plan (IFSP) is developed by a team, which includes the parents or caregivers and all providers who work with the child and the family including the child's educator or caregiver (**https://www.cdc.gov/ncbddd/actearly/autism/case-modules/pdf/early-intervention/sample-ifsp.pdf**). With consent, appropriate program staff members can join the IFSP team. The staff members must understand both the role the program is to perform and the resources available through the IFSP to support the child's family and the work of their team.

The IFSP describes the child's developmental, therapeutic, and health needs; summarizes assessments that have been done; describes early intervention services and family support that will be provided; and lists the expected functional outcomes of services. Figure 10.1 outlines the steps in the IFSP process.

Evaluations must be conducted using a strengths-based framework focusing on children and their families' abilities rather than their deficits. The IFSP and all service providers emphasize the child's strengths and capabilities rather than perceived weaknesses. Service providers strive for progress by enhancing and supporting the family's strengths, focusing on their resources, priorities, and concerns about the child rather than on correcting "deficiencies."

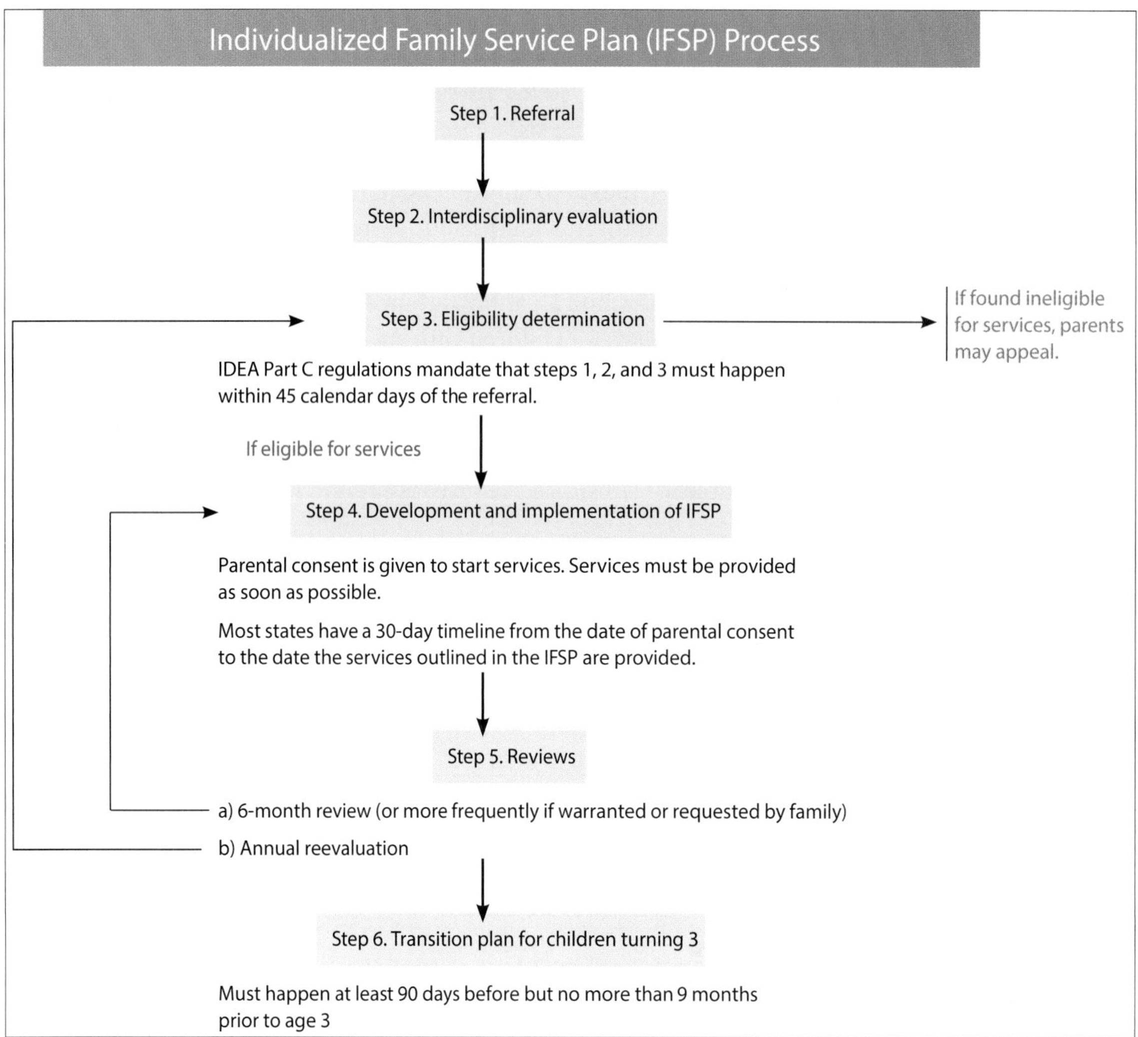

Individualized Family Service Plan (IFSP) Process
Step 1. Referral
Step 2. Interdisciplinary evaluation
Step 3. Eligibility determination
If found ineligible for services, parents may appeal.
IDEA Part C regulations mandate that steps 1, 2, and 3 must happen within 45 calendar days of the referral.
If eligible for services
Step 4. Development and implementation of IFSP
Parental consent is given to start services. Services must be provided as soon as possible.
Most states have a 30-day timeline from the date of parental consent to the date the services outlined in the IFSP are provided.
Step 5. Reviews
a) 6-month review (or more frequently if warranted or requested by family)
b) Annual reevaluation
Step 6. Transition plan for children turning 3
Must happen at least 90 days before but no more than 9 months prior to age 3

Figure 10.1.

Reprinted, with permission, from P. Brillante, *The Essentials: Supporting Young Children with Disabilities in the Classroom* (Washington, DC: NAEYC, 2017), 10.

Part C of IDEA requires delivery of services in environments defined as settings that are "natural or normal for the child's peers who have no disabilities." Such environments include the child's home, neighborhood, community programs, early learning programs, parks, recreation centers, stores, museums, and so on. Family and educators incorporate elements of the child's regular, everyday environment in the planning and delivery of services and supports. In this way, they can best discover the child's talents and gifts. These can then be used as a foundation on which to promote the child's progress in the normal course of play, relationships, and caregiving. Learning about and understanding the child's routines and using real-life opportunities and activities, such as eating, playing, and interacting with others, greatly enhances adults' ability to work on the child's developmental skills. This approach helps the child achieve the functional outcomes identified in the IFSP.

Part B, Section 619 of IDEA: Children 3–5 Years Old

Part B, Section 619 allocates funds specifically for special education and services for eligible children ages 3–5 years old. Each state administers its own IDEA Part B programs for children with suspected or identified disabilities. The Part B regulations outline eligibility requirements and procedures for seeking services, as well as the timelines for when the steps in the referral and evaluation processes must happen.

These services are generally served through a written Individualized Education Program (IEP). In some states and communities, the IFSP may still be used for preschoolers. As with the early intervention process, terminology varies from state to state and may change over time, but the basic steps are similar (see Figure 10.2). The teacher may be able to participate, with prior informed written parental/caregiver consent, in the IEP review meetings to share valuable insight and information regarding the child's needs in the early learning setting.

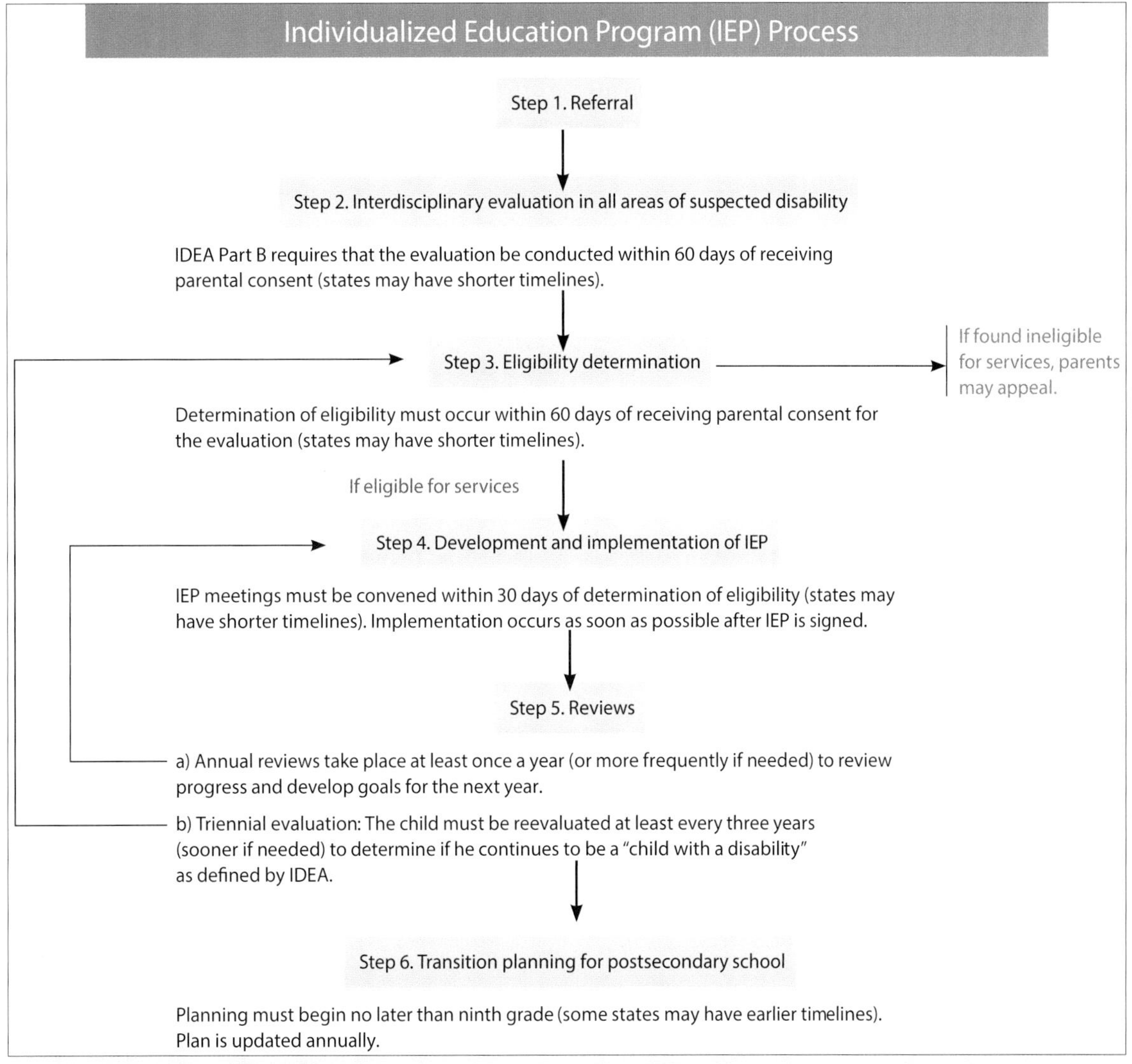

Figure 10.2.

Reprinted, with permission, from P. Brillante, *The Essentials: Supporting Young Children with Disabilities in the Classroom* (Washington, DC: NAEYC, 2017), 16.

Early Learning Program Responsibilities and Resources

There are numerous resources available that detail the responsibilities that early learning programs share with other agencies to serve a child with special healthcare needs. ADA's website (**www.ada.gov/resources/child-care-centers**) and the Department of Health and Human Services in each state are good places to look. However, some children with special healthcare needs who do not have developmental delay are not eligible for education-based services like an IFSP or IEP, but the procedures outlined in the standards should be used, nonetheless.

The steps described in the standards include the following:

1. Planning for inclusion, including delineating the tasks to be accomplished pre-enrollment:
    - Assessment of the child's strengths and special needs
    - Developing a service plan that identifies the type and frequency of special services required
    - Formulation of an educational action plan
2. Identifying a staff member to coordinate the child's care in the program and specifying that person's role going forward
3. Arranging for contracted services and reimbursements
4. Developing measurable objectives and providing documentation in written reports to all those involved in the child's care
5. Conducting periodic re-evaluation of the child and of the facility's performance in meeting the objectives
6. Conducting individualized planning and support to help the child develop their strengths and meet learning standards that apply to all children

IMMEDIATE IMPACT

Look for Examples and Seek Advice

Teachers can visit other programs where children with similar special healthcare needs receive educational services or speak with specialists, particularly those who have evaluated or worked with the child. They usually have valuable suggestions and may be able to offer training and other resources.

If the child is younger than 3 years old and eligible for early intervention services under Part C of IDEA, early intervention staff members will be a valuable resource. Ideally, the program staff members should be ongoing members of the team who plan for the child in the formal process involved in establishing and updating the IFSP and informally on an ongoing basis. Remember to obtain required Health Insurance Portability and Accountability Act (HIPAA) forms signed by the parent/caregiver or legal guardian to communicate with the child's healthcare provider and with others who work closely with the child.

FAMILY CONNECTIONS

ChildCare.gov

ChildCare.gov is one resource that provides families with resources to allow them to understand the laws that affect children with special healthcare needs in order to promote advocacy. This material can also be informative for early learning programs and includes links that provide details about services in each state within the United States (**https://childcare.gov/consumer-education/services-for-children-with-disabilities**).

To obtain general information about disabilities and chronic healthcare conditions, one can search the National Center on Birth Defects and Developmental Disabilities website (**www.cdc.gov/ncbddd**). Relevant information regarding a wide range of medical conditions is available on this website by searching the A to Z links provided. One can also find credentialed organizations affiliated with a particular type of health condition.

To provide competent care, be sure to review all of the relevant standards in *Caring for Our Children* (**https://nrckids.org/CFOC**). This collection of standards provides methods and suggestions for inclusion for children with special healthcare needs with a section on infants and toddlers as well as preschoolers. Details are also included regarding supporting the family, environmental considerations, and fostering communication.

AAP RESOURCE

The AAP has an easy-to-use resource called *Managing Chronic Health Needs in Child Care and Schools: A Quick Reference Guide* to help education professionals understand and address the chronic conditions of children who are seeking to enroll or are already enrolled in their programs. This book uses the broad definition of special healthcare needs that includes developmental disabilities and includes Quick Reference Sheets on topics such as allergies, asthma, attention-deficit/hyperactivity disorder, autism spectrum disorder, Down syndrome, and visual impairments. The Quick Reference Sheets each describe a medical condition, how frequently it is seen, the characteristics of children with the condition, the professionals who make up the treatment team for this condition, common adaptations needed, considerations in an emergency, types of program policies that may be required, and resources that provide additional information about the specific condition.

Program Modifications to Support Children with Special Healthcare Needs

Modifications in a program's policies, practices, equipment, or routines may be needed to facilitate the active participation of children with special healthcare needs. The primary goal of inclusion is to enable all children to participate as much as possible in educational activities. The Division for Early Childhood (DEC) and the National Association for the Education of Young Children (NAEYC) created a joint position statement on inclusion that encompasses the following:

> Early childhood inclusion embodies the values, policies, and practices that support the right of every infant and young child and his or her family, regardless of ability, to participate in a broad range of activities and contexts as full members of families, communities, and society. The desired results of inclusive experiences for children with and without disabilities and their families include a sense of belonging and membership, positive social relationships and friendships, and development and learning to reach their full potential. The defining features of inclusion that can be used to identify high quality early childhood programs and services are access, participation, and supports. (DEC & NAEYC 2009, 2)

A program that enrolls children with special healthcare needs and children with medical complexity should meet these objectives:

- Develop a program that ensures successful participation of all children.
- Promote a child's feelings of competence and independence.
- Encourage peer acceptance.
- Avoid overprotection and isolating activities.
- Strengthen teamwork among the family, teachers, and other specialists.

IMMEDIATE IMPACT

Identifying the Supports Children Need

To help children be successful in the general education classroom, first identify your expectations for all children within the typical routines, activities, and lessons of the day. Doing so lets you see the barriers a child with a disability may have with access or participation, and then you can start problem solving to remove those barriers and meet children's specific needs (Brillante 2017).

Physical Adaptations

Selecting and adjusting materials and activities for children with special healthcare needs sometimes requires problem solving and creativity. Unique supplies may be required, many of which can be used by typically developing children as well. Examples of such materials are

- Eating utensils with special grips or edges
- Puzzles with large pieces and/or knobs for children with fine motor needs
- Books with large pictures for children with visual impairments
- Hypoallergenic art materials
- Foods that avoid ingredients that could be problematic for children with allergies, food intolerance, or other nutritional issues

In many cases, staff members can modify materials already available. For example, they can

- Apply masking tape to thicken brush handles and crayons to give children a firmer grip
- Slit a small rubber ball and slide the paintbrush or crayon through it to allow for easier grabbing
- Paste fabric of varying textures on a storybook to make it more tactile
- Lower an easel or coat hooks
- Incorporate visuals to accompany classroom discussions for children with impaired hearing as well as auditory activities for those with visual difficulties
- Use a wedge, standing table, or step stool to help support children physically
- Remove pets or plants from the room or center if they aggravate a child's asthma or allergies

Necessary adaptations depend on the type and severity of a child's needs. For example, to accommodate a child who uses a wheelchair, staff members can

- Measure pathways to ensure that the child can maneuver from one area to another without obstacles present
- Check the height of tables to ensure that the arms of the wheelchair fit under them, add blocks to slightly increase the height, or find an alternate seating arrangement
- Explore the use of a scooter board instead of a wheelchair, if appropriate, for mobility around the classroom
- Ensure ready access to, from, and around the building with the addition of ramps if necessary
- Position an activity table or food table so the child can reach it

"Appendix A.10.1: Adaptive Equipment or Devices" provides a list of adaptive equipment for children with special healthcare needs and includes many materials that may already be available in a program serving typically developing children. Reviewing this list may help reassure staff members when considering enrolling a child who has a disability.

Promote Peer Acceptance

Children must be provided with positive role models so they can learn to interact with others in a kind, accepting way. When given opportunities to watch adults relating comfortably to children with special healthcare needs, typically developing children take the first step toward learning peer acceptance. Early childhood educators must use person-first language, especially when working with children with disabilities or medical conditions. This places the emphasis on the child rather than their condition and is helpful modeling for other children. Children should be given factual information about disabilities to dispel misunderstandings and diminish fear. Staff members can encourage the acceptance of a child with special healthcare needs in the following ways:

- Always answer children's questions accurately, using language they can easily understand.
- Reassure children that they cannot "catch" a disability.
- Plan activities that allow the other children to see the child with a special healthcare need in a successful role.
- Include materials that reflect diversity available, such as books about children with special healthcare needs in the reading area and dolls or puppets with disabilities (e.g., a stuffed animal with a gastrostomy tube).
- Invite adults with disabilities into the classroom to participate in activities.
- Focus on a variety of similarities and differences among people.
- Operate from a viewpoint of competence and adaptation rather than from a deficit model that emphasizes weakness.

Avoid Overprotection

Overprotection limits a child's opportunities to grow to full potential. Both pity and fear may make a teacher reluctant to allow a child with special healthcare needs to take risks, have the opportunity to respond to limits before the teacher intercedes, engage in conflict, and experience *real* success and failure. Staff members can avoid overprotection by remembering to do the following:

- Set limits that apply to *all* children (e.g., all children must wait for a turn on the slide).
- Provide many classroom options and activities for children that they can do without needing to wait for adult guidance or assistance.
- Encourage all children to try new activities if they do not choose to do them on their own.
- Communicate a positive attitude and sincere feelings to the children; children see their teachers as important role models.

Strengthen Teamwork

Including a child with special healthcare needs in the program makes teamwork an even greater necessity. Parents, caregivers, teachers, and administrators must communicate closely and regularly. With family consent, periodic communications with the child's source of healthcare and any specialists who provide special care or services is essential too. Collaboration on the following tasks is especially important:

- Identifying the child's strengths, needs, areas of progress
- Planning and implementing a program responsive to the child's needs, including transitional activities when the child moves on to the next source of care
- Noting any changes in the child's condition
- Talking or meeting with other specialists providing therapeutic services
- Sharing information, observations, concerns, and the child's growth

- Obtaining special materials and resources to help work with the child
- Promoting and tracking the connection of the child to a medical home

Medical Needs to Consider

Medical Procedures

Caring for Our Children Standard 3.5.0.2 provides guidance for accommodating the growing number of children who require some medical procedure during their usual day. Such procedures can include tube feedings, airway suctioning, supplemental oxygen, postural drainage, urine catheterization, blood sugar checks, or injections. These measures may need to be performed routinely every day or urgently for a specific circumstance. Some children with these special healthcare needs, especially older children, know how to do certain procedures on their own.

For all children who require medical procedures while in the early learning program, educators should obtain a written report from the healthcare provider who prescribed the special treatment. This report should include any special preparation needed to perform urgent procedures that are unique to the child with special healthcare needs. The clinician's report should also contain instructions for performing the procedure, how to receive training, and what to do and who to notify if complications occur. Families are responsible for ensuring any equipment needed for a procedure is available in the program, and the program should allow sufficient time for staff members to carry out necessary procedures.

The skills required to implement special medical procedures are not traditionally taught to teachers as part of their academic or practical experience. In some instances, a child may have a home health nurse who accompanies them to school and is responsible for these procedures. Even so, very few children's needs are so complex that they require specialized facilities with health personnel as teachers. Remember that reasonable accommodation is legally required by ADA. Therefore, teachers must do their best to make the accommodations required to enroll and ensure the safe care of the child who requires one or more medical procedures. Some state laws require that certain procedures be done only by family members or by a licensed health professional who follows written medical orders. Adding a licensed health professional, if one is not already a staff member, can be costly. Sometimes the expense is covered by health insurance or payments covered by funds from IDEA identified in the IFSP or IEP. Under ADA, the early learning program cannot charge the family for the costs involved in reasonable accommodations to meet their child's needs. In some states, medical procedures may be performed by teachers who receive training in the procedures and have the oversight and supervision of a licensed health professional. After checking with the requirements of the state board of medicine and nursing, one can then work with the family and the child's healthcare provider to comply with these requirements.

Emergency Planning Considerations for Children with Special Needs

To prepare for emergency episodes with a child with a chronic illness, ask the family to describe situations that required such action in the past. Explore the potential and likely causes as well as how the child may behave before, during, or after such episodes. It is worth asking the child's caregiver(s) and physician to describe and, as appropriate, demonstrate what to do during and following such an incident. Ask if these actions are something you can reasonably be expected to perform alone or if you will need someone else's help, as well as whether an ambulance will need to be called to facilitate management in an emergency department (ED) setting.

In conjunction with the federal Maternal and Child Health Bureau of the Health Resources and Services Administration, the American College of Emergency Physicians (ACEP) and the American Academy of Pediatrics (AAP) developed a tool called the "Emergency Information Form for Children with Special Health Care Needs." This form provides the key information that emergency medical services (EMS) and ED personnel need for treating a child, including current medications and doses, usual baseline findings on physical examination, and rapid treatment options that may be appropriate for the child. Families should request their primary care physician or pediatrician to complete this form and share it with the program. It should be kept up-to-date and always physically available with a child who has special medical needs that might require EMS and ED personnel. This form can be accessed online at the ACEP website (**www.acep.org**).

Prepare other children in the group for possible health crises by giving them a simple explanation as part of a discussion about other types of emergencies. Assure children that staff members can handle such situations. If an event occurs, matter-of-factly review with the children what happened. Allow them to play out what they experienced, draw pictures, tell stories, and ask questions related to the event until their interest wanes, indicating that they have become comfortable with it.

Facilitating Communication Among All Care Providers

During enrollment, but before a child actually participates in the program, staff members should request detailed information from the family about the child's health issues and unique needs. (See "Chapter 3: Enrollment, Health Documentation, Assessments, and Screenings.") Ask specific questions about how a condition may affect the child's ability to participate in the program and what services staff members will be expected to provide that differ from those provided for typically developing children. Identify the professionals involved with the child's care. Families should complete HIPAA forms to enable information to be shared directly between health professionals and appropriate staff members on a regular basis. Such correspondence streamlines recommendations regarding accommodations for a child and regarding measures that are required in caring for the child on a daily basis or during an acute illness or emergency.

To care for children with special physical, mental, behavioral, or developmental needs, teachers need to be part of a professional team. Children with disabilities and special healthcare needs should have a multidisciplinary, interdisciplinary, or transdisciplinary assessment by appropriately qualified professionals. The following components should be included in a comprehensive assessment of a child:

- A care plan developed by the child's healthcare providers, preferably those in the child's medical home with potential input from the child's subspecialty physicians
- Results of medical examinations and developmental assessments
- Evaluations of the child's behavior, cognitive functioning, and current overall adaptive functioning, such as autism diagnostic observation schedule (ADOS) or neuropsychological testing
- Evaluations of the family's needs, cultural and linguistic differences, concerns, and priorities

Comprehensive Healthcare Plans

Teachers need as much information as possible about the daily and emergency needs of all children. Any child who has a medical condition or a special healthcare need that may require unique attention from teachers should have a care plan. A care plan informs staff members about special training they may need, what procedures they might need to follow, and any modifications to the program's usual routines. The care plan may be very simple or complex depending on the child's needs.

Caring for Our Children Standard 3.5.0.1 explains the recommended content of a care plan for such children. Any child who meets these criteria should provide the school with a Comprehensive Health Care Plan completed by their primary care provider in their medical home that includes the information like that listed in Table 10.1.

Care plan templates vary, but the child's healthcare provider should complete those parts of the care plan that they think the child care program needs to know to take care of the child. Some children will have more than one medical and educational specialist, each of whom should contribute information to a care plan. The teacher should compare the care plan with the information contained in the Developmental History Form (see "Chapter 3: Enrollment, Health Documentation, Assessments, and Screenings" and "Appendix A.3.1: Developmental History"). If there are conflicting instructions (for example, if the family listed different allergies in the Developmental History Form than what is included in the care plan), the teacher will need to contact the parties involved or engage the help of the program's child care health consultant (if available) to resolve the areas that seem to be incompatible.

Table 10.1. Required Content for Healthcare Plans

1. The child's diagnosis/diagnoses
2. Contact information for the primary care provider and any relevant subspecialists (e.g., endocrinologists, oncologists)
3. Medications to be administered on a scheduled basis
4. Medications to be administered on an emergent basis with clearly stated parameters, signs, and symptoms that warrant giving the medication written in lay language
5. Procedures to be performed
6. Allergies
7. Dietary modifications required for the health of the child
8. Activity modifications
9. Environmental modifications
10. Stimulus that initiates or precipitates a reaction or series of reactions (triggers) to avoid
11. Symptoms for caregivers/teachers to observe
12. Behavioral modifications
13. Emergency response plans—both if the child has a medical emergency and special factors to consider in programmatic emergency (e.g., a fire)
14. Suggested special skills training and education for staff members

The information in the care plan should be reviewed collaboratively by the program's child care health consultant, if available, and staff members to plan and provide training for necessary accommodations. Each time the child receives care from a healthcare professional or from other specialists, the care plan should be reviewed again and updated. It is also worth re-evaluating the care plan at the start of each new school year. More frequent changes to the care plan may be necessary should aspects of the child's care fluctuate due to age, illness, or other circumstances. Therefore, it is essential to optimize communication between family, healthcare professionals, teachers, and developmental specialists (e.g., physical therapists, occupational therapists, speech therapists, nutritionists). Multiple approaches can be utilized to accomplish this type of correspondence, such as email communication, phone calls, or scheduled care conferences where all care providers are included. Though an arranged meeting ensuring all parties are available can be difficult, the COVID-19 pandemic has changed the landscape (Fleming 2021). People have become more comfortable with certain technology that is also more readily accessible, thus allowing for live communication to occur virtually as well.

Summary

For educators, working with and caring for children with special healthcare needs and medical complexity can be demanding, but it is always rewarding. Inclusion of these children in the educational environment is beneficial for them, their peers, and for teachers and staff members. IDEA has enabled this integration to happen and be successful over time. It is crucial for early learning programs to prepare for the inclusion of these children by implementing environmental accommodations, utilizing community resources, incorporating developmental specialists in the classroom, and engaging in communication with medical providers. Having a recognized, appropriate plan of care in place that is continually reassessed helps facilitate a wonderful experience for these children in the early learning program and empowers teachers to care for them and allow them to thrive.

Child Maltreatment: What It Is and What to Do

NIKKI GAMBHIR

LEARNING OBJECTIVES

- To define the term *child maltreatment*
- To explain the four types of maltreatment: neglect, physical abuse, emotional (psychological) abuse, and sexual abuse
- To understand that the presence of risk and protective factors can increase or decrease the likelihood of experiencing or carrying out child abuse and neglect
- To determine the elements of a child maltreatment policy and reporting procedure
- To understand that early care and education providers are required by law to report child abuse and neglect and should not be disciplined or fired for making the report

(continued)

LEARNING OBJECTIVES (*continued*)

- To understand that early learning programs can provide a therapeutic environment for families under stress, and thus play a key role in preventing child abuse and neglect

In planning a safe, healthy early learning program, child maltreatment is a critical and complex issue that must be addressed. Early childhood educators can support families through preventive measures and efforts to identify and report child maltreatment, but first they must understand what child abuse and neglect are, how they impact children and families, and what the laws require. In this chapter, the terms *abuse* and *neglect* are clearly defined, and the responsibilities of early childhood educators to protect children and report abuse or neglect are discussed.

Child Maltreatment: Abuse and Neglect

Child maltreatment, often used interchangeably with *child abuse* and *neglect*, is more common than one may think and an important public health concern. In 2020, at least one in seven children experienced child abuse or neglect in the United States (Finkelhor et al. 2015). It is the duty of individuals, communities, and local, state, and federal governments to protect our children's safety and well-being. Furthermore, rates of child abuse and neglect reflect economic disparities and poverty. While child abuse and neglect do occur in families of relative higher socioeconomic status, rates are five times higher in those of lower socioeconomic status (Fortson et al. 2016). It is hypothesized that poverty increases stress placed on caregivers in meeting their family's basic needs, accessing resources, and engaging with social support. Additionally, the parents or caregivers abilities may be negatively impacted by changes in their mental health, behaviors, and family dynamics (Lefebvre et al. 2017).

Children who are abused or neglected experience both immediate and long-term consequences. Children may suffer acute physical injuries, such as bruises, burns, or broken bones, and/or delayed access to medical and dental needs. They may also have emotional disturbance and mental health problems, such as anxiety, depression, or posttraumatic stress (Fortson et al. 2016).

Over the long-term, and of particular concern for those in early childhood education and interested in optimizing early childhood development, maltreated children are at increased risk of delayed brain development, lower educational attainment, and limited employment opportunities. They are also at risk of experiencing future violence victimization and perpetration, substance abuse, and sexually transmitted infections.

Thus, child abuse and neglect have been recognized as adverse childhood experiences (ACEs) and are linked to toxic stress, a process by which brain development is affected and individuals are susceptible to learning, attention, and memory difficulties; mental health issues; and chronic medical problems (Shonkoff et al. 2012). By building upon family strengths, resilience and supportive environments can be established. In turn, the negative impact of risk factors and ACEs can be overcome.

How Common Is Child Maltreatment?

Before addressing the problem, it may be helpful to further understand the magnitude of the problem. Learners may find the number of child maltreatment cases upsetting and staggering. Cases of child abuse and neglect are prevalent across all types of communities and population groups.

Due to variations in definitions of abuse and treatment, and reporting practices among states, it is difficult to ascertain the annual number of children abused and neglected each year, and numbers are likely an underestimate as many cases are unreported. Measures have been undertaken to create uniform definitions for child maltreatment and associated terms and recommended data elements. It is hoped that definitions and data elements will provide a framework for use by local and state health departments and thereby promote and improve quality of child maltreatment surveillance for public health practices (Leeb et al. 2008).

The scope of the problem is outlined in annual reports on child maltreatment from the Children's Bureau, an office Administration for Children and Families, which is part of the US Department of Health and Human Services (HHS). In the most recent publication (Children's Bureau 2022), data was collected from child welfare agencies in the 50 states, the Commonwealth of Puerto Rico, and the District of Columbia. According to this document, in 2020, child protective services (CPS) received 3.9 million (3,925,000) referrals alleging maltreatment of approximately 7.1 million (7,100,000) children. An estimated 618,000 children were found to be a victim of child abuse or neglect with higher rates of victimization seen in children younger than 1 year old, girls, and American Indian or Alaska Native children. Data demonstrated that about 76.1 percent of victims were neglected, 16.5 percent were physically abused, 9.4 percent were sexually abused, and 0.2 percent were sex trafficked. In 2020, an estimated 1,750 children died of child abuse and neglect. Higher rates of fatality were seen in those younger than 1 year old (46.4 percent). Boys and African American children also had higher rates of child fatality compared to girls and White and Hispanic children, respectively (Children's Bureau 2022).

Data showed that more than half (52 percent) of perpetrators were female, and majority (77.2 percent) of perpetrators were a caregiver to their victim. Two-thirds (66.7 percent) of reports of suspected child maltreatment were made by a professional (i.e., someone who had contact with the child because of the individual's work role). Examples of professionals include legal and enforcement personnel, education personnel, and medical personnel. Educators made less than one-fifth (17.2 percent) of reports. Nonprofessionals (e.g., friends, neighbors, and relatives) also made less than one-fifth (17 percent) of reports (Children's Bureau 2022).

Prevention services are aimed at preventing child abuse and neglect and may be directed at at-risk populations and may be aimed at increasing parent and caregivers' confidence and competence in their parenting abilities, increasing strength and stability of families, and affording a stable and supportive environment. In 2020, approximately 2 million (1,963,369) children received prevention services. Postresponse, or postinvestigation, services, on the other hand, are delivered within the first 90 days of the report's disposition. Postresponse services are "provided or arranged by the child protective services agency, social services agency, or the child welfare agency for the child or family [because of] needs discovered during the investigation. [Activities] include such services as family preservation, family support, and foster care" (Children's Bureau 2022, 122). In 2020, approximately 1.2 million (1,159,294) children received postresponse services from a CPS agency. Approximately two-thirds (59.7 percent) of victims and one-third (27.1 percent) of nonvictims received postresponse services (Children's Bureau 2022).

CAPTA and the Definition of *Child Abuse and Neglect*

Federal legislation, in the form of the Child Abuse Prevention and Treatment Act (CAPTA) (Public Law 100-294), aims to address child maltreatment by providing federal funding as well as a framework and guidance for states to prevent, identify, assess, prosecute, and treat child abuse and neglect.

Originally enacted in 1974, CAPTA was reauthorized by the CAPTA Reauthorization Act of 2010 (Public Law 111-320) and most recently amended in 2019 by the Victims of Child Abuse Act Reauthorization Act of 2018 (Public Law 115-424). CAPTA established the Child Welfare Information Gateway, a national clearinghouse of information relating to child abuse and neglect; the Office on Child Abuse and Neglect within the HHS; and grants to public agencies and nonprofit organizations, including Indian Tribes and Tribal organizations, for demonstration programs and projects.

CAPTA defines *child abuse and neglect* as, at a minimum, "any recent act or failure to act on the part of a parent or caregiver that results in death, serious physical or emotional harm, sexual abuse, or exploitation, or an act or failure to act that presents an imminent risk of serious harm." The Justice for Victims of Trafficking Act of 2015 (Public Law 114-22) expanded federal definitions of *child abuse and neglect* and *sexual abuse* by including a child who is identified as a victim of sex trafficking or severe forms of trafficking in persons. A child is identified as any person younger than 18 years old who is not an emancipated minor. A perpetrator is the person who is responsible for the abuse or neglect of a child (Child Welfare Information Gateway, n.d.).

Though CAPTA sets minimum standards in the definition of child abuse and neglect, each state is thereafter responsible in setting its own definitions of child abuse and neglect. Definitions may vary across states; however, most states recognize four major types of maltreatment: neglect, physical abuse, sexual abuse, and emotional abuse. Abandonment, parental substance use, and human trafficking are often identified as abuse or neglect. It is important to recognize that different types of maltreatment may occur separately and/or in combination.

Types of Child Maltreatment

This section covers the different types of child maltreatment. Definitions have been adopted from the Child Welfare Information Gateway and Centers for Disease Control and Prevention (CDC), which aimed to set standardized definitions to aid in consistent surveillance and public health data collection of child maltreatment (CDC 2022a; Child Welfare Information Gateway, n.d.; Leeb et al. 2008).

Putting the CAPTA definition of child abuse and neglect in simple terms, child maltreatment includes all types of abuse and neglect of a child under age 18 by a caregiver or another person in a custodial role (such as a religious leader, coach, or teacher) that results in harm, the potential for harm, or threat of harm to a child (CDC 2022a; Leeb et al. 2008). If a child arrives with an injury requiring immediate medical attention, arrange for a visit to a doctor or to an emergency department for treatment. If you notice bruises, cuts, burns, or other injuries on a child, ask the parent or caregiver how the injury occurred, what treatment was provided, and what care or precautions must be taken.

Physical abuse is the intentional (nonaccidental) use of physical force that results in, or has potential to result in, physical harm to the child. Examples include "hitting, kicking, punching, beating, stabbing, biting, pushing, shoving, throwing, pulling, dragging, dropping, shaking, strangling/choking, smothering, burning, scalding, and poisoning" (Leeb et al. 2008, 14). Physical abuse injuries include minor bruises, acute head trauma, severe fractures, and death.

› There are certain types of injuries that strongly suggest abuse. These include burns on the skin, handprints on the child's body, striped bruises that suggest the child was hit by a cord or stick, other types of imprints of objects on the child's body, or a swelling, bruise, or cut on a body part that the child tells you happened as the result of a deliberate injury.

- Sometimes there are no obvious external physical signs of injury or violence, and caregivers may attribute various signs and symptoms to other causes, such as viral illnesses. For example, violently shaking an infant by the shoulders, arms, or legs, tossing in the air, and/or with impact (hitting a surface) can cause the infant's head to move violently back and forth and result in traumatic and sometimes fatal brain injury. This type of injury (called *shaken baby syndrome*), presents in those younger than 2 years old and can present with different signs and symptoms, including unresponsiveness, loss of consciousness, breathing problems (irregular breathing or not breathing), no pulse, dilated pupils, seizures, drowsiness, irritability, uncontrollable crying, inability to be consoled, abnormal posture, vomiting, and inability to nurse or feed (NPIC 2010).
- Use of physical discipline, such as spanking or paddling, though not recommended, are not by CAPTA considered reportable abuse if it is "reasonable" and with no resulting bodily injury to the child.

Sexual abuse is any completed or attempted (noncompleted) sexual act, sexual contact with, or exploitation (i.e., noncontact sexual interaction) of a child by a caregiver. It involves pressuring or forcing a child to engage in sexual acts. It includes behaviors such as fondling; penetration; incest; rape; exposing a child to other sexual activities; and exploitation through prostitution, the production of pornographic materials, or sexual trafficking.

Emotional abuse (or *psychological abuse*) refers to a pattern of behavior that negatively impacts a child's self-worth and/or emotional well-being and development. This type of abuse can be "continual (e.g., chronic and pervasive) or episodic (e.g., triggered by a specific context or situation: caregiver substance use/abuse)" (Leeb et al. 2008, 16). Examples include name-calling; shaming; constantly criticizing; belittling; blaming; degrading; intimidating; spurning; rejecting; threatening; isolating; terrorizing; and withholding love, support, or guidance. Without evidence of harm or mental injury to the child, emotional abuse may be difficult to prove and address but should still be reported when observed or disclosed.

Neglect (or *failure to provide*) is the failure to meet a child's basic needs or combination of needs. It is important to ascertain whether co-occurring poverty, cultural values, and community standards of care are contributing to concerns for neglect as this may indicate that the family needs access to information and community resources. If a family fails to use available information and support to care for their child with resulting risk to the child's health or safety, then intervention could be required. Neglect may include the following categories: physical, medical/dental, emotional, educational, parental substance abuse, human trafficking, and abandonment (Child Welfare Information Gateway 2019).

- Physical neglect occurs when there is a failure to provide necessary food, hygiene, clothing, housing (shelter), and/or lack of appropriate supervision.
- Medical/dental neglect occurs when there is failure to provide attention to necessary medical, vision, dental, or mental healthcare and treatment and/or withholding medically indicated treatment from children with life-threatening conditions. Access should be timely. Per CAPTA, treatment may include adequate nutrition, hydration, and medication. Many states may offer exceptions to parents or caregivers who choose not to seek medical care for their children due to religious beliefs. For example, though all 50 states require children to receive specific vaccinations before entering public school, every state also grants medical exemptions for children who cannot be vaccinated. Forty-four states and Washington, DC, allow religious exemptions to vaccinations. Among these states, 15 also allow exemptions to immunizations due to any type of parental or caregiver nonreligious belief (e.g., personal, moral, or other) (NCSL 2022).

- Emotional neglect occurs when there is inattention to the child's emotional needs and/or failure to provide psychological care.
- Educational neglect occurs when there is a failure to provide access to adequate education, including attention to special education needs.
- Parental substance use includes prenatal exposure to harmful legal or illegal drugs or other substances, caregiver substance use/abuse and use of controlled substances that impairs the caregiver's ability to care for the child, and selling, distributing, or permitting a child to use alcohol or illegal drugs.
- Human trafficking includes both sex trafficking and labor trafficking. "Sex trafficking is recruiting, harboring, transporting, providing, or obtaining someone for a commercial sex act, such as prostitution, pornography, or stripping. Labor trafficking is forced labor, including drug dealing, begging, or working long hours for little pay" (Child Welfare Information Gateway 2019, 4). Reporters should be aware that children in child welfare are vulnerable to being victims of human trafficking.
- Abandonment occurs when the parent or caregiver's identity or whereabouts are unknown, the parent or caregiver has failed to maintain contact with the child and/or provide adequate support and supervision, or the child has been left alone in circumstances that can risk or result in serious harm to their health or safety (e.g., leaving a child in a car). It is important to note that states' child abuse and neglect reporting laws may vary in specifying a minimum age for a child to be left home alone or unattended in the car. Many states, such as Texas, do not specify what age is old enough for a child to be left alone but insist that an adult caregiver must be accountable for providing adequate supervision. You may want to contact your local police department or child protective services agency for information about specific local regulations or ordinances (Child Welfare Information Gateway 2018).

Identification of Child Maltreatment

Identification of child maltreatment is important in the protection of the child and helping the family receive needed support and assistance. A child may disclose, directly or indirectly, that they have experienced abuse or neglect. However, for others who are reluctant to speak about their experience, recognition of risk factors and signs and symptoms by an adult is the first step needed to help identify suspected cases of child maltreatment.

Caregivers and educators are not expected to diagnose or investigate child abuse and neglect (*CFOC* Standard 3.4.4.1). However, it is important for educators to be aware of common risk factors and common physical and emotional signs and symptoms of maltreatment. As previously noted, children from families in lower economic situations are more likely to be victims of neglect or abuse, but one must always remain vigilant and unbiased in their assumptions about families and the different strengths and challenges they face. "Teachers of young children—like all people—are not immune to such bias . . . [I]mplicit biases are associated with differential judgments about and treatment of children by race, gender, ability and disability, body type, physical appearance, and social, economic, and language status" (NAEYC 2019, 15).

Risk Factors Related to Child Maltreatment

The presence of individual, relational, community, and socioeconomic risk factors may contribute to an increased likelihood of children experiencing or of an adult carrying out child abuse and neglect. Stressors can contribute to certain circumstances that result in child abuse and neglect.

It is important to note that the following list is not comprehensive. Additionally, the presence of the following risk factors, signs, and/or symptoms does not necessarily mean that the child is a victim of maltreatment. An alternative physical, emotional, or environmental explanation may be true. However, the presence of these attributes and signs, particularly when multiple ones coexist or occur repeatedly, reflects the need to pay further attention to a child's welfare and consideration of potentially abusive situations.

The following risk factors are adapted from the CDC (2022b):

- Individual child risk factors include early age (younger than 4 years old) and special healthcare needs that increase caregiver burden (e.g., prematurity, disability, mental health issues, chronic physical illnesses).
- Individual caregiver risk factors include difficulty bonding and nurturing with the child, isolation without support, unresolved mental health issues, drug and/or alcohol use, prior history of child abuse or neglect or other trauma, lack of education, low income, young age or single parent with or without multiple children, high levels of parenting or economic stress, caregivers in the home who are not a biological parent, and caregivers with attitudes accepting of or justifying violence or aggression.
- Family risk factors include having household members in jail or prison, isolation from others, experiencing other types of violence (including domestic or relationship violence), and those with conflict and negative communication styles.
- Community risk factors include high poverty rates, high unemployment rates, violence, crime, and limited educational and economic opportunities. Unstable housing, food insecurity, low community involvement, and easy access to drugs and alcohol are additional factors.

Signs of Maltreatment

Table 11.1 describes the signs of maltreatment categorized by the type of maltreatment as well as by child and/or parent/caregiver.

Table 11.1. Signs of Maltreatment

General Maltreatment	
A child who exhibits the following signs may be a victim of maltreatment.	• Shows sudden changes in behavior or school performance or unusual/concerning behaviors • Has not received help for physical or medical problems brought to the parents/caregivers' attention • Has learning problems (or difficulty concentrating) that cannot be attributed to specific physical or psychological causes • Is always watchful, as though preparing for something bad to happen • Lacks adult supervision • Is overly compliant, passive, or withdrawn • Comes to school or other activities early, stays late, and does not want to go home • Is reluctant to be around a particular person • Discloses maltreatment

(continued)

Table 11.1. Signs of Maltreatment (*continued*)

General Maltreatment	
The possibility of maltreatment should be considered when the parent or other adult caregivers exhibits the following actions or behavior.	• Denies the existence of—or blames the child for—the child's problems in school or at home • Asks educators or other caregivers to use harsh physical discipline if the child misbehaves • Sees the child as entirely bad, worthless, or burdensome • Demands a level of physical or academic performance the child cannot achieve • Looks primarily to the child for care, attention, and satisfaction of the parent/caregiver's emotional needs • Shows little concern for the child
The possibility of maltreatment should be considered when the child and parent or other adult caregivers exhibit these actions or behavior.	• Touch or look at each other rarely • Consider their relationship entirely negative • State consistently they do not like each other
Physical Abuse	
A child who exhibits these signs may be a victim of physical abuse.	• Has unexplained injuries, such as burns, bites, bruises, broken bones, or black eyes • Has fading bruises or other noticeable marks after an absence from school • Seems scared, anxious, depressed, withdrawn, or aggressive • Seems frightened of their parents or caregivers and protests or cries when it is time to go home • Shrinks at the approach of adults • Shows changes in eating and sleeping habits • Reports injury by a parent or another adult caregiver • Abuses animals or pets
The possibility of physical abuse should be considered when the parent or other adult caregivers exhibits the following.	• Offers conflicting, unconvincing, or no explanation for the child's injury or provides an explanation that is not consistent with the injury (including one that is not consistent with the child's development) • Shows little concern for the child • Sees the child as entirely bad, burdensome, or worthless • Uses harsh physical discipline with the child • Has a history of abusing animals or pets
Neglect	
A child who exhibits the following signs may be a victim of neglect.	• Begs or steals food or money • Lacks needed medical care (including immunizations), dental care, or adaptive devices (e.g., glasses) • Has poor hygiene (e.g., consistently dirty and has severe body odor, lacks weather-appropriate clothing) • Is frequently absent from school • Abuses alcohol or other drugs • States that there is no one at home to provide care

Table 11.1. Signs of Maltreatment (*continued*)

Neglect	
The possibility of neglect should be considered when the parent or other adult caregivers exhibits the following.	• Appears to be indifferent to the child • Seems apathetic or depressed • Behaves irrationally or in a bizarre manner • Abuses alcohol or other drugs
Sexual Abuse	
A child who exhibits the following signs may be a victim of sexual abuse.	• Has difficulty walking or sitting • Experiences bleeding, bruising, or swelling in their private parts • Suddenly refuses to go to school • Reports nightmares or bedwetting • Experiences a sudden change in appetite • Demonstrates bizarre, sophisticated, or unusual sexual knowledge or behavior • Becomes pregnant or contracts a sexually transmitted disease, particularly if under age 14 • Runs away • Reports sexual abuse by a parent or another adult caregiver • Attaches very quickly to strangers or new adults in their environment
The possibility of sexual abuse should be considered when the parent or other adult caregivers exhibits the following.	• Tries to be the child's friend rather than assume an adult role • Makes up excuses to be alone with the child • Talks with the child about the adult's personal problems or relationships
Emotional Abuse	
A child who exhibits the following signs may be a victim of emotional abuse.	• Shows extremes in behavior, such as being overly compliant or demanding, extremely passive, or aggressive • Is either inappropriately adult (e.g., parenting other children) or inappropriately infantile (e.g., frequently rocking or head-banging) • Is delayed in physical or emotional development • Shows signs of depression or suicidal thoughts • Reports an inability to develop emotional bonds with others
The possibility of emotional abuse should be considered when the parent or other adult caregivers exhibits the following.	• Constantly blames, belittles, or berates the child • Describes the child negatively • Overtly rejects the child

Informed by Child Welfare Information Gateway 2019.

Preventing Maltreatment in Early Learning Programs

Caring for Our Children (*CFOC*) is a set of national standards that represent the best practices for quality health and safety policies and practices in early learning programs. The standards are based on evidence, expertise, and experience. In efforts to prevent maltreatment of children in their care as well as protect the program from being wrongly suspected of allowing maltreatment to occur and future legal challenges, programs should implement the following essential practices (*CFOC* Standards 3.4.41–3.4.4.5).

Child Maltreatment Policy and Considerations

Every early learning program should have a written policy on child abuse and neglect. The policy should include the following elements:

- Procedures for investigating job applicants and volunteers prior to hiring and whenever suspicion is raised concerning a staff member.
- Requirements for mandatory staff training on the prevention, identification, and reporting of suspected child abuse and neglect
- A code of conduct for staff members relating to their behavior with children, including permissible methods of classroom management, guidance, and discipline
- Strategies to ensure caregiving tasks, particularly those in which children receive assistance with dressing, undressing, and toileting, occur in open and accessible areas within the facility
- Program commitment to providing stress management when needed and breaks for educators (e.g., 15 minutes every four hours and at least a 30-minute break for lunch; paid time off)
- A method for educators to signal for and receive immediate relief by a substitute when they feel they cannot continue to provide safe and nurturing care
- Procedures for reporting suspected maltreatment, including details on who must be informed, who makes the report, and who communicates with the other families, staff members, and the press
- Approaches to management of children who have been victims of maltreatment, including special training for staff members by experts in behavior management of child abuse victims

Per *CFOC* Standard 3.4.4.1, every program is responsible for providing staff members with copies of the written child abuse and neglect policy.

Physical Contact

It is recognized that physical contact and positive touch are parts of high-quality programs and are important for fostering meaningful and trusting relationships with families and the child's social and emotional development. The program's touch policy should be "direct in addressing that children may be touched when it is appropriate for, respectful to, and safe for the child" (*CFOC* Standard 2.1.2). Therefore, a children's comfort or discomfort with physical contact, regardless of their age, should be respected.

Understandably, educators may voice hesitation and fear that contact with touching children in certain contexts in any manner might be mistaken for maltreatment. Thus, parents and caregivers should be informed in advance about program practices and policy safeguards that are in place to ensure touch is appropriate (e.g., training, visibility, presence of other staff members), what curriculum activities that may or may not include contact or comfort, and the many types of appropriate physical contact the staff members usually have with the children as a regular part of caregiving. Appropriate situations include nurturing methods of holding, hugging, cuddling, comforting, and soothing (e.g., when upset, falling asleep) and assisting with feeding and diapering. Inappropriate touching includes acts that induce or coerce children in a sexually suggestive manner or for the sexual gratification of the adult, such as inappropriate touching, kissing, and/or sexual penetration (sexual abuse) (*CFOC* Standard 2.1.2.1). Parents and caregivers should be encouraged to discuss any concerns or questions about physical contact as part of caregiving.

IMMEDIATE IMPACT

Become Acquainted with Different Child Maltreatment Policies

Ask different early learning programs to share a copy of their written policies. Which of the items listed in this chapter are covered? Which are not? After reading this chapter, would a new staff member at each of these facilities know what was expected of them in reporting suspected child abuse and neglect?

Screening and Background Checks

Child maltreatment preventions should be incorporated into the general screening and selection process that programs are already undertaking when choosing candidates. Screening and selection policies, including the order and timeline for the application and hiring process, should be diligent, standardized, and consistent across the organization. Policies should identify screening criteria, areas of concern, how information gained in screening will be used to determine applicant eligibility for the role, and who will be making the determination. Screening and selection policies should not violate federal or state laws prohibiting discrimination in the workplace; consultation with an attorney may need to be considered. Prospective employees and volunteers should be made aware that background checks are required, and they are not eligible for the job without it. Candidates must give written consent for background checks.

If early learning program administrators carry out employment background checks independently, state child care licensing agencies should be able to provide appropriate background check documentation as required by the state's licensing regulations. Local social services and law enforcement agencies can aid in accessing and documenting information gained for background checks. Alternatively, program administrators can also obtain employment background check services through private companies.

Program directors of centers and large family child care homes and educators in small family child care homes should conduct complete background checks before employing any staff member (adults or adolescents) who will be on the premises or in vehicles when children are present. This includes substitutes, cooks, clerical staff members, transportation staff members, bus drivers, and custodians. Also, all individuals, including family members older than age 10 that live in large and small family child care homes should also have background screenings.

If licensing or regulation of individual educators is required by the state, background checks may already be integrated into the licensing process and thereby reduce the burden of an individual program. However, this does not excuse programs from being vigilant and may repeat screening if deemed necessary.

If work history and criminal background checks are unavailable for adolescents, further screening measures, such as written applications and personal interviews, may be needed. More thorough screening should be undertaken for those employees and volunteer applicants who will work more independently with the children. Prior familiarity or acquaintance of an applicant does not exempt them from the screening process.

Background screening should include the following (*CFOC* Standard 1.2.0.2):

- Name, address, and Social Security number verification
- Education verification
- Employment history
- Alias search
- Driving history documented by state Department of Motor Vehicles records
- Background checks of
  - State, tribal, and federal criminal history records, including fingerprint checks
  - Child abuse and neglect registries
  - Licensing history by any other state agencies (e.g., foster care, mental health, nursing homes)
  - Sex offender registries
- Mention in court records (misdemeanors and felonies)
- Verifications of legitimacy and reliability of information given by references; these should come from a variety of employment or volunteer sources and should not be limited to an applicant's family and/or friends
- In-person interview; including open-ended questions about establishing appropriate and inappropriate boundaries with young children as well as verbally asking about previous convictions and arrests, investigation findings, or court cases with child abuse/neglect or child sexual abuse.

Programs can screen in a stepwise process. Once identification information (e.g., name, address, Social Security number, education, employment history, and references) is verified and the candidate considered suitable, further background checks can be completed.

Unfortunately, absence from child abuse registries does not mean an individual does not have a history of abuse. Though adults are unlikely to disclose past or current abuse to another person, employment applications should include a question regarding previous experience with hitting, shouting, losing control, or sexual misconduct. Questions may discourage potentially abusive individuals from applying to the program and alert candidates that such behaviors are unacceptable and not tolerated.

Candidates should not be hired or allowed to work or volunteer if they acknowledge a history of any abuse, being sexually attracted to children or having physically or sexually abused children, or if they are known to have committed such acts. Failure of a candidate or current staff member to disclose previous history of child abuse or neglect or child sexual abuse is also grounds for not hiring or dismissal.

All background screening records should be checked before allowing any employee or volunteer to have contact with children. Arrange to have another background-checked person present to observe and always intervene if the individual is needed before all screening steps are complete. Per state laws and/or requirements or if program concerns arise about an individual's performance or behavior, background screenings should be repeated or conducted as needed.

More information can be gained about the candidate's suitability for the position by observing the candidate performing the job she is applying for and offering a trial or probationary period for new employees and volunteers. All other staff members involved in the care of the children and families can observe and discuss the individual's performance.

Education and Professional Development for Educators and Staff Members

Programs also have responsibility to deliver both initial and continuing education and training to assist educators in staff member conduct and the prevention, identification, and reporting of child abuse and neglect. Staff members should be educated on identification of risk factors (including repeated exposure to violence, stress in families, children with special healthcare needs), prevention and identification of shaken baby syndrome/abusive head trauma, promotion of protective factors to prevent child maltreatment, how to provide support, and referral to resources (*CFOC* Standard 1.4.5.2).

Employees and volunteers should be made aware of program, local, state, and federal standards and reporting procedures regarding child abuse and neglect. Systems may differ among early learning programs and states. Staff members should be informed that reporting suspected abuse and neglect is confidential and that they will be "immune from discharge, retaliation, or other disciplinary action for reporting suspected abuse and neglect in settings where they work" (*CFOC* Standard 3.4.4.2).

It is important to develop partnerships among early learning programs, healthcare professionals, and other community service agencies. Collaborations can include local- and state-level organizations offering community partners, such as early learning programs, hands-on training in recognition and implementation of methods for preventing child abuse and neglect. Other training and educational opportunities may include providing local- and state-specific information and instructions for mandated reporting and/or how to respond when a child discloses abuse. By improving understanding of child welfare issues, we can promote better outcomes for children and families.

IMMEDIATE IMPACT

Role Playing

Role-play with other staff members to become familiar with your program's child maltreatment policy and procedures.

Example scenarios include

- Informing a new family about the measures taken by the program to prevent child maltreatment and encourage protective factors
- Informing a family that a CPS report has been filed and how the program will help them during this time

EDUCATING CHILDREN ABOUT THEIR BODIES AND TOUCHING

Abuse prevention also involves teaching young children about their bodies, when it is okay to touch others, and when it is okay for others to touch them. Children often show interest in their bodies by 3 years old. Rather than using silly euphemisms, parents, caregivers, and educators need to be comfortable using correct terminology for body parts, such as *genitals, penis, vulva, testicles, breasts,* and *buttocks*. Though a child may have a special name for a body part, the proper name should be used as well so not to give the idea that there is something bad about the proper name (AAP 2023). For example, if asked "How do girls pee if they don't have a penis?" The adult may respond by saying "Everyone pees, for some people that comes out of their penis, for other people that may come out of a small opening in their vulva."

Also, children should be taught there are different private parts on their body (the mouth, breasts, genitals, and buttocks or parts covered by a swimsuit) and that no one can see or touch them without permission. Though young children are not expected to recognize and resist inappropriate touching, they should be taught that some people may check parts of their bodies that feel private to ensure they are healthy and developing. That may include a dentist examining a child's mouth or a doctor asking them to take off their clothes for an exam. If someone wants to see or touch their bodies in a way that is scary, uncomfortable, confusing, or not right, they have the right to say *no* and request that another trusted adult, such as a parent or caregiver, be present with them. An adult who is touching children with appropriate intentions will respect the child's boundaries and resistance to give consent. They should tell a trusted adult about what has happened. They should not feel blamed or at fault for what has happened. (See the section "Child's Disclosure of Maltreatment.")

Program Operations

Parents and caregivers should be aware that in addition to extensive background screening of staff members, further practices have been adopted to prevent potential child maltreatment within the program.

Program directors should adopt important operational measures to reduce the risk of child maltreatment. These measures include background screening of staff members; keeping appropriate, accurate, and current records; and creating safe physical spaces (*CFOC* Standard 1.2.0.2; 9.4.1.9; 3.4.4.5).

As a routine practice, the program should keep careful records about every child, noting all injuries that children have when they arrive at the program and any injuries that happen while the child is at the program. Include a description of their injury; the date, time, and place it happened and how it occurred; details of reporting staff member; a statement by the parent or caregiver or child; and the treatment the child received (*CFOC* Standard 9.4.1.9). Keeping records allows for the identification of injury patterns and child abuse and neglect and assists in developing preventive measures (*CFOC* Standard 9.4.1.9).

It is imperative that there is adequate daily supervision of all staff members. Multiple educators should be present so to reduce time in isolation for individual educators with a child. Children should be kept in areas that allow for easy viewing by other adults. They should not be taken to any area where they cannot be easily viewed by other staff members. Therefore, careful consideration should be given to the program's physical layout of toileting and caregiving spaces. It is recommended that the physical layout allows for high levels of visibility in the inside and outside areas as well as diaper-changing areas and toileting areas that are used by children (*CFOC* Standard 3.4.4.5). This also reduces the likelihood of isolation or privacy of individual educators with children, especially where children may be undressed or have their private parts exposed.

IMMEDIATE IMPACT

Additional Recommendations

- Incorporate windows and mirrors in areas to provide more visibility.
- Consider child-height toilet partitions.
- Remove doors on toilet stalls and toileting rooms for children who need assistance with toileting so that all adult-child interactions can be seen and heard. Of note, most children understand the concept of privacy by 6 years old and may start to request respect for their modesty.

Implementation of these measures aims to deter abuse or accusations of abuse by eliminating or reducing privacy to adults and increasing possibility of observation by another adult. In those situations in which educators work in isolation, such as in early or late child care or in family child care homes, there is screening of the teachers and other adults who will be in the building when children are in care. Parents and caregivers and outside health, educational, and regulatory therapists who come into the early learning program to provide specialist services to a child should adhere to the program's visitor protocols. Visitor protocols should ensure that individuals must check in upon entering the building and use the program's sign-in and sign-out system for accurate documentation of their interactions with or on behalf of the child. The visitor protocol should also detail parents and caregivers' ability to visit the classroom and access to other children in the classroom.

Behavior and Class Management

As noted in the American Academy of Pediatrics policy statement, "Effective Discipline to Raise Healthy Children," *discipline* means to teach, train, or guide. "Effective disciplinary strategies, appropriate to a child's age and development, teach the child to regulate his or her own behavior; keep him or her from harm; enhance his or her cognitive, socioemotional, and executive functioning skills; and reinforce the behavioral patterns taught by the child's parents and caregivers" (Sege et al. 2018, 2). It does not imply punishment. *Corporal punishment is not acceptable under any circumstances.*

Thus, rather than focusing on punishment, effective guidance and classroom management techniques teach the child how to behave and equip educators with how to approach undesired behavior by children. Educators should give guidance and model self-control, appropriate social behaviors, and strategies to resolve conflicts, manage transitions, engage in a challenging situation, and express one's feelings, needs, and wants. Children should be taught positive and appropriate words, actions, and ways of relating to other children and adults. To develop control of their own actions and behaviors, children should be taught expectations for their behavior.

In addition to being developmentally appropriate, behavior management methods should be consistent, reinforce desired behaviors, and offer natural and logical consequences for unacceptable behaviors.

- Natural consequences are consequences that occur in response to a behavior without an adult's influence or intervention. For example, if a snack bowl is knocked onto the floor, the food can no longer be eaten.
- Logical consequences are consequences that require the intervention of an adult to impose a reasonable consequence acceptable by the child's parents or caregivers. The adult sets the consequence. Logical consequences should be related to the behavior, respectful of the child and not involve shame or blame. Logical consequences may result in the loss of participation or the opportunity to do something. They do not include a denial of daily functions of living, such as eating, sleeping, and/or toileting. They should create a helpful learning experience that might encourage children to choose responsible cooperation (Nelson 1985). For example, if a snack bowl is knocked onto the floor, the adult will ask them to help clean it up. Other examples may include if a child draws on the wall, they should be directed to clean up what they drew, or if a child has hit another child, they should be gently moved away from other children while being given opportunities to express frustration and anger in more acceptable ways (rather than being moved away and scolded).

If a consequence feels close to punishment, another positive behavior management strategy should be used. Disciplinary methods such as physical punishment and/or abusive, shaming language are not acceptable.

It is recommended that all early learning programs have a philosophy and written policy that provide positive methods and developmentally appropriate guidelines for preventative and responsive strategies. Age-appropriate expectations for children's behaviors and the program's discipline policy should be effectively communicated to staff members and families. Parents and caregivers should be encouraged to use similar positive discipline methods at home and provide more consistency to management of children's behavior and emotions.

The following disciplinary practices have been adopted from *Caring for Our Children* Standard 2.2.0.6. By promoting positive interactions, these strategies can also be perceived to help mitigate child maltreatment.

- Form a positive relationship with the child; this can influence their ability to follow directions.
- Use sound child development principles to set expectations and realistic limits for children.
- Establish simple rules children can understand and be proactive in teaching and supporting children learn the rules.
- Ensure indoor and outdoor play and child care environments are well-designed, engaging, and supportive of appropriate development behavior and learning in children.
- Create a predictable daily routine and schedule. This may reduce anxiety and related acting out.
- Individualize behavior management strategies based on the individual needs and appropriate developmental level of children.
- Use enthusiasm, clear encouragement, and descriptive, positive praise for appropriate behaviors. Encouragement and praise should label the behaviors, not the child (e.g., "It's really helpful when you clean up your toys, that keeps our classroom safe").
- Give clear, simple directions that children can easily follow and use positive language to tell the child *what to do* (an alternative) rather than *what not to do* (e.g., "please walk in the hall" instead of "no running"). By doing so, children are more likely to follow them.
- Use if/then and when/then statements with logical and natural consequences. These practices help children understand they can make choices and that choices have consequences.
- Model desired behavior.
- Use redirection strategies when possible. The redirection should be prompt and focus on teaching the child what they should or might do. For example, if a child is drawing on the wall, one could say, "I will not let you draw on the wall. Here is some paper if you want to draw." Another example may be if a child is playing with something you do not want them to have, then it can be replaced with another object or toy of interest.

Reporting Child Abuse and Neglect

Legal Considerations

CAPTA requires that all US states and territories have laws that mandate that certain professionals and institutions report suspected or known cases of child maltreatment. In addition to protecting children from child abuse and neglect, reporting also enables delivery of support and assistance to families.

Though states vary regarding when and to whom to report concern, reporting should be made to child protection agencies and/or police. A copy of a particular state's child abuse and neglect reporting statute can be obtained from the regional HHS office, district attorney's office, local department of social services, or law enforcement agency. It is useful to review and understand the statute for one's own clarity on the reporting and investigation process and when informing the family about your responsibility to report a suspicion.

Mandatory reporters are legally required to report suspected child maltreatment. Certain types of professionals, particularly those who have frequent interface with children, are mandatory reporters. Social workers, child care providers, educators and other school personnel, physicians and other healthcare workers, mental health professionals, clergy, and law enforcement officers are examples of mandatory reporters. Failure to report child abuse and neglect is a crime and may lead to legal penalties.

Ethical Considerations

In addition to legal standards, the prevention and reporting of child abuse and neglect are addressed in the NAEYC's (2016) *Code of Ethical Conduct and Statement of Commitment*. The following principles are related to child maltreatment:

> P-1.1—Above all, we shall not harm children. We shall not participate in practices that are emotionally damaging, physically harmful, disrespectful, degrading, dangerous, exploitative, or intimidating to children. *This principle has precedence over all others in this Code.*
>
> P-1.8—We shall be familiar with the risk factors for and symptoms of child abuse and neglect, including physical, sexual, verbal, and emotional abuse and physical, emotional, educational, and medical neglect. We shall know and follow state laws and community procedures that protect children against abuse and neglect.
>
> P-1.9—When we have reasonable cause to suspect child abuse or neglect, we shall report it to the appropriate community agency and follow up to ensure that appropriate action has been taken. When appropriate, parents or guardians will be informed that the referral will be or has been made.
>
> P-1.10—When another person tells us of his or her suspicion that a child is being abused or neglected, we shall assist that person in taking appropriate action in order to protect the child.
>
> P-1.11—When we become aware of a practice or situation that endangers the health, safety, or well-being of children, we have an ethical responsibility to protect children or inform parents and/or others who can.
>
> P-2.13—We shall maintain confidentiality and shall respect the family's right to privacy, refraining from disclosure of confidential information and intrusion into family life. However, when we have reasons to believe that a child's welfare is at risk, it is permissible to share confidential information with agencies, as well as with individuals who have legal responsibility for intervening in the child's interest.
>
> P-2.15—We shall be familiar with and appropriately refer families to community resources and professional support services. After a referral has been made, we shall follow up to ensure that services have been appropriately provided.

P-3B.4—If we have concerns about a colleague's behavior, and children's well-being is not at risk, we may address the concern with that individual. If children are at risk or the situation does not improve after it has been brought to the colleague's attention, we shall report the colleague's unethical or incompetent behavior to an appropriate authority.

P-4.6—We shall be familiar with laws and regulations that serve to protect the children in our programs and be vigilant in ensuring that these laws and regulations are followed. (NAEYC 2016, 8, 10, 14, 17, 20)

Child's Disclosure of Maltreatment

Prior to discussing the coordination of making a report of suspected or confirmed child abuse and neglect, individuals should be knowledgeable about what to do if a child makes a disclosure. Programs are advised to plan how to support the child through the disclosure, reporting process, and next steps.

In many cases when a child discloses abuse, it may not be obvious. The child may speak vaguely, disguise details, or make gestures in hopes that the adult will be able to understand what the child is trying to say. It is important to respect and recognize the courage undertaken to speak out and ask for help. Let other staff members know that you are speaking with the child and provide a safe setting for the discussion.

Hearing a child disclose maltreatment may be uncomfortable. Table 11.2 lists dos and don'ts that may be helpful in guiding the conversation.

After disclosure, report the abuse per program procedures.

Table 11.2. Dos and Don'ts for Guiding Child Disclosure Conversations

Do	Appropriate Example Statement/Question	Don't	Inappropriate Example Statement/Question
Be certain to give undivided attention	*"It seems that you are sad. I am here if you want to talk."* *"I am listening."*	Scold the child for not disclosing sooner	*"Why didn't you tell me before?"*
Listen calmly to the child without denial	*"What has happened is not okay."* *"You have done the right thing in telling me."*	Interrupt the child to do something else or get someone	*"Just a minute. I think Ms. Smith needs to listen to you too."*
Reassure the child that they are supported, believed, and not alone	*"It must be so hard to talk about this."* *"You are brave for telling me."* *"I believe you."* *"You are not alone. I am here for you and will support you. I want to help you be safe."*	Make assumptions or judgements or pass blame or fault to the child for what has happened	*"Why were you there? What did you do to make this happen to you?"*

(continued)

Table 11.2. Dos and Don'ts for Guiding Child Disclosure Conversations (*continued*)

Do	Appropriate Example Statement/Question	Don't	Inappropriate Example Statement/Question
Encourage the child to explain what has happened in their own words	*"Tell me more about that."* *"I am concerned because I heard you say/or I saw a bruise."* *"I understand if you are afraid to tell me. Please know you can tell me anything."*	Attempt problem solving or offer to speak to the alleged abuser. The child may love and care for that person or fear repercussions from telling someone.	*"I'm sure that isn't what they meant to do."* *"I am sure this is all a misunderstanding. Would you like me to speak to them?"*
Document exact quotes of what the child says. This information may be useful for authorities.		Interrogate or pressure the child for details or ask leading questions. The authorities will ask further questions and are trained in asked sensitively and with the goal of avoiding multiple interviews.	*"Did this or that happen?"* *"Did your [family member] hit you on the arm?*
Limit questions to the following (if not already disclosed by the child)	*"What happened?* *When did it happen?* *Where did it happen?* *Who did it/how do you know them?* *Is there anything else that you want to tell me?"*	Make promises of not telling anyone else	*"I promise I will not tell anyone. Your secret is safe with me."*
Let the child know about the next steps	*"You are not in trouble. My job is to protect you and keep you safe, so I will be speaking to other people whose job it is to also keep you safe."* *"I am always here if you want to talk again."*	Question the child's honesty and integrity	*"Are you telling the truth? Are you sure that happened?"*

The Reporting Process

Educators and other program personnel may hesitate to make a report if not all details are known or confirmed; however, remember that responsibility is to the child and their safety, and educators are mandated reporters. Therefore, if there is *reason to believe* that child maltreatment has occurred, the program should make a report. Any rational suspicion is appropriate. *Proof that child abuse or neglect has occurred is not required.*

How to Report

All states require that a verbal or written report (or both) be made to the specified agency.

Reporting forms and the contents of reports of suspected child abuse and neglect vary from state to state. State-specific information sheets and reporting forms are often available on respective state and agency department websites. Obtain and familiarize yourself with copies of your state's reporting form so you can be prepared to give all the information during the telephone report.

What to Report

States may specify the type of information required when submitting a report. This usually includes

- Child's name, age, gender, and address
- Parent's or caregivers' name and contact details, including address
- Details about the injury (e.g., mechanism/cause if known, extent of injury/condition, where it occurred)
- Details of prior injuries, if any
- Actions taken by the reporter (e.g., medical attention, talking with the child, managing injuries)
- Reporter's name, location, and contact information. While this information may be useful to CPS staff, most states *do* allow individuals to report anonymously. States must protect the confidentiality and identity of the reporter from the person suspected of abuse or neglect. It is important to provide a complete and honest account of what was observed and/or disclosed that led to the suspicion of child abuse or neglect. Therefore, any additional information may be helpful, including previous injuries observed by the reporter to the child or to a sibling, information about the suspected perpetrator, if previous reports have been made, and any relevant information about the child and family that would help CPS in their risk assessment of suspected maltreatment.

Administrators are responsible for ensuring that staff members know they will not be disciplined or fired for making the report.

Where and When to Report

If a parent or caregiver has concerns that a child is being maltreated, they should be encouraged to contact CPS directly. If a staff member has concerns that a child is being maltreated, they should report concerns to the appropriate staff member with administrative or supervisory authority as well as to the agency (e.g., CPS) responsible for taking such reports.

Volunteers and staff members should report their concern to the child abuse reporting hotline, department of social services, CPS, or police as required by local and state laws. Current reporting system protocols and contact information for the appropriate agency for reporting suspected abuse should be easily accessible to caregivers and educators.

Suspected child abuse and neglect must be reported *as soon as it is suspected* because delay may expose the child to significant harm. If there is an urgent, emergency, or life-threatening situation, call 911 or the local law enforcement agency. If unsure about the urgency of a situation or concerned that a situation needs to be investigated within 24 hours, call the state toll-free hotlines or Childhelp National Child Abuse Hotline for assistance. Urgent situations include, but are not limited to, those involving serious injuries, injury to a child 5 years old or younger, immediate need for medical treatment, sexual abuse where the abuser has or will have access to the victim within the next 24 hours, children 5 years old or younger who are alone or likely to be left alone within the next 24 hours, or anytime you believe the situation requires action in less than 24 hours.

For more information about where and how to file a report for suspected child maltreatment, contact local CPS agency, social services department, or police department as required by local and state laws. States have child abuse and neglect toll-free reporting numbers.

For 24-hour-a-day, 7-day-a-week access to crisis counseling, information about where to call or make a report in your state, resources, and referrals to support services, call the previously mentioned Childhelp National Child Abuse Hotline (1-800-4-A-CHILD or 1-800-422-4453) or visit its website (**www.childhelp.org/hotline**). The hotline does not take a report of abuse directly, but staff members can counsel about whether a report should be made, refer to the appropriate reporting agency, and assist in making the call. For information about how to report online sexual exploitation of a child or if it is suspected that a child has been inappropriately contacted online, call the CyberTipline (1-800-843-5678) or visit its website (**www.missingkids.org/gethelpnow/cybertipline**).

Case Reported: Next Steps

Once a suspected or confirmed case of child abuse or neglect is reported, it will be sent to CPS. A CPS worker will review the information, collect further information, and determine whether further assessment and investigation is needed. The process may involve speaking with the child, family, and others.

Further steps for the child and parent/caregiver will depend on numerous factors, including state or local policy, severity of the maltreatment and whether it prompted the child's removal from the home and/or protective court action, the assessment of the child's immediate safety, the perceived risk of continued or future maltreatment, and available services to address family needs. The categories of perceived risk for future maltreatment are little or no risk, low-to-moderate risk, moderate-to-high risk, and high risk. Interventions may range from helping in accessing community services, resources, and education to removing the child from the home or affirming the agency's prior removal of the child. The child may be placed with a relative or in foster care.

Communicating with Authorities

While making a report, ask whether, when, and how someone from the agency will give feedback to the original reporter about the result of the investigation. In most circumstances, only limited information is provided by the social service agency to the person reporting the suspected child maltreatment, and the only feedback may be whether the investigation confirmed legally defined child maltreatment. Early learning programs are also encouraged to ask agency staff to advise appropriate staff members about supporting the family during the reporting experience and with the outcome.

Communicating with Families

At time of enrollment, parents and caregivers should be informed of the program's child maltreatment reporting requirements, procedures, and staff members' legal obligations to report any suspected child abuse or neglect.

Despite ethical and legal considerations and potential support and assistance received by the family as result of reporting, employees and volunteers may (understandably) continue to experience mixed feelings about reporting suspected child maltreatment. Staff members may hesitate to make a report because they

- Feel that they lack the skills required for accurate identification
- Fear that the relationship with family and other staff members will be affected and anonymity is hard to avoid by nature of information contained in report
- Do not want to become involved
- Believe that families have the right to discipline their child in their own way
- Are worried about the family reacting with anger and hostility, and/or remove the child from the program
- Know someone who is being accused of being abusive
- Have had previous negative reporting experiences (e.g., social worker was unresponsive, discouraged reporting, or did not handle the case or the abuse continued or escalated)

The previous scenarios are valid; however, they should not be deterrents to filing a report. Hesitations must be overcome to fulfill obligation to a child's health and safety. Children cannot be protected from maltreatment unless they are first identified, and the situation is reported.

It can be difficult to determine when to notify a family that a report has been filed. Each case requires individual handling. In general, it is recommended to inform the family that a child abuse or neglect report has been made. However, depending on the situation, this is not always advisable.

Notification is *not* recommended if a child is in imminent danger and/or the parent/caregiver may disappear with the child. Instead, call the appropriate agency immediately and do not tell the parent or caregiver.

Notification *is* recommended when the child is not in imminent danger.

If a decision has been made to inform a family, an individual skilled in communication and experience in navigating these situation (e.g., administrator, social worker) should be identified. It should not be the individual that has filed the report. When informing the family, the following discussion points and explanations should be considered:

- Educators are required by law to report all instances of suspected child maltreatment.
- It is the job of the investigators to determine whether there is actual maltreatment.
- The goal of child welfare and CPS involvement is to help families care for their children successively and promote the well-being and safety of children and families.
- Services aim to ensure family permanency and prevent unnecessary separation of children from their families.

- Part of the reporting process is to determine what help and assistance families need in attempts to remedy conditions that brought the children and family to the attention of the agency (Children's Bureau 2022).
- In addition to meeting basic needs, programs exist that address educational and economic advancement and prevention of child abuse and domestic violence.

It is hard to predict how families will respond to the news of a report. Reactions may vary from denial to relief to hostility, and staff members and child protection agencies can support the family through this challenging time. For example, although parents or caregivers may be very irate, or even act in a threatening manner, staff showing concern for the child may help them see that there was no choice in the matter. Abusive adults need help, and some are grateful when they receive it. In other situations, parents or caregivers are unaware that their child is being abused by another adult. Failure to inform families about making a report may lead them to feel betrayed or deceived. Even if the person adamantly denies any abuse or neglect or knowledge of abuse by others, filing of suspected abuse or neglect is required so child protective services can investigate and initiate action if appropriate. Of note, be sure to inform the social service agency and the police if aggression and hostility are experienced.

Debriefing among relevant staff members (or even between the reporting staff member and supervisor) is encouraged to learn from the event and assist processing of a potentially emotionally difficult situation.

Supporting Stressed Families and Maltreated Children

High quality early learning programs play a pivotal role in preventing child abuse and neglect. They are the only places where young children are seen regularly for an extended time by professionals trained to observe their appearance, behavior, and development. By establishing teacher-parent/caregiver relationships, both parties should be able to engage in sharing of concerns, including assistance in accessing community resources and staff member recognition of signs of stress in the children and family. A teacher may be the first person to suspect (and to report) child maltreatment. Educators should immediately follow program reporting policies and procedures when they suspect something is amiss.

Often, children who are victims of maltreatment are not able to learn or participate to their full potential. They may carry physical and emotional scars throughout life. Depending on the kind and/or severity of abuse or neglect, long-term effects can include motor impairment, loss of hearing or vision, cognitive disabilities, and/or learning and emotional difficulties. Thus, it is essential that educators take action to interrupt the cycle of abuse and neglect by helping children and parents receive needed treatment. The teacher's trusting relationship with children is a major factor in helping children and families cope with and resolve such difficult situations.

Protective Factors

The presence of protective factors may help build upon the strengths and resilience of parents and caregivers in caring for children and lessen the likelihood of experiencing or carrying out child abuse and neglect. Promoting early relational health, or stable, safe, and nurturing child-parent/caregiver relationships is important. The following factors are adapted from the CDC (2022b), Child Welfare Information Gateway (n.d.), and the Strengthening Families framework developed by the Center for the Study of Social Policy (n.d.). Individual child protective factors include safe, nurturing, emotionally supportive and positive caregiver-child relationships, social and emotional competence, and access to basic needs (food, shelter, health, and education).

- Individual parent and caregiver protective factors include parent/caregiver resilience, knowledge of parent/caregiver and child development, engaged and attentive caregivers, education and employment status, and stress management strategies.
- Family protective factors include supportive and reliable social networks and stable mentoring relationships.
- Community protective factors include access to safe and stable housing, high-quality and nurturing early education and child care, economic and financial assistance, and work opportunities with family-friendly policies.
- Early learning programs can use recommended strategies to foster protective factors and prevent child maltreatment. In addition to providing quality care, staff members have a unique opportunity to observe insights into child-family interactions. They are privileged to form positive, long-term, and trusting relationships with parents or caregivers that encourage communication and strengthening nurturing parent or caregiver-child relationships. Facilitate friendships and mutual support with parents and caregivers and guardians. Provide a place where parents and caregivers can have positive social interactions in a child-friendly setting.
- Strengthen parenting and childrearing skills. Model and teach positive, effective guidance techniques with explanations about appropriate expectations based on child development.
- Value and support parents and caregivers. Help them develop confidence and link them to community agencies that provide support services and resources, such as respite care, mental health and counseling, temporary shelter, drug treatment, and food stamps. Include both responsive services and relationship/community building resources.
- Respond to family crises. Connect stressed families with community resources when needed.
- Facilitate children's social and emotional development. Provide children with a healthy, nurturing environment that encourages trust and attachment.
- Observe and respond to early warning signs of child abuse and neglect.

FAMILY CONNECTIONS

Family Resource List

Become familiar with professional help and community resources available to stressed families who are at risk of abuse or have already abused their children, and consider speaking with your local child welfare agency or social work contacts. Then make a list of community resources that families can easily access for more information and assistance in addressing stresses at home.

Child and Family Support Programs

Many child and family support programs exist on the local community, state, and national levels. In general, programs aim to support parents and caregivers by promoting economic and social well-being, optimal development, and the safety of their child. Services aim to build upon the strengths of a family while also identifying needs and challenges being faced. Programs can focus on specific goals or offer comprehensive services, as well as differ in target groups (e.g., ethnic and cultural minorities, young parents, families facing mental health or substance use issues).

› Federal programs and services through the HHS include those that focus on child abuse and neglect, child care/child support, adoption, foster care, early childhood development, family violence prevention and services, Head Start, healthy food financing, job opportunities for low-income individuals, low-income home energy assistance, and substance abuse and mental health treatment. Eligibility and contact information about all federal programs can be found on the Benefits.gov website (**www.benefits.gov**).

› Child Welfare Information Gateway has compiled a list of child abuse and neglect prevention organizations, as well as child welfare-related state and national organizations. The listed organizations provide direct services and consultation for the prevention of maltreatment and offer other professional, family, and policy support. For updated contact information, visit **www.childwelfare.gov**.

› Stop It Now! aims to prevent child sexual abuse by providing parents and other adults with resources and offering direct help to those with questions or concerns about child abuse, prevention advocacy, prevention education, and technical assistance and training. The website is available at **www.stopitnow.org**.

› Prevent Child Abuse America is a national organization that provides information on child maltreatment and its prevention. The website is available at **http://preventchildabuse.org**.

Promotion of Child Development and Early Relational Health

It is important to empower parents, caregivers, and families to develop stable, nurturing, and safe relationships with their children. Numerous resources are available to equip families with knowledge and skills. Educators can also direct families to resources available in the community.

› The CDC's "Child Development" webpages outline child development basics, including milestones (and useful mobile app), developmental screening, positive caregiver tips, and more. Visit **www.cdc.gov/ncbddd/childdevelopment**.

› The CDC's "Essentials for Parenting Toddlers and Preschoolers" webpages include guidance on communicating with children, giving directions, setting a routine/structure, and use of consequences and time out. Visit **www.cdc.gov/parents/essentials/toddlersandpreschoolers/index.html**.

› The Office of Early Childhood Development's "Tips and Resources for Families" webpage links to a range of tip sheets and other information. Visit **www.acf.hhs.gov/ecd/child-health-development/watch-me-thrive/families/tips-and-resources**.

- Vroom is a free set of evidence-based tips, tools, and activities to help caregivers connect with children in positive and back-and-forth moments while also building developmental and life skills. The resource aims to encourage families to turn “everyday moments” into “brain building moments” by layering activities that are essential to healthy brain development onto existing routines. Vroom is available at **www.vroom.org** and/or on a mobile app.

Summary

Given the numerous individual, family, and community contributing factors at play, there is no doubt that there is complexity in the identification, treatment, and prevention of the different types of child maltreatment. However, complexity is not a good enough reason to ignore signs or suspicions of child abuse and neglect. By maintaining a child maltreatment policy, early learning programs can have a framework from which to operate and help protect children. Educators are uniquely placed to observe behaviors, model positive strategies, assist in developing nurturing relationships among children and families, and report and signpost those that need further attention.

PART 4

Program and Facility Management

JENNIFER NIZER,
MANJULA PAUL, AND LOUIS A. VALENTI

Emergency and Disaster Preparation and Planning

JENNIFER NIZER, MANJULA PAUL, AND LOUIS A. VALENTI

LEARNING OBJECTIVES

- To understand the importance and the requirements of written action plans to prepare for and respond to emergency or disaster situations
- To explain the roles and responsibilities of parents/caregivers and teachers to review and update emergency preparedness plan, policies, and procedures
- To develop collaborative communication and action plans with community agencies, families, and the licensing organization
- To ensure the plan demonstrates clear roles and responsibilities of each participating community organization including the early learning and family communities

(*continued*)

LEARNING OBJECTIVES (*continued*)

- To train all staff members on their designated roles, responsibilities, and engagement to respond to emergencies of all types as per the written plan
- To conduct and document periodic drills as required and include all staff members and children
- To identify various nondisaster emergencies involving one or multiple children in care and provide appropriate care and intervention to minimize the injuries and damage
- To protect the health and safety of children and adults with special medical needs and chronic medical conditions during an emergency

Child care emergency preparedness is an early learning program's business and licensing responsibility. It is a collaborative action plan that requires public, private, family, and community participation. Federal and state licensing programs require that all licensed and regulated early learning programs develop, review, and update this plan to stay current with emergency procedures and adaptable to changing situations. In addition, the Child Care and Development Block Grant (CCDBG) Act of 2014 requires both center-based and family child care providers to prepare written plans for responding to emergency situations or natural disasters. These written action plans should include preparation and response practices and procedures for hazards or disasters that could occur in any location, including acts of violence, biological or chemical terrorism, exposure to hazardous agents, facility damage, fire, a missing child, power outages, and other situations that may require evacuation, relocation, lockdown, lockout, or shelter in place. In this chapter, we discuss specific procedures and responsibilities of administration and staff members to prepare for and respond to emergency situations.

Plans and Procedures

It is recommended that a program's emergency and disaster preparedness plan include certain elements that will guide the early learning program personnel to implement procedures to prevent, mitigate, respond, and recover in the event of an emergency. In addition, the plan must provide for the safe care of all children and have procedures to care for children with disabilities and chronic health conditions needing emergency medications or interventions. The plan also must identify the basic elements required to relocate to a safe alternate area for continuation of child care services; resumption of normal services, including communication for reunification and provision of emergency and temporary child care services; and temporary operating. Emergency preparedness plans should also include policies and procedures for training staff members to manage, document, and report these incidents (*CFOC* Standard 9.2.4).

A comprehensive and well-structured plan can help to minimize psychological impact (trauma) and promote resilience in children and adults. The program operators, owners, and directors must make sure that all personnel, regardless of their employment status, are trained and oriented to the plan to respond to the emergencies promptly and appropriately. Likewise, preparedness and readiness to respond to unpredictable emergencies can reduce injuries and adverse effects, such as loss of lives and resources. Organizations and programs that are dedicated to child safety must build and maintain organizational resilience with the capacity to reduce vulnerability to disruptive shocks and to respond effectively while maintaining delivery of core services.

Emergency Preparedness Planning: The Four Phases

Phase I: Prevention and Mitigation. This phase aims to avoid or reduce the occurrence of incidents and the harm and negative consequences (e.g., physical, emotional, financial) resulting from disastrous incidents. For example, having equipment to monitor the main entrance of the school or program and keeping all other external doors locked is a preventive measure against unwanted intruders entering the school or program.

Phase II: Preparation. Preparation includes training staff members in threat assessment. The program staff must invite local law enforcement to inspect the premises (indoor and outdoor) for risk assessment and develop a collaborative preparedness plan. The best practice recommendation is that the program receives input from the community partners, including, but not limited to, the local health department, department of social services, representatives from local chapter of the American Academy of Pediatrics, mental health professionals, staff members, and children's families.

Preparedness is an ongoing process of planning, practicing, and evaluating actions and then modifying the plan to focus on a collective response to prevent the incidents and reduce damages and adverse outcomes affecting the facility, children, and staff both physically and psychologically.

Phase III: Response. The response phase is where the preparedness plan is put into action and steps are taken to protect the children and staff members during an incident. When responding to an incident, staff members should always check their mental readiness or how they feel—overwhelmed, frozen, uncertain, or scared. During such moments, taking a pause and a deep breath can help to reset the physical and emotional level of the individuals to effectively follow the plan and be able to explain and provide support to the children as needed. With this in mind, it is important that programs and staff members invest their time and resources to receive training and perform ongoing drills and communications to promote a positive and supportive environment. How staff members respond in emergencies plays a vital role in keeping the children safe and deescalating harmful behavior before it becomes a threat to the safety of the children and staff members.

Phase IV: Recovery. Recovery is a three-level approach. *The initial and the first level* of the recovery phase is debriefing through structured and guided reflections to uncover the emotions experienced during the traumatizing incident, such as an active shooter inside the early learning premises. The program should underscore the importance of social and emotional health and promote an understanding that the young children's and staff members' individual needs will vary based on a postemergency situation and their lived experiences. Young children, including infants, express their thoughts and emotions through different ways in their daily activities with words, behaviors, and play. Educators need to pay close attention to any changes in behavior to provide support. It is important to understand when children hear staff members talking about their experience, children feel that they too can express and talk about their feelings.

As much as possible, keep regular structure, schedules, and routines while expecting that children may need extra attention and reassurance. Communicate with children's parents and caregivers. Listen to their concerns and share with them any concerns you have. Work together to find ways to best support the children. Facilitate referral to needed resources such as food, shelter, medical and psychological supports.

The second level of recovery is focused on returning back to normalcy or resumption through physical and psychological healing and reassurances and restoring the physical environment to ensure safety and protection to children and staff members. In addition to the physical restoration of the early learning areas, restoring the positive and protective caring and learning environment is essential. Extending support to children and families is key, but it is also critically important that the staff members have their physical and mental health status assessed, are supported to sufficiently recover, and are equipped to welcome back the children with a positive and reassuring atmosphere.

The third and final level of the recovery phase includes evaluation of the incident and the response to analyze and update the preparedness plan. The plan needs to be updated based on experience, research, and changing vulnerabilities. Examples of updates to the preparedness plan include providing training (e.g., new staff member training, annual training); holding meetings (e.g., parent and teacher meetings, preparedness partnership meetings); improving measures that are in place (e.g., outdoor and indoor security, shelter-in-place arrangements, communication equipment and network connections); conducting drills; and garnering support and resources from community organizations. The significant first response public organizations include local government, public health, department of social service, law enforcement, emergency medical services, education, and licensing. The examples for nonpublic community organizations include local businesses, parent-teacher organizations, and the local chapter of the American Red Cross. Coordination and a formal memorandum of understanding (MOU) with key response partners strengthen connections and clarifies roles and responsibilities to implement streamlined response actions.

Check points:

- What policy does your program have for staff training?
- When is your emergency preparedness plan updated?
- Who are your public and nonpublic first response partners?
- Are you ready for environmental assessment for threat monitoring and developing a MOU?
- What security measures do you have in place?
- Do you have only one main entrance where people may enter?
- Is your main entrance monitored at all times with all other outside doors locked?
- Did you check with your fire marshal for fire code regulations for how doors should be secured?
- Do you have a requirement instituted to limit access to one main, monitored entrance?
- Does your program have cameras to monitor the premises, including the parking area?
- Does your program have requirements for visitor sign in and increasing the visibility of visitors, including parent and caregivers' wearing name badges, as increased security measures?

Disasters

The Centers for Disease Control and Prevention (CDC 2012) defines a disaster as "a serious disruption of the functioning of society, causing widespread human, material, or environmental losses that exceeding the local capacity to respond, requiring external assistance" (iii).

Natural disasters like wildfires, floods, tornadoes, hurricanes, and earthquakes are the most common types of disaster. However, other types of disasters, such as hazardous material spills, building fires, and disease outbreaks, can happen anywhere and at any time. Because children

Helping Children Cope During and After a Disaster

A Resource for Parents and Caregivers

The amount of damage caused from a disaster can be overwhelming. The destruction of homes and separation from school, family, and friends can create a great amount of stress and anxiety for children. They may not fully understand what is going on. A child's reaction and signs of stress may vary depending on age and previous experiences and typical coping behavior with stress.

What You Can Do to Help Children Cope with a Disaster

Set a good example by managing your own stress through healthy lifestyle choices, such as eating healthy, exercising regularly, getting plenty of sleep, and avoiding drugs and alcohol. When you are prepared, rested, and relaxed, you can respond better to unexpected events and can make decisions in the best interest of your loved ones.

The following tips can help reduce stress before, during, and after a disaster or traumatic event.

Before

- Assure your children that you are prepared to keep them safe.
- Review safety plans before a disaster or emergency happens. Having a plan will increase your children's confidence and help give them a sense of control.

During

- Stay calm and reassure your children.
- Talk to your children about what is happening in a way that they can understand. Keep it simple and appropriate for each child's age.

After

- Give your children opportunities to talk about what they went through. Encourage them to share concerns and ask questions.
- Encourage your children to take action directly related to the disaster so they feel a sense of control. For example, children can help others after a disaster, such as volunteering to help community or family members in a safe environment. Children should NOT participate in disaster cleanup activities for health and safety reasons.
- Because parents, teachers, and other adults see children in different situations, it is important for them to work together to share information about how each child is coping after a traumatic event.
- Help your children to have a sense of structure, which can make them feel more at ease or provide a sense of familiarity. Once schools and child care opens again, help them return to their regular activities.

CS305921-A May 3, 2019

Figure 12.1. The CDC provides free resources on caring for children in disasters for families and caregivers.

(continued)

CDC Continued

Common Reactions

The common reactions to distress will fade over time for most children. Children who were directly exposed to a disaster can become upset again and behavior related to the event may return if they see or hear reminders.

If children continue to be very upset or if their reactions hurt their relationships or schoolwork, parents may want to talk to a professional or have their children to talk to someone who specializes in children's emotional needs.

Learn more about common reactions to distress below:

For Infants to 2-Year-Olds

Infants may become more cranky. They may cry more than usual or want to be held and cuddled more.

For 3 to 6-Year-Olds

They may have toileting accidents, bed-wetting, tantrums and a hard time sleeping, or be frightened about being separated from their parents/caregivers.

For 7 to 10-Year-Olds

Older children may feel sad, mad, or afraid that the event will happen again. Correct misinformation the child may get from others.

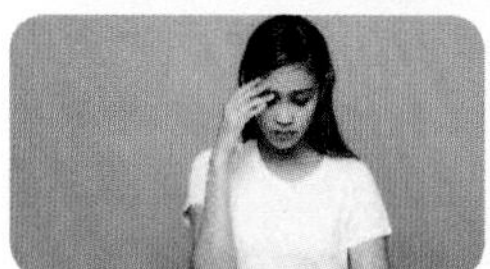

For Preteens and Teenagers

Some preteens and teenagers respond to trauma by acting out or feeling afraid to leave the home. Their overwhelming emotions may lead to increased arguing and even fighting with siblings, parents/caregivers or other adults.

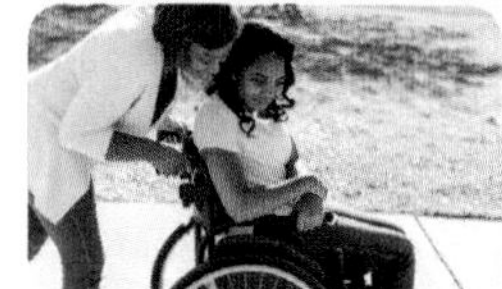

For Special Needs Children

Children with physical, emotional, or intellectual limitations may have stronger reactions to a threatened or actual disaster. Children with special needs may need extra words of reassurance, more explanations about the event, and more comfort and other positive physical contact such as hugs from loved ones.

Want to learn more?
https://www.cdc.gov/childrenindisasters/index.html

CS305921-A May 3, 2019

Figure 12.1. (*continued*)

From Centers for Disease Control and Prevention (CDC), (Atlanta: CDC, 2019), www.cdc.gov/childrenindisasters/pdf/children-coping-factsheet-508.pdf.

are more vulnerable than adults during disasters, it is important that early learning programs and community organizations work together to protect children before and during an emergency. All early learning programs should have procedures in place to address natural disasters relevant to their location (e.g., earthquakes, tornadoes, tsunamis, floods/flash floods, storms, volcanoes). Basic preparation and ongoing practice will help programs be ready to protect the children and staff and to also mitigate damage to the physical environment.

Emergency and Evacuation Drills

It is required that early learning programs have a written policy and a log for listing and conducting periodic drills per state and federal licensing organizations. Staff members must adhere to the drill schedule and practice with all staff members (including volunteers), children of all ages, children with special health needs, and children with devices for functional needs (*CFOC* Standard 9.2.4). The drills must be documented and logged according to the policy. Table 12.1 list types of drills and recommended practice frequency.

Check points:

- Carry communication devices, the building and premises entry and exit map, and communication plan.
- Limit children to drills they are developmentally ready for (e.g., excluding them from very intense drills that realistically simulate hostile or harmful events).
- Include children with special healthcare needs and disabilities in drills to determine if accommodations are needed.
- Carry each child's individual health plan, medications, and equipment during each evacuation drill.
- Review plans for moving children, including infants and children with special healthcare needs or disabilities, and the assigned staff members from areas of potential danger.
- Carry a first aid supply box and emergency snacks and water.
- Practice drills at different times, including naptime and during different activities, and from all exits.
- Use the daily roster during the drill to account for all children. Refer to *Caring for Our Children* Standard 9.2.4.6: Use of Daily Roster During Evacuation Drills.
- Document all drill practices, as described in *Caring for Our Children* Standard 9.4.1.16: Evacuation and Shelter-In-Place Drill Record.

Table 12.1. Types of Drills and Recommended Practice Frequency

Drill Type	Action Required	Example	Frequency
Evacuation	Leaving the building or area	Bomb threat, fire, flood, gas leak, chemical spill	Every six months or per licensing requirement
		Fire	Monthly
		Flood	Every six months and before flood season
Shelter in place	Finding a safe place to stay temporarily	A perceived or real hazard or threat (e.g., tornado, earthquake)	Every six months or per licensing requirement
Lockdown	Being locked inside classrooms	A violent or hostile intruder (e.g., active shooter)	Every six months or per licensing requirement
Lockout (reverse evacuation)	Bringing inside children and staff members who are outside and securing the building	A perceived or real hazard or threat outside the building (e.g., dangerous person reported in the area, threatening animals)	Every six months or per licensing requirement

IMMEDIATE IMPACT FEATURE

How to Make Drills More Fun and Engaging for Young Children

Here are some ideas to build skills and knowledge for emergency disaster drills:

- Play games like follow-the-leader so that children can learn to move together in an orderly way.
- Plan a field trip to the fire station or have your local firefighters visit your program.
- Add costumes for firefighters, first responders, and emergency workers for dress up and dramatic play.
- Develop a science theme with books and activities about earthquakes, tornadoes, floods, blizzards, and so on.
- Play "turtle" and have children pretend to be turtles by crouching down, covering their heads, and holding still.
- Play "lizards under rocks" and have children pretend to be lizards seeking shelter under a sturdy table.
- Practice using a walking rope for children to hold onto when walking as a group. (UCSF CCHP 2016, 1)

Emergencies Involving Injuries

Ensuring safety and preventing injuries is one of the top priorities for early learning program staff members. Children experience falls and injuries every day, but an emergency is when you believe an injury or illness may be severe and is threatening the child's health or may cause permanent harm. In these cases, a child needs emergency medical treatment right away. Injury prevention for children of all ages requires awareness and careful integration of developmentally appropriate skills. Active supervision and monitoring of the children and the environment is also needed to promote safety and prevention of injuries, disabilities, and death.

As young children learn to walk, run, and climb, they are wobbly and often misjudge distance and danger. Their heads are large in relation to the rest of their bodies, and it is often the head that breaks a fall. Head injuries can be minor bumps or can cause serious injury to the brain. A head injury can be internal, external, or both. Any blow to the head can cause the brain to bang against the inside of the skull or cause bleeding within the skull that can harm the brain. Younger children are also at a greater risk for accidents that lead to head injuries, broken bones, and burns, which are the leading causes of death and disability among children.

It is important that the staff members in early learning settings are knowledgeable of safety and injury prevention standards to identify and prevent injuries and promote a safe environment. (See also "Chapter 7: First Aid and Injuries.") Unintentional injuries are preventable, and early learning program staff members need to be prepared and ready to prevent injuries and reduce their impacts. Every educator has the chance to not only keep the children safe but also find ways to teach them how they can prevent injuries by modeling and explaining safe behaviors in a way that is appropriate for the age and developmental level of the children in their care.

Three recommended best practices to prevent and be ready to response to injuries include

1. Ensuring safety precautions are in place at all times and in all places (e.g., hallways, classrooms, playground, play equipment)
2. Maintaining proper child-to-staff member ratios
3. Ensuring active adult supervision at all times

Providing active adult supervision during indoor and outdoor activities is the most effective way to create a safe learning and play environment that can prevent avoidable injuries and emergencies. Handling specific incidents will require notifications to the appropriate agencies and parents or caregivers and adherence to the licensing and regulatory responsibilities.

IMMEDIATE IMPACT

Post Emergency Contacts and Phone Numbers

- In each classroom and in common areas, post a list of the names and contact information of those who should be contacted in the event of an emergency.
- In each classroom and in common areas, post a list of community contacts and phone numbers who may need to be called in the event of an emergency (911, licensing office, local health department, poison control).
- Make sure contact information is kept up to date.

Injuries Requiring Emergency Medical Treatment

The injuries and accidents that result in broken bones, skull and brain injuries, or concussions can be fatal or life threatening. Mobile and curious infants and children are at risk for falls and crush injuries due to their unstable movements and lack of mature visual-spatial awareness.

According to the National Centers on Health, active supervision is the most effective practice in keeping children safe and preventing injuries (NCH 2022). Unintentional injuries are the leading cause of child death after age 1. From ages 1 to 14, unintentional injuries represent about one-third of all deaths. Unintentional injuries include those caused by being cut or pierced, drowning, falling, fire and heat, firearms, machinery, natural and environmental, overexertion, poisoning, being struck by or against something, suffocation, transportation-related accidents, and unspecified incidents (Gielen et al. 2019).

The program must have a written policy on how to handle these emergencies, Including calling 911 and contacting the parents and emergency contacts. (See "Chapter 7: First Aid and Injuries.")

To ensure safety and protection of the children in the play areas, the staff members should always use active supervision to keep children safe. Staff members should also inspect the premises for potential hazards each day and address them immediately.

SAFE PLAYGROUNDS

The US Consumer Product Safety Commission (**www.cpsc.gov**) created the following playground safety checklist:

1. Make sure surfaces around playground equipment have at least 12 inches of wood chips, mulch, sand, or pea gravel, or are mats made of safety-tested rubber or rubber-like materials.
2. Check that protective surfacing extends at least 6 feet in all directions from play equipment. For swings, be sure surfacing extends, in back and front, twice the height of the suspending bar.
3. Make sure play structures more than 30 inches high are spaced at least 9 feet apart.
4. Check for dangerous hardware, like open "S" hooks or protruding bolt ends.
5. Make sure spaces that could trap children, such as openings in guardrails or between ladder rungs, measure less than 3.5 inches or more than 9 inches.
6. Check for sharp points or edges in equipment.
7. Look out for tripping hazards, like exposed concrete footings, tree stumps, and rocks.
8. Make sure elevated surfaces, like platforms and ramps, have guardrails to prevent falls.
9. Check playgrounds regularly to see that equipment and surfacing are in good condition.
10. Carefully supervise children on playgrounds to make sure they're safe. (US Consumer Product Safety Commission, n.d., n.p.)

Check points:

- Availability of staff members certified with pediatric and adult first aid and cardiopulmonary resuscitation (CPR)
- Prompt provision of first aid and or CPR by the certified staff members
- First aid kit and replenishment plan
- Call 911
- Contact the parent or caregiver listed on the child's emergency contact form
- Communicate with child's healthcare provider or specialist. You must have written permission from the parent to contact child's health care provider.
- Administer medication or emergency treatments as per the health care provider's order and facility policy by approved staff and note on updated healthcare and special needs care plan

- Documentation (e.g., child's record, communication, licensing)
- Supervising and supporting other children while attending to the child who is injured
- Reporting as per licensing requirements (injury/adverse event report)
- Follow-up with the injured child's family
- Debriefing
- Reassessment of the incidents and the triggers and development of a corrective action plan, including environmental assessment, staff training, and supervision

Poisoning

Poisoning is another medical emergency that can happen in child care. About 60,000 young children end up in emergency rooms each year because they got into medicines while an adult wasn't looking. These emergency visits can be prevented by always putting every medicine up and away and out of children's reach and sight every time you use it (CDC 2023a).

Chemical substances and personal care products, including medications that might be safe or harmless to adults, can cause irreversible damage to young children. Poisoning in children can happen through different means, including ingestion (eating or drinking), absorption (contact with the skin or eyes), inhalation (breathing in dust, fumes, or droplets), and injection (puncture or open cut wounds). (See "Chapter 7: First Aid and Injuries.")

Poison Control is available 24 hours a day to provide free, expert, and confidential guidance in a poison emergency. When you call, a poison specialist will ask you questions to determine the severity of your case, and then provide recommendations. To get help from Poison Control, call 1-800-222-1222 or visit **www.poison.org** to get specific recommendations for your case online.

Check points:

- Provide staff training on when to call local poison control center.
- Medication storage should be accessible to approved staff members and inaccessible to children.
- Label medications and infant feeds with the right child's name, their date of birth, and the expiry date and time.
- Store harmful substances, including cleaning, laundry, and disinfectant products.
- The number for Poison Control (**1-800-222-1222**) should be readily available and near the phone.
- Communication plan
- Clutter and smoke-free environment
- Free from poisonous fumes and plants

Communicable Disease Outbreak

Early learning programs are an important part of the infrastructure of communities as they provide safe, supportive learning environments for students and children and enable parents and caregivers to be at work (CDC 2023b). As part of their normal day-to-day operations, the program must follow a core set of infectious disease prevention strategies at all times, including layered or multitier prevention strategies specific to the particular infectious diseases at the community levels. (See also "Chapter 9: Preventing and Managing Infectious Diseases.")

The program should work closely with local health departments to report the signs and symptoms of any communicable diseases that the children and or staff members experience and receive guidance for isolation, quarantine, early treatments, and prevention so that the disease outbreak is prevented and controlled at the program and community levels. The program must stay updated on the disease outbreak and its impact on the local healthcare and hospital system; absenteeism; and follow the licensing, local, and state health department's recommendations and reporting requirements.

Check points:

- Check and comply with children and adult immunization requirements and vaccine records (record review policy)
- Daily health check and screening policy
- Exclusion for acute illness/stay-home-when-sick policy
- Separate room or space for isolation
- Reporting requirement (health department and licensing organization)
- Hand hygiene and respiratory etiquette
- Cleaning and disinfection
- Ventilation system check
- Safe disposal of biohazard and biological contaminates

Mental Health Emergencies

A mental health crisis or emergency is when a child is at risk of harming themself or others, or when a child's emotions and behavior seem extreme and out of control. Children's mental health crises can occur without warning and are unpredictable. The early learning program staff members must be knowledgeable of the triggers, such as stress, changes in family situations, bullying, substance use, trauma, and violence at home or in the community, that may incite the sudden appearance of or an increase in behaviors or symptoms that lead to a mental health crisis.

During the mental health crisis or emergency, the child becomes overwhelmed and may not always clearly communicate what is happening to them, such as their thoughts, emotions, and actions. It is important to empathize and connect with the child's feelings, try to deescalate the crisis, and assess the situation to determine the need for emergency assistance, including calling 911. (See also "Chapter 6: Social-Emotional and Mental Health.")

Check points:

- Available Behavioral health plan/Individualized Education Program (IEP)/Individualized Family Service Plan (IFSP)
- Staff mental health first aid training
- A quiet room/first aid room

- Trained staff members to address developmentally appropriate social skills, conflict resolution, and emotional regulation
- Collaborative family meetings
- Understanding of the triggers (e.g., family situations like death, sickness, separation, violence; community social climate), behaviors (e.g., persistent sadness, anxiety, social withdrawal), and mitigation measures
- Call for support, 911 first, then the parent or caregiver and mental health or behavioral health specialist
- Usage of age-appropriate therapeutic communication
- Staff member wellness policies on availability of sick days and mental health time and resources

Drowning

Drowning is a leading cause of death for children. In the United States, more children ages 1–4 die from drowning than any other cause of death except birth defects. For children ages 1–14, drowning is the second leading cause of unintentional injury death after motor vehicle crashes (CDC 2022a). For every child who dies from drowning, another eight receive emergency department care for nonfatal drowning. Most drownings in children ages 1–4 happen in swimming pools. Drowning can happen anytime, including when children are not expected to be near water, such as when they gain unsupervised access to pools.

The factors that contribute to higher rate of drowning in young children include

- Inability to swim
- Missing or ineffective fences around water
- Lack of close supervision
- Location

The early learning programs can prevent injuries and deaths associated with accidental drownings. Follow the licensing requirement and approval from the licensing agency conforming to all state and local health regulations. Safety and injury prevention must be a top priority, and staff members following simple measures at all times promotes safety and protects their employment and the license.

Check points:

- Staff training on pool safety, ratio, supervision, readiness, and use of life saving equipment/rope
- Fully enclosed pool or bodies of water that are separate from the program's building, with self-closing and self-latching gate
- Enclosure must be four to six feet in height or higher, and the barrier distance must be three feet horizontal to the swimming pool or body of water.
- Pool alarms, sensors, and/or remote monitors as additional safety features not as a substitute for enclosures (fence) or active supervision
- Age-appropriate child–staff member ratios and supervision for swimming, wading, and water play
- Constant and active supervision should be maintained when any child is in or around water.

- Pool safety rules (e.g., staff training, pool area safety for toys, trash)
- Caregiver consent/permission slips, emergency contact form
- Exclusion policy for sick children
- Emergency response policy and procedures (e.g., 911, CPR and first aid, communication devices, and responsible staff members)
- Staff member readiness and behaviors (e.g., distractions, such as chats, reading, or phones; looking away or leaving the area; physical and mental abilities; health conditions that may impair close monitoring; influences of alcohol, substances, or prescription or nonprescription medication)
- Signage, visibly posted, that clearly communicates pool safety rules and provides general guidelines for staying safe in and around water
- Lifesaving equipment in good condition for immediate access. A lifeline (rope and float line) should be provided at the five-foot break in grade between the shallow and deep portions of the swimming pool.

When a Child Is Lost or Missing

A child is considered missing if they are not located in the physical custody of the program or if their whereabouts are unknown to the program staff members. The safety and security of the children must be ensured at all times from the time the child enters into the approved child care area to exiting the premises. This will include indoor and outdoor program areas, including field trip activities. Every attempt must be made, through the implementation of policies and procedures, to ensure the security of children. The program must have a clearly written, easy-to-follow, systematic, step-by-step procedure for a child who goes missing on the premises or while on a field trip or other off-premises activity.

When a child is missing during program hours, the staff members must immediately report the situation to law enforcement and the parents, caregivers, or emergency contact and follow their written policy, which should include reporting to the licensing office. Every effort must be taken to locate the child and reunite the child with the family.

Suspected Maltreatment or Abuse of a Child or an Adult (Staff Member, Family Member, or Visitor) While on the Program's Premises

All states have laws mandating the reporting of child abuse and neglect to Child Protective Services (CPS) and/or police. Failure to report abuse and neglect is a crime in all states and may lead to legal penalties.

Educators should receive initial and ongoing training to help them prevent and recognize the signs of child abuse and neglect. There are different types of child abuse and neglect. The program staff members should be trained to understand their role as mandated reporters and learn how to respond to a child who discloses abuse or neglect. (See "Chapter 11: Child Maltreatment: What It Is and What to Do.")

The program must have clearly written policies and procedures on what, when, and how to report child abuse and neglect. Every staff member should be familiar with reporting requirements and sign the policy annually to ensure understanding of their role. The program should have important phone numbers posted for easy access, such as the CPS hotline, Department of Social Services, and police as required by state and local laws. It is important that the parents or caregivers are notified of the program's child abuse and neglect reporting requirements when the child is enrolled. The program staff members must complete required training and must be familiar with the reporting requirements including completion of the required forms, reporting channels, and availability to the regulatory agencies (e.g., licensing, CPS, law enforcement), and others for follow-up actions.

Check points:

- Staff training on recognizing child abuse, neglect, and mandated reporting
- CPS reporting form (the mandate to report for timely support and legal ramifications)
- Licensing reporting (written and verbal communication and report, participation in joint investigation)
- Multidisciplinary approach (CPS, law enforcement, licensing, forensic team, and metal health/ social work support)
- Protecting child's privacy
- Communication with family and participating agencies

Loss and Grief

Though human beings are considered resilient and able to endure loss, and loss is perceived to be a natural part of life, it can still lead to long periods of sadness or depression. Children understand about death at different ages. Grieving is an important process in order to overcome the feeling of loss, guilt, and/or confusion. What a child's grief might look like varies from child to child. The early learning program staff members need to be knowledgeable of the grieving process and the ways they can support the children and family members (APA 2020). Staff members can sometimes find it overwhelming to relive their own loss. Supporting someone as they struggle through loss and grief can be extremely difficult, especially when the bereaved individual is a child. Due their developing emotional and coping strengths, limited experiences in dealing with loss, and dependency on the adult care provider for their emotional support, children are vulnerable and have difficulty understanding and coping with the loss of a loved one. Children express their loss and grief in different ways. Some stay quiet while others may want to talk about what has happened, and some develop challenging behavior, acting out or perhaps having tantrums. (See "Chapter 6: Social-Emotional and Mental Health.") Certain behaviors should be referred for professional assistance. Psychologists and other mental health consultants are the trained professionals who help people better handle the fear, guilt, or anxiety that can be associated with the death of a loved one and can help children build their resilience and develop strategies to get through their sadness.

Early learning program staff members can attend training and workshops to acquire knowledge and skills on how to handle these situations with positive role modeling. Training and workshops help the staff members learn how to be supportive, what to say, and what not say during their mourning and grieving process.

IMMEDIATE IMPACT

Grief and Healing Resources

The National Child Traumatic Stress Network has developed many resources to provide help and guidance to educators and caregivers when working with children with traumatic grief (**www.nctsn.org**).

Check points:

To support a child who may be experiencing grief (APA 2020):

- Ask questions to assess the child's emotion and perceptions of the event.
- Allow time for children to talk or to express thoughts or feelings in creative ways.
- Provide age- and developmentally appropriate responses.
- Practice calming and coping strategies such as reading, drawing, coloring, storytelling, writing, or doing other activities.
- Maintain routines as much as possible.
- Take care of yourself and model coping strategies for the child.

Preparing and Responding to Immediate Dangers

All emergencies require quick and effective responses to keep children and staff members safe, but some events require an even higher level of training and response. Measures to prevent and respond to fire and firearms and gun-related emergencies fall into this category.

Fire Precautions and Response

Injury prevention efforts in early learning programs include fire alarm safety checks, adherence to regulations mandating a smoke-free environment (smoking of any kind of cigarette, including vaping), child-resistant safety lighters, smoke alarms, and developing and practicing a fire evacuation plan.

The best practice prevention measures include smoke alarms that are properly installed and maintained, maintaining smoke alarms, having and practicing an escape plan in the event of a fire, cooking with care, and maintaining a safe hot water temperature.

In the event of a fire, staff members must assess the situation quickly. If the fire spreads beyond the spot where it started or if it could block your exit, don't try to fight it. If you have the slightest doubt about whether to fight or not to fight—then don't. Get out and call the fire department.

Check points:

- Update and review fire evacuation plan.
- Train staff members and orient new staff members during onboarding, including location of fire extinguishers.

- Demonstrate and acquire skills with correct use of fire extinguisher (learn PASS—pull, aim, squeeze, sweep).
- Have fire extinguishers inspected annually. Place them where they can be reached easily. Know when and when not to use a fire extinguisher.
- Test fire and smoke alarms at least once each month.
- Post a diagram showing the main shutoff switches for electricity, gas, and water.
- Post diagrams of exits and escape routes in each room.
- Mark exits clearly, and do not block them with furniture or other objects.
- Teach and practice with children who can follow these instructions to stop, drop, and roll if their clothing is on fire and to crawl under smoke to get out of a smoke-filled building.
- Teach and practice with younger children to come to the adult person when spotting something hot or something scary happens.
- Practice leaving the building with the children at least once a month so that they recognize the sound of the alarm and know where to go.
- During a fire, get out of the building, and then call 911 to alert the fire department.

USING A FIRE EXTINGUISHER

1. Stand back about eight feet from the fire.
2. Aim at the base of the fire, not the flames or smoke.
3. Squeeze or press the lever while sweeping from the sides to the middle of the fire (remember to learn PASS—pull, aim, squeeze, sweep).

Firearms and Active Shooter Protocols

Firearm-related injuries are among the five leading causes of death for people ages 1–44 in the United States (CDC 2022b). The CDC reported that in 2019, there were 39,707 firearm-related deaths in the United States with approximately 109 people dying from a firearm-related injury each day. In addition, more people suffer nonfatal firearm-related injuries with many leading to permanent disabilities and trauma. Seven out of every 10 medically treated firearm injuries are from firearm-related assaults, and two out of every 10 are unintentional firearm injuries (CDC 2022b). Unintentional shootings happen to children of all ages. In homes with guns, the likelihood of accidental death by shooting is four times higher. In 2020, there were at least 369 unintended shootings by children, causing 142 deaths and 242 injuries. During the 2020 COVD-19 pandemic, the unintended shooting deaths by children went up more than 30 percent compared to the same time period in 2019 (Schaechter 2023).

The different ways that individuals can get hurt that can be fatal or nonfatal include

- Intentionally self-inflicted (suicide, self-injury)
- Unintentional, which is an accidental firing
- Interpersonal violence that can be homicide or nonfatal assault
- Legal intervention
- Undetermined intent

The presence of any type of firearm in an early learning program may lead to intentional and unintentional/accidental risk for injury to and death of young children. According to *Caring for Our Children* Standard 5.5.0.8, firearms of any kind are not approved within the premises at any time for storage nor can they be brought onto the premises. The child care regulatory/licensing agency will monitor the firearm safety measures during inspection/monitoring visits. The examples of firearms include loaded or unloaded guns of any type (including pellet or BB guns), darts, bows and arrows, cap pistols, stun guns, paintball guns, or objects manufactured for play as toy guns.

FAMILY CONNECTION

Home Gun Safety

If a gun is kept in a home, safe storage and safe use provide protective efforts to prevent and reduce unintentional fatal and nonfatal injuries to children and adolescents. A gun license is required, and guns should be kept unloaded, equipped with child protective devices, and kept under lock and key (e.g., trigger locks, lock boxes) with the ammunition locked separately in areas inaccessible to the children and other family members.

Active Shooter Training

It is important that programs conduct active shooter drills that provide opportunities to play out staff members' designated roles and responsibilities as well as their mental readiness. It is also key to have conversations among staff members that incorporate feedback, including additional training for staff members, and conversations with the children and parents or caregivers.

Regularly review your active shooter plan with parents and caregivers and keep updated contact information. Keep your plan updated. If you are going to regularly have active shooter drills, be sure that both the parents/caregivers and the staff members are prepared with the same information for how to talk to and support children before and after the drills. Be aware from the initial intake of children who may have been exposed to violence or trauma and may be more reactive during or after the drills. Parents and caregivers need to be prepared to talk to their children in advance of the drills and describe what will happen, why it is being done, and reassure their children that they will be safe and it is just an exercise that the program is doing to be prepared and that staff members will be available to answer any questions and provide support.

ACTIVE SHOOTER INCIDENT RESPONSE ACTIONS

The recommended steps during an active shooter incident are as follows:

1. Lockdown/evacuation (if possible),
2. Shelter-in-place/hide (if evacuation is not possible),
3. Take action (Direct confrontation is a last resort if your life or the lives of the children are in danger.),

4. Evacuation, and
5. Reunification.

1. **Lockdown/evacuation if possible.** Call 911 and secure the doors. This is the immediate first step when there is supervision of intruders resulting in an immediate or imminent threat to the children and staff members. The assigned staff members will make sure to immediately call 911. Alert and lock all exterior doors. The designated staff members will make sure to lock or secure the classroom, activity rooms, and cafeteria/lunch room doors. Monitor the children and staff members in the bathroom, outdoors, and on field trips, and follow the protocol. The staff members must lock the classroom doors and start moving the children to the designated secure locations.
2. **Shelter in place/hide/reverse evacuation.** After the doors are locked and secured, the staff members will follow the preparedness plan to take the children to the designated hiding place. The preidentified designated shelter in place may be inside the building or an outside location that has been approved with safe outdoor passage. Some preparedness plans may use steps such as drop, cover, and hold.
3. **Take action.** This is the last resort during the vulnerable situation when the staff members recognize the direct threat/danger to children. The staff members confront the situation with the tools and techniques received from the training and the preparedness plan.
4. **Evacuation.** This is the final step in removing the children and staff members from the dangerous situation. Upon receiving the message/code language from the designated person that the conditions outside are safer than inside, the staff members can initiate evacuation from the inside building to the outside designated location. Bringing the children and staff members outside of the building must be done in an orderly fashion to minimize the damage and emotional trauma. The most vulnerable, who are yet to verbalize and have difficulty communicating and ambulating, must be given priority. During the evacuation, start with infants, children with special needs, and children in wheelchair/ambulatory equipment. Head counts needs to be taken so that no child is left behind. Ensure emergency lighting in the corridors and stairwells to guide safe passage to emergency exits or shelter-in-place locations. Open flames, such as candles, flares, and lanterns, are not safe.
5. **Reunification.** The program will follow the preparedness communication plan to contact the parents/caregivers/emergency contacts to safely reunite the children. The designated staff members will follow the plan and protocol for communication and the reunification process. This task is not complete until all children and staff members are accounted for.

(Illinois EMSC; Office of Safe and Healthy Students 2013).

When a disaster like an active shooter in the early learning setting occurs, it profoundly and negatively affects all children and staff members, not to mention the despair it brings to the families and local community. Even though some children may be too young to comprehend the magnitude of the situation directly, they experience the fear, anxiety, uncertainty, and stress of the caregivers around them. Even when programs have comprehensive plans in place and have prepped and drilled regularly, sometimes a situation goes beyond anyone's control. It is always the adults' responses to, interactions with, and relationships with the young children during an emergency that provide them with the psychosocial protective barrier to handle the situation. Be a steady and calming presence to assure physical and emotional safety.

Regardless of children's age and their ability to verbalize, it is important that the staff members talk to children about what is happening and assure them that they are there to keep them safe. Age-appropriate, honest conversation with simple language will garner their support to effectively mitigate the situation. The children understand and respond to the staff members' voices when their tone and volume of the speech changes, and they can understand the magnitude of their vulnerability or safety from emotions, facial expressions, and body language of the adults around them.

Remember that it is important to pay attention to what you say to other adults even when you do not think children are listening. You don't want to unintentionally alarm or confuse the children.

1. What educators might say or do when caring for infants during an active shooter situation:
   - As you pick up each infant, whisper, "It's not safe; we're all going to sit together."
   - Sit in the middle of the room, remember to silence your cell phone, and quietly hum as you rock the children.
2. What educators might say or do when caring for toddlers or young children:
   - Say, "Children, I need you to all follow me" or "Follow my directions."
   - If a child says, "That was a gun," you might respond, "That was a gunshot."
   - Say, "We're going to sit right here together and be really quiet."
   - Remember to mute your cell phone and put your finger to your lips to remind the children to be silent.
3. What educators might say or do when a coteacher begins to cry:
   - Whisper to the children, "Ms. Becky is crying. I think she may be scared. I think we all may be scared."
   - Say, "Let's all practice our belly breathing."
   - You and your coteacher might wrap your arms around as many children as possible.
   - Notice if other children are holding each other's hands.

After a traumatic event like this, educators and staff members can help children feel safe, stable, and supported. The strength of the relationship between educators and children serves as a protective factor for children who are later impacted by a violent incident.

Check points:

› Conduct ongoing active shooter drills.

› Regularly review active shooter plan with parent, caregivers, and families.

› Keep the plan updated.

Emergency Rescue: When to Call 911

All individuals in early learning should be aware of the phone number 911 and how to use it correctly and effectively. The program must have a written policy and procedure for the incidents that require 911 to be called, including who is authorized to call. Staff members should be trained in the policy. It is critical to have immediate access to a working telephone in all areas of the premises, including indoor, outdoor, and field trip activities. ("Chapter 7: First Aid and Injuries" and "Chapter 8: Understanding Common Illnesses and Conditions" also provide specific guidance for when to seek higher care and call 911 in certain situations.) **Call 911** if you are experiencing an emergency that requires immediate assistance from the police, fire department, or ambulance.

Johns Hopkins Medicine (2022) reported that The American College of Emergency Physicians recommends calling 911 or reaching out for immediate help if a child exhibits any of the following:

- Significant change from normal behavior
- Confusion or delirium
- Decreasing responsiveness or alertness
- Excessive sleepiness
- Irritability
- Seizure or abnormal shaking or twitching
- Strange or withdrawn behavior
- Severe headache or vomiting, especially after a head injury
- Uncontrolled bleeding
- Inability to stand up or unsteady walking
- Unconsciousness
- Abnormal or difficult breathing
- Skin or lips that are an unusual color (blue or purple for lighter-skinned children, gray for darker-skinned children)
- Feeding or eating difficulties
- Increasing or severe, persistent pain
- Fever accompanied by a change in behavior (especially with a severe, sudden headache accompanied by mental changes, or neck or back stiffness or rashes)
- Severe or persistent vomiting or diarrhea
- Choking
- Severe burns (second and third degree)
- Drug overdose
- Someone makes a credible threat to hurt or kill themselves or someone else
- Allergic reaction, especially if there is any difficulty breathing
- Seizures that last over five minutes, person appears unusual or is injured. Remember, you are the best judge of the situation.
- Any crime in progress (e,g., robbery, burglary, prowler, fights)

- Any type of fire (e.g., structure, vehicle, brush)
- A vehicle collision, especially if someone is injured
- When you or the person you care for feels at risk

Summary

An emergency preparedness plan provides a systematic approach and guidance to protect young children and staff members from physical, emotional, and psychosocial trauma resulting from emergencies. In early learning programs, emergency plans are developed to institute age- and developmentally appropriate communication and response actions to prevent emergencies; manage the emergency incidents; and support children, families, and staff members after the emergency. Though emergencies and disasters are not common, they do happen from time to time and can be natural or man-made. Emergency preparedness is the key to mitigating the negative effects.

ADDITIONAL RESOURCES FOR MANAGING EMERGENCY SITUATIONS AND EVENTS

AAP (American Academy of Pediatrics). 2022. "School Safety During an Emergency or Crisis: What Parents Need to Know." *HealthyChildren.org,* last modified September 9. www.healthychildren.org/English/safety-prevention/all-around/Pages/actions-schools-are-taking-to-make-themselves-safer.aspx.

CDC (Centers for Disease Control and Prevention). 2021a. "Grief and Loss." www.cdc.gov/mentalhealth/stress-coping/grief-loss/index.html.

CDC (Centers for Disease Control and Prevention). 2021b. "Injuries Among Children and Teens." Last modified September 22. www.cdc.gov/injury/features/child-injury/index.html.

Bartlett, J.D. 2018. "Resources to Help Children in the Wake of a School Shooting." *Child Trends,* February 15. www.childtrends.org/blog/resources-help-children-wake-school-shooting.

Save the Children. 2013. "Tips for Protecting Children in Violence-Based Emergencies." Tip sheet. Fairfield, CT: Save the Children. www.savethechildren.org/content/dam/usa/reports/emergency-prep/GRGS-VIOLENCE-EMERGENCIES-TIPS.PDF

Save the Children. 2016. *Prep Rally Guide: Prep Step Lessons Preschool.* Fairfield, CT: Save the Children. www.savethechildren.org/content/dam/usa/reports/emergency-prep/GRGS-PREPSTEP-PRESCHOOL.PDF

Creating a Safe Environment

JENNIFER NIZER, MANJULA PAUL, AND LOUIS A. VALENTI

LEARNING OBJECTIVES

- To understand how the physical environment of an early learning program influences health, safety, learning, and behavior of the individuals who use the facility
- To value the expertise in design; engineering; fire safety; plumbing; heating, ventilation, and air conditioning (HVAC); and lighting to positively influence the quality of a program
- To adhere to standards of cleaning, sanitation, and disinfecting and follow the key elements to ensure a safe and healthy setting
- To monitor, mitigate, and control the exposure of toxic substances
- To describe and follow transportation requirements of passengers, drivers, and vehicles

A well-designed and maintained early learning program facility promotes physical access, way-finding, communication, growth and development, social and emotional learning, and developmentally appropriate behavior and skill formation. It also prevents, mitigates, and minimizes health and safety risks to the greatest extent possible. The critical elements involved in the structural design of an early learning program center include entrance doors; entrance vestibules; interior doors; corridors; toilet rooms; telephones; drinking fountains; visible and audible alarms; signage; and wheelchair-accessible and accommodative spaces in assembly areas, dining facilities, service counters, corridors, rest-rooms, and ramps or elevators where changes in level are necessary (US GSA 2003).

Many early learning facilities are located in buildings that were not designed for young children in group care, such as family homes that are older, especially those built before 1978; churches; stores; warehouses; and office spaces. These spaces can be approved for licensed child care if they meet certain requirements.

When new facilities are built, areas with high levels of air pollution, loud noises, heavy traffic, deep excavations, toxic materials in the indoor and outdoor paint and surrounding soil, and radiation hazards should be avoided.

An environmental audit is essential before choosing a new site, and if one has not been conducted at the site of a facility already being used for child care, it should be arranged so that hazards can be identified and abated. In this chapter, exterior and interior building design and maintenance standards are discussed.

Code Requirements

Early learning facilities should comply with all applicable building codes. The state child care licensing agency requires that child care facilities meet local codes for zoning, building, lead dust testing, plumbing, water and sewer, and fire. These requirements are typically included in each agency's statewide regulations. The facilities must ensure that the permits and licenses are up to date, ensure uninterrupted services, and protect the safety of the children and staff members.

Fire Warning and Safety Systems

All facilities should have a smoke detection system that is hardwired or a battery-operated wireless system that signals an alarm when batteries are low or during a hazardous situation. The detectors should be placed in front of doors to stairways and in corridors, adult break and meeting rooms, and areas that children occupy at any time. Generally, local fire or building inspectors will specify how these systems must be installed and how they should be tested and maintained. Portable fire extinguishers should be installed and properly maintained. They should be accessible to adults but not children. Staff members must be taught how to use them correctly. Fire extinguishers vary by the type of fire on which they should be used. Some are specifically designed for fires that involve electrical equipment, some are for use on flammable liquids, and others are for fires involving wood, cloth, or paper. (See "Chapter 3: Enrollment, Health Documentation, Assessments, and Screenings" and "Chapter 12: Emergency and Disaster Preparation and Planning" for more discussion about fire safety.)

Space and Structural Design

The early learning program's physical environments, including structural and aesthetic designs, are built to develop and strengthen physical, social-emotional, and developmental milestones for children. The physical spaces include indoor and outdoor areas designated and approved for care and early learning. The spaces are designed in such a way to provide developmentally appropriate scheduled child care activities and to assist children in being curious, solving problems, observing, gaining environmental understandings, being creative, developing their physical abilities, and interacting socially. The children's learning is supported through play and interactions in both indoor and outdoor areas. The space and the structural design of the physical facility allow for the free flow of children between the indoor and outdoor learning environments and provide stimulation, interest, variety, change, and challenge.

Facilities need to consider Americans for Disabilities Act (ADA) requirements for reasonable accommodations and local codes to serve children with disabilities. The program environment's design must be functional, safe, accessible, and sustainable.

The design of areas that children and adults use influences how they behave and feel in those spaces. Open spaces accommodate activities that require the use of large muscles to move around, while object-filled spaces confine movement and offer a smaller frame of things to be seen, touched, or used in some way. Odors, sounds, sights, textures, temperatures, and aesthetic preferences all play a role in the experience that an environment provides.

The physical environment must provide access and equitable opportunities for all children to fully participate in all program activities. All children, regardless of health status or condition, must have ongoing access to learning without interruptions due to illness and injury.

The health and safety components of the indoor and outdoor spaces must promote safety and wellness and minimize risks and hazards for all children. The classroom and child care spaces must allow for clear access to different spaces focusing on placement of permanent and movable equipment, furnishings, storage, and materials. The physical spaces must also promote the social-emotional health of children by promoting equitable access, providing space for group learning and social activities, and encouraging acquisition of social-emotional health and linguistic-communication competencies. Both indoor and outdoor physical spaces and classrooms should promote early learning through art, science, music, math, language, and communication. The space design, furniture and their layout, lighting, and learning materials must be designed to encourage multiple learning modalities—observe/visual, hear/sound, write/letters, touch/practice, speak/articulate, express, reflect, and retain—so that individualized developmentally appropriate learning is promoted and achieved. The classrooms, meal rooms, and activity areas must allow for the teacher to conduct individual assessments to evaluate learning and behaviors. Finally, a program must always have a designated space for staff members, family meetings, and caregiver participation activities. The programs can test their spaces for their usability, functionality, and applicability by simply having the children to use the space. Getting feedback from the children also allows them to feel part of reconfiguring their spaces.

Amount of Indoor Space per Child

It has been recommended that 35 square feet of free space per child is allowed to meet the space needs of a group of children younger than school-age, and 40 square feet per child for children with special healthcare needs. Programs must follow their respective state licensing standards for the number of square feet per child of classroom space. *Caring for Our Children* Standard 5.1.2.1 cites research that these commonly used space requirements are inadequate and recommends a minimum of 42 square feet of usable floor space per child, preferably 50 square feet per child. This does not include space used for walkways, staff member work areas for classroom support, furniture, administrative areas, restrooms, food service areas, storage, laundry, mechanical equipment, or rooms for care of ill children. Lack of space is associated with challenging behavior and increased density of air pollutants, including disease-causing germs. Sleep equipment may be placed in areas used at other times for play, and against furniture or walls, but the total area must be sufficient to provide three feet of space between sleep equipment of adjacent children who are resting. The best layout is one that ensures that teachers can monitor all the children from wherever they or the children are at any moment. Space for school-age children, space for children who have special medical needs, and spaces with low ceilings are addressed in *Caring for Our Children* Standards 5.1.2.2 and 5.1.2.3.

Planning Safe Spaces for Activities

The type and placement of furnishings in a space helps to direct people to activities that will take place in that space. If chairs and tables are placed in an area, children and adults will tend to sit down to do an activity there. If wide open spaces are left unfurnished, children will be tempted to run across them. If furniture is placed near windowsills, children are more likely to climb to look out the window or climb on the windowsills. The types of activity centers and tools that are available determine how well children and adults carry out the program's philosophy. Whatever is chosen should incorporate principles of health and safety. Sinks must be located where handwashing should take place. Food preparation surfaces must be intentionally and obviously separate from surfaces used to change diapers. This is critical so that no one is tempted to put food on the diapering surface or diapers on the food preparation surface. Diaper changing tables should have nothing on them that can't be disinfected easily after each diaper change.

To avoid injury, equipment used for play should be sized to children's developmental abilities. All equipment, materials, furnishings, and toys should be sturdy, safe, in good repair, and meet the recommendations of the Consumer Product Safety Commission (CPSC) for control of known hazards. More stringent requirements apply to furnishings in early learning program facilities.

Communal water tables have a high probability of spreading infectious disease in an early learning facility. Using communal water tables requires considerable attention to detailed arrangements. It is permissible only if the children are closely supervised. The table should be clean, sanitized, and disinfected before and after each use and must allow sufficient time between each use. The water table should be filled with fresh water right before use or supplied with free-flowing water. To provide clean, slowly flowing water indoors, set up a hose that is connected to the sink tap so it empties into the inside of the water table. Then put a bucket under the table drain or attach another hose connected from the drain in the bottom of the water table to a wastewater drain.

IMMEDIATE IMPACT

An Alternative to Water Tables

As an alternative to a communal water table, use separate basins with fresh water from the drinkable water source for each child to engage in water play. The bins can be put on a table, although putting each child's bin into the water table to catch the splashes might cause fewer slippery floors and smaller messes to clean up. Only children free of cuts and runny noses should be allowed to play in the water. Children should wash their hands before water play. No child is allowed to drink the water from the table.

Access and Mobility

Early learning program facilities must comply with ADA requirements. The design must accommodate children and adults with disabilities. According to Fund for Quality (2020), though early learning facilities may be exempted from certain codes and legal requirements due to the specific zoning rules set forth by the local government codes, they must comply with ADA guidelines. Some of the examples listed under best practice recommendations include.

- Furniture (including reception counter) shall accommodate wheelchair users and adults of short stature.
- One cubicle shall be provided in the children's toilet that is large enough for assisted access with space for helpers on both sides of the toilet.
- Universal access shall be provided to doorbells, security control panels, switches, and controls.
- Considerations will be made for the needs of individuals with impaired vision, hearing, and severe sensory issues, sometimes referred to as "low incidence disabilities." (Fund for Quality 2020, 16)

Exit routes must lead to a sheltered place if children and staff members cannot reenter the building. Alternate exit routes should be available in case the most convenient way out is blocked. Consideration should be given to how nonambulatory or less cooperative children can be evacuated to an area where they may need to stay for long periods in an emergency.

Surfaces and Fabrics

The finishes used on room surfaces and the type of furnishings placed in rooms should be chosen based on consideration of where nonporous surfaces are needed for sanitation and where it makes sense to use soft elements that are covered with washable fabrics to absorb sound and provide comfort. For example, an upholstered chair or love seat should have a washable slipcover and should not be next to the diaper-changing table. It might be placed in the reading area of the room next to a washable rug.

Figure 13.1. Example of adaptive ADA approved playground equipment. **(Copyright @ Getty.)**

Many articles of differing fabrics are used in early learning facilities. Sheets, pillowcases, cot covers, dress-up clothes, furniture covers, and other soft articles accumulate soil and become contaminated by drooling, emissions from skin sores, toileting accidents, and vomit. Avoid large area carpets that cannot be laundered. To help control sound, you can use carpets that are easily vacuumed, washable fabrics on walls, and tiles made for sound absorption on ceilings. Centers should have a mechanical washing machine and dryer on site or a contract with a laundry service. The laundry equipment must wash or dry at above 140°F, or an approved sanitizer must be used in the rinse cycle. Dryers must be vented to the outside. Store soaps, bleaches, and other laundry supplies in locked cabinets. The young children's linen can be sent home for laundering so that the crib and cot covers, sheets, and other washable items stay clean for daily use.

Outdoor Play Areas

The outdoor play area must be ample and well designed for the intended users. For example, play areas for different age groups should be developmentally appropriate for children based on three age ranges, birth to 23 months old, 2 to 4 years old, and 5 to 12 years old. Playgrounds designed for school-age children should not be used by preschoolers and toddlers. Programs should plan for 75 square feet of space per child using the playground at any one time. Then, plan enough space so that each group of children can use the playground area for the recommended outdoor time.

The outdoor space should be designed for play value and safety. Because the greatest number of serious injuries occurs during active play, playgrounds deserve special attention. Playground safety has so many technical issues that program directors should be sure that a Certified Playground Safety Inspector (CPSI) reviews existing playgrounds and any plans for additions. To find a CPSI near you, follow the instructions available on the National Recreation and Park Association's website (**www.nrpa.org**).

It is critical to provide opportunities for children with disabilities to use play areas, so additional space may be needed. Playground accommodations need to meet the needs of children with mobility impairments, cognitive delays, and sensory dysfunctions (Figure 13.1). The outdoor playgrounds need to be made accessible for children with disabilities. Indoor play areas should augment outdoor space and be sufficient to meet the needs for physical activity when inclement weather limits outdoor play. The same issues apply to indoor areas used for active play; for example, the need for cushioning surfaces under climbing equipment is often overlooked, but it is just as important inside as it is outside.

The program may choose to follow Early Childhood Education Linkage System's (ECELS) "Safety Checklist and Planning Tool for Active Play Areas." (**http://ecels-healthychildcarepa.org/tools/checklists/item/587-active-play-safety-checklist-planning-tool.html**)

TEACHER SAFETY

Equipment should be organized to reduce the risk of back injuries for adults wherever possible. Select furnishings that enable teachers to hold and comfort children while minimizing the need for bending, lifting, and carrying heavy children and objects. Teachers should not routinely be required to use child-size chairs, tables, or desks.

Animals

Animals can be integrated into early learning activities and can be a way children learn how to take proper care of the animal. This creates a caring, nurturing, and empathetic environment when children are caring for a living thing together. Although this can be a great asset to the classroom, there are things that you need to keep in mind while thinking about bringing in a live animal. Small pets can carry germs even if they look healthy and clean. Germs are shed in their droppings and can easily contaminate their bodies, habitats, toys, bedding, and anything in areas where they live. These germs can spread to people after they touch these animals or anything in their habitats.

Check Points for Safe Animal Interactions:

- Pets or visiting animals have documentation from a veterinarian or an animal shelter to show that the animals are fully immunized (if the animal should be so protected) and that the animal is suitable for contact with children.
- Check local regulations, program policies, parental permissions, and children's health conditions (Asthma, Allergy) before bringing animals into child care settings (CDC 2022)
- Before having an animal come to visit or stay in the facility, check with a veterinarian about what risks a particular animal might pose to humans, especially children. Any farm animal or zoo programs that bring animals to children's facilities should be inspected and licensed by the U.S. Department of Agriculture. Review the inspection reports before making any arrangements.
- Any animal coming into the facility or with which children have contact must be adapted to be with young children, be in good health without fleas or ticks, be fully immunized and maintained on an intestinal parasite program, and have a current (time-specified) certificate from the animal's attending veterinarian on file in the facility.
- Before allowing children to have any contact with animals, teachers must explain and demonstrate how to have safe, humane interactions. Teaching staff must supervise all interactions between children and animals and instruct children on safe behavior when in close proximity to animals.
- Program staff make sure that any child who is allergic to a type of animal is not exposed to that animal.
- Reptiles are not allowed as classroom pets because of the risk of salmonella infection. (NAEYC Early Learning Accreditation Standard 5.C)

- Do not allow any animals in areas used for preparing, eating, or storing food; areas where children wash their hands; supply rooms; or areas where children play.
- Do not allow adults or children to carry toys, use pacifiers, or have any food or beverage item in animal areas.
- Animals' food dishes should be inaccessible to children. When feeding animals, separate the animals from one another and from children with barriers that prevent interaction. The barrier may allow children to observe from a safe distance.
- Clean animal areas frequently. Keep all animal litter boxes out of children's reach. Do not use food service facilities to clean anything related to a pet. Children and adults who touch animals or their equipment should use hand hygiene immediately afterward.
- Separate animal food and cleaning supplies from food service supplies.
- Pregnant women are at risk from infections carried by apparently healthy cats and rodents. They should discuss these risks with their obstetrical health providers.

Air Quality, Ventilation, Heating, and Cooling

Rooms that children use should be heated, cooled, and ventilated not only to achieve the desired temperatures but also to prevent accumulation of disease-causing germs, odors, and fumes.

A draft-free temperature of 68°F–75°F at 30–50 percent humidity should be maintained in the winter months, and a temperature of 74°F–82°F at the same range of humidity should be maintained in the summer months. Air exchange should be a minimum of 15 cubic feet per minute per person of outdoor air. Heating and air-conditioning equipment should be inspected and maintained by qualified contractors, usually those who follow the guidelines of the national standard-setting organizations. Heating devices should not expose children to surfaces hot enough to burn them or expose them to toxic fumes. Programs must follow approved outdoor weather and air quality index charts for planning indoor and outdoor activities. For details, see *Caring for Our Children* Standard 5.2.1.

Ventilation is one component of maintaining healthy environments. Good ventilation can reduce the number of disease producing microorganisms, toxic/poisonous substances, and the likelihood of spreading disease. Ensure HVAC settings are maximizing ventilation. Make sure your ventilation systems are serviced and meet code requirements. They should provide acceptable indoor air quality, as defined by American Society of Heating and Air-Conditioning Engineers Standard 62.1-2022 for the current occupancy level for each space (ASHRAE 2022). Home-based child care programs should meet requirements established by their state and local regulatory authority (CDC 2021).

It is recommended that early learning programs have a routine check of their ventilation system. A ventilation consultant can assess a building's current natural or mechanical ventilation systems to ensure proper functioning and determine if appliances meet technical standards or require maintenance. Follow the Centers for Disease Control and Prevention (CDC)'s recommendation for "Cleaning, Disinfecting, and Ventilation" at **www.cdc.gov/coronavirus/2019-ncov/community/clean-disinfect/index.html.**

IMMEDIATE IMPACT

Healthy Air

Healthy Air in Your Child Care Facility

The quality of the air we breathe affects the health and well-being of both children and adults. Poor air quality can also affect children's learning and behavior. To increase the quality of air at your facility, follow these three key guidelines:

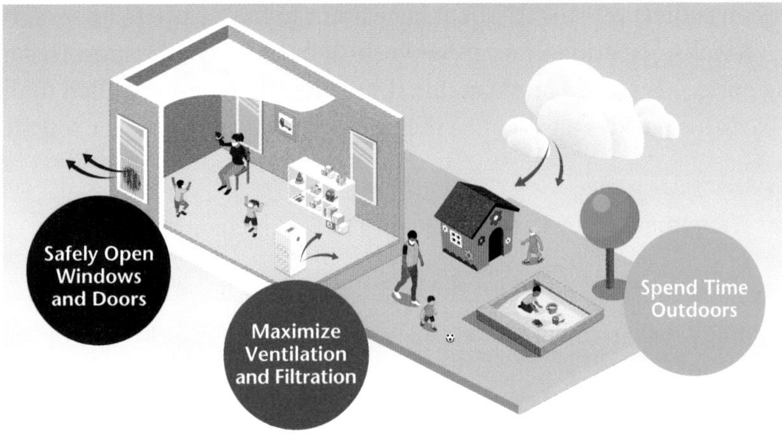

UCSF California Childcare Health Program • cchp.ucsf.edu 02/2021

This poster was made possible with funding from the Heising-Simons Foundation.

Lighting

The dominant human sense is vision, and light is the source of vision. The quantity, quality, and variety of light exposure shape young children's experiences and understanding of the world around them. Studies on school performance suggest that children learn better in classrooms with daylight and the opportunity for natural ventilation. Incorporation of a range of natural and artificial light from a variety of sources through increasing the number of windows between spaces and the outdoors would positively impact the quality of the early learning environment. Reducing glare in the room will support all children but especially those who may have vision challenges. Natural lighting should be provided in rooms in which children work and play for more than two hours at a time. Where possible, install windows at children's eye level so they can see the outdoors while inside. Visual stimulation is developmentally appropriate practice. Natural lighting provided by skylights exposes children to variations in light during the day that is less perceptually stimulating than eye-level windows but is still preferable to artificial lighting. *Caring for Our Children* Standard 5.2.2 covers specific levels of illumination by type of activity in a particular area, safety precautions for light fixtures, and limitations on the use of certain types of lamps. There should be adequate outdoor lighting to ensure the safety of persons entering and leaving the center when it is dark outside.

Noise Levels (Acoustics)

Noise in early learning spaces should not exceed 35–40 decibels at least 80 percent of the time (CFOC 5.2.3.1). In practical terms, this means that it should be easy to hear and understand a conversation spoken without raising one's voice. Use of noise-absorbing materials can help, such as acoustical tiles on ceiling or walls. While it is best not to have carpeted floors, it is acceptable to put carpeting on walls, partitions, and other vertical hard surfaces to absorb sound. All sound-absorbing materials should be cleanable (by vacuuming) and installed to meet fire safety requirements. Check local codes and reduce the noise level of alarms to the lowest decibel level acceptable

The best practices recommended by Fund for Quality (2020) include

- Keep the ceiling height under 14 feet for the best therapeutic noise level.
- Reduce background noise from both inside and outside as it interferes with the sound travel and understanding of the words.
- Use movable furniture with rubber feet or tennis balls to minimize sound.
- Use ceiling tiles with a noise reduction coefficient (NRC) that is not less than 0.70 over 40 percent of the ceiling.
- Fill gaps between spaces (e.g., gaps where the wall meets the ceiling, the wall meets the floor; behind outlets, switches, and ceiling lamps; around plumbing pipes) with flexible acoustic sealant to reduce sound traveling across spaces and minimize disruptions.
- Consider installing a voice amplification system so the teacher can be heard from anywhere in the room without raising their voice. (Learn more about these and other systems from the local assistive technology program.)

Electrical Items

Electricity is a potential source of injury. All outlets in areas where children are developmentally younger than kindergarten age should be of the tamper-resistant type or have screwed-on safety covers that accomplish the same objective. Some contain a shutter mechanism that prevents children from sticking objects in them. Others have internal design that prevents current flow unless a two- or three-pronged plug is inserted. Safety covers and shock-protection devices are essential where young children are in care. Safety plugs are not acceptable because children can remove them, and adults often forget to put them back after using the outlet.

Water and electricity pose special hazards and must be kept separated. Ground-fault circuit interrupter (GFCI) outlets should be installed in all areas where electrical appliances or wires might come into contact with water. These GFCIs need to be tested by pushing on the test button every one to three months. Electric cords must be kept beyond the reach of children who mouth objects. Avoid electric extension cords whenever possible. All cords should be inaccessible to children. Inspect all electrical fixtures and appliances, wiring, and outlets to be sure they do not pose a fire or shock hazard.

Electrical items and machines used in class rooms, and lunch or feeding rooms must be inaccessible to children and under direct staff supervision when used.

Drinking Water and Plumbing

Programs should have hot and cold running water, with hot water temperature not exceeding 120°F. Children should have safe and easy access to drinking water. Do not locate drinking water in a toilet or bathroom, and do not use handwashing sinks as a source for drinking water. Drinking water can be supplied by an angle-jet drinking fountain with mouth guard, or with individual cups. Licensed bottled water in the original container is acceptable.

Safe Water

We generally take safe water for granted or make assumptions about safe sources of water that are not necessarily correct. For example, many people prefer to drink bottled water yet the bottled water industry is essentially unregulated and the content of water bottles, even from the same company, has been found to vary substantially. Plumbing plays a role in not only providing safe drinking water but in controlling the spread of disease.

Water should be from a source approved and tested by the local public health authorities to be sure it contains no unhealthy bacterial or chemical contaminants. Drinking water should be freely available to children indoors and outdoors. Drinking water, including the output at drinking fountains, should be tested for lead and copper content.

Handwashing Sinks

Handwashing sinks are critical to infectious disease control in early learning programs. If plumbing is unavailable to provide a handwashing sink, facilities should use a portable water supply and a sanitary catch system approved by the local public health authority. The water in handwashing sinks should be at a temperature of at least 60°F and no hotter than 120°F. The water should flow for at least 30 seconds without having to reactivate the faucet. Hands-free faucets are widely available and provide a significant reduction in hand contamination.

Handwashing sinks should be adjacent to the surface used for changing diapers and soiled underwear. Use of hand sanitizers is permissible only for adults and children older than 2 years and only when there is no visible soil. Visible soil will be present sometimes with diaper changing, so using hand sanitizers does not eliminate the need for a sink in these areas. Provide step stools that allow children to use the sinks comfortably. Handwashing sinks should be separate from those used for preparing food or washing out contaminated items. All children should wash hands during critical transitions, including infants and toddlers. Washing an infant's hands after diapering creates lifelong practices that protects their health and safety.

Swimming facilities used for children in child care must meet applicable local standards of health, sanitation, and safety. An above-ground swimming pool may not be used for swimming activities and shall be made inaccessible to children in care. Children should not use fill-and-drain molded plastic or inflatable pools. Pools should be enclosed with child-resistive fences and gates. In addition, they must be monitored for water quality and have equipment that is routinely used for sanitation. Few early learning facilities have the resources to undertake safe maintenance of swimming and wading equipment. Those that choose to do so should check standards in *Caring for Our Children* for detailed requirements and guidelines for working with local public health authorities.

Diaper-Changing Area

The typical components of a diaper-changing area include the counter or changing table (which is typically 42–45 inches long, 36–40 inches high, and 24 inches wide), sink, cabinets for diaper and supply storage, and covered trash and diaper receptacles. Cabinetry can be built to hold each individual child's diapers and wipes and so that the teacher can reach the supplies without taking both hands off the child. A built-in changing counter will typically be four feet long and two feet wide. Generally, the sink is placed immediately adjacent to the counter, resulting in a total counter length of five to six feet. Some centers opt to have steps built into the changing tables so that older children can climb up to the table rather than having teachers lift them.

Containers for Soiled Diapers

Containers for soiled diapers should be washable, plastic lined, tightly covered, and hands free (i.e., a container with a motion-sensor lid or a step can). These containers should be located within arm's reach of changing surfaces. Individual bagging of soiled diapers is unnecessary unless they will be sent home for laundering. Do not use containers that require pushing the diaper through a narrow opening or touching the exterior surfaces with a hand or with the diaper. Do not use containers that have exterior surfaces likely to be touched while discarding contaminated or soiled material or those that have lids with handles.

Separate containers should be used for disposable diapers, cloth diapers (if used), and soiled clothes and linens. All containers should be placed away from areas where children are allowed to go without close adult supervision and should be tall enough to prevent children from reaching into the receptacles or from falling into them headfirst. Do not use short, poorly made domestic step cans because the foot pedals break easily, requiring teachers to use their hands to open the lids. Instead, invest in commercial-grade step cans big enough to hold all soiled diapers before they are taken out to a trash receptacle. These cans are used by doctor's offices, hospitals, and restaurants. A variety of sizes and types are available from restaurants and medical wholesale suppliers. Electric-eye-operated trash cans and other types of hands-free containers can be used as long as teachers can place diapers into the receptacle without touching the exterior of the container with their hands or with the soiled diaper.

Check points:

- Location of diaper area allows teacher to continue to supervise classroom.
- Sink location is separate from food preparation area.
- Diaper sink is separate from other sinks and adjacent to diaper area.
- Changing table/surface has safety rail and nonporous surface.
- Soiled diapers are placed in convenient, hygienic, and air-tight storage bins.
- Diapering and sanitizing/disinfecting supplies are stored securely.

- For toddlers, the changing table has steps.
- Area is ventilated with mechanical exhaust fan.
- Diaper and wipe storage is accessible with one hand while teacher still has one hand on the child.
- The sink features wrist-controlled faucets.
- A hand washing sign is posted at the diaper changing area as a reminder.

Facility Maintenance

Early learning programs should have written policies and procedures for the routine cleaning and maintenance of the facility. These policies and procedures should specify the type of cleaning and chemicals used, as well as the method and schedule for cleaning and sanitizing (see *Caring for our Children* "Appendix K: Routine Schedule for Cleaning, Sanitizing, and Disinfecting"). They should also name the person responsible for supervising and monitoring cleaning and other maintenance activities.

Cleaning, Sanitizing, and Disinfecting

Use an application of US Environmental Protection Agency (EPA)-approved disinfectant agents, follow the manufacturer's information, and wear appropriate personal protective equipment (PPE) for safe use of the product on the specific surface, equipment, toy, and frequently touched area. Follow the guidelines provided in *Caring for Our Children*. Keep the facility neat, clean, and free of trash.

Check points:

- Clean the facility in a way that avoids contamination of food and food-contact surfaces.
- Keep soiled linens or aprons in laundry bags or other suitable containers.
- Wash all windows inside and outside at least twice a year.
- Do not use deodorizers to cover up odors caused by unsanitary conditions or poor housekeeping. Instead, ventilate and clean to eliminate the smell.
- Keep storage areas, attics, and cellars free from refuse, furniture, old newspapers, and other paper goods. These items are a fire hazard and may provide a home for vermin.
- Keep flammable cleaning rags or solutions in closed metal containers in locked cabinets.
- Label each waste container to show its intended use. The containers should be cleaned daily to prevent buildup of soil in them.
- Be aware that techniques that some people recommend as green, or environmentally sustainable, approaches for cleaning, sanitizing, or disinfecting may require more labor and may not be effective. Look for products that bear the EPA's Design for the Environment (DfE) logo on their label to quickly identify and choose products that have been tested as green products. The inclusion of this logo on a product means that the DfE scientific review team has screened each ingredient for potential human health and environmental effects and that—based on currently available information, EPA predictive models, and expert judgment—the product contains only those ingredients that pose the least concern among chemicals in their class. Thousands of products, including cleaners and disinfectants, are listed on the EPA website at **www.epa.gov/dfe**. Follow the manufacturer's instructions for use.

Keep equipment and cleaning supplies clean, in good working condition, and stored safely.

Check points:

- Keep on hand wet and dry mops, mop pails, brooms, cleaning cloths, and at least one vacuum cleaner.
- Store housekeeping equipment in a separate, locked space, such as a closet or cabinet, *not* in bathrooms, in halls, on stairs, or near food.
- When possible, use a separate sink to clean equipment (not the same one used for food preparation) that has hot and cold running water.
- Use disposable rags rather than reusable sponges. Sponges allow germs to grow in trapped organic material. If you must use sponges, store them in bleach solution between uses.
- If potty chairs are used, use a separate sink to wash, rinse, and disinfect them. This sink should not be used for handwashing or any other purpose. Because potty chairs pose a significant sanitation hazard, their use is strongly discouraged.

Using an Integrated Pest Management (IPM) Program

Pests can pass along disease-causing germs by biting (e.g., mosquitoes, ticks) or by spreading contamination from one surface to another (e.g., flies that land on feces and then on food surfaces). They can damage property (e.g., termites, rodents) and disrupt learning when people become upset or get sick when infestations occur indoors (e.g., lice, ants, cockroaches) or outside (e.g., mosquitoes, stinging insects, weeds). Many pesticides are toxic and especially hazardous for children because children's bodies are still developing. Pesticides enter children's bodies through their mouths, skin, and lungs, and even through their mother's exposure during her pregnancy.

Integrated Pest Management (IPM) is the safest approach for controlling pests that minimizes harm to people and the environment. The first step is to use measures that keep pests out of the facility and outdoor play areas. For example, all the exterior openings of the building should be tightly caulked or otherwise sealed. Any foods brought into the facility should be checked to be sure no pests are hiding in the packaging or in the food. IPM focuses on reducing pest access to food, water, shelter, and hiding places. IPM requires keeping areas clean and uncluttered, using tightly closed waste receptacles, plugging holes and cracks, using traps and fly swatters, using bacteria that are harmless to humans or insect-eating animals like birds and frogs to control specific pests, and choosing the least toxic pesticides when a pesticide is needed.

By monitoring for pests, IPM pest control focuses any necessary pest treatment only where it is needed. Monitoring is usually pest-specific; for example, using roach traps or looking for rodent feces. When pests are found during monitoring, IPM treatments like enclosed baits, gels, diatomaceous earth, and dusts (e.g., boric acid) are used. Aerosols, concentrates, foggers, bombs, and sprays—especially those labeled *danger* or *warning*—are not first-line IPM approaches. For more information, fact sheets, and guidelines for hiring a pest management professional who is likely to practice IPM, see *Integrated Pest Management: A Toolkit for Early Care and Education Programs* on the University of California San Francisco California Childcare Health Program website at **https://cchp.ucsf.edu/resources/training-curricula/integrated-pest-management-toolkit-early-care-and-education-programs**.

Food Preparation and Service Area

Make sure food is handled and used properly and that the food preparation and service area is clean and all appliances are fully operational.

Check points:

- Appliances and equipment in the food preparation area shall be
  - Cleaned and sanitized
  - In good repair
  - Capable of normal operation
  - Not conducive to the harboring of insects and rodents
- Food contact surfaces shall be
  - Nontoxic
  - Smooth
  - In good repair
  - Free of breaks, open seams, cracks, pits, and similar imperfections
- Refrigeration shall be
  - Of sufficient capacity to store all food and beverages that require refrigeration
  - Operated at or below 40°F
  - Equipped with an indicating thermometer graduated at 2°F intervals
- All frozen food units shall be
  - Operated at 0°F or less
  - Provided with an indicating thermometer
- Food preparation and utensil washing sinks may not be used for handwashing.
- A cooking exhaust hood shall be provided when routine cleaning does not eliminate condensation or greasy film.
- Utensils and equipment used for the preparation and service of food and beverages shall be
  - Cleaned
  - Sanitized
  - Air dried
  - Stored in a manner approved by the office
- Floors and walls in a food preparation area shall be
  - Easily cleanable
  - Maintained in a clean condition

Procedure for Washing Dishes and Mouthed Toys

The easiest way to wash dishes and mouthed toys is with a dishwashing machine. Commercial dishwashers should meet the requirements of the National Sanitation Foundation (NSF) and be used according to the manufacturer's instructions. The dishwashing machine must incorporate a chemical or heat-sanitizing process.

Three types of household dishwashers are capable of producing the cumulative heat factor to meet the NSF time-temperature standard for commercial, spray-type dishwashing machines. Two of the three are capable of doing so only if the temperature of the water coming into the machine is 155°F or higher, but this temperature exceeds what is considered a safe temperature to prevent scalding of skin.

Washing dishes by hand requires more diligence in group care facilities than doing so at home because of the risk of sharing germs across multiple families. First, you need a three-compartment dishwashing arrangement. This can be a combination of dishpans and sink compartments to wash, rinse, and sanitize dishes. (If this is not possible and you don't have the required type of dishwashing machine, use paper cups and plates and plastic utensils that are thrown away after every use.)

Using the three-compartment setup to wash reusable food service equipment and eating utensils requires the following procedure:

1. Scrape off any leftover food.
2. Use the first compartment to wash all surfaces thoroughly in hot water containing a detergent solution.
3. Rinse all surfaces in the second compartment.
4. Sanitize all surfaces by one of these methods:
    - Immersion for at least two minutes in a lukewarm (not less than 75°F) chemical sanitizing solution and then air-drying the sanitized items
    - Immersion in an EPA-registered sanitizer following the manufacturer's instructions on the product label
    - Complete immersion in hot water and maintenance at a temperature of 170°F for no less than 30 seconds, followed by air-drying
    - Another method approved by the local department of health

These procedures provide for proper sanitizing and control of viruses and bacteria. Instead of using a sponge for washing dishes, use a cloth that can be laundered. The structure of natural and artificial sponges provides an environment in which microorganisms thrive.

To manually sanitize dishes and utensils in hot water at 170°F, a hot water booster is usually required. To avoid burning the skin while immersing dishes and utensils in this hot water bath, use special racks designed for this purpose. If dishes and utensils are being washed by hand, the chemical sanitizer method using household bleach is usually a safer choice.

Handling Clean Dishes and Utensils

Pick up and touch clean spoons, knives, and forks only by their handles, not by any part that will be in contact with food or put in someone's mouth. When children help set the table, be sure they have washed their hands thoroughly and remind them not to touch the parts of the tableware that will have contact with food and go into the mouth. Handle clean cups, glasses, and bowls so that fingers and thumbs do not touch the inside or the lip-contact surfaces.

Managing Hazardous Substances and Garbage

Storing and Managing Toxic Substances

Be sure that all potentially toxic items remain in their original labeled containers, except for diluted solutions. Label diluted solutions with the product name, dilution, date the dilution was prepared, and place to find the container (with the manufacturer's label on it) of the concentrate from which the dilution was made. Substances that are likely to be toxic include cleaning materials, detergents of any sort (e.g., for general use, for use in dishwashers, for cleaning rugs), aerosol cans, pesticides, medications, landscaping chemicals, and any other products labeled with warnings about their toxicity. The Occupational Safety and Health Administration (OSHA) requires that a Material Safety Data Sheet (MSDS) must be available on site for each hazardous chemical present. The MSDS is a standard document that describes the product's properties, hazards associated with using it, and instructions for using it safely. Manufacturers are legally required to prepare and make the MSDS documents available for their chemical products.

When toxic substances are used, they must be handled and applied so they do not pose a hazard to staff members or children. They should be stored in a locked closet or cabinet that is inaccessible to children and separate from substances that could be contaminated by them. Staff members should be informed about the presence of toxic substances in the facility. The EPA requires that toxic products regulated by the agency have labels that provide one of its signal words: *caution, warning,* or *danger* (in ascending level of risk). Always choose the least toxic product that will accomplish the task.

Monitoring Radon and Carbon Monoxide

Facilities should be monitored for the presence of hazardous levels of radon and carbon monoxide. For radon, there are protocols to test facilities that follow EPA specifications. Facilities that have any fuel or product that can produce carbon monoxide should have detectors that monitor for this odorless, invisible gas on a continuous basis. Check with local building inspectors for information on types of detectors to install and how to maintain them.

Exposure to toxic substances through inhalation, ingestion, skin contact, and other methods may cause injury and disability in children and adults. Work with your local code enforcement office to measure the levels of each and follow local codes and regulation and national laws and standards to prevent exposures and to mitigate their impacts. Examples include the following (Fund for Quality 2020):

- Carbon monoxide
- Mold and mildew
- Volatile organic compounds

- Sewer gas
- Radon
- Lead
- Mercury
- Toxic fumes and smells

Monitoring Asbestos and Other Friable Materials

A facility with asbestos, fiberglass, or any other friable (easily crumbled) material must monitor its condition and arrange for removal when there is a dangerous condition. Removal or repair requires a certified contractor who can do the work in compliance with EPA regulations. Children and staff members should not be present in the facility when such work is being done.

Garbage Storage and Disposal

Keep the facility free of accumulated garbage. Garbage containers attract animals and insects. When trash contains organic material, decomposition creates unpleasant odors. Therefore, facilities must choose and use garbage containers that control sanitation risks, pests, and offensive odors. Lining the containers with plastic bags reduces the contamination of the container itself and the need to wash the containers. Washing garbage containers can spread the contamination into the environment.

Trash and garbage should be removed from all occupied spaces of the facility every day and from the premises at least twice a week. Use plastic-lined, durable metal or plastic containers that keep out pests, do not leak, and do not absorb odors. Enough containers should be present to hold all waste properly until it is removed. Using plastic bags as overflow waste storage without an outer rigid metal or plastic container is not acceptable; this practice invites pest infestations. Store toxic wastes and infectious wastes separately from other refuse, in clearly labeled containers. Dispose of these materials according to instructions from your local department of health.

Each trash/waste and diaper container should be labeled to show its intended contents. Clean these containers daily to keep them free from buildup of soil and odor. The wastewater used for cleaning should be discarded by pouring it down a toilet or floor drain. Wastewater should not be poured onto the ground or into handwashing sinks, laundry sinks, kitchen sinks, or bathtubs.

Transportation

Transportation is an important aspect of all early learning programs. Whether you drive the children to and from their homes each day, have them dropped off and picked up by their families, or schedule only an occasional field trip, the cars or buses and walkways that participants in the program use are part of your environment. Motor vehicle pedestrian and passenger injuries represent the greatest threat to a child's life. You can reduce the chances of vehicle-related injury to children and staff members by being alert to potential dangers, eliminating or avoiding these dangers, and knowing what to do when an emergency occurs. Detailed resources about vehicular safety are available from the National Highway Traffic Safety Administration at **www.nhtsa.gov**. This regularly updated website has information about selecting, installing, and using appropriate seat restraints, as well as information about how to prevent injury to children.

The facility should have and communicate with everyone a plan for safe, supervised drop-off and pickup. The locations allowed for these transitions should be protected from traffic and have designated pedestrian pathways. Someone should be assigned to make sure that children are not in the path of moving vehicles. Family members and staff members must ensure that responsibility for each child is clearly transferred from one adult to another.

No child younger than 13 years old should ride in the front seat. Before using a seat restraint, an adult should check all metal parts to be sure they are not hot enough to burn the child. Interior temperatures should be controlled with fresh air, air conditioning, or heating so that the temperature is in the range of 65°F–82°F. Drivers must know the quickest route to the nearest emergency medical facility along the route to be traveled.

Decisions to transport children involve consideration of family needs and legal, regulatory, moral, and ethical concerns. By learning about safe transportation, providers can reduce their liability and teach families and children how to avoid injury related to transportation by foot, car, bike, and bus.

Legal Requirements and Standards

Whenever motor vehicles are used to transport children, special safety measures are necessary. When child transportation is conducted to or from the program by staff members, there shall be at least one adult, other than the driver present in the vehicle, who has successfully passed federal and state criminal background checks and a review of child and adult abuse. When at least one child in care is being transported to a local school district or an off-site activity by an independent contractor, the center operator shall ensure that there is at least one adult other than the driver present in the vehicle. The driver must be experienced and licensed with an excellent driving record and no history of substance abuse, criminal record, or any medical condition that could impair driving ability. The driver must be mature enough to assume responsibility for passengers' safety. Some of the training requirements for bus drivers include

- Classroom instruction and on-the-road skills training prior to transporting children
- Safe operation of a fixed route
- First aid and emergency situations
- Routine maintenance, safety checks, and recordkeeping
- Additional training topics as outlined in the Head Start Program Performance Standards

Caring for Our Children standard 6.5.1.1 recommends that drivers check the vehicle before and after each trip for children who might be hiding in, under, and behind the vehicle. The driver needs to lock the vehicle after it has been emptied and checked. A staff member should count the children before the vehicle leaves, when the children arrive at a destination, when they enter the vehicle at the trip location, and when they return to the facility. A staff member should conduct a "sweep" of the vehicle every time it is parked to be sure that no child is left in the vehicle.

Carefully assess all pickup and drop-off locations. Each facility is unique in its proximity to local traffic, parking lots, driveways, and pedestrian areas. Drivers of vans and school buses cannot see children who may be walking close to the vehicle; some children have died as a result. The danger zone for pedestrian injuries is 10 feet in front of and beside the vehicle. Teach children to take the number of giant steps required to move them 10 feet from the vehicle as soon as they exit it.

All drivers and staff members must be familiar with emergency plans, the use of safety restraints, supervision requirements, and pediatric first aid in the event of an injury. When transporting children, meet or exceed the facility's staff-to-child ratios set by state requirements. Keep in mind that these ratios are minimum standards. Drivers must be able to focus entirely on driving tasks, leaving supervision of the children to other adults in the vehicle. They should not be counted in the staff-to-child ratios.

Staff members are responsible for supervising every child at all times, including when the children are going to or coming from vehicles and getting in or out of them at the facility. When volunteers assist with transportation, they must follow the program's policies. After each trip, be sure that family members and volunteers escort children into the building and stay with them until responsibility for the children is transferred to another adult. It is essential to do a careful name-to-face attendance check of children entering and exiting vehicles.

Transporting Children with Special Healthcare Needs and Disabilities

Automotive safety devices have been designed to protect children with special physical and behavioral needs when they are riding in motor vehicles. Devices are available for children of various weights and heights with conditions like prematurity, muscular and skeletal problems, head and spinal cord injuries, temporary orthopedic conditions (e.g., a fracture), neurological diseases, developmental disabilities, recent surgery, obesity, and emotional or behavioral issues that might distract a driver. Wheelchairs should face forward, not sideways, during transport. Crash-tested wheelchair tie-downs, *not* homemade devices, should be used to secure wheelchairs in a van. All restraint systems must be crash-tested according to federal safety standards and retested even if only a small modification is made. Other equipment, such as an oxygen tank, should be secured so that it does not become a projectile should a collision occur.

Drivers and adult passengers who will transport children with special healthcare needs should receive training related to the needs of the children they are transporting. All vehicles should be equipped with a two-way radio or mobile phone. The following should be assessed:

- Children's seating arrangements to accommodate different motor abilities and activity levels so that everyone can move about
- Whether the flooring is safe for all children to move

Necessary Information for Travel

Specific information about the children and the route should be kept in a notebook or similar secure holder in the vehicle. Make sure the information is up to date and the driver and other staff members can find it easily. Include the following:

- A map of the route with estimated mileages and travel times and the names and addresses of children in the vehicle
- An information/emergency card for each child that describes how to reach caregivers and emergency contacts and contains special medical or health information

- Information regarding children with special healthcare needs, including descriptions of the condition and medications, behavior patterns, and warning signs for medical attention
- Telephone numbers of emergency services (e.g., local police, fire station, hospital, ambulance service), the name and telephone number of the early learning program, and a contact person who should be called in the event of any difficulty
- Pen and paper to record information from the families at pickup so this information can be passed on to teachers

Equipment to be kept in the vehicle includes

- **First aid kit.** Use the list of suggested items included in "Chapter 7: First Aid and Injuries" to assemble your kit.
- **Wireless communication device, such as a cell phone.** Use this only for emergencies and then only by an adult passenger or the driver when the vehicle is stopped.
- **Emergency supply of toys.** Bring along songs, books, and other activities to help keep children occupied during an unscheduled wait.
- **Travel rope.** Use this for children to hold on to for easy evacuation or for walks from the vehicle to a safe place.
- **Fire extinguisher, extra water, flashlight, and tools for minor repairs.** These may be indispensable in the event of a breakdown.

The following suggestions can help staff members safely transport children during special trips.

Check points:

- When the destination is known in advance, review the route mentally (or with a map if the distance is great). Practice the route if you have time and the vehicle is available. When using a GPS device to assist in navigating the route, the driver should also carry a map to serve as a backup.
- Make sure you have a signed authorization for every child and a list of all adults who will be traveling. Check your insurance coverage for car pools.
- Make sure both the driver and other adults (e.g., volunteers, staff members) know who is responsible for providing behavioral guidance to children. Let the children know who is in charge and what the rules are.
- Make sure that all children and adults use age- and size-appropriate safety restraints (e.g., child car seats and safety belts).
- Never have more passengers than seat restraints.
- Help the driver concentrate by keeping children occupied with soft books or toys, songs, and conversation.
- If children become unruly or remove their safety restraints, stop and pull off the road to calmly address the situation. **Do not attempt to provide behavioral guidance while the vehicle is moving.**
- Make sure all passengers know when and where they are supposed to return to the vehicle.

- If more than one vehicle is used for the trip, make sure all passengers know which vehicle they are to ride in during the return trip.
- **Never leave children alone in or near the vehicle.**
- Use a trip sheet to record destination, mileage, times of departure and return, and a list of passengers.
- Ensure that every child is buckled, unbuckled, and removed from the vehicle. People who are in a hurry may make unsafe "just this time" decision.
- Ensure children's nutritional and toilet needs are met and, hands are washed before transporting the children.

Passenger Safety Education

Preschoolers are old enough to understand simple concepts of passenger and pedestrian safety. Consistent use of safe behaviors helps children continue to practice them in later years. There are four major messages to emphasize with children and parent or caregiver passengers:

1. Everyone in the car must buckle up—including drivers and passengers in the front and back seats—no matter how short the trip is.
2. Safety belts go across the hips, not the stomach, with the shoulder portion across the chest.
3. The back seat is the safest place for child passengers.
4. Good passengers ride quietly.

You might make pretend cars out of cardboard boxes and make chairs, seats, and safety belts from fabric scraps. Practice in the classroom or on the playground by playing games such as Simon Says to encourage the use of safety belts and entering and exiting vehicles correctly. Practice taking giant steps after exiting the vehicle and count how many steps are needed to reach 10 feet, which is the distance that allows the driver to see a child. These games are fun role-playing and dramatic play activities. Invite the safety officer from your community to come to the program to talk about traffic safety.

Pedestrian Safety

Teach pedestrian safety to children from infancy onward. Adults who discuss and personally practice these rules consistently effectively teach children how to walk safely.

Teach children to safely use riding toys that are pedaled and have a wheel base more than 20 inches in diameter. Start teaching these rules when children first learn to ride any riding toy with pedals (e.g., big wheels, tricycles, bicycles):

- Always wear a properly fitted helmet.
- Ride only on something that is the right size for you.
- Ride on the right side of the road.
- Learn hand signals and clear commands and guide the children to follow (e.g., turning right and left, stopping) as soon as you can.
- Stop before crossing any street to look left-right-left, scanning for cars. Use your eyes like a flashlight to sweep the area to look for cars.

Involving Families

It is important to involve families in all educational activities; they can promote concepts presented in the classroom. Keep them informed through letters, parent and caregiver education meetings, and personal contacts. With transportation topics, send home suggestions and activities that families and children can work on together (e.g., counting the number of seat belts in the car). Focus on three main issues:

1. Children must use child safety seats and safety belts for every ride.
2. Select a suitable child safety seat.
3. Use child safety seats and seat belts correctly. Children younger than 2 years old should be seated facing the rear of the vehicle. Newer seat restraints are being sold to allow this positioning.

FAMILY CONNECTIONS

Checking Family Safety

Observe passenger safety restraint use by standing at the curb outside an early learning facility during an hour when the largest number of children in the program are arriving or leaving. What proportion of the adults are wearing seat belts? Are all of the children in seat restraints? Are all of the children younger than 2 years old seated facing the rear of the vehicle? The American Academy of Pediatrics (AAP) regularly updates materials on family transportation safety. Go to **www.aap.org** and use the search terms *child passenger safety* and *child pedestrian safety*.

Summary

Early learning program spaces provide safety and promote the health of all children attending the program. The internal and external environments and the atmosphere facilitate age-appropriate growth and development, enhance each child's learning, and, most of all, provide a caring and nurturing environment for all children. The space, its location, layout, arrangement, configurations, equipment, furnishings, lighting, sounds, indoor temperature, and ventilation all have their own way of communicating with the occupants, especially the young learners. Ensuring a safe and healthy early learning environment is everyone's responsibility and requires enforcement of related rules, regulations, laws, and codes; regular monitoring; and maintenance. The participation and assurance of continued support from all participating agencies, including the parents, caregivers, children, the local community, and licensing and regulatory boards, are vital for providing a safe and healthy environment for children to learn, play, and grow when they are way from their homes.

Early learning program administrators and families can use the following checklist (Head Start ECLKC 2022) as a guide to ensure all areas covered in this chapter are being addressed by the program:

- **Building approval document.** Inspection by building inspector to ensure compliance with applicable state and local building and fire codes before the building can be used for the purpose of early care and education.
- **Fire marshal approval.** Compliance with the fire prevention code.
- **Environmental audit.** Inspection by an environmental specialist to assess and certify that the site is free of (1) potential air, soil, and water contamination on program sites and outdoor play spaces; (2) potential toxic or hazardous materials in building construction, such as lead and asbestos; and (3) potential safety hazards in the community surrounding the site.
- **Electrical device or apparatus.** These should be inaccessible to children and located so it could not be plugged into an electrical outlet while a person is in contact with a water source, such as a sink, tub, shower area, water table, or swimming pool.
- **Integrated pest management.** Practice pest exclusion, sanitation, clutter control, and elimination of conditions that are conducive to pest infestations.
- **Toxic substances.** Use and storage of cleaning and sanitizing products and other toxic substances should be inaccessible to children and should not be used when children are present.
- **Carbon monoxide detectors.** Follow state or local laws regarding carbon monoxide detectors, including circumstances when detectors are necessary.
- **Safety of equipment, materials, and furnishings.** Equipment, materials, furnishings, and play areas should be sturdy, safe, in good repair, and meet the recommendations of the CPSC.
- **Telephone or wireless communication devices.** Make available for general and emergency use on the premises and offsite, including field trips and transporting the children.
- **Cribs and play yards.** Comply with current CPSC and ASTM International (formerly American Society for testing and Materials) safety standards including ASTM F1169-10a Standard Consumer Safety Specification for Full-Size Baby Cribs, ASTM F406-13 Standard Consumer Safety Specification for Non-Full-Size Baby Cribs/Play Yards, or the CPSC 16 CFR 1219, 1220, and 1500—Safety Standards for Full-Size Baby Cribs and Non-Full-Size Baby Cribs; Final Rule.
- **First aid and emergency supplies.** Maintain up-to-date first aid and emergency supplies in each location. A transportable first aid kit should be in each vehicle that is used to transport children to and from the program.

APPENDIXES

Appendixes Referred to in Chapters

A.3.1 Developmental History

A.3.2 Observation and Symptom Record

A.4.1 Storage and Preparation of Breast Milk

A.9.1 Sample Letter to Families About Exposure to Communicable Disease

A.10.1 Adaptive Equipment or Devices

Book Appendixes

B.1 Glossary and Acronyms

APPENDIX A.3.1

Developmental History

[Name of Center/Logo]

All information is confidential and for staff use only.

Today's date:

Child's name:

First:

Last:

Preferred:

Birth date:

Preferred method of communication: Email Text Phone

Family Information

Language used in home:

Members in home:

Names	Relationship to Child	Age

Are there other people in your child's life you would like us to know about?

Has your child ever had a traumatic experience? O Yes/No O If yes, please explain.

Has your family experienced any major changes over the last year? O Yes/No O If yes, please explain.

Eating habits:

1. Are there any foods your child cannot eat? O Yes/No O If yes, please explain.

2. What is mealtime like at home?

3. What are your child's favorite foods?

Naptime (infants and preschoolers):

1. How does your child fall asleep at naptime? Do they have a comfort item (toy or blanket)? Do they listen to music? Please explain.

Physical Health

1. Does your child have a current health problem or condition? O Yes/No O If yes, please list and explain.

2. Has your child had any health problems or conditions in the past? O Yes/No O If yes, please list and explain.

3. Does your child have allergies? O Yes/No O If yes, please list and explain.

4. Does your child take any medications? O Yes/No O If yes, please list and explain reason and frequency.

5. Has your child received a diagnosis of a disability (e.g., cerebral palsy, dyslexia)? O Yes/No O If yes, please explain.

6. Has your child ever been hospitalized? O Yes/No O If yes, please explain.

7. Do you have concerns about your child's health? O Yes/No O If yes, please explain.

Developmental Milestones (Relative to Children in the Same Age Group)

1. Does your child have any problems talking or making sounds? Please explain.

2. Does your child pull up, crawl, and/or walk? Please explain.

3. Does your child use diapers? If yes, cloth or disposable?

4. How does your child indicate toilet needs?

APPENDIX A.3.2

Observation and Symptom Record

Child's name:

Date:

Observations and symptoms:

Describe when the observations were made. When any symptoms or atypical behavior occurred, describe how often, how long, and how intense they seemed:

Circle any symptoms the child shows:

- runny nose
- trouble breathing
- itching
- sore throat
- stiff neck
- trouble sleeping
- cough
- rash
- earache
- vomiting
- trouble urinating
- headache diarrhea
- pain
- stomach ache
- wheezing

Other symptoms:

Exposure to medications, animals, insects, soaps, new foods:

Exposure to other people who were sick (names and what sickness):

Child's other problems that might affect this illness (such as allergy, asthma, anemia, diabetes, emotional trauma):

What the program would like the child's healthcare provider to share with the child's family and teachers:

Program staff member completing this form:

Response from the child's healthcare provider:

Name of child's healthcare provider completing this form:

Adapted, by permission, from S.S. Aronson, ed., *Model Child Care Health Policies*, 5th ed. (Elk Grove Village, IL: American Academy of Pediatrics, 2014), 185–186.

APPENDIX A.4.1

Storage and Preparation of Breast Milk

ACCESSIBLE VERSION: https://bit.ly/2dxVYLU

STORAGE AND PREPARATION OF BREAST MILK

BEFORE EXPRESSING/PUMPING MILK

Wash your hands well with soap and water.

Inspect the pump kit and tubing to make sure it is clean.

Replace moldy tubing immediately.

Clean pump dials and countertop.

STORING EXPRESSED MILK

Use breast milk storage bags or clean food-grade containers with tight fitting lids.

Avoid plastics containing bisphenol A (BPA) (recycle symbol #7).

HUMAN MILK STORAGE GUIDELINES

TYPE OF BREAST MILK	STORAGE LOCATIONS AND TEMPERATURES		
	Countertop **77°F (25°C) or colder** *(room temperature)*	**Refrigerator** **40 °F (4°C)**	**Freezer** **0 °F (-18°C) or colder**
Freshly Expressed or Pumped	Up to **4 Hours**	Up to **4 Days**	Within **6 months** is best Up to **12 months** is acceptable
Thawed, Previously Frozen	**1–2 Hours**	Up to **1 Day** *(24 hours)*	**NEVER** refreeze human milk after it has been thawed
Leftover from a Feeding (baby did not finish the bottle)	Use within **2 hours** after the baby is finished feeding		

STORE

Label milk with the date it was expressed and the child's name if delivering to childcare.

Store milk in the back of the freezer or refrigerator, not the door.

Freeze milk in **small amounts of 2 to 4 ounces** to avoid wasting any.

When freezing leave an inch of space at the top of the container; breast milk expands as it freezes.

Milk can be stored in an insulated cooler bag with frozen ice packs for **up to 24 hours** when you are traveling.

If you don't plan to use freshly expressed milk **within 4 days**, freeze it right away.

THAW

Always thaw the oldest milk first.

Thaw milk under lukewarm running water, in a container of lukewarm water, or overnight in the refrigerator.

Never thaw or heat milk in a microwave. Microwaving destroys nutrients and creates hot spots, which can burn a baby's mouth.

Use milk **within 24 hours** of thawing in the refrigerator *(from the time it is completely thawed, not from the time when you took it out of the freezer).*

Use thawed milk **within 2 hours** of bringing to room temperature or warming.

Never refreeze thawed milk.

FEED

Milk can be **served cold, room temperature, or warm.**

To heat milk, place the sealed container into a bowl of warm water or hold under warm running water.

Do not heat milk directly on the stove or in the microwave.

Test the temperature before feeding it to your baby by putting a few drops on your wrist. It should feel warm, **not hot.**

Swirl the milk to mix the fat, which may have separated.

If your baby did not finish the bottle, leftover milk should be used **within 2 hours.**

CLEAN

Wash disassembled pump and feeding parts in a clean basin with soap and water. **Do not wash directly** in the sink because the germs in the sink could contaminate items.

Rinse thoroughly under running water. Air-dry items on a clean dishtowel or paper towel.

Using clean hands, store dry items in a clean, protected area.

For extra germ removal, sanitize feeding items daily using one of these methods:

- clean in the dishwasher using hot water and heated drying cycle *(or sanitize setting).*
- boil in water for 5 minutes *(after cleaning).*
- steam in a microwave or plug-in steam system according to the manufacturer's directions *(after cleaning).*

June 2019

Centers for Disease Control and Prevention
National Center for Chronic Disease Prevention and Health Promotion

FOR MORE INFORMATION, VISIT:
https://bit.ly/2dxVYLU

296657-B

APPENDIX A.9.1

Sample Letter to Families About Exposure to Communicable Disease

Name of Child Care Program:

Address of Child Care Program:

Telephone Number of Child Care Program:

Date:

Dear Parent or Legal Guardian:

A child in our program has or is suspected of having:

Information about this disease:

The disease is spread by:

The symptoms are:

The disease can be prevented by:

What the program is doing:

What you can do at home:

If your child has any symptoms of this disease, call your doctor to find out what to do. Be sure to tell your doctor about this notice. If you do not have a regular doctor to care for your child, contact your local health department for instructions on how to find a doctor, or ask other parents for names of their children's doctors. If you have any questions, please contact:

______________________________ at (______)______________

(Educator's name) (Telephone number)

Reprinted, with permission, from S.S. Aronson, ed., *Model Child Care Health Policies*, 4th ed. (Elk Grove Village, IL: American Academy of Pediatrics, 2002), 189.

APPENDIX A.10.1

Adaptive Equipment or Devices

PAMELA BRILLANTE

Adaptive equipment, or *adaptive devices*, can be specifically designed for an individual or they can be common materials that are temporarily modified in some way to improve a child's access and ability to participate in classroom activities and/or to provide ways for a child to be independent.

- Adaptive equipment for young children with sensory disabilities (vision and hearing loss)
  - Low vision/blindness
    - Large-print books
    - Brightly colored materials
    - Braille materials
  - Hard of hearing/deafness
    - Vibrating toys
    - Frequency modulation (FM) units
- Adaptive equipment for young children with disabilities that impact mobility
  - Positioning issues
    - Chair inserts/positioning pillows
    - Beanbag chairs
  - Mobility issues
    - Walkers
    - Wheelchairs
  - Safety concerns
    - Helmets
    - Knee and elbow pads
- Adaptive equipment for young children with disabilities that impact self-help skills
  - Feeding issues
    - No-spill cups
    - Lipped plates and bowls
    - Weighted plates and bowls
    - Adapted utensils
  - Dressing
    - Clothing adapted with Velcro
  - Toileting/diapering
    - Raised toilet seats
    - Grab bars near toilet
    - Adapted changing tables

- Adaptive equipment for young children with disabilities that impact play skills
    - Large knob puzzles
    - Switch adapted toys
- Adaptive equipment for young children with disabilities that impact communication
    - Low-tech communication systems with pictures and icons
    - Single- and multiple-message devices

Glossary and Acronyms

acute: Adjective describing an illness that has a sudden onset and lasts a relatively short period of time.

adverse childhood experiences (ACEs): "Potentially traumatic events that occur in childhood [. . .]. Also included are aspects of the child's environment that can undermine their sense of safety, stability, and bonding" (CDC 2019, 7).

agent: In medical terms, an element such as a microorganism, chemical substance, or a form of radiation that can lead to an effect either by causing or exacerbating a disease or as a therapy.

anaphylaxis: An allergic reaction to a specific substance (e.g., food, pollen, pets, mold, medication) that can have dangerous and possibly fatal complications, including the swelling and closure of the airway that can lead to an inability to breathe.

antibody: A protein substance produced by the body's immune defense system in response to something foreign. Antibodies help protect against infections.

antigen: Any substance that is foreign to the body. An antigen is capable of causing a response from the immune system.

audiologist: A healthcare professional who evaluates, diagnoses, treats, and manages hearing and balance disorders.

BIPOC: Black, Indigenous, People of Color

BMR: Basalmetabolic rate

botulism: A rare but serious illness caused by a toxin that attacks the body's nerves.

Child Abuse Prevention and Treatment Act (CAPTA): The key federal legislation addressing child abuse and neglect, originally enacted in 1974. It establishes national definitions regarding child abuse and neglect and assigns certain responsibilities to the federal government, particularly relating to data collection and technical assistance.

Children with medical complexity (CMC): Children with medical complexity (CMC) have multiple significant chronic health problems that affect multiple organ systems and result in functional limitations, high healthcare needs or utilization, and often the need for or use of medical technology (Cohen et al. 2018; Cohen, Kuo, & Agrawal 2011; Kuo et al. 2011). An example of a CMC is one with a genetic syndrome with an associated congenital heart defect, difficulty with swallowing, cerebral palsy, and a urologic condition (Kuo, Houtrow, & Council on Children with Disabilities 2016).

communicable/infectious disease: A disease caused by a microorganism (bacterium, virus, fungus, or parasite) that can be transmitted from person to person via infected body fluids or respiratory spray, with or without an intermediary agent (such as a louse or mosquito) or environmental object (such as a table surface).

congenital: A condition that has existed from the time of birth.

corporal punishment: Physical harm inflicted on the body as punishment, such as spanking.

CYSHCN: Children and youth with special healthcare needs.

dental caries: A disease process that leads to holes in the teeth; also referred to as *dental cavities*.

early intervention: Services and supports that are available to infants and young children with developmental delays and disabilities and their families. These may include speech therapy, physical therapy, and other types of services based on the needs of the child and family (CDC 2022a).

early learning settings: Programs serving children from birth through age 8. *Setting* refers to the locations in which early childhood education takes place—child care centers, child care homes, elementary schools, religious-based centers, and many others.

electrolytes: Substances that have a natural positive or negative electrical charge when dissolved in water. They help your body regulate chemical reactions and maintain the balance between fluids inside and outside your cells. Examples include potassium and magnesium.

EMR: Electronic medical record

fecal-oral transmission: Transmission of a disease via fecal particles passed from one person to the mouth of another person. Fecal contamination of food is a form of fecal-oral transmission. Not washing hands properly after changing an infant's diaper or after performing anal hygiene on a child are examples of how this type of transmission can happen.

food insecurity: A household-level economic and social condition of limited or uncertain access to adequate food (ERS USDA 2022).

gastroenteritis: Gastroenteritis is an inflammation of the lining of the stomach and intestines. The main symptoms include vomiting and diarrhea.

germs: Small particles or organisms (viruses, bacteria, fungi, or parasites) that may cause infections. Some germs are harmless.

health disparity: A difference in health that adversely affects disadvantaged populations in comparison to a reference population based on one or more health outcomes, including a higher incidence and/or prevalence of a disease or premature or excessive mortality from specific health conditions. All populations with health disparities are socially disadvantaged due in part to being subject to racist or discriminatory acts and are underserved in healthcare (National Institute on Minority Health and Health Disparities 2023).

Health Insurance Portability and Accountability Act (HIPAA): Federal act that provides protections for personal health information held by covered entities and gives patients an array of rights with respect to that information.

hematocrit (HCT): The ratio of the volume of packed red blood cells to the total volume of whole blood.

hemoglobin: An iron-containing protein that transports oxygen to tissues in the body, such as the lungs.

immunity: The body's ability to fight a particular infection.

IEP: Individualized Education Plan

IFSP: Individualized Family Services Plan

Individuals with Disabilities Education Act (IDEA): Federal law that makes available a free and appropriate public education to eligible children with disabilities throughout the nation and ensures special education and related services to those children.

malnutrition: Deficiencies, excesses, or imbalances in a person's intake of energy and/or nutrients. The term covers two broad groups of conditions: *undernutrition*, which includes stunting (low height for age), wasting (low weight for height), underweight (low weight for age), and micronutrient deficiencies or insufficiencies (a lack of important vitamins and minerals); and *overweight, obesity,* and *diet-related noncommunicable diseases*, such as heart disease, stroke, diabetes, and cancer (WHO 2020).

Medicaid: A program that "provides health coverage to millions of Americans, including eligible low-income adults, children, pregnant women, elderly adults, and people with disabilities. Medicaid is administered by states, according to federal requirements" (Medicaid, n.d., n.p.). The program is funded jointly by states and the federal government.

medical home: Central primary medical facility or office in which the child healthcare professional works in partnership with the family and patient to ensure that all the medical and nonmedical needs of the patient are met.

microorganism: An organism that is too small to be seen with the naked eye, including bacteria and fungi.

mortality: The death state. Fatality.

obesity: An excess percentage of body weight, or a body mass index (BMI) equal to or greater than 95 percent, due to fat that puts people at risk for many health problems. In children older than 2 years old, obesity is assessed by a measure called BMI.

OSHA: Occupational Safety and Health Administration

osteoporosis: A bone disease that develops when bone mineral density and bone mass decreases, or when the structure and strength of bone changes. This can lead to a decrease in bone strength that can increase the risk of fractures (broken bones). (National Institute of Arthritis and Musculoskeletal and Skin Diseases 2023).

pathogen: An organism that causes infection; also referred to as an *infectious agent*. The human body's immune system acts as a defense against pathogens.

predisposition (genetic): Having an increased chance of developing a certain disease based on genetic makeup.

quality rating and improvement system (QRIS): A systemic approach to assess, improve, and communicate the level of quality in early learning programs. Similar to rating systems for restaurants and hotels, QRIS awards quality ratings to early learning programs that meet a set of defined program standards.

radon: A radioactive gaseous element formed by the disintegration of radium that occurs naturally in the soil. Radon is considered to be a health hazard that may lead to lung cancer.

respiratory tract: The nose, ears, sinuses, throat, and lungs.

standards: The national standards formally adopted by a profession to define the essentials of high-quality practice for all members of that profession.

telehealth: The delivery of healthcare and health-related services from your healthcare provider through the use of remote technologies rather than an in-person office visit; also referred to as *telemedicine*. (HRSA 2023).

toxicity: The state of being poisonous.

transmission: The passing of an infectious organism or germ from person to person.

types 1 and 2 diabetes: Type 1 diabetes is when the pancreas doesn't make insulin or makes very little insulin. Insulin helps blood sugar enter the cells in the body for use as energy. Without insulin, blood sugar can't get into cells and builds up in the bloodstream. High blood sugar is damaging to the body and causes many of the symptoms and complications of diabetes. Type 1 diabetes was once called *insulin-dependent* or *juvenile diabetes*. It usually develops in children, teens, and young adults, but it can happen at any age. Type 1 diabetes is less common than type 2 diabetes (CDC 2022b). With type 2 diabetes, cells don't respond normally to insulin; this is called *insulin resistance*. The pancreas makes more insulin to try to get cells to respond, but eventually it can't keep up, and the blood sugar in the body rises, setting the stage for prediabetes and type 2 diabetes. (CDC 2023).

vegan: An individual who does not eat meat, poultry, fish, eggs, or dairy products; the individual only eats plant-based foods.

vegetarian: An individual who does not eat meat, poultry, or fish. Variations of vegetarians include lacto-ovo vegetarians (who consume eggs, dairy products, and plant foods) and lacto-vegetarians (who eat dairy products and plant foods but not eggs).

virus: A microscopic organism, smaller than a bacterium, which may cause disease. Viruses can grow or reproduce only in living cells.

Index

Note: Page numbers followed by *f* and *t* indicate figures and tables, respectively.